High-Return,
Low-Risk
Investment

High-Return, Low-Risk Investment

Using Stock Selection and Market Timing

Thomas J. Herzfeld

Robert F. Drach

Second Edition

McGraw-Hill, Inc.

New York   San Francisco   Washington, D.C.   Auckland   Bogotá
Caracas   Lisbon   London   Madrid   Mexico City   Milan
Montreal   New Delhi   San Juan   Singapore
Sydney   Tokyo   Toronto

Library of Congress Cataloging-in-Publication Data

Drach, Robert F.
  High-return, low-risk investment : using stock selection and market
timing / Thomas J. Herzfeld, Robert F. Drach.—2nd ed.
      p.   cm.
  Includes index.
  ISBN 0-07-028449-0 (alk. paper) :
  1. Stock-exchange. 2. Stocks—Mathematical models. 3. Portfolio
management. 4. Closed-end funds. I. Drach, Robert F.
II. Title.
HG4551.H44 1993
  332.6'78—dc20
                                                            93-9690
                                                            CIP

1 2 3 4 5 6 7 8 9 0   DOC/DOC   9 9 8 7 6 5 4 3

ISBN 0-07-028449-0

*The sponsoring editor for this book was David Conti, the editing
supervisor was Fred Dahl, and the production supervisor was Suzanne
Babeuf. It was set in Baskerville by Inkwell Publishing Services.*

Printed and bound by R. R. Donnelley & Sons Company.

 This book is printed on recycled, acid-free paper containing a
minimum of 50% recycled de-inked fiber.

This publication is designed to provide accurate and authoritative
information in regard to the subject matter covered. It is sold with the
understanding that the publisher is not engaged in rendering legal,
accounting, or other professional service. If legal advice or other expert
assistance is required, the services of a competent professional person
should be sought.
                    *—from a declaration of principles jointly adopted by a committee
                    of the American Bar Association and a committee of publishers*

Dorothy F. Drach Joyce
Marian Herzfeld

Contents

Part 3. The Actual Processes: Market Timing, Investment Selection, Portfolio Modeling

8. Basic Market Timing and Specific Stock Selection   169

Authors' Note

The design of this book is to describe the opinions and investment techniques of the authors.

Any investment is effectively a projection into the future, and certainty of the future is not within the ability of mankind. There is no way any investment strategy can be guaranteed to result in success.

No two investors have identical needs, goals, and resources. Individuals, therefore, cannot be properly served by any duplicated publication. Before embarking on any investment strategy, the investor should utilize expert, competent, professional services suitable to the individual.

Portions of this book contain the actual results of the testing and application of the authors' theories. Readers are advised not to assume that future use of the described techniques will be profitable or equal past performance.

The authors and the publisher specifically disclaim any personal liability, loss, or risk incurred as a consequence to the use and application, either directly or indirectly, of any advice or information contained herein.

The authors welcome questions and comments concerning the contents of this volume and its practical application.

Inquiries concerning closed-end fund chapters may be directed to:

Thomas J. Herzfeld, President
Thomas J. Herzfeld & Co., Inc.
The Herzfeld Building
PO Box 161465
Miami, FL 33116
(305) 271-1900

Inquiries concerning general market theory, timing, stock selection, as well as stock, bond, and option portfolio modeling and/or the current Master List, may be directed to:

Robert F. Drach
Drach Market Research
PO Box 490092
Key Biscayne, FL 33149
(305) 361-5461

The authors wish to sincerely thank Patrick Joyce, Cecilia Gondor, Bridgette Fraschetti, Marjorie Bowen, and Jane Slaughter for their valuable contributions to this writing.

Thomas J. Herzfeld
Robert F. Drach

High-Return,
Low-Risk
Investment

PART 1

Separating Fact
from Fiction

1

A Professional Viewpoint of the Stock Market

The Elements of a Total Strategy

This book is about winning.

The reader is going to experience a journey into the stock market guided by two internationally recognized professionals who have demonstrated their capacity for attaining consistent profitability where most others fail.

It is a voyage into the real world of market participation based on our years of experience. There is no concern for impractical academic theories beyond exposing the fallacious aspects of many widely held beliefs as to both the structure of the market and the methods of participation. The concern is to describe logical theory, how it is utilized in actual market endeavors, and the results derived.

As professional investors, our livelihood depends heavily on consistent, accurate price forecasting. Since our market involvement is on a continuing, full-time basis, it is mandatory for us to minimize risk. Large losses would effectively put us out of business.

The importance of risk minimization is deeper than simply avoiding the discomfitures associated with loss. Profit consistency allows the full, often dramatic, benefits of compounding. It also functions to reduce psychological pressures that can create mistakes. In addition, it makes capital base management (the decision as to the amount of funds applied to any specific investment) much easier.

To minimize risk, we have developed a method of *market timing* that assists:

- In confining common stock investment to those periods in which probabilities indicate that the market will advance.
- In minimizing exposure (or incorporating short selling) when probabilities indicate the market will decline. Risk minimization can be extended beyond that associated with accurate market timing by proper *stock selection*. With the basic elements of risk reduction (market timing and specific stock selection) in place, a logical foundation has been constructed from which profit expansion can be emphasized without increasing risk.

The result is a total strategy of high-return, low-risk investment that can be extended beyond basic timing and specific stock selection—including the trading of bonds, options, index futures, and closed-end funds.

Describing the development and implementation of complete investment strategies requires the blending of realistic basic market theory, market timing, specific selection, closed-end funds, and other investment types. Each of these areas has a value in itself. You will see, however, when any of the elements are properly combined, the resulting strategy is far more rewarding than the benefits to be derived from any individual factor.

Hello, Reality!

As we proceed in providing an understanding of our strategies, we will be describing the market from the perspective of proven, professional stock traders.

This book differs from most financial writings in that time is not wasted on hypothetical nonsense as to what could have happened, should have happened, or would have happened given a particular market condition. We will detail what did happen, what we anticipate in the future, and why we think so. This includes fully disclosed, published portfolio modeling over a 16-year period, which has included a variety of market conditions; including the crash of 1987. The results, to date, are that 95+ percent of the stock positions specified for purchase concluded profitably. The ability to achieve these (and better) results is simply understanding and accepting the market for what it is: a business.

Whether the reader is a novice or an experienced investor, understanding our viewpoint requires a review of basic market realities. We have found that many widely held assumptions concerning the stock market are erroneous. What many consider to be fact is actually fiction, with erroneous beliefs forming the basis for subsequent disappointment from poor investment results. To facilitate consistently successful market participation, misconceptions must be replaced by realism. This education (or reeducation) process requires some discussion of the basic characteristics of common stock itself, as well as trading mechanisms.

Some of this material, at first, may appear elementary to the experienced investor. However, as you will soon realize, we are developing a realistic psychological approach to the stock market, as well as describing specific theories and techniques.

A basic concept central to the development of an appropriate frame of mind is the clear recognition that your purpose in the market is to win—to win money. The money has to come from somewhere. Obviously, it has to come from other market participants. We are therefore involved in the process of taking someone else's money.

The personal source of our profit is irrelevant. It matters not if those from whom we extract gain are widows, yuppies, or felons. What is important is to recognize that through the mechanics of stock trading we consciously want and fully intend to take money away from fellow market participants.

This simple, perhaps brutal, attitude is widely overlooked by those who view the market as an inanimate machine that effectuates price change by whim or some magical mathematical formula. As we shall see, consistent profit can be achieved by specific methods and formulas, but the core of such profitable techniques rests with the human factor, for it is money of living, breathing, human beings that we are going to acquire. And the chances are that these folks would prefer a result directly the opposite of our objective.

We are entering into a predator-prey relationship. Our potential victims all share two requirements necessary to participate in the stock market: (1) They have some cash, and (2) they are legally able to contract. That is, they are not too young (no minors allowed) or too crazy. Occasionally, those who do not meet requirement 2 sneak in, but that is not our concern as long as they satisfy criterion 1. The name of the stock market "game" is money. People like money and have been known to go to great lengths to acquire it. Although securities trading functions are under strict guidelines, there are those who push the rules to their limit in the attempt to profit at the expense of others. As you participate in the market, expect no quarter and give none.

The stock market is not a team sport.

The Professional

The term *professional* does not imply ability. Boxers who fight poorly but have obligated themselves to have their brains battered for pay are still considered pros. To qualify as a professional simply means to do something for money. It does not mean the "professional" does anything well.

In this book, we feel it is necessary to differentiate between the *true professional* and the *pseudoprofessional.* The pseudoprofessional is one who professes to be capable in market endeavors but is unable to profit consistently. It can be the individual investor who lies about his or her investing expertise. Or it can be someone closely associated with the securities industry who projects an image of capability but who is dependent on salary, fees, or commissions without any relationship to the ability to profit in actual market endeavors. If everyone who was unable to achieve reasonable profit in the market was required to have the word *vacancy* printed across their forehead, the average investor would be shocked at the number of authors, professors, brokers, and institutional portfolio managers so marked.

This does not mean that everyone on campus, within brokerage firms, or involved in discretionary management is a loser. There are competent personnel. The reality, however, is that incompetence is present even among those widely assumed to be the most astute. In addition, as we will describe in detail in future chapters, the very structure of the securities industry can destine some participants to poor performance, irrespective of their ability, conscripting otherwise logical and intelligent beings into the pseudoprofessional ranks.

Incompetence (from whatever cause) is not to be scorned. Once you have learned to differentiate between the true and pseudoprofessional, the incompetence of other "investors" is clearly desirable. The weakness of others—be it mental and/or structural and/or financial—provides us the opportunity to fulfill our purpose: taking money. Pseudoprofessionals, because they will always be present, are a constant source of profit to the true professional.

The true professional is *anyone* who has learned to utilize the trading of securities as a consistent source of monetary gain. In this context, true professionalism is not limited to those who are involved in the market on a full-time basis. Professionalism can be found among investors who rarely become involved. It is within the reach of the small, intermediate, and large investor, once he or she has learned to accept and function in the market in a realistic framework.

Functioning as a true professional does not require any unique intellectual abilities, complicated equipment or special educational background.

The fact is that the realistic, practical education needed to facilitate market success is not to be found in an ivory tower. The only means of obtaining such knowledge is by learning from true professionals whose livelihood depends on the ability to predict price change correctly. This ability is not inbred; it is learned and refined into systematic methods. The development of an understanding that allows any investor to function at a true professional level is a building process that entails four distinct steps:

1. Acquiring a basic knowledge of the rules and characteristics of common stock trading.
2. Learning how to recognize and concentrate on areas of opportunity.
3. Understanding and implementing techniques to minimize loss from the basis of market timing and proper stock selection.
4. Developing methods to expand gain while maintaining controls for reduced risk.

Intimidation

The market is a brain game. The trading structure provides a great degree of anonymity as to the specific identification of buyer and seller. Consequently, physical coercion to influence opponents has no place. With few exceptions from those broken by extended leverage, our opponents must make a willing, conscious decision to take a loss at the expense of our gain.

We are not referring here to intimidation involved in the actual trading of securities or psychological stresses *after* market participation has been initiated. We are speaking and attempting to reinforce the necessity to develop self-confidence *before* participation is initiated.

The market can appear (superficially) tough. It *must* be that way to enhance the process of profit extraction. To stand up and be ready is one thing; to be able to withstand subliminal pressure is another.

The securities industry takes in billions of dollars contributed by multitudes of people who have been (mis)led into believing that the markets are a complicated monster beyond their intellectual grasp and that the only way they can hope to participate successfully is to blindly entrust their monies to the investment decisions of others. This is basically intimidation which is the direct result of efforts to portray the market as complex.

Such portrayals have developed for two basic reasons. First, the large number of investment vehicles, the voluminous and complicated literature, and the specialized degrees of financial "professionalism" all tend to make many people feel that successful market participation requires a specialized academic background. Second, financial institutions that derive their subsistence from commissions and management fees advertise market success as being attainable only through the use of "astute" services—their own.

Neither special equipment nor special education is necessary. The market is, in fact, deviously simple. The images conveyed to the outside public carry no clout on the market inside, where the actual exchange of money takes place. It is the inside that is important.

To help put yourself at ease at the prospect of competing with others in the market, remember that the total strategy described in this book has, to date, resulted in the correct forecasting of common stock price changes at a level far above that attained by the vast majority of "professional" money managers, regardless of the image they project.

In addition, this strategy can be simplified so that it can be implemented swiftly and simply with the aid of only a telephone and newspaper. Economic platitudes and bookshelf-lined offices are unnecessary. You can acquire the ability to outperform most of the largest financial institutions within the confines of your home, with minimum time and expense.

The attainment of this market ability is the result of proper understanding. Success is not dependent on secret formulas, cheating, or native intelligence. It requires only that misconceptions be exposed, misdirections corrected, and realism instilled.

This does not mean you should never seek assistance and guidance. The help of a competent advisor and/or the use of a truly professional portfolio manager can be of great benefit. The individual investor must, however, understand the strategy and methods being utilized. It is *only* through such understanding that investors can protect themselves against possible abuses inherent in *blindly* entrusting others.

You are learning to function as a true professional when you realize that, for investment success, the best insurance is self-assurance.

What It Means to Be a Common Stockholder

Having refused to be intimidated and consciously aware that our purpose is to take money, we can now step into the market. Looking about, we can see that the gist is the redistribution of wealth via the trading back and forth of common stock.

Common stock is nothing more than a piece of paper stating the proportionate ownership of the corporation that issues the stock. For example, at the time of this writing, American Telephone and Telegraph had 1,335,609,000 outstanding shares of common stock. Therefore, if you own 100 shares of AT&T, your shares represent 1/13,365,090 of the corporation.

This example helps you put into proper perspective the absurdity of developing an emotional attachment to an individual corporation. For the vast majority of investors, their proportionate share of ownership is insignificant. The "piece of paper" does not care who owns it or why. Those who transpose ownership into a symbol of status or ego support are both wasting their time and making themselves more susceptible to a variety of common errors.

We all remember Dear Old Uncle Charlie. Right before he choked to death on his gruel, he said, "If anything ever happens to me, don't sell National Zipper. I bought the stock in 1920 for $10 a share and now it's $200. It has been good to us. Hold on!"

Uncle Charlie was emotionally locked into National Zipper by the common lure of witnessing paper profitability without a true understanding of the value of compounding. No matter that Uncle Charlie was eating lumpy gruel because he refused to cash in on National Zipper. No matter that, if National Zipper had managed to grow at only 10 percent a year, the stock would be worth $7000! Uncle Charlie was simply in love with a piece of paper.

Over the years, National Zipper (as the name implies) fluctuated in price. Profit maximization, as well as risk minimization, required getting in when Zipper was down and getting out when Zipper was up. The fact that, no matter how much Uncle Charlie loved National Zipper, the National Zipper stock cared nothing about him.

One-sided love affairs are tragic, as are the results of those who indulge in stock marriage. For those so affected, the divorce can be made painless by means of a realistic understanding of the true nature of common stock.

There are intrinsic merits to common stock ownership because the holders of the stock are entitled to certain privileges or rights. These major rights can be divided into three categories:

1. The right to information
2. The right to vote
3. The right to corporate earnings

The use, or misuse, of these rights can influence stock price. A basic understanding of these rights is necessary to prevent one from being misled by the volumes of literature that portray stock ownership in an unrealistic context.

The Right to Information

Each stockholder is provided with quarterly and annual reports concerning various aspects of corporate activity.

These reports contain financial information as well as a discussion of current corporate highlights and future prospects. The discussion generally begins in the form of a message from the corporate president, who is usually making a case for his retention: taking credit if the company is doing well and blaming others if it is doing poorly. After all, it is his message. For practical purposes, this discussion is of little concern because there is little the individual stockholder can do even if the management is incompetent.

The financial data presented in the reports is also of little benefit to the average investor. The accountant's statement will usually state that the accounting was conducted using "generally accepted accounting principles." All this means is that there is a great deal of variance in the methods of accounting allowed. Since things can be accounted for differently, the earnings of a corporation can vary with the type of accounting utilized. In many cases, the published financial data is quite misleading and is presented in such a way that it results in confusion rather than an understanding of the corporation's actual financial condition.

Many analysts who thrive on dissecting financial data pay little attention to the annual report provided to shareholders, preferring the much more detailed information in corporation's 10K filings with the Securities and Exchange Commission, which is available to the public.

The most important things to remember are that the information is provided to the general public as well as to the shareholders and that it is always presented *after the fact* of recorded corporate events. Stock prices related to this information have therefore almost always occurred by the time the stockholder or anyone else receives the information through corporate printing.

In its proper context from the perspective of stock trading, the stockholders' right to information is relatively meaningless since the information is usually late and is available to all.

The Right to Vote

As owners, stockholders have a right to determine some major corporate decisions concerning the selection of directors, the authorization of additional shares, the acceptance or rejection of takeover bids, the selection of accountants, and other issues. The vote does not concern the day-to-day management activities of the corporation except through the selection of directors.

Unless some matter of extreme concern should arise, voting is confined to an annual meeting. These are usually rather dull affairs where the president gets up and generally follows the same pattern as in the discussions in financial reports: commending himself and management if the speech brings good news and blaming others if there are problems. A vote is then taken on the issues with the majority, almost invariably, following management's suggestion.

Many corporations, including some of the largest, have a majority of outstanding shares under the control of one family or some other tightly knit group, which effectively controls the vote. Control of the vote does not necessarily mean personal control of the majority of outstanding stock. As a company grows, often the original dominant stockholders sell their interest to many different entities, thus creating widely dispersed ownership. This dispersion of stock can have the effect of eliminating communication among stockholders. Therefore, the logistics of organizing displeased stockholders is a difficult and costly task.

Perhaps the most common shareholder complaint is to see huge salaries paid to managers who have very little (or no) investment in the form of personal stock holdings in the corporation. This clearly demonstrates how corporate management can often perpetuate and fatten itself at the expense of stockholders and without the risks inherent in stock ownership.

For the majority of stockholders and from a trading perspective, except for those rare instances when each vote really counts, the right to vote is as meaningless as the right to information.

The Right to Earnings

This right is the most important single characteristic of common stock, for it (at least in most theories) is the dominant factor in determining stock price. The corporate earnings (theoretically) belong to the owners (stockholders), who therefore have the potential to realize tremendous profit if the corporation is successful.

One must not blindly assume, however, that if corporate profits rise the stock will also appreciate. As will be described in detail in later chapters, the exact opposite can occur. The fact is that there is no automatic correlation between corporate profitability and common stock pricing. It often takes more than earnings gains to create an advance in the market price of a stock.

Corporate management has the choice of doing any one (or a combination) of three things with earnings:

1. Retain them within the corporation to finance future growth.
2. Distribute them to stockholders.
3. Steal them.

Most texts on the market ignore theft, considering such nastiness a rare event that it is not important. The general perception of corporate theft is that of a slimy little over-the-counter stock sold to the public at a ridiculous price by management or a seedy embezzler packing misappropriated cash in a suitcase and running to Brazil. Theft at the expense of shareholders can take many forms and can occur in dramatic amounts in the largest corporations. There are two basic types of theft:

1. *That in direct violation of law.* All you need to do is look at the paper to see the Mr. Boesky types being taken away for stealing millions, or the billions in fraud that contributed in making the insurance protection for the entire savings and loan industry of the United States insolvent. Such behavior cannot be shrugged off or considered a laughing matter because of the light penalties; remember whose pockets—stockholders' and taxpayers'—were fleeced.

2. *That not in direct violation of law.* This includes management's paying itself exorbitant salaries, perks, options, and other compensation without merit. It also includes such practices as putting friends and relatives on the payroll at inflated costs or making corporate contracts at a price above real market value because of personal interest. In the most abrasive form, management sells corporate assets (or the entire corporation) to itself or "others," where management has an interest at a significant discount. In effect, any managerial "decision" that unethically takes from the rightful owners (stockholders) is stealing. Such activities are common and easily identified, but, since they fall into the classification of "business judgment," they are beyond statutory prosecution.

The point: There are very nice people and very nasty people involved in both the structure of securities trading and in the corporations represented by that trading.

As we will discuss in Chap. 2, there are methods to significantly reduce the chance of becoming victimized by scoundrels, but the reality of the market must include clear, ongoing recognition that the environment involves some unsavory characters. To repeat, it is not a team sport.

Setting thievery aside for the moment, can concentrate on whether corporate earnings should be retained to fund future growth or distributed to stockholders via dividends.

The generally "taught" academic approach is that the corporation (extrapolated to read "stockholders") is most benefited by applying earnings to future growth; consequently, a low dividend policy expands future potential.

From the perspective of professional investing, however, an exceptionally low (or inconsistent) dividend policy is a weak point. There is a real correlation between the degree of potential price decline and the dividend when the stock price descends to the point where the dividend payment is offering an exceptionally high yield in relation to the market price of the stock. In other words, people will buy the stock simply because of the dividend. This buying can help support the market price of the stock and minimize risk. It should be noted that, although the dividend yield may help soften the decline of a stock, there is no significant evidence that a high dividend in itself will help the price of a stock to advance.

We have found the three basic stockholder rights to be shallow at best, with only the right to earnings providing a general benefit. Even this right, stolen or not, provides no guarantee that the market price will appreciate.

As an investor, your primary concern is *optimal* utilization of common stock in your own capital growth. In this context, stockholder rights in themselves do not warrant any emotional attachment. The advantage of the stock market is liquidity. That is, you can easily move in and out of the stock market as well as within the market. By being long (buying) in anticipation of rising prices, or by going short (selling) in anticipation of lower prices you can benefit either way, as long as you correctly anticipate the direction, with very low transaction costs. It is a function of easy maneuverability to whatever area is providing the most opportunity at any given time.

To identify yourself with an individual stock issue is effectively to identify with the "rights." The rights are often illusion and in any form do not guarantee success. Emotional attachment to the rights only encourages relatively poor performance because it does not allow either objective reasoning or full utilization of the liquidity factor.

Face it. As a holder of common stock from a professional trading perspective, you are involved for the price ride. And, like it or not, to maximize profit, the ride has to be for a limited duration. No matter what the stock, the time will come to get out of the market entirely or obtain a position in another stock for another ride. To function as a professional, you must accept in fact that *stock is a piece of paper to be utilized as a medium of exchange in acquiring the monies of others.*

The Importance of Emotion

We have now taken one of our most important steps in learning to function successfully in the market. We have detached ourselves emotionally from common stock. We *have not* detached ourselves emotionally from the process of trading. We are very emotional about making money. We like it! It feeds ourselves and our families. Emotion, therefore, is not to be avoided. It is to be properly directed to the acquisition of the *cash* of others.

Most texts describing trading methodologies stress the need to be devoid of emotion, imposing a rigid "mechanical" process of market participation. The vast majority of such strategies fare poorly over time with their difficulties usually directly traceable to the elimination of the human (emotional) element.

As we proceed into the development of the understanding of total strategies and their implementation, it will become increasingly clear that the market is a mechanical business. It is silent. It is brutal. But *certainly it is not* devoid of emotion. Emotion is, in fact, often the most dominant force in the market. As such, when recognized and properly understood, it is a source of profit.

Masochists excluded, all investors (from the wild-eyed speculator, to the most conservative retiree, to ourselves) share one common emotion: greed.

Greed

Greed is the motivational core of the marketplace, and recognition of its pervasiveness is an integral element in implementating a successful market strategy. Although not considered one of the best human traits, greed is perfectly acceptable in the market. It accompanies a genuine desire to win, and it aids in the acquisition of disproportionate amounts of money.

The recognition and acceptance of greed in yourself is not the advantage. The successful investor is able to recognize and quantify the importance of greed in his fellow market participants. When greed results in our opponents' losing rational perspective, opportunity develops. This loss of perspective is especially significant during periods of euphoria, whether in the market as a whole or in a particular stock group. In effect, greed provides buyers at inflated stock prices.

As you shall see in future chapters, the degree of greed in the market can be measured by various means, such as the amount of margin debt, put:call premium and volume ratios, surveys of analysts' opinions, and other measures of sentiment. By utilizing these measurements, you can take stock positions with the reasonable expectation that the stock can be sold at higher prices to investors motivated solely by greed. Greed can also be a factor in stock positions taken for reasons other than preying on the emotions of others. Any particular stock can become attractive to the misdirected greedy for a variety of reasons. Recognition of the greed factor allows us flexibility; so we can raise our selling price more than in "normal" trading strategy, thereby increasing our profit.

Despair

Next to greed, the most important emotion to be recognized in professional market participation is despair. Just as greed can lure people into the market at inflated prices, despair can compel people to sell at excessively low prices. Often, underlying despair leads to panic selling, a situation that allows unique opportunities. For example, suppose we decide to buy a stock for reasons other than taking advantage of investor emotions, only to find that the despair of others has become a factor. We then can lower the price that we are willing to pay. As with greed, despair can be measured by a variety of sentiment indicators.

Necessity

Another factor in the market that carries emotional connotation and is important to the professional is necessity. Whenever necessity, whether psychological or financial, becomes the primary criterion for a buy or sell decision, the decision is being made under duress. Duress puts the investor at the mercy of the market—more specifically at the mercy of other market participants, including ourselves. Neither charity nor compassion is a trait of the true nature of the market. The investor acting out of necessity will be financially brutalized, with the profits accruing to those who function professionally.

A good example of necessity associated with selling is the crash of 1987. As we will describe in detail in later chapters, our timing technique indicated that the market was due to splat. A variety of factors were involved, including excessive margin debt. When prices began to descend rapidly, those who had employed excessive borrowing (margin) were "called." That is, they either had to put up more cash to collateralize the declining value of their stock purchases or have their stock sold: no other choices. For many, the cash (or psychological resolve) was not available, and they were sold out as prices plunged. This is selling by necessity. When the final smash occurred, it sent Wall Street wailing. We were positioned to buy heavily and did so at very discounted prices. To us, the "infamous" day of October 19, 1987 was absolutely delightful.

Necessity associated with nonprofessional buying often involves excessive nonprofessional short selling. Short selling will be dealt with later in detail. At this point all you need to know is that selling a stock does not require true (physical) ownership, but the short seller must post sufficient assets to be able to buy the stock at the current market price. The short seller is betting that the market will go down, thereby profiting by buying back the "short" stock at a lower price.

When the short sellers have overextended themselves and prices rise, they are forced to buy at higher prices. They become "necessitated" by the financial (or psychological) strains associated with collateralizing their short positions. In effect, their own buying activity out of necessity helps to elevate prices, making their condition proportionately worse. (Heh, heh.)

Necessity is mentioned as a source of profit at this time to emphasize the predator-prey relationship and to show that wide price fluctuations can occur because of maneuverings within the market that have no relation to standard fundamental analysis.

Hope and Luck

Hope and luck are basic elements present to some extent in all aspects of everyone's life. In professional stock market participation, hope and luck play very minor roles. Profitability in the market depends on the development and implementation of the ability to forecast price change accurately. This price prediction is a very logical process, in which hope and luck have no objective role. However, hope and luck are important because they are the guiding force of thousands of investors from whom we can profit.

The most rewarding aspect (for us) about investors who rely on hope and luck is quite simply that they will lose. If they are initially successful, they will attribute their result to what they consider "rational" reasons. The basic reason for their success was pure luck; yet they will isolate factors that will lead them to believe their gain was due to intelligent logic. This process traps the unwary because, when the illogical factors again present themselves, the investor will apply an increased amount of capital and expect results similar to those previously attained. Eventually, the investor will lose because the illogical strategy will sooner or later demonstrate its lack of merit. Reliance on hope and luck, therefore, is not only dangerous, but will cause certain eventual failure. As in a gambling casino, a great many winners will keep on playing until they have given the winnings back plus a portion (if not all) of their own money. The professional functions as the "house," which has designed the odds to be in its favor.

The Market as a Business

Greed, despair, necessity, hope, luck. When associated with one's financial fate, these unpleasant terms denote, to many, a certain degree of amorality in the process of professional market participation. This is not the case.

Whenever one attempts to preserve and/or expand capital, whether by hiding cash in a mattress or by becoming involved in the stock market, he or she is in business. The nature of the market, like the nature of any business in a free enterprise system, is competitive. The early installation of this reality is imperative in establishing a firm psychological base from which to expand and succeed through investment.

In an uncertain economy, the stock market is one of the few areas that provide consistent profitability at acceptable rates of return. The holding of cash, conventional savings, and most debt instruments can pose inordinate risk through the eroding effects of inflation. The advantages of real estate are largely a myth, because of possible illiquidity, high transaction costs, and excessive leverage. Commodities, because of the leverage aspect, are exceptionally dangerous. For us, the answer lies in the stock market. But the market is an environment unto itself to which the investor must adapt before consistently successful participation can be achieved.

The market is neither immoral, amoral, or moral: *It is a business*. As in any business, the most successful are keenly aware of the realities associated with both the characteristics of the industry and competitors.

Basic Factors Creating Price Change

The forces that shift stock prices can be divided into two categories.

1. *Extrinsic.* These factors are outside the mechanical trading structure of the market and include standard fundamentals: corporate earnings, interest rates, general economic conditions, political policies, etc.

2. *Intrinsic.* These factors are related to market structure: the mechanics of trading, emotion, repetitive behavioral characteristics of various market participants, and any other force that can effectuate price change resulting from internal market conditions.

As those of us who endured the rituals associated with the attainment of graduate degrees in finance can attest, intrinsic factors are largely ignored. Very few investors, both institutional and individual, seem to fully comprehend the tremendous effect that intrinsic factors can have on price change—often greater than the extrinsic factors.

Consistently successful market participation is simply a matter of realistic adaptation. This involves clear recognition of the existence of both extrinsic and intrinsic factors, as well as the blending of these elements into a total investment strategy.

Why There Will Always Be Losers

The authors of this text, either jointly or individually, have been featured in every major financial publication, have been regularly interviewed on both national and international television networks, have had their writings distributed worldwide by some of the largest publishers, and manage many millions of dollars.

This can lead to a concern. If the authors distributed their techniques too widely, would the result be fewer losers and the loss of all the advantages? Rest assured, the losers will always be there. Some of the reasons are as follows:

1. The vast majority of the financial media is concerned with reporting the sensational, *after-the-fact* "reasons" for price change. The result is a huge industry busy in the constant process of reinforcing false concepts of what the market is and what causes the market to "move."
2. Many of the most widely held academic theories have been developed by theoreticians who have no practical experience in the market. These theories are basically erroneous and/or of little use unless combined with other aspects that are either unknown to the "teacher" or ignored. Those so taught will follow and adhere to what they have been told to believe.
3. The structural framework of many financial institutions is such that from time to time they are literally forced into situations where advantage can be taken.
4. The securities industry is based on sales, income derived from commissions and management fees. Naturally, its efforts to attract customers gravitate to and concentrate on whatever most easily produces a sale. Securities are intangibles. They are pieces of paper denoting ownership and/or debt, and for most investors they are more theoretical than

tangible. Financial sales, therefore, inevitably incorporate more emotional decisions than the marketing of other products. The misdirected emotion of others is a partial source of our profit. The securities industry is a multibillion-dollar force working day and night to bring funds into the market and provide a constant source of profit for the professional.

5. The bulk of published literature, purportedly and with good intent designed to be of assistance, falls into two basic categories.

  a. *Fundamental.* Stressing standard economic concepts and their presumed effect on common stock pricing, but ignorant of intrinsic factors. Such writings are fine, except that the result is analogous to designing a boat well, but building only the front portion. It sinks.

  b. *Technical.* This includes charting, waves, time "cycles," astrology, and anything else that concentrates on price and/or volume measurements without regard for fundamental and/or internal structural factors. As we shall see, some of this data is beneficial but the bulk is nothing more than nonsensical applications of misdirected hindsight. Standard "technical" analysis can provide only tiny pieces to the "puzzle" of total strategy. The pure technician's boat will sink far more swiftly than that of the pure fundamentalist's.

6. Let's not forget the thieves. As anyone who has been sold investment lemons (by broiler room operations and the like) has experienced, very real members of the financial "community" have no intention of making the investor more intelligent and are benefited only by reinforcing misunderstanding.

Summary

In this single chapter we have attempted to provide the foundation necessary to quickly begin the building process of a total investment strategy.

The market is an environment unto itself. It is superficially "tough." It involves a variety of characters of varying ethical intent, both in the mechanical/structural aspects of trading and in the management of the corporations being traded. Reality is mandatory, including the recognition of predator-prey relations.

For the unwary, pressures from both intrinsic and extrinsic misconceptions can elicit behavior resulting in loss. Avoiding such discomfiture requires building a total, objective strategy, as well as being acutely aware that such efforts must blend all psychological, structural, fundamental, and technical elements.

In the opinion and experience of the authors, once the learning (adaptation) process is completed, the stock market provides both the easiest source of profit consistency and the dramatic benefits of compounding capital growth. In addition, with controls of the stock market in hand, you can extrapolate the knowledge to a variety of other investment types.

The central element of this writing is not hypothetical. It involves actual, fully documented results. That does not mean the "investment world" will be as kind to us in the future as it has in the past. But we have not witnessed any techniques, to date, that are better than those the authors' have developed, relative to the objectives of profit consistency and compounding. If we found better methods, be assured we would utilize them in our quest for maximizing gain while controlling risk.

2
The Tools:
Common Stock
Selection

The Importance of
Stock Selection

The market is composed of millions of people, each of them attempting (knowingly or unknowingly) to profit at someone else's expense. The market is also composed of thousands of individual stocks.

To the uninitiated, the magnitude of the number of possible alternative decisions, both as to specific stock selection and as to the investment method to utilize, can appear overwhelming. Simplification is easily accomplished. As a first step, consider market participation as analogous to hunting. The successful hunt requires the proper choice of weapon as well as the identification and isolation of quarry. It is a predator-prey relationship. There is a primary difference between conventional hunting and that in the market. In the market the prey we seek is also armed and on the hunt for us. The successful market participants know that the hunt is not for sport but to ensure financial survival.

Our choice of weapon is common stock.

The decision as to the specific stock(s) we will use is extremely important for three reasons.

1. The maximum benefit to be derived from any given market situation is enhanced by *timing*. that is, knowing when the market as a whole is likely to rise or fall. Timing is very helpful because the majority of

individual stocks will (almost always) go in the same direction as the popularized averages. The method of market timing utilized in this book (Chap. 8) involves the monitoring of properly selected individual stocks as an indicator of future overall market movement. Consequently, a basic understanding of the selection techniques in this chapter is necessary to fully comprehend the actual timing method described later.

2. The design of this timing method is such that the same stocks used to determine future overall market direction can be utilized for actual investment. This *combines* what are generally considered two separate *processes*: a process for timing future market moves, plus a process of determining which specific stocks to purchase or sell to take maximum advantage of the move. Not only does this technique save time and energy; it also helps minimize risk.

3. Although all stocks (simply because their prices fluctuate) can be shown through hindsight to have provided profit opportunity, not all stocks can be utilized in a program designed to derive profit on a consistent basis. You should be able to use the stocks selected *repeatedly* to extract profit.

This approach involves benefits beyond those associated with timing and repeated use. The confusion that can occur in the task of attempting to select specific individual issues from among the thousands available is greatly simplified by having the entire market condensed to a manageable list. With concentration focused, the investor is provided the time necessary to become knowledgeable about any unique characteristics of the stocks being monitored. The market is wrought with psychological pressures which can be greatly reduced through the development of confidence brought about by familiarity.

Each of the vast number of stocks traded publicly has its individual characteristics and associated potential of reward and degree of risk. The process of differentiating among stocks to determine which provide acceptable risk with respect to potential reward have kept, and will always keep, hordes of academicians and theoreticians busy. Many who have burned out their brains on the task conclude that the process is impossible, stating that the future direction of stock prices is random, and that therefore the stock market is suitable only for "venture capital." By this they mean the stock market is not predictable and as such carries inordinate risk. What they really mean is they have not been able to figure out risk/reward relationships or much else. The forest remains invisible because of the trees.

The professional lives and thrives in that "invisible" forest. As in any environment, survival and growth are function of proper adaptation. Venture capital concepts are fine as long as the capital consistently ventures from someone else to ourselves.

Extrinsic and Intrinsic Factors
Relative to Stock Selection

The stock selection process is simplified by taking a professional stance from the onset. Our basic objectives are to select stocks that allow us two things:

1. *Our continued existence.* We are in the market to stay and profit, and that requires money. We will have no money if we purchase stocks that disappear through bankruptcy. Brilliant concept! Do not buy garbage.

2. *A reasonable probability that someone else will be willing to buy our stock at a higher price than we paid.* Another brilliant concept! Try to make sure there will be someone in the future who will provide profit.

At first, our objectives may seem so elementary as to be foolish. However, the market as a whole is elementary. We have already taken important steps into the forest. We are blending intrinsic and extrinsic factors, a basic necessity of professional participation and a basic factor overlooked by tens of thousands of investors. In other words, we are just as concerned with identifying who will provide us profits as we are with the corporate characteristics of the stocks selected.

This approach varies significantly from that of most investors. The general assumption is that, if a stock with good earnings (or other) prospects is selected, the prospects will materialize and suddenly the price will rise providing easy profit. This is a childish belief in surprise. The investor is buying something presumed to be undervalued in the hope that its real value is going to become suddenly apparent to someone who until then was too ignorant to foresee the real value. This unknown someone is presumably going to be eager to buy at the higher price.

This is folly. The concentration is solely on extrinsic factors (corporate characteristics), without clear thought about the intrinsic factors. Your actual profit has to come from a fellow market participant and the corporation's stock is only the tool. To put it bluntly, why *assume* there is someone more stupid out there who is going to provide profit because of surprise? Granted, no great intellectual capability is required for market involvement, but what if the dullards are broke? Or what if they are so ignorant that they never see the great value the original investor thought he discovered? Or, as is a very common event, the great surprise was already factored into the price of the stock when the original "discovery" was made?

Our stock selection process therefore involves two elements:

1. *Extrinsic.* We want to become involved in the stock of corporations that meet reasonable criteria for quality in respect to economic fundamentals.

2. *Intrinsic.* We want stocks that can be utilized easily and repeatedly within the mechanical trading structure of the market. This involves the potential of attracting a variety of identifiable market participants from whom we can acquire profit.

In effect, there are two risks in the market. One is the fundamental quality of the corporation, and the other is within market structure. Risk (in any investment type) can never be totally eliminated, but it can be lessened by attempting to minimize unknowns from both extrinsic and intrinsic factors.

The actual selection of specific common stock can be a tedious process. Fortunately, the market often favors the lethargic, and it is fair play to utilize the work of others. Information concerning the ongoing research of individual stocks is usually readily available and often free.

Value Line, Standard & Poor's, and other fairly well respected publications provide stock ratings and other information on a regularly updated basis. These publications are available by subscription and are often subscribed to by libraries, so that the information can be obtained without cost. Brokerage firms and other financial institutions often provide their own research which scans a large number of stocks and then categorizes them according to fundamental quality. Note, however, that such research is usually designed to assist in sales and the quality of such material is quite variable. Also note that the size of the research department is not necessarily indicative of quality. Bigger does not automatically translate to better in the world of securities analysis. Small, specialized firms often significantly outperform those much larger who spend millions to project an "image" of special ability.

The Authors' Method of Stock Selection

In our method of stock selection, we first determine which specific stocks warrant investment consideration. Qualification for consideration does not necessarily translate into actual investment. Consideration is only the first step. The actual implementation of purchase and sell decisions depends on a number of other factors which will be described after we have determined the general group of stocks we want to utilize. The qualification process is a filtering technique, through which thousands of different stocks are condensed down to a manageable number. This is not a hypothetical process. It is the actual method we use, and it is the basis from which our extraordinary high degree of accurate price forecasting (demonstrated in following chapters) was developed.

While very logical, the stock selection procedure is possibly too lengthy for the average investor. *Do not be alarmed.* After explaining the long method, we will describe a greatly simplified approach that is easy and quick, and that approximates the results of the longer method. The following lengthy explanation, however, is necessary for an understanding of the logic of the selection process.

The Criteria

The following qualifications are considered mandatory for the stock of any corporation to be of sufficient quality to warrant possible inclusion in our market strategy.

1. Earnings Predictability. If you are involved in a serious hunt for a dangerous prey, your primary concern is the reliability and working condition of your weapon. Our weapon is common stock, and its specific selection is a serious (core) concern. The probability of error must be minimized to help assure survival.

As discussed in the previous chapter, earnings are generally the most important factor in the value of a corporation. It was also mentioned that earnings generally are not easily predicted. Some corporations, however, have demonstrated a consistent record of earnings predictability. Because of the existence of such corporations there is no need to rely on corporations whose earnings are less predictable.

As a rule, we consider the earnings predictability factor acceptable if the corporation has managed to meet earnings projections ±15 percent during each of the previous seven years. Disqualifying corporations that have not demonstrated a satisfactory past predictability as to earnings helps to eliminate fundamental surprises, as well as about 80 percent of all common stocks.

2. Earnings Growth. Predictable earnings does not mean acceptable earnings. Because of the availability of corporations with demonstrated patterns of earnings growth, it is only logical to direct investment toward these issues.

The reason for this criterion is deeper than psychological reassurance. Corporations with demonstrated earnings growth get wider publicity within the investment community, and consequently they are considered for investment by a larger number of investors, both individual and institutional. It is from other investors that profits are taken. The greater the number and different types of investors involved, the easier the task of prey identification.

Keep in mind, however, that past earnings growth in itself is not enough. Future earnings projections must also indicate a pattern of growth. The market is most influenced by anticipation of the future. Limiting investment to corporations with both earnings predictability and earnings growth concentrates attention on quality, which can (but won't necessarily) help in supporting market price.

This earnings growth criterion generally halves the number of issues that were able to survive the test for earnings predictability.

3. Dividend Protection and Growth.   Dividends play a role both in added income and in risk reduction. To maximize these benefits, a corporation's dividend policy must be established and stable. The decision as to what portion of earnings will be paid to shareholders in the form of cash dividends, relative to the amount retained to finance future corporate growth, must be reasonable.

A consistent dividend policy, providing adequate assurance that the dividend will continue to be paid (protection) as well as increase (growth), reduces the possibility of unpleasant "surprises." It also reduces the number of stocks we find suitable for investment consideration.

4. Liquidity.   As discussed in the previous chapter, one of the primary advantages of common stock as an investment type is maneuverability; the investor can buy or sell quickly with very low transaction costs. This ease of movement is termed *liquidity*.

Liquidity involves two elements, which vary as to the characteristics of individual stocks:

1. The number of shares a stock trades daily. This is the standard measurement of liquidity. It is only reasonable to confine interest to those issues that provide sufficient trading volume so that orders can be accommodated without disrupting price.

2. The "mix" of investors in the stock's market. To us, the liquidity factor also involves an aspect largely ignored in conventional analysis. Profes-

sional participation mandates the realization that success depends on the actions of other investors. It is only logical, therefore, that the more varied the market participants interested in a particular security, the more areas of potential profit.

In later chapters we will detail that market participants can be isolated and categorized (public, institutional, market makers, etc.) as to their repetitive behavior, which can provide us opportunity. The more varied and abundant the prey, the easier the task of the predator. Consequently, our liquidity requirements provide a dual function in filtering for both the number of shares traded and the number of different participants. Accordingly, the list of qualifying stocks is decreased.

5. Shareholder Concern.   Unfortunately, a corporation's fundamental (earnings) success does not automatically translate into the success of shareholders. In a variety of ways, management can intervene to block owners (shareholders) from experiencing presumed benefits. *Greenmail* is the corporate acronym for blackmail. The usual form is a "hostile buyer" (supposedly independent of management) who purchases a relatively small amount of outstanding shares and then threatens to buy controlling interest. The connotation is that with such control it will oust current management and ravage the corporation's assets.

To avoid the greenmailer's threat (and retain their paychecks), a common reaction is for the management to deem it "wise" to buy the greenmailer's stock at a price above "market." That is, "pay off" the greenmailer at prices higher than those available to other owners (shareholders).

Although greenmail could conceivably be justified in some instances, in general we question the credibility of managers that engage in such practices, thereby disqualifying their corporations from investment consideration.

The capitalization structure of corporations (that is, the monies the corporation utilizes to fund its activities) involves two basic sources: *equity* (monies contributed by and/or earned for stockholders) or *borrowings* (debt). The capitalization "structure" is simply the ratio of debt versus equity.

To avoid "hostile takeovers," greenmail and other activities that could interfere with management's security, a popular maneuver is to *restructure*. The general pattern of restructuring is for the corporation to add debt to the point that the new debt load makes the corporation less attractive to potential buyers. The excessive debt has the net effect of reducing the corporation's fundamental quality, with the excessive interest charges detract from earnings and making it more difficult for the corporation to survive adverse economic conditions.

In the middle to late 1980s, the restructuring binge financed by junk bonds resulted in many previously superior corporations degenerating to bankruptcy. Despite past records of earnings predictability and growth, we usually delete corporations that have restructured with excessive debt because they are less likely to meet earnings projections.

Inordinately *high compensation* (in the form of salary or options) to senior management and/or their families and friends is another managerial practice that can disqualify a corporation from our list of issues suitable for investment consideration.

Many corporations have various *classes of common stock.* The most important differentiations among the classes are usually concerned with rights involving dividends and/or voting. The various classifications are usually distinguished alphabetically—Class A, Class B, and so on. Note that alphabetical positioning is not necessarily indicative of the merit of the class of stock. For example, Class A may be nonvoting and Class B voting.)

Of particular concern is the restriction of the voting right and/or preferential right to dividends to a class that is not available to the public. This characteristic is usually found when a family or other tightly knit group is able to sell the public the lower classes of stock. The public is, in effect, capitalizing the holders of the preferential stock and accepting disproportionate risk. Although such "class" issues are defended rather vigorously, those most vocal in the defense are those holding the preferential stock.

It is a general policy of ours to disqualify such stock issues, but not because of the voting right. As discussed in Chap. 1, the vote is relatively meaningless to the vast majority of stockholders. Our objection is to the basic attitude of the issuing corporation. The motivation demonstrated by any corporation selling "ownership" (via common stock) and then not allowing the stockholder even the gesture of a vote, carries the implication of pomposity at best and hypocrisy at worst. Neither of these traits is desirable in any form and the avoidance of such issues is prudent.

Family-held/publicly-traded situations are similar to those involving stock classes, except that all outstanding stock has voting privileges and equal rights to dividends. The majority of outstanding shares, however, remain under the control of one family. Thus, nonfamily stockholders are effectively as powerless as if their stock has no voting rights.

Such circumstances, although quite common, are not an automatic reason to disqualify the stock issue from investment consideration. Almost all publicly traded corporations will eventually fall under the control of a few individuals whether or not they personally control the majority of outstanding stock.

Family-controlled corporations must, however, be closely monitored to isolate those instances in which management is passing from one generation to the next.

Managerial ability is not a genetic trait. Quite often, when the second and/or successive generations become dominant, the intelligence and drive that initially allowed the corporation to prosper tend to lessen. Another potential problem is sibling rivalry, which can result in effective stagnation of corporate growth.

In summary, the basic intent of our criteria is to select corporations that are stable and predictable. We want to minimize "surprise" from fundamental corporate events. By doing so, the process of actual market participation becomes greatly simplified because attention can be focused on intrinsic market mechanisms (timing and the other aspects of trading that are most affected by internal market structure).

Also important is the fact that our filtering process is a search for the quality of two elements: the corporation's business and its record in conducting that business, as well as the individual managers directing the corporation.

Master List of Common Stocks

The following list of common stocks are those that meet all of the previously discussed criteria at the time of this writing. The stocks have been listed by symbol, according to the principal exchange on which they are traded.

New York Stock Exchange

ABT	Abbott Laboratories
ABS	Albertson's, Inc.
AHP	American Home Products
AIG	American International Group
AWK	American Water Works
BUD	Anheuser-Busch Companies
ADM	Archer-Daniels Midland
AUD	Automatic Data Processing
ONE	Banc One Corp.
BOH	Bancorp Hawaii
BDG	Bandag,, Inc.
BDX	Becton Dickinson
BMS	Bemis Co.
HRB	Block (H&R)
BA	Boeing

BMY	Bristol Myers
CZNB	Citizens Utilities Cl. B
KO	Coca-Cola
CAG	ConAgra, Inc.
CRD.B	Crawford & Co. Cl. B
CNK	Crompton & Knowles
DLX	Deluxe Corp.
DDS	Dillard Department Stores
DNB	Dun & Bradstreet
EMR	Emerson Electric
FSS	Federal Signal
GE	General Electric
GPC	Genuine Parts
GWW	Grainger (W.W.)
HRD	Hannaford Bros.
HNZ	Heinz
HSY	Hershey Foods
HB	Hillenbrand Indus.
HRL	Hormel
HUBB	Hubbell Cl. B
IPG	Interpublic Grp. Cos.
K	Kellogg Co.
KMB	Kimberly-Clark
LLY	Lilly (Eli)
LTD	Limited Inc.
LOR	Loral Corp.
MKC	Marion Merrell Dow
MA	May Dept. Stores
MCD	McDonald's Corp.
MES	Meville Corp.
MRK	Merck & Co.
MMM	Minnesota Mining/Manufacturing
NWL	Newell Co.
PLL	Pall Corp.
PBY	Pep Boys-Man,Mo,Ja
MO	Phillip Morris Co.
PBI	Pitney Bowes
RTN	Raytheon Co.
RBD	Rubbermaid, Inc.
SLE	Sara Lee Corp.
SVM	Service Master L.P.
SCY	Society Corp.

STI	Sun Trust Banks
SVU	Super Valu Stores
SNV	Synovus Financial
SYY	Sysco Corp.
TMK	Torchmark
UST	UST, Inc.
WAG	Walgreen Co.
WMT	Wal-Mart Stores
WEC	Wisconsin Energy Corp.

American Stock Exchange

FES	First Empire State
SMO	Santa Monica Banks
TFX	Teleflex, Inc.
VAL	Valspar Corp.

NASDAQ (Over-the-Counter)

ASBC	Associated Bancorp
BLOCA	Block Drug
BRNO	Bruno's, Inc.
CFBS	Central Fidelity Banks
FITB	Fifth Third Bancorp
FABC	First Alabama Bancshares
FHWN	First Hawaiian
FRME	First Merchant Corp.
FDLNB	Food Lion, Inc. Cl. B
LSNB	Lake Shore Bancorp
NOBE	Nordstrom, Inc.
OKEN	Old Kent Financial
RPOW	RPM, Inc.
SHLM	Schulman (A.)
SIAL	Sigma-Aldrich
STRZ	Star Banc Corp.
STBK	State Street Boston
USBC	U.S. Bancorp
WILM	Wilmington Trust

Remember that the list is designed to isolate issues that are suitable to be *considered* for investment. The *actual* selection during any given buy point depends on a variety of factors to be discussed in later chapters.

How much time is necessary to spend on each stock to employ the methods to be described in later sections of this book? Very little time need be spent. The only thing you need to do is to note the stock's price and volume at regularly spaced time intervals. That's all. The information is in the financial pages of most newspapers. The spaced time intervals depend on the individual investor and will be discussed in detail in other chapters. At this point, however, note only that the most optimal intervals for individual investors can be anywhere from one week to several months, depending on the chosen level of involvement in trading activity. The lower the level of trading activity, the further spaced the time intervals will be.

What the List Does

It may appear that our filtering process is nothing other than the application of a subjective, academic process to isolate stocks that have demonstrated superior fundamental quality, which could be of little benefit in the "ever changing" investment environment. This is not the case. The use of the list is far more practical than theoretical for several reasons.

1. A major cause of investor disappointment is misdirection created by *confusion*. It is virtually impossible for an individual investor or money manager within the largest institution to personally be able to differentiate the merits of the tens of thousands of specific alternate investments. Those who espouse such ability have transcended both physical and mental possibilities. So be warned.

By focusing on the Master List, you reduce the entire spectrum of alternate investment types to a manageable number. In effect, the list becomes *your investment world*. Nothing outside that world matters. Almost all industry groups are covered. Transaction costs can be minimized. You can buy within this world in anticipation of higher prices or sell (short) within this world in expectation of lower prices, or employ a variety of other techniques. Although the "market" has been condensed to reasonable proportions, there has not been a proportionate reduction in the number of opportunities. In fact, by confining investment to a core of basic alternatives, the probability of profit in any given transaction, as well as higher annualized return over time, is greatly enhanced.

2. As addressed in Chap. 1, the market is largely a brain game in which the decision to buy or sell can be greatly influenced by emotion. *Psychological pressure* can displace logic and thereby enhance the possibility of error. Our goal is to attempt to eliminate error.

For most investors, the problems associated with mental stress are complicated by the financial press, which (in doing its job) concentrates on the sensational. The sensational, by definition, is not the rule. However, because of the constant media attention to the exceptions, such exceptions can easily become misjudged and become the "rule." The investor can begin to chase exceptions, losing sight of basic realities and eventually becoming trapped by the professional. Neither the exceptional nor the sensational are consistent. Consistent profit is our objective.

By reducing the number of corporations that warrant investment consideration to a relatively small number, the investor is provided with the benefit of familiarity, which greatly reduces possible errors induced by emotion.

In later chapters, where we detail our actual positions over the years, the process of profit extraction can appear extremely simple (which it is). However, most positions were taken directly *against* prevailing analytical/media sentiment. From this it might be inferred that, because we have profited in 48 of 50 positions taken, the dominant feeling among analysts and the media is in error around 95 percent of the time when dealing with *our* stocks. Having pocketed their money, we feel that is exactly the case, the Master List being our primary bulwark against enticement by emotional nonsense.

3. In an attempt to eliminate the effect of extrinsic factors, our Master List criteria stress predictability and quality. We are not part of corporate management. We cannot make corporate decisions. The fundamental activities of the corporation are not within our direct control.

We do have some control over *intrinsic factors*, those that determine stock price change because of market structure. As market participants, we must compete and (hopefully) profit within this inner world. By attempting to confine interest to corporations with demonstrated predictability, we have some assurance that matters beyond our control will not catch us unexpectedly. We can therefore concentrate attention on those aspects over which (by our actual buying and selling) *we do have some control*, including discretion as to whether we will even participate. As functioning professionals, we exist in the market, not within the corporations whose stock we are using to acquire profit.

The result of this reasoning is that we are involved with stocks whose prices are more a function of the market than a function of some particular corporate event that may (or may not) occur. Since corporations have been selected on a basis of both earnings predictability *and* earnings growth, the unexpected has been minimized. Price changes of the stock, therefore, will be more affected by overall changes in the market than by events within the corporations themselves. Consequently, the benefits associated with market timing become more easily attained.

4. As the investor may perceive, by limiting our interest to the Master List, we are shifting the entire investing situation to our favor. The variables that concern us most are those involved with internal market structure. Since we have a reasonable understanding of the earnings and dividend traits of *our* stocks, we can easily evaluate them as reasonable or unreasonable relative to market price.

As a result, we can do two things. First, we can make a disciplined determination as to which individual stocks appear relatively over- or underpriced, thereby allowing us to concentrate on the undervalued stocks as buying possibilities and the overvalued stocks as potential selling possibilities. Second, by determining if the entire list is overpriced or underpriced (Chap. 8), we can develop a method of market timing. Both facets (relative positions within the list and the relative position of the list as a whole) are interrelated. The combination of the two (Chap. 9) forms the basis of Drach Market Research as being able to predict price change with an accuracy of 95+ percent for specific common stocks over many years and in a wide variety of market conditions.

The value of confining interest to stocks appearing on the Master List, therefore, goes far beyond the rather simplistic criteria used in the List's construction. We not only have concentrated attention on specific potential investments, but have taken an important step in constructing a *method of market timing*. And, as detailed in later chapters, the timing aspects are not limited to common stocks. They can be applied to a variety of investment types including closed-end funds.

Condensing the List

The more stocks there are on the list, the higher the probability of success, simply because of the greater number of individual stocks from which selections can be made. However, the list can be substantially reduced without any significant loss of accuracy. For those who desire to work with fewer stocks, the elimination of specific issues depends on individual investor's circumstance.

For U.S. investors, Canadian issues may hold disadvantages because of the added taxation on dividends and potentially added costs/risks associated with currency exchange.

If you do not work closely with over-the-counter stocks, the sometimes excessive spreads, the possibility of double charging (commissions plus markups/markdowns), the lack of accounting for order priority, and other factors can make this market less desirable than listed stocks.

This leaves the New York and American Stock Exchange issues. From these, the process of elimination becomes one of personal preference. If you do not like the name of a corporation, never heard of it, dislike an industry, then go ahead and scratch it. Throw darts. Let the kids decide. It is a matter of whim because the criteria used in developing the list are such that it mathematically makes little difference in the long term which stocks are selected.

Only two things must result after this condensation.

1. The list should contain a minimum of 20 issues.

2. The list should not be altered except to more issues from the Master List. No subtractions should be made unless they have been deleted from the original Master List. To do otherwise injects after-the-fact emotion, which can seriously detract from the probability of success and effectively destroys objectivity.

Whether you choose to follow all stocks or the minimum, the most important aspect is clear recognition that this is now *your* market. The principles and methods described in later chapters can be employed with the stocks selected.

Expanding the List

Some investors might feel that condensing the entire market to under 100 individual stocks is overly restrictive. Others might feel that the list should be altered to more closely duplicate the specific stocks comprising popular averages.

The statistical fact is that, in our method, the addition of issues that fail to meet the fundamental quality standards results in a net loss of accuracy as to both the percentage of individual positions including profitably and annualized return.

Changes in the List

Although additions and deletions to the Master List are rather infrequent, over time the list does change. Takeovers, buyouts, mergers, and the loss of fundamental quality reduce the number of acceptable issues, while the list can expand via corporations establishing the characteristics required by our criteria.

Whether you construct your own list or use ours, review it occasionally. Our current list has been made available, free of charge, since the initiation of the publication of their portfolio modeling (January 1, 1977) through Drach Market Research at the address given in the author's note and at the end of Chap. 11.

Summary

In this chapter we have taken an essential step in the process of developing our strategy to reduce risk while maintaining a relatively high rate of return.

We have reduced the entire "market" to a rather small number of individual issues, making participation in actual market endeavors both easily understandable and manageable. At first, it may appear that we have excessively restricted our possible investment alternatives, with the result that we are denying ourselves benefits associated with a greater number of choices. This is not the case.

What we have accomplished with the Master List is a central base which, as detailed in later chapters, can be greatly expanded to investments beyond the stocks on the Master List without a proportional reduction in profit consistency. Without this base, such accuracy would be impossible.

In Chap. 1 we portrayed the market as a predator-prey relationship, such as with spiders and flies. We prefer the spider's role. The Master List provides us the necessary ingredients for the construction of our web, our environment—an environment giving us an advantage over others who dare enter.

We also now know specifically what tools (issues) we are going to use in our attempt to extract profit.

With this background, we can shift our concentration to the factor that provides the basis for profit: price change.

3
The Rules

Although dividend and interest payments play important roles in deriving income, the bulk of profit and almost all aspects of risk minimization are a function of correctly anticipating price change. It is foolish to attempt to participate in the market without some concept as to what actually causes market values to fluctuate.

Almost all fundamental literature on the stock market considers price change in terms of a cloudy, fanciful concept that reads something like this: "When good things happen, prices go up; and when nasty things happen, prices go down." Such naive reasoning permeates the financial press and most research services to the point that a broad spectrum of investors assume that everyone agrees on what makes stock prices go up and down. The result is a sort of mass idiocy.

In reality, the relationship between fundamental economic events and stock pricing is not necessarily parallel. Both individual stocks and the market as a whole can experience price changes directly opposite to the optimism or pessimism regarding current fundamental economic events.

Price advances on bad news and price declines on good news have created followers of pure technical analysis, which attempts to forecast price changes without any fundamental considerations. Pure technicians rely on a variety of sources: charts, waves, astrology, football scores, and anything else their minds can conjure as a guiding "force" for price change that is unaffected by standard fundamentals. The thought processes of this group can rightfully be considered weird and their results usually correspondingly disappointing. However, as discussed in later chapters, the followers of such nonsense are present in sufficient numbers to represent a significant segment of the "investment" community.

Quite naturally, because of the lack of consistent and/or adequate profitability by either the pure fundamentalists or pure technicians, a variety of hybrid theories have developed with variable doses of the "fundamental" and "technical" aspects. The most common hybrids have a general theme that the market discounts the present and is looking into the future. For example, if the market advances when the economy is "bad," these theorists say that the market is discounting the current situation, looking ahead, and "seeing" better times in the future. Conversely, when the market is declining during a "good" economy, the reason is that the market is "seeing" rough economic times ahead. This concept is assumed to be true among thousands of individual and institutional investors. It is fostered by a wide range of "services" purported to have discovered "lead" indicators. We have found most of these theories to be erroneous.

If you reverse these theories, saying that the market is discounting the current situation and looking backward into the past (not the future), the same results will usually occur. Of course, it is absurd to think the market is moving backward, but it is just as absurd to think the market has eyes to look anyplace. The volumes of paper devoted to the mythical belief that the market discounts current events and foresees the future would serve better purpose in litter boxes than in misleading investors. The only thing "learned" by those following discounting theories is that market prices fluctuate, that is, they go down and up—a fact obvious to anyone. [Prices never go straight up, and (in any stock that maintains its existence) prices never go straight down.] That is all discounting theories have discovered.

Our intention is not to discredit all aspects of fundamental and/or technical analysis. Indeed, each of these analytical methods involves elements useful in price forecasting. In our opinion, both the fundamentalists and technicians experience difficulties because they tend to overlook a third area of stock analysis: structure, which involves the mechanical design of trading rules and specific human behavioral patterns (intrinsic factors). People and *only* people, through their buying/selling activities, create price change through conscious decisions. Any analytical method that ignores the human element in searching for a formula to predict price change is destined to experience difficulties. Nonetheless, structural analysis is widely disregarded.

The question may now be asked: Since very little written concerns the importance of intrinsic (structural) factors, does this mean the bulk of literature concerning how to participate successfully in the market is insufficient? To us, the answer is essentially yes.

It is within the market that the real, physical aspects of price change occur. It is only by beginning on the inside and then expanding outward that you can adequately comprehend the causative agents of price change. With such an understanding, you can easily grasp such phenomena as prices sometimes advancing on bad news and sometimes declining on good news.

The "mystique" of the market disappears, replaced by logic. The game becomes a business.

Supply and Demand

Let's review some of the simple logic beaten into the heads of anyone subjected to Economics 101. When demand (buying) exceeds supply (selling), prices go up. Conversely, when there is more supply than demand, prices go down.

This basic, elemental concept is essentially correct. However, in the stock market, "normal" supply/demand relationships can become convoluted. In fact, both the mechanical aspects of market structure and investor emotions can twist demand or supply to the extent that the results on price are directly opposite those of conventional economic theory.

Let's also review a few terms that will be used extensively in this and later chapters regarding the placement of orders.

Market. An order "at market" means the investor does not specify a price; he or she is willing to accept the best price available. Market orders will usually be executed (filled) as soon as they reach whatever exchange or over-the- counter market maker is trading in the stocks.

Limit. When an investor specifies a price, the order is "limit." All limit orders connote "or better," that is, the investor will accept a price better than the limit. Limit orders, since they might not be executed because the desired price is unavailable, must carry a notation as to how long the order is to remain in force.

Day. This is a limit order specified to be in force only for the trading day in which the order is entered.

GTC. A limit order specified to remain in force until cancelled by the investor is termed "good till cancelled" (GTC). Limit orders that are in effect (that is, have not been filled, have not expired, or have been not cancelled) are termed *open orders.*

Basic stock quotations involve three terms:

Last. This is the most recent price at which a trade was consummated.

Bid. The highest price of all open orders to purchase the stock is the "bid."

Ask. This is the lowest price of all open orders at which someone is willing to sell the stock. It is also called the *offer.*

For stocks traded on major exchanges (rather than over-the- counter), most orders are directed to the primary exchange where trading is conducted through a specialist. In the process of keeping track of the open orders in a given issue, the listing of the orders is called the *book.* Some stocks are traded (*listed*) on more than one stock exchange, and stocks listed on exchanges can also be traded over-the-counter. Consequently, different markets may involve different trading rules. Important differences in trading rules are discussed in later chapters.

To explain some of the basic principals (or lack thereof) relative to price change and supply/demand, we will refer to Fig. 3.1 as our hypothetical example of a book. This example is greatly simplified, but will explain the basic concepts of price change.

If you were to ask for a quote of the status of the stock, you would be told:

Last 20. This is the most recent transaction price.

Bid 19. The highest price anyone is willing to pay is the open order for 100 shares at 19¾.

Ask 20¼. The lowest price anyone is willing to sell is the open order for 100 shares 20.

Now let's say the "book" is that appearing in Fig. 3.1 and we want to buy 400 shares "at market," that is, we are willing to pay the best price that is available. Our order would be filled by:

100 shares that were offered at 20¼
200 shares that were offered at 20½
100 shares that were offered at 20¾
400 shares total

Price	
21	500 shares offered
20¾	100 shares offered
20½	200 shares offered
20¼	100 shares offered
20	Last trade—no bids or offers—closing price previous day
19¾	100 shares bid
19½	300 shares bid
19¼	200 shares bid
19	400 shares bid

Figure 3.1. The book for XYZ Corp.

Our order is filled. We have bought stock at the prices the sellers wanted. Because of our buying, we have increased the price to 20¾. The quote would now be last 20¾, bid 19¾, ask 21.

The price increased because of buying demand.

Go back to the original book (Fig. 3.1) and reverse the process. We have 400 shares and want to sell them at market. Our order would be filled by:

100 shares that were bid at 19¾

300 shares that were bid at 19½

400 shares total

Again, our order is filled. We have supplied stock at prices the buyers wanted. Because of our selling, we have decreased the stock price to 19½. The quote would now be last 19½, bid 19¼, ask 20¼.

The price decreased because of selling supply. So we see good old basic economics at work: Prices go up when there is excessive "at-market" buying demand, and prices go down when there is excessive "at-market" selling supply.

This elemental, classical supply-demand relationship is true, and recognition of this is an important ingredient in the development of a successful market strategy. Understanding this fundamental concept, however, is only the first step, for (as we shall see) various factors often make actual stock market pricing function directly opposite to conventional economic theory.

Let's return to our example when we purchased 400 shares. Because of our buying demand, the price of the last trade increased to 20¾, leaving the bid 19¾ and the ask 21. Now let's say that, right after we bought, someone else decided to sell 100 shares at market. They would be given the bid, 19¾. And then let's say there were no more trades that day.

The buying demand would have been 400 shares, the selling supply would have been 100 shares. The closing price would be the last trade at 19¾, down¼ from the previous day's close on a total trading volume of 500 shares. This could be perceived by shareholders as, "The stock's goin' down . . . maybe something's wrong." There was actually more at-market buying demand than at market selling supply, a very positive aspect for price advance in classical economic theory. The impression, however, because of the day-to-day price change of minus ¼ is that the stock is going down, which could stimulate some people to sell.

The book in our hypothetical example is, of course, oversimplified. In actual trading of the stocks selected in Chap. 2, there are (almost always) much smaller price increments at which the stock is being bid and offered, usually at every ⅛ point. Also, much larger volumes are involved than the few hundred shares in our example. And, usually many more people are involved in the stock's trading, so that new bids and asks come in frequently. Lastly, open orders tend to be concentrated at even points rather than at points and a fraction. Larger groupings of limit orders in lower-priced stocks are often bunched at $5 increments (15, 20, 25, etc.), while higher-priced stock limit orders congregate at $10 increments (80, 90, 100, etc.). For our purposes, however, our example is sufficient: It provides a foundation from which we can clearly understand how "normal" demand-supply relationships can be altered because of both market structure and investor behavior.

It is *extremely important* to realize that demand and supply in the market are often more influenced by emotional impression rather than classical economic "reason."

To dramatize this point, let's stray from concentration on stock to our stomachs. Let's say we find green beans and peas equally palatable. The price of green beans goes up and the price of peas stays the same. We opt for the peas because they are cheaper. In effect, by making a reasonable economic choice, we have lowered the buying demand for the more expensive green beans and have increased the buying demand for the peas. If the majority of people follow our reasoning, the price of peas will go up because they will be demanded by buyers as long as the price remains below green beans. Because of the lack of buyers for green beans (excess supply), the price of green beans will come down until it is at least equal to peas.

This is a case of classical supply and demand. Prices increase because of excessive buying demand, and prices decrease because of excessive selling supply. In this example we are dealing with tangibles, something we can put our hands on and, in this case, into our mouths.

The market is different. Stock is an intangible. Its merit is not that it can satisfy some real physical need directly. The benefit of stock is only that it can be used to extract profit. Because of this, emotional impressions are extremely important and can be dramatically more influential than corporate financial fundamentals in causing price change. If a stock's price goes down, the lower price *in itself* may give the impression that something is wrong with the corporation and stimulate more selling. Conversely, if a stock's price goes up, the higher price *in itself* may create the impression that something good is happening to the corporation and stimulate more buying. In effect, emotional investor behavior can often be isolated as the source for dramatic stock price changes when there is no change in the fundamental characteristics of the corporation.

As you will see, the emotional aspects of price change are extremely important and easily measured. Once involved in the market, thousands of seemingly logical people can get their reasoning so twisted by emotion that they behave like idiots—buying high and selling low, the precise formula for loss.

Before expanding on the effects of emotional motivation, it is helpful to understand some of the factors in the internal market structure that help create demand/supply imbalances.

Margin

Margin is simply the term used for borrowing money to buy stock. It is another word for the amount of credit used. The maximum amount of margin used is determined by the Federal Reserve. At the time of this writing the margin requirement was 50 percent. This means that for every $1 worth of stock (that qualifies for margin) purchased, the investor could put up only 50 cents (50 percent). Individual brokerage firms may impose their own "house rules" regarding margin requirements, which can be more restrictive than the Federal Reserve requirement.

The amount of interest paid on margin debt is determined by the rules of the brokerage firm the investor utilizes. The rate usually varies with the size of the debt (more debt, lower rates), and with the basis of the rate (usually related to the prime lending rate posted by major New York banks).

The importance of margin in a supply/demand context is that it aggravates the situation beyond the imbalances that would occur if prices have to be paid in full with cash—no borrowing allowed.

The reason for this aggravating effect is that investors do not have to use margin, That is, the amount of margin utilized varies in different market conditions. The "rational" investor would choose to use margin only when the profit to be achieved is going to exceed the cost of the funds borrowed. As a result, the use of margin depends on investors' expectations. In an atmosphere of optimism, the use of margin goes up, often dramatically. Buying demand, already out of balance with supply because of the optimism, is increased by the use of margin. Everything else being equal (even though everything else is never equal in real life), the increased use of margin in buying adds buying demand, causing prices to advance faster than if margin were not available.

Conversely, margin can help prices spiral downward. If those who have aggravated buying demand by margin become pessimistic or are unable to endure the financial strains associated with borrowing costs, they may, in mass, decide to sell in an environment with insufficient buyers.

Therefore, because its usage is not constant, margin has the effect of making prices more volatile.

Your first reaction may be, so what? The "so what" is that the amount of margin is published, readily available, and known by the professional. When excessive buying demand enters the market by margin, those aware of this condition can often hold out for higher selling prices, knowing that there are buyers willing to borrow to fulfill their optimistic expectations. Conversely, when those margined decide to sell, the excessive amount of stock they want to get rid of allows the professional to lower prices from levels that would have been otherwise acceptable.

In effect, during euphoric periods, we can watch the margin debt expand, as prices rise and curtail our selling until the margin debt begins to level off. This can help ensure selling near the top. When margin debt and prices begin to decline, we can reverse the process. We know margined investors will be forced to sell because of their (self-induced) financial and/or psychological pressure. We can lower our purchase prices knowing those margined will be forced to accept the lower prices.

This is basic, but provides the beginning of an understanding of both professional strategy and the importance of investor emotion. By preying on those who have trapped themselves by margin, the professional adds to the demand/supply imbalance already aggravated by the use of leverage (borrowing).

The point is not to criticize margin. Indeed, real estate and other investments are more heavily leveraged than stock. And, through the use of stock options and stock index futures, the degree of leverage available is far greater than that allowed by the Federal Reserve requirement. In some circumstances, margin can be incorporated into extremely conservative strategies. Our emphasis in this discussion is to provide a first step in developing an understanding as to why stock pricing can vary dramatically from conventional economic "wisdom."

Short Selling

Just as, by using margin you do not have to have the full amount to purchase stock, you do not have to own stock to sell it. Selling stock you do not own is called *selling short*. (If you sell stock you own, you are *selling long*.)

In selling stock short, the person who sold *must* eventually buy the stock back. Making a profit by selling short requires that the stock declines in price so that it can be bought back at a lower price. (This is exactly opposite to having a long position.)

To sell short requires that the investor have, at all times, sufficient funds in his or her account to buy the stock. And, although there is (usually) no time limit as to how long a short position can be kept, the stock will eventually have to be purchased. Selling short is not getting something for nothing.

Whether or not you ever sell short, recognition of short selling is imperative because it creates an imbalance in the normal demand/supply relationship. In effect, there can be a supply of stock for sale, even though the sellers do not own the stock. Note that because the stock sold short has to be borrowed, short selling takes place in margin accounts.

Most short selling is done by market makers and other professionals, but often nonprofessional short selling becomes excessive. The amount of short sales in specific stocks on major exchanges and on the national over-the-counter list is regularly published.

If there is an excessive amount of short positions in a stock, we know the short sellers will eventually have to buy the stock back. We also know the general investor is not an avid short seller. The usual nonprofessional short seller is a speculator attempting to trade in brief time periods. We know this group has to buy, and their staying power (because of emotional or financial weakness) is limited. The short sellers can be trapped (in what is termed a *short squeeze*) when prices advance. Having isolated a group forced to buy, we can hold out for higher prices than we would accept in a more normal situation.

Short selling, as with margin, is a structural facet within the market that can distort conventional demand/supply relationships.

The Inverse Relationship Between Supply and Demand in Stock Price

Several things lure people into and out of the stock market. The most important is *price change*. In our example of peas and green beans, basic logic made the lower-priced vegetable preferable. That is the case in the logical world of tangibles and classical economics: the lower the price, the greater the buying demand.

With intangibles, common stock included, the investor often lacks any clear concept as to the true merits (or lack of them) of the investment. It is, after all, nothing more than a piece of paper whose value is largely based on hypothetical assumptions. By their very nature, it is no great surprise that intangibles can develop nonsensical pricing. However, to relegate the "reason" for ridiculous stock pricing purely to the intangible aspect is both superficial and misleading. All investments—whether intangible or tangible (such as real estate, gold, antiques, etc.)—experience periods when pricing has no relationship to fundamental value.

The fact is that all investment types are influenced by emotion. *Greed and fear care nothing about classical economics.* Greed and fear are concerned with price change. Period.

Those who lose in the stock market (and they are in the majority) are stimulated to buy *after* the market has advanced. They have witnessed higher prices. They have seen (at least on paper) that profits have been made. *The higher prices function as psychological proof of the value of the investment.* Elevated pricing in itself conjures optimism and euphoria: "If the other guy can do it, why not me?"

The reverse applies when prices decline. Those (again, the majority) who lose are stimulated to sell *after* the fact of lower prices. *The lower prices function as psychological proof of the investment's faults.* Pessimism develops. The fun was in the hope of winning and now the fun is gone. What better way to salvage what is left (both financially and emotionally) than just to sell out?

The investing "process" becomes a brain game in which seemingly logical adults place themselves in an environment that can easily encourage totally illogical behavior. The end result is both exactly the opposite of classical demand/supply dynamics and the precise formula for loss: buying high and selling low.

The proof of this repetitive, destructive behavior is far from theoretical. Anyone with experience in the brokerage industry has witnessed a sudden increase in both individual and institutional investors wanting to buy during periods of euphoria and high prices. The same types will sell after the market declines. Such activity is nothing more than the manifestation of emotion, fear, and greed, creating a condition inverse to conventional demand/supply relationships.

The inverse relationships is also clearly demonstrated by reviewing illegal manipulative schemes. A central ingredient in almost all such activity is that the manipulators raise prices to stimulate greed among the victims who, consequently, buy at inflated prices.

Blending the Elements

Starting from a very elementary basis, we have now advanced to a level that allows us to combine the factors discussed into a format of practical strategy.

The primary theoretical concept guiding our actual market participation is the recognition that the market is an environment unto itself and successful participation involves adaptation to the market rather than expecting the market to adapt to personal preference or whim.

We acknowledge that the environment contains some nasty characters who engage in blatant, illegal, manipulative schemes to fleece the unwary. These unsavory types generally confine their activities to smaller, low-quality issues where they can most easily exercise manipulative control. Our Master List, because it concentrates on larger, high-quality corporations, provides a logical attempt for protection from most forms of manipulation.

We recognize the market involves both structural and emotional factors that function to create prices that defy conventional economic logic. However, when the causative agents of price change are understood, the market is actually quite simple.

We fully realize the market can appear both brutal and irrational, but we have found it to be nothing more than a repetitive business providing more opportunity than any other investment area. The investor can go long (in anticipation of higher prices), go short (in anticipation of lower prices), or stay away. Movements into, out of, or within the market can be accomplished quickly with very low transaction costs. In effect, profit can be derived from any set of market conditions. Drach's accuracy rate (fully disclosed and documented), profiting in 95+ percent of concluded positions, attests to the simple truth that the stock market is exceptionally predictable.

Common sense dictates that buying demand is neither constant nor perpetual. From a purely mathematical standpoint, prices cannot rise to an infinitely high level because there is not an infinite supply of money. From a practical standpoint prices do not rise forever because the individuals creating the buying demand,

1. Run out of money.
2. Or see the price advance stop (reducing or eliminating the greed factor) and curtail their buying.
3. Or shift interest to another investment (with more greed appeal), which is usually another stock.

Whatever the reason, those who forced the price up will want to sell. Having made their decision to sell, there are insufficient new buyers for a number of reasons. The supply/demand situation was thrown out of balance by those buyers stimulated by greed. The situation could have been further imbalanced by the use of margin. The principal stimulus for purchase (price advance) no longer exists. Professionals (knowing sellers are coming) lower the price at which they have a buying interest. The price begins to spiral downward, usually faster than it advanced. Panic selling can ensue, compounding the price decline. Then the selling pressure is finally extinguished and prices begin the next advance—an ongoing cyclical process.

Expanding on this basic cyclical process, we can gain an insight into conflicts within the market. For example, let's say the price of a stock begins to go up, and investors become interested to the point that they increase their buying demand by using excessive margin. Now let's say a professional decides the price is too high and begins to sell short. If he is powerful enough, the short selling can stop the price advance. In other words, all buy orders will be met by short sales. The price cannot advance. The stimulus (price advance) that caused the initial buying demand no longer exists. Those on margin are experiencing losses from the cost of their borrowing. The result can be that those margined become discouraged and begin to sell. For reasons previously explained, prices can spiral downward; allowing the short seller to profit.

The main point of this example is not to show how to identify opportunities; this is dealt with in detail in Part 2. The objective is to demonstrate that stock prices can be dramatically influenced by factors that are totally intrinsic. It is quite common for the price of a stock to gyrate widely while the fundamental characteristics of the underlying corporation remain unchanged.

Now, the elimination of confusion as one of the reasons for the careful construction of our Master List becomes increasingly clear. If investors base their decisions *solely* on extrinsic factors (corporate activities and expectations), the market price can be so affected by intrinsic factors that the interpretation based on extrinsic factors can be totally unfounded. For example, suppose a corporation is selected for purchase solely because of good earnings prospects, but then the price declines because of a struggle between margin buyers and professional short selling. The investor may misinterpret the cause of the downward price movement by thinking the lower price is the result of some fundamental corporate problem. The investor so influenced might sell because of fear attached to the price change when in reality the lower price makes the fundamentally sound corporation a better buy.

In the stocks we have chosen to utilize, we have done the best we can to make sure there are no unexpected corporate events. When supply and demand become out of balance and cause wild price fluctuations, we do not need to spend inordinate amounts of time looking for a fundamental reason. Some examination of the corporation's current activities is prudent, but the price change has more than likely occurred because of some intrinsic factor. We can isolate the factor and proceed to take advantage.

In other words, we have avoided unnecessary abstraction and worry, as well as minimized risk by reducing the possibility of reacting emotionally rather than logically.

Placing Orders

The place to take advantage in the market is at every point you can. You stand a better chance of doing that if you understand how to order stock positions. In fact, many investors place themselves at a disadvantage from the outset through faulty ordering. The different ways of placing orders should be known and understood to help ensure profit.

The first, and most basic concern, is price. As mentioned earlier in this chapter; whether buying or selling, there are two ways of stipulating price. Market orders mean the investor will take whatever price is available at the time the order is entered; in limit orders, the investor stipulates the price. Limit orders also carry the connotation "or better." For example, if we enter a buy order with a limit of 20, it would mean we will pay 20 or any price under 20. Conversely, if we were selling and our limit was 20, we would accept a price of 20 or any price higher than 20. Unlike market orders, there is no guarantee that the limit order will be filled since there might not be another investor willing to meet the limit price.

In deciding which order type to use, the first thing to eliminate from consideration is any hope of getting "or better" on limit orders. Even if you are a saint, there is no reason to assume anyone is going to be nice to you in the market. They do not even see you, only your money. Although a better price than the limit will occasionally be achieved, it can be considered as just plain luck, having no objective role in professional strategy.

It is important to realize to whom you are speaking when ordering. The broker, whose income depends on commissions, will be compensated only if the transaction is consummated. Some brokers, through their own initiative or as the result of prodding by their employer, will stress the merits of market orders. The market order guarantees that (if the stock is being traded) the transaction will occur and the commission generated. The justification for encouraging the use of market orders usually goes something like, "If you really want it, why not pay a little more and make sure you get it?" You may "get it" all right, by paying too high a price repeatedly.

In following the strategies presented in this book, if it costs a little more than your preferred limit, you may not want it because it may not be worth it. There are times when a market order should be used, but there is reasonable cause to be suspicious of whose interests are really being served if the broker is continuously pushing to buy or sell at market. Most of the time, market orders can be shown to have resulted in overpayment when buying and underpayment when selling. In other words, they create an expense that should be minimized.

As a general rule, we use limit orders and are aware of the possibility that the price we desire might not be available. For example, let's say a stock is acceptable to us at a price of 20 and the quote is bid 19¾, ask 20¼. We place our order at 20. It is our bid at 20 (the quote now bid 20, ask 20¼). Now let's say the price goes up without ever trading at 20. Our limit order is not filled.

The investor in such a circumstance may sit and watch the stock advance without participating. This can lead to, "I knew I should have gone ahead and paid a little more. Next time I'm just going to pay the ask and not get left out." This type of experience and resultant attitude can cause frustration, anger, obscenities, foaming at the mouth, and the like. Those who experience such emotional agitation should just go ahead and place market orders. They might as well overpay from the beginning since their emotion is probably going to create a loss for them anyway.

In the use of limit orders, it can be expected that from time to time stocks will move away from the specified price and sometimes (rarely) it will be necessary to move the limit order correspondingly. The occasional missing of stock positions by the use of limit orders should be expected and accepted without emotional involvement.

The portfolio strategies described in this book are therefore designed (with a few exceptions) to utilize limit orders. Remember that several stocks are being monitored (Chap. 2), a process that can be accomplished quickly and easily, as will be described in later sections (Parts 1 and 4). By following several stocks with similar characteristics as to fundamental quality, determining the merit of any particular issue (or its lack) relative to other stocks is not difficult.

To illustrate, let's say we are interested in buying either stock A or stock B. They both are quoted 19⅞ bid, 20⅛ ask, and we find both issues equally acceptable at a price of 20. We place a limit order to buy stock A at 20. Stock A goes to 20½ without trading at 20. Our order is not filled. Rather than chase the stock by moving our bid up, we check stock B and see that it has declined to 19½. *Now* the relative merit of B is greater than A. In other words, the two stocks were of equal value at 20, but now that B has gone down it represents a better value. We than cancel our bid for A and bid on B. Through this relative process, the shortcomings of the limit order are generally overcome quite easily.

In applying this technique of shifting unfilled orders in response to price change, the broker might become irritated because of the added paperwork. In such an event, do not get discouraged—get another broker. The data is quite firm that, over time, the constant use of limit orders and shifting both reduces cost and enhances profits.

By knowing the differences between market and limit orders, the investor can recognize a danger in those brokerage firms that offer extra discounts if the order is market, especially if they require the market orders to be placed before the stock exchange opens. In so doing, they have guaranteed both that the order will be executed and that they will receive the commission. In addition, since they know you are going to buy or sell at whatever price is available, they can (theoretically) place themselves in the position of being the entity with whom you are trading. In other words, they themselves (or their buddies) may be the ones you are selling to or buying from. The net effect can be a double cost, which is most easily accomplished in the over-the-counter market where (because many different brokerages might be acting as market maker) order precedent can be hard to trace.

For example, let's say a stock is bid 19¾, ask 20¼. Customer A wants to sell at market and customer B wants to buy at market. The broker accommodates customer A by purchasing the stock at the bid of 19¾ in the broker's own account. The broker then accommodates customer B by selling the stock at the quoted ask price of 20¼ out of the broker's own account (that is, the stock he just bought from customer A). The broker has made two profits, the commissions for sell of A and the buy of B, plus a profit of a half point. This type of trading practice can be structured so that it is quite legal, but the ethical aspect is clearly lacking. Customer A and customer B could have transacted at 20, beneficial to both buyer and seller and within the broker's control.

This example is not meant to imply that the brokerage industry is filled with cheats. Our point is to demonstrate that, without proper understanding, the investor can be disadvantaged in the most simple transaction. In this case, splitting the differential between the bid and ask by both customer A and B (limit orders at 20) would have been to their mutual benefit.

Since we are touching on devious trading tactics, let's describe an (greatly simplified) example associated with the benefits of shifting limit orders rather than chasing price. With the stock quoted at 19⅞ bid, 20⅛ ask, the investor places a firm buy order for 10,000 shares at 20 with his friendly broker, Mr. Slink. Knowing the investor's desire to purchase is firm, Mr. Slink buys 10,000 shares at the ask price at 20⅛ for himself. Mr. Slink's position is nice. If the stock advances, he has the chance for (theoretically) unlimited profit. His downside risk is limited to $\frac{1}{8}$ since he knows he has a buyer at 20—his own customer.

Now, let's say that Mr. Slink and his accomplice Ms. Slinky manipulate the stock up by "painting the tape," that is, selling the stock back and forth to each other (a zero sum game between themselves) until the stock moves to 21. The bidder at 20 has the impression of being left out)—opportunity is fleeing! Slink, Slinky, or pure emotion convinces the investor to move his bid to 21: He just bought the stock (unknowingly) from Mr. Slink who pocketed a one-point profit. The investor is out $10,000, Slink is up $10,000 plus his commission as the stock returns to its fundamental value of $20. The investor's financial discomfort could have easily been avoided by the strict adherence to a policy of shifting limit orders.

As previously discussed, the time duration of orders can also be of importance. In this category the only differentials of practical concern are (1) *day*, meaning that the order (if not filled) is automatically terminated at conclusion of the day's trading, and (2) *GTC* (good till cancelled), meaning that the order remains in force until it is filled or cancelled by the investor.

Our actual trading generally involves both a large number of individual stocks and relatively large volume. The movement and shifting of limits is often rapid and incorporates computerized scans of various investment alternatives. In this type of trading structure, we generally use day orders because the ability for rapid shifting will usually get all accounts properly placed during the trading day.

However, for most investors who are concerned with a lower number of issues and less volume, the GTC order has advantages. Because there is sometimes a slightly higher cost to the brokerage firm in processing GTC orders, some brokers (usually the same ones who attempt to talk their clientele into market orders) will stress the use of day orders. Their reasoning may be something like, "What if you get squashed by a train? Your GTC order will still be in effect and [shudder] you will not know if the order has been filled." Of course, if you should get squashed, you would really not care if the order was filled. Another reason might be, "What if you forget about the order?" This brings images of your being aged and poor, on the brink of being forced to rummage through garbage for subsistence when you are suddenly informed that the order you placed 43 years ago during better times has been filled. Now it will take all your savings to pay. Such fears are basically nonsense: Few investors are so stupid, and it is part of the broker's function to keep clientele aware of open orders.

The GTC order is generally preferable because it allows maximum flexibility without sacrificing any type of advantage. Although any type of order can be cancelled at any time, it is only reasonable to leave the time of expiration at your option. Note that, if no time duration is specified when placing an order, it will usually be entered as a day order. To ensure that the order carries the GTC stipulation, specify GTC when ordering.

In many respects the market is analogous to a card game, in which you lose advantage if the opponent sees your hand. For example, let's say you want to buy a stock at $19\frac{7}{8}$ and the quote is $19\frac{3}{4}$ bid, $20\frac{1}{4}$ ask. You place a *day* order at $19\frac{7}{8}$. It is now your bid with the quote being $19\frac{7}{8}$, $20\frac{1}{4}$. In well regulated markets, you are the first one to bid the higher price and as such are generally first in line if anyone is willing to sell at your price. Now, let's say that, right after you bid $19\frac{7}{8}$, another investor bids $19\frac{7}{8}$ using a *GTC* order. The day ends with the stock not trading as low as $19\frac{7}{8}$. Your order is automatically cancelled; its time duration has expired. The GTC order placed after your day order is now first in line. Now, let's say you still want to buy the stock and reenter your order at $19\frac{7}{8}$. You have lost your priority: The GTC order is now ahead of you, creating the possibility that the order ahe ..d will be filled and not yours. If you had used a GTC order, you would still have been able to cancel the order at the end of the day; but you also could have let the order stand if you so wished and not lost your priority.

The ramifications of using GTC are somewhat deeper than the possible loss of order priority. You could, by the use of day orders, help someone else. Using the illustrative quote of $19\frac{3}{4}$ bid, $20\frac{1}{4}$ ask, you enter a day order at $19\frac{7}{8}$ and are first in line. Someone else wants priority on the bid. To be assured he is first in line, he must raise the bid to 20, that is, over your bid at $19\frac{7}{8}$, and he knows that your order is going to expire. He may wait until your order has expired and then bid $19\frac{7}{8}$; effectively shoving you out of line.

One type of order deserves special attention: the *stop loss order.* Although suggested by a large number of brokers, analysts and financial publications, *the stop loss order has no place in our methods of professional market participation.* With the exception of some rather wild trading schemes, we consider the intellect (possibly the ethics) of those who insist on using stop limit orders to be suspect. If these terse statements are not enough to discourage the use of this type of order, perhaps the following discussion will explain its perils.

The stop loss order is "designed" to limit the amount of possible loss associated with any stock position. For example, you buy a stock at 30 and do not want to lose more than 4 points. To ensure (the term *ensure* is used loosely) that your loss will not be greater than 4 points, you place a stop loss order at 26. If the stock goes down to 26, your position will be automatically sold.

In the processing of this order, you have effectively stated that you will sell at a price lower than the current market price, in this example taking a loss. The disadvantages of this type of ordering are many, from both theoretical and practical standpoints:

1. No investor intending to profit consistently should ever purchase a stock that does not represent a better value at a lower price. To dispose of what is fundamentally a better value based *solely* on price decline is simply stupid. The decline may be because of intrinsic factors and very temporary.

2. If a stock should decline in price and (for whatever reason) no longer warrants investment consideration, there is no rational reason to stipulate a *specific* amount of price decline before selling. To do so involves irrational motivation.

3. As we will discuss in those chapters devoted to specific portfolio modeling, a central reason Drach has been able to maintain his exceptionally high accuracy in the percentage of positions concluding profitably is that the buy/sell points are determined by market condition, *not* by specific prices. This involves adhering to the attitude, "Don't count it till you cash it." In these methods, price fluctuations between predetermined (by condition) buy/sell points are of no concern because there is no reason to alter positioning without a specific buy/sell indication. To be influenced by price gyrations between the buy/sell points injects unnecessary emotion and deters from risk minimization, profit consistency, annualized return, and benefits of compounding.

4. If a stock is so volatile and unpredictable that it might decline dramatically, it may gap the stop loss limit. For example, let's say you purchase at 30 and place a stop loss at 26. The stock then declines to 26½ and then stops trading. It reopens at 20. That is, it "gapped" (skipped all prices) from 26½ to 20. The stock did not trade at your price, and (by definition of the stop loss order) the stop loss will take the next "best" price under 26 which, theoretically, is the best possible price to minimize loss. The real loss in this example turns out to be 10, far greater than the 4-point presumed to be the maximum. The point is that the stop loss "protection" is essentially theoretical and is no way guaranteed.

5. Now, let's play the role of a sneaky player to illustrate how advantage might be taken of someone who has entered a stop loss order. Using the same stop loss limit of 26, let's say the stock price has declined to 26¼. Mr. Slink considers 26¼ a good price to buy. Now, by whatever

means (be assured stop loss limits are not confidential), Slink discovers there is a stop loss order at 26. *He has identified a willing seller at a lower price.* Slink drops his bid to 26 and takes out the stop loss limit. If he were a super Slink, knowing of the stop loss limit order he might have artificially lowered the price to 26 by means of short selling. In a normal demand/supply situation, Slink's desire (demand) to buy the stock at 26¼ would have allowed the stock to trade at that price and perhaps not descend lower. By lowering his bid (and perhaps pushing the price of the stock down to the stop loss limit), Slink was able to get stock cheaper while still being on the demand side.

The "Slink" example in the last paragraph is somewhat simplified, but demonstrates another disadvantage in publicizing your exact strategy. In doing so you can be preyed upon. Again, it is the card game analogy.

Aware of the disadvantages associated with letting others know your specific stop loss limit, stop loss advocates suggest using a "mental stop," which simply means do not tell anybody and, when the limit is reached, place the order. This eliminates the dangers posed by the Slinks of the world, but does not eliminate the pitfalls associated with the other disadvantages. A variety of other order types are used infrequently, such as fill-or-kill and all-or-none. *Fill-or-kill* means that, if the order is not executed when it reaches the trading area, it is to be automatically cancelled. *All-or-none* means that all the shares in the order must be taken or the order is not to be executed. These, and others, are applicable only in specialized situations. For the practical application of the strategies presented in this text, knowing the advantages of limit and GTC orders (and the disadvantages of stop loss order) is all that is necessary.

Summary

At this juncture, starting from a very elementary basis, we have been able to isolate and identify danger areas that cause millions of dollars of loss for the unwary. In doing so we are stripping away aspects of the market that can lead to confusion. In effect, we are in a process of simplification that allows us a realistic understanding of the market.

We have discussed how price advance and decline are caused by the classic demand/supply relationship. Prices will rise if there is excessive buying demand, and prices will fall if there is excessive selling supply. We have shown that elements of market structure (such as margin and short selling) can alter "normal" demand/supply relationships. More importantly, we have realized that emotion (greed and fear) can totally reverse classical demand/supply theory, creating more demand at high prices and more supply at low prices.

With this background, we are learning to function independently. Combining the material in this chapter with that of Chaps. 1 and 2, we are developing the essential understanding that the market is an environment unto itself, to which we are adapting. We know specifically which stocks we will use and how to place orders. We are examining the market from within.

Accepting the market as a predator-prey situation, we recognize that to survive and prosper we must have some idea as to the identity and characteristics of those who share our environment. We are keenly aware that our profit must come at the expense of fellow participants. In the next chapter we will begin to look around at others to form a judgment as to their strengths and weaknesses.

4
The Players

In thinking about who constitutes the market, you must keep two things in mind.

1. Of tens of thousands of individual market participants, each is bound to all others by a common purpose: to make money that must come from someone else. They are in a competitive environment; so, naturally, all of them cannot succeed. By the very definition of individuality, all are not equal.

2. For any transaction there has to be a buyer and a seller, each of whom has consciously chosen to act.

These very elementary facts are often overlooked by investors who view "the market" as a thing in itself. But the market is not its own entity; it is the result of human design and behavior. It is humans who choose to move their monies, not "the market." It is this movement, and *only* this movement, which creates price change. Understanding the market, therefore, requires that you understand the characteristics of the participants.

This involves categorizing investors. At first, because of their large number, the task may seem immense, but, in practice, the process is not that difficult. Market participants can be divided into seven basic groups, each with its own particular psychological base and physical position within the market structure. Categorizing investors gives us a logical foundation for predicting behavior and therefore pricing. The identification of those prone to consistent loss effectively isolates areas of consistent profit.

In this chapter we are going to discuss the *general* characteristics of each group. From these generalizations, we can expand in Part 2 to isolate the traits that allow recognition of specific opportunity.

Identifying the different types of market participants does more than make it easy for us to see opportunities. It also shows us trading strategies that seem to be within the reach of individual investors, but that in reality are impossible to utilize effectively because of market structure. With a basic knowledge of the existence of favored groups within the market, you will be able to recognize many danger areas, as well as acquire a firmer understanding of the benefits associated with utilizing the methods presented in later chapters.

The Public

This group consists of individual investors who determine, either alone or through some type of advisor, their own specific investment decisions.

The public is often portrayed as the perpetual loser. This is not an accurate generalization. The individuals who learn to conduct themselves properly have very distinct advantages. Because of the liquidity in the stock market, the public's primary advantage is maneuverability. That is, an individual's position in a stock is generally small enough so that the purchase or sale can be consummated without severely affecting the demand/supply balance. With low transaction costs, the individual can compete against the largest institutions with distinct advantages.

Another misconception concerning the public is that the market has become so dominated by institutions that the small investor is of no practical importance. The public sector can often be the most important factor in creating price change, either by a consensus of opinion concerning specific investments or by dictating institutional behavior by varying the amount of funding the public provides the institutions.

The public can be divided into two loosely termed basic groups: investors and speculators.

Investors

Investors are those who enter and exit the market infrequently. The general pattern of this group is that they buy because of some presumed fundamental reason and then hold the stock "long term."

The simplified pattern of the investor is to buy a stock, put it into a safe deposit box, and leave it there for an extended time period. In the "long term," of course, the investor dies and the heirs will probably cash in the stock as soon as they can get their hands on it.

If the stock selected turns out to be one of those *very few* that significantly outperform the general market over time, long-term investing can be demonstrated to have some merit. Within the brokerage industry, these long-term *exceptions* are often stressed. The usual reason for such emphasis is that the investor buys something expecting a rapid appreciation—the belief, perhaps, resulting from a broker's sales pitch. Then the investment sits flat or depreciates. Questioning the reason for the disappointment, the easiest answer is, "The holding period has not yet been long enough." Of course, unless the investment disappears, the long- term reasoning can be used forever.

The most successful public long-term strategies are usually those associated with a constant dollar amount involved with each purchase and purchases made at constant intervals. This practice is termed *dollar cost averaging*. Its benefit is that, because the dollar amount is constant, more stock will be purchased when the stock is low and less when the price is high. This method is often stressed by mutual fund salespeople. However, since most investors leave such programs, the usual successful "dollar cost" players are those who have a constant amount deducted from their salary, generally to purchase stock of their employer (assuming the employer stays in business and prospers). Since the money is not physically experienced, it is not keenly missed.

As discussed in later chapters, potentially disastrous problems can occur in a dollar cost program (whether conducted by individuals or institutions). This type of program is mentioned here because of its prevalence in sales promotions directed to the public "investor" sector. For the vast majority, the dollar cost method produces unsatisfactory results. One reason they can be portrayed as successful is the public's ignorance of the effects of compounding. For example, someone buys some real estate for $10,000, holds it for 25 years, and sells it for $30,000. The result appears to validate the merit of the investment. The fact is that, if the $10,000 had appreciated at 10 percent per year (shown to be very easily accomplished by a variety of stock market strategies), the value after 25 years would be $108,000; 15 percent ups the return to $329,000; 20 percent (our usual goal in conservative strategies) would result in an end amount of $950,000. You cannot get these returns if you buy at high prices, which is required by dollar cost averaging, even though you have bought lesser amounts at inflated prices.

Speculators

Speculators incorporate more active, shorter-term strategies in an attempt to experience exceptionally high levels of profitability. Unfortunately (for them), this group fares poorly. Many of the methods the speculators find attractive, including some of the most heavily advertised, have no real practical application, effectively guaranteeing loss.

We will discuss the specifics of these losing strategies in future chapters. The main point at this time is that the public speculative sector provides an area for ongoing profit opportunities.

The Public Investor's Behavior

Our interest in the public (as well as in all other groups) is to identify their strengths and weaknesses: incorporating the strong aspects in our strategies and preying on their losing characteristics. The public's primary advantage is maneuverability. Their weaknesses are financial and psychological: Both are directly related to a lack of available information concerning the realities of the market environment.

The public often overlooks and/or misunderstands a very important factor in professional portfolio management: *capital base management,* which is simply the decision as to the amount of money to be applied to a specific investment type at any given time. For example, a common condition of the speculative public sector is being excessively leveraged (over borrowing) in buying stock on margin. When the margined stock declines and more money is needed to prevent a forced sale, overextended investors cannot protect the position; that is, they are forced to sell at a loss.

The public's behavior is most affected by extrinsic factors, because knowledge of intrinsic factors is not widely disseminated. You can assume that significant numbers of individual investors will be influenced by sensationalism and therefore will tend to concentrate their activity in whatever market area is receiving the most attention in the media. The reasons for this are twofold. First, the repetitive press coverage of the sensational area acts as a natural reinforcement process. Having been subjected by various media to similar reasons to buy and sell, investors' natural impulse is to do as they are told. Second, financial sales are easiest in areas receiving the most publicity. Individuals are more receptive to an investment type of which they have acquired some information. If a broker appears to be in agreement with the publicity, it may be the only reinforcement necessary to make the investor act and consequently generate a commission. It is only logical in sales not to discourage prospects if they have already sold themselves. This is not necessarily a devious broker tactic. Brokers can be similarly influenced by the sensationalism.

Public reaction to sensationalism is generally after the fact. The major market price changes in response to the sensationalist publicity usually occur before the individual investor has become psychologically assured of the merit of the investment decision. Often, the result is that the public is among the last to be influenced to buy before a price decline. As the sensationalism shifts to other areas, the stream of new buyers dries up and prices begin to falter. The price that once appeared reasonable could turn out to have been inordinately high.

The process is the same on the sell side. If influenced in mass, the sellers tend to come to market all at once, creating a serious supply/demand imbalance and causing price to decline severely. Once this mass of sellers is gone, however, the supply/demand balance will bounce back to a more normal level. Because of the lack of sellers, the balance can easily turn back to the demand side, causing the price to advance. Many investors who have sold because of the psychological effect of negative sensationalism have been stunned to watch the price suddenly go back up soon after they have sold at a much lower price.

The maximum benefit of recognizing sensationalism is in realizing that the monies rushing into the dramatic investment area are leaving other areas. The "forgotten" investment areas can become excessively low-priced as the flow of money causes the sensational areas to become overpriced.

By monitoring a list of stock meeting our selective criteria, you can quickly isolate those areas relatively depressed in price. Money has already flowed from these stocks, which can reduce the probability of further decline. In other words, the sellers have already had their effect on the depressed stock. Knowing that investor interest will shift, you can select the most promising depressed stock for purchase—then sit back and wait for the shift. Because of the high quality of the stocks monitored, there is a reasonable probability of the shift occurring within a relatively short time.

As you shall see in later chapters, the probability of consistent success can be greatly increased by coupling the sensational-depressed relationship with market timing methods. In doing so, you can isolate both the individual stock showing the greatest probability of gain and the periods during which the probability of advantageous overall market movement is greatest.

Note that individual investors are often the most willing buyers during periods of general market euphoria without the need for inordinate sensationalism in any specific stock or stock group. In other words, because of the natural reaction to buy during periods of euphoria (after prices have advanced), the public can be enticed to indiscriminately purchase a wide variety of stock types. Having witnessed the possibility of gain, the perception can develop that, "Stock is stock and I want some." In effect, they'll buy just about anything when the greed factor becomes pronounced. It therefore should come as no surprise that periods of extreme public optimism coincide with the sale (to the public) of large numbers of new stock issues, many of dubious quality. Such behavior, however, is not what profits are made of, and purchasing at high levels of investor euphoria (and high prices) is generally the opiate of the naive. The usual result is short-lived optimistic delusion, followed by painful, prolonged financial withdrawal. In addition to the warning signs associated with the expanding number of new issues during market highs, there is a tendency during such periods for an inordinately large number of stock splits which (for no logical reason) tend to reinforce public confidence at precisely the wrong time.

The main point is that public buying euphoria can become so widespread, and the corresponding overall market condition so dangerous, that the safety factor associated with confining interest to the most discounted issues on our Master List loses validity. In other words, when the public becomes exceptionally crazy in their buying, the broadly based market can become so dangerous that abandonment (effectively being out of the market entirely) is warranted. A recent example of this condition was prior to the crash of 1987. Monitoring public behavior was a principal reason Drach's research was able to stipulate being out of the stock market during the highs, prior to the historical splat in 1987, as well as before other periods of significant decline.

Those prone to euphoria are also prone to despair. In depressed market conditions, the public will often tend to hold on and ride stocks down in price until forced to sell. The forced sale can result from financial necessity or from the psychological depression associated with downward price movement. If pressures are sufficient, brief (but very significant) panic selling can ensue. This is generally a good buying opportunity since these sellers are often the last of those who can be panicked. After they have been eliminated, the supply/demand balance can easily shift to demand dominance and a resultant sharp price advance.

Fortunately for us, the public's market behavior is very easy to measure:

- Margin debt is regularly reported.

- The calendar of new issues and announced stock splits is continuously updated in many easily obtainable publications.

- Option activity is published daily by major financial papers: The public speculator sector tends to buy calls when prices are too high and buy puts when prices are overly discounted.

- Odd lot short sale statistics—although (we feel) not as valid an indicator of public sentiment as they are widely perceived—are constantly available.

- Mutual fund statistics are closely followed, both as to performance and to the ratio of sales versus redemptions. When mutual fund sales (that is, public buying) are inordinately high, the market is generally due for a fall after the buying spree wanes. Conversely, when redemptions (or public selling) dominate, the market is usually due for a rise after the selling has had its effect.

The preceding list concentrates on intrinsic measurements of public behavior. Extrinsic data relative to the overall economy (statistics relative to employment, manufacturing, taxes, construction, inflation, etc.) can also be informative. The ability of the public to participate in the market is largely a function of disposable income. When money supply is expanding and the public has excess cash, they will generally be net buyers. Conversely, in adverse monetary conditions the public can find itself in need of cash and will generally be net sellers.

Institutions

This group consists of pension funds, mutual funds, mutual insurance companies, bank trust departments, brokerage firms that accept discretionary accounts, and any other entity that invests monies on behalf of those who have entrusted their funds. The institution may use pooled monies (mixing together the monies of many different individuals) or invest for others on an individual basis.

There is a significant difference between institutional money management and most other professions. Doctors can (sometimes) bury mistakes. Attorneys can befuddle their clients about why their case was lost. Administrators can attribute mistakes to staff. Politicians can cast blame on predecessors. But institutional money managers have nowhere to hide: Either they have made money or they have not.

To check institutional results, all you need to do is see how the money under management performed relative to some predetermined standard, the most popular standard being major market averages. Many investors might be surprised that most institutions are unable to outperform the market and/or profit consistently.

This is not to imply that institutional managers are ignorant, for many of them are quite competent. The difficulties, even for the most astute manager, can be inherent in the structure of the institutions themselves and the market.

The primary advantage of institutions is their financial power. Because of the large amounts of money at their disposal, their investment actions can significantly affect the supply/demand balance and consequently price changes.

The Problems of Institutional Investing

This financial power can also function as a disadvantage because of a lack of maneuverability and liquidity. Dealing with large dollar volumes, institutions often find themselves with very large stock positions. When the time comes to sell, there might not be enough buyers to purchase the large amount of stock unless the price is lowered significantly. In such instances, institutions can be forced to accept lower prices when they sell. Conversely, when they buy, they can be forced to pay higher prices because of the large amounts of stock involved. Of all investor groups, institutions are the most predictable, and as such they are frequently preyed upon by true professionals.

In isolating the institutional characteristics that afford profit opportunity, it is possible to categorize institutions as to type (pension funds, mutual funds, etc.), ethical standards (high, low, none), investment strategies (fundamental, technical, etc.), method of funding (constant or variable), and taxation (immediate or deferred).

Specific institutional investment strategies (strengths and weaknesses) and associated factors will be dealt with in later chapters. In this discussion our concern is with general characteristics.

The institutional manager is, by definition, in the business of investing the monies of others and consequently is influenced by both the attitudes and actions of clientele. The source of the capital can have a significant influence on performance. The greater the stability of the funds that are being added/withdrawn, the easier the task of management.

The stability factor can be clearly demonstrated in open-end mutual funds where the investors can add money (that is, buy mutual fund shares) or withdraw money (through mutual fund redemptions) at any time. Mutual fund sales are highest during periods of euphoria when the public's greed has been stimulated *after* seeing stock prices advance significantly. The fund manager is forced to invest the monies coming in because that is what those investing expect. In effect, the manager is being forced by the institution's structure to buy at high prices. When prices falter and the investors become fearful and/or disgusted, they want to redeem. To meet the investor's demand for cash, the institutional manager is forced to liquidate stock positions at low prices. In effect, through no fault of personal investment ability, the manager so placed is forced to buy high and sell low—the precise formula for disappointment. Even without net redemptions, this basic problem is further compounded by the fact that there is more money to be invested when stocks are overpriced than when stocks are underpriced.

The Sheep Syndrome

Irrespective of the stability aspect, almost all institutional managers are under pressure to achieve acceptable relative performance. That is, the manager does not want to look bad when compared to other managers. This results in what we term the "sheep syndrome," which is the predictable herdlike behavior of the majority of managers who make identical judgments as to their movement into, out of, and within the market. As with their animal counterparts, those who stray or straggle behind are easy targets for the crafty predator. And the herd itself, relatively defenseless because of predictability, has no great strength in numbers when attacked.

To understand this phenomenon, try to empathize with the institutional manager. He or she has certain goals and needs, among which survival through job preservation is of prime consideration. Most portfolio managers, although tending to exhibit little individuality, believe themselves to be in a very competitive environment and are keenly aware if they are over- or underperforming their peers. As long as everyone is doing about the same thing, the status quo is maintained and all proceeds relatively smoothly. The manager who does not stay with the crowd is easily singled out and comes under the scrutiny of others. The manager who demonstrates exceptionally profitable performance has effectively shown up the others and, as a result, may be resented rather than applauded. A manager who underperforms only draws attention as being inferior to the crowd.

In the market, it is mathematically impossible to be correct all the time. Therefore, when a maverick manager (even though consistently doing better than others over time) does make a mistake, it attracts inordinate attention. The result can be analogous to a baboonlike cuffing when one of the adolescents gets out of line. In a more civil context, it is peer pressure. This pressure can intimidate a manager into thinking that the investing public is focusing attention on the error and into magnifying the imagined detrimental effects to his or her image.

This real and/or supposed pressure can make even the most original manager fall into line with the others. In other words, the manager may be forced into what may be considered a herd of other managers. But not all managers choose the herd because of peer pressure. It is also a convenient place to disguise incompetence or lethargy. Just do what the others do and you will never be singled out as less capable. This also reduces the possibility of being disliked, which enhances the chances of obtaining alternate employment if it should become desired or necessary.

Our observation of the effects of peer pressure among institutional managers is far from theoretical. It is not unusual to see institutional managers have their personal funds managed under strategies far different from those employed by the institution itself.

How the Institutional Investor Behaves

The net value of understanding the behavior of institutions is that they will conduct themselves in similar patterns. When you know what the future action of another investor will be, the opportunity for profit is crystalized.

It is not necessary to wait until the whole institutional herd acts. You need only watch for one or a few leaders [analogous to Judas Goat(s) in many instances] to begin to move. You may be reasonably assured that others will follow. This is not done by watching any particular institution, as the lead will shift from time to time because of various factors, including personnel changes. The correct anticipation of institutional herding is best achieved by examining what causes the lead institution to begin the move. Note that the lead institution is not the one from whom profit is most easily obtained. Profit extraction is primarily from those who follow the lead.

The most common lure for institutional involvement is a price advance caused by another investor group. Institutions who were not heavily invested in common stock when the price advance was beginning to see the results of those institutions who happened to be more heavily invested. The institutions with the lower investment level feel they are going to be outperformed: the more rapid the advance, the stronger the feeling. The lagging institutions, therefore, begin to bid up prices among themselves.

Initially this buying will be in the same types of stocks that have shown the most rapid gain and have received the most publicity. By including these issues in their portfolios (albeit after they have already advanced), the lagging institutions can at least give the impression that they were "astute" enough to recognize the better performing (more sensational) stocks.

However, the lagging institutions will not continue to concentrate buying in the same stock groups because in doing so they can never catch up to the performance of the initial institution who bought the stocks at lower prices. These later buyers look around for groups of stocks that have not yet advanced in the hope that the newly "discovered" bargains will outperform the stocks that have already advanced and thereby allow acceptable relative performance. *Rotational* institutional buying patterns develop, which are easy to observe. One stock group will advance for awhile and then stall, as buying demand shifts to another group because the lagging institutions are attempting to "catch up."

Knowing institutional rotational patterns, it is easy for the true professional to take advantage. All that needs to be done is take positions in those areas that have yet to attract institutional buying. That is, buy into those areas that are relatively discounted, sit back, and wait for the institutions to shift their buying preference. Let them bid prices up among themselves, and sell to them at a profit. (As described in later discussions of specific portfolio modeling, this process is quite simple.)

This attempted catching up eventually causes institutional selling and loss, because there is not an infinite amount of money and buying demand is never constant. Institutional buying has its strongest effect on price when buying is concentrated in a relatively small group of stocks. As the buying begins to dissipate over a wider number of issues, the effect on price diminishes. This can cause some hesitation in future buying as dramatic price moves lessen. If, during the slack period, there is continued selling by other investor groups (including true professionals), the result can be a swift downward price movement. Seeing the weakness, a lead institution may begin to sell and the herd will be quick to follow. There are, however, insufficient buyers to offset the sudden mass of sellers. Prices can quickly spiral downward.

In effect, when price advance is the lure for professional buying demand, price decline is eventually the lure for selling supply. The result (especially for lagging institutions) is buying high and selling low, obviously not the type of activity from which profits are made.

Note that during periods of extreme speculation (such as preceded the 1987 crash), the usual institutional rotational patterns are absent. During these conditions, which are very easy to identify (discussed in detail in later chapters), preying on the general rotational behavior of lagging institutions is not applicable.

Although price is the most common stimulus for institutional behavior, there are other factors. A variety of institutions are formed to strictly adhere to a predetermined strategy (ranging from rational to absurd). The benefits (or the lack of them) will be the subject of later chapters. The main point here is that such strategies allow the professional to know what will dictate the behavior of these participants. As always, knowing what your opponent will do in a competitive environment provides tremendous opportunities.

Whether institutions follow a strict or variable investing pattern, one thing is assured: They are acutely aware of their relative performance, and many grueling hours are spent around conference tables in attempting to determine where errors are made. The fact that the difficulty might be inherent in the institutional system itself is rarely admitted. The final outcome of such discussions may only be the scolding of whoever has the least seniority. Then business gets back to normal with the overriding thought, "That'll never happen again." Of course, because the real weakness was never addressed, it *will* happen again.

The analysts using variable investment strategies will pore over past market data in an attempt to discover what factors preceded past market advances. Once factors are believed to be isolated, the institution will be quick to act if the factors present themselves again. This is, of course, a firm belief in pure historical repetition (discussed in Chap. 6), which does not in itself provide profit consistency and can create significant loss. The factors awaited can be anything that can pass as something rational, including chart patterns, interest rates, price/earnings ratios, margin debt, political events, astrological cycles, hem lines, and so on. The important thing to recognize is that, when the factors next appear, they will likely be the stimulus for the lead institutions.

In real life, no two market environments (cycles) can be exactly the same. The elements that precede significant advances/declines are always present but in varying mix. The specific combination of factors institutions consider important because of their most recent experience may not even be significant during the next cycle. Belief in the precise "identification" of the factors by the consensus of institutional thought, however, is all that is really important because the belief in itself can cause the buying/selling stampede.

To isolate such factors is not difficult. Institutional thinking is far from complex. All one need to do is check what factors were getting the most attention at the beginning of the most recent major market move. The key words in the preceding sentence are "most recent." Memories tend to be very short within the analytical community. The specific cause of the brief memory spans can vary: rapid personnel changes, identifying with the concerns of clientele that are most influenced by recent events, the mental comfort associated with forgetting periods of financial pain, stupidity, or anything else. The important aspect is that opportunities or dangers associated with various market conditions tend to be ignored proportionately to the time lapse since the condition last appeared. This frequent (often very convenient) memory loss we refer to as Wallstreetheimer's disease. In its most extreme form, those affected continuously see any market condition as absolutely new and behave without concern for historical/statistical precedent. The more usual symptom is being able to recall only the most recent emotional market condition, in effect, participating in the market on the basis of a sample size of one. The fact is that the market functions within the boundaries of some very rigid parameters that are repeatedly demonstrated over time. Those suffering from Wallstreetheimer's disease are easily preyed on by the professional simply because they repeatedly make the same mistakes.

We have isolated the three key ingredients that cause a repetitive behavioral trait among institutions that professionals can almost continuously prey on: (1) institutions function under tremendous pressure to demonstrate satisfactory relative performance, (2) institutions undergo the regular patterns of rotational shifts in their buying demand, and (3) institutions suffer from Wallstreetheimer's Disease:

All this adds up to a great need among institutional investors for window dressing. Almost all institutions have to publish, at regular intervals both their results and their specific investments. The most common interval is quarterly with the most common quarters being those ending the last days of March, June, September, and December. Knowing their portfolios are going to be published and (theoretically) scrutinized, it is a "natural" reaction among many managers to want their portfolios to look as good as possible. The adjusting of holdings to look their best when published is termed *window dressing*.

Try to empathize with the thought process of the institutional manager; holding stocks that show significant losses reflects the possibility that the manager will look stupid. Conversely, holding stocks that show significant gains can create the impression that the manager is brilliant. Consequently, the common window dressing behavior is to sell the losers and keep the winners so that the published portfolio looks wonderful, with all those nice gains in print and the losses gone.

Many financial writings stipulate that selling the losers and holding the winners provide superior results. However, as common sense dictates, these strategies fall short of expectations because they involve selling at low prices rather than high prices.

Keeping in mind that most institutions are unable to outperform the popular averages over time, note that some types of portfolio management react directly *opposite* to the "window dressing" behavior and that have doubled the return in the popular averages. The basic reason these exceptionally simple anti-window dressing programs do so well is nothing more than concentrating buying in those issues that have become relatively discounted and selling when the issues become relatively high. It's elementary: Buy low, sell high. Because of the psychological pressures (real and imagined) inherent in the structure of institutional management, the advantages afforded to antiwindow dressing strategies will always be present.

Another basic factor that contributes to institutional weakness (as well as other sectors) is the process of *marking to market* to determine the degree of profit or loss. This is very logical process of determining the value of a portfolio's holdings based on the current market price. Marking to market is a reasonable practice because it is the only way to realistically estimate the true value of holdings. The difficulties develop when the marking to market results are overemphasized to the extent that they inject psychological pressures that deter from overall strategy. If the marking to market results show high profits, the attitude can develop, "Oh, yea! I am rich!" This nice feeling can result in positions being held too long, enhancing the possibility of making frivolous decisions from the sensation of wealth. Conversely, if the marking to market results show losses, the attitude can be, "Oh, woe! I am going broke!"—an uncomfortable feeling that can stimulate selling at a loss just to eliminate the mental strain.

The difficulties due those who become overly enamored with marking to market can all be traced to the reality that the concentration is on *paper* profit/loss rather than actual profit/loss in the form of cash. The paper valuations (and the associated emotions) can shift dramatically and quickly. Cash is cash. Those who become myopic in marking to market are vulnerable to the professional who will buy or sell based on condition rather than on specific prices because prices are a function of condition. In other words, relative over- or underpricing is a function of prevailing market factors and price (profit) accompanies the factors. There are two truisms among old market sages that can be helpful in avoiding the mark to market lure.

1. Mark to pocket, not to market.
2. Don't count it until you have cashed it.

The mark to market illusion is repeatedly demonstrated by the public flocking to the mutual funds that have demonstrated the best short-term results in terms of the market value of their holdings. Because most institutional results over time fall into a normal bell-shaped curve, the probabilities are that the lead institution during any time period will underperform the next time period so the end result is that the institution's actual performance will be the average. By buying the institution with the "best" marked-to-market performance, investors are actually increasing their chance for loss. The same dangers are involved in institutions themselves in their selection of individual managers.

For those individual investors who are attracted to mutual funds whose holding show large gains, there is a danger beyond the probability that the institution will likely underperform during the next time period. If the fund sells a position that involves a gain, the investor could be taxed on the gain even though the gain was never realized. For example, let's say a fund is priced at $10 (the value of its portfolio) and the investor buys at $10. Then the fund sells $1 worth of stock that represents a capital gain (that is, the fund bought the stock at a low price before the investor bought the fund). The investor is now even ($9 worth of fund + $1 cash from the sale = $10, the cost of buying the fund). However, the investor has a tax liability on the $1 received. The actual result is a loss because of the taxes. Those who experience this are often shocked.

Because of the immense size of the institutional sector and the wide variety of investment strategies represented, it can appear that monitoring this group is exceptionally difficult. This is not the case. Detailed data concerning the positioning (and coinciding behavior) of this sector is more detailed and more widely available than any other group of participants.

Not only are institutions' holdings and buy/sell decisions closely monitored (which allows maximum opportunity through rotation), but their levels of cash reserves are constantly reviewed and updated. When cash reserves are high, institutions have the power to apply buying demand and push prices higher. When cash reserves are low, the institutions do not have the ability to support prices through buying and the market becomes more likely to decline. The interactions of the public and institutions is also readily available from data such as mutual fund sales versus redemptions, which can force repetitive institutional behavior.

We will go into more detail later as to the methods of taking advantage of institutional characteristics, at this point we are providing only an overview of market participants in order to identify the general aspects that provide profit opportunity. As you will see in Chap. 8, when simple methods of market timing are applied, the process of identifying institutional behavior that provides tremendous opportunities requires no special information and takes only minutes to calculate.

Brokerage Firms

Many investors are unaware that the brokerage firm, upon which they rely for advice and/or the placement of orders, is often a direct market participant and as such is potentially a direct competitor. Brokerage firms, on a corporate level as well as through individual officers and employees, are often actively involved in the market on their own behalf.

The reasoning of those who ponder the merits (or lack of them) of broker participation generally gravitates toward one of two categories:

1. *It is good.* After all, if the broker is so convinced of the merits of a particular stock that he or she purchased it, it seems only ethical to share this reasoning with the clientele. And, if a broker suggests a stock, it is an indication of demonstrated good faith that the broker has placed monies alongside those of his or her clientele. If the broker is wrong, all will suffer. Such personal participation may influence the broker to be more astute and work harder in stock selection to ensure success.

2. *It is bad.* If a broker has a position in a stock and then recommends the stock to customers, the broker faces a potential conflict of interest. The broker's clientele could be used to support the price of the stock the broker owns. That is, the clientele, through their buying, will help increase the price of the stock and may even end up conveniently buying the stock owned by the broker at an elevated price.

There are many scholarly (and not so scholarly) discourses as to which line of reasoning is more accurate. The usual compromise is to advise clients (generally in the form of very small print on the bottom of a research report) if the broker has a position in the stock, so that clients can make up their own minds about the potential advantages or disadvantages.

Such research reports are designed to aid both individual and institutional clientele in becoming informed as to the investment merits of a particular stock. They are sales tools. Naturally, if the brokerage firm owns the stock, the research report is generally favorable.

From our perspective, it makes no difference whether the involvement of brokerage firms as direct market participants is good or bad. We are only concerned that it exists. It is a factor in the market environment that can influence supply/demand, and as such it can provide opportunity for profit.

If large brokerage firms concentrate their own buying and/or the efforts of their sales force on a particular stock or stock group, you know you have buyers regardless of the ethical motivation behind the buying. With the influx of buyers, you can be reasonably assured the demand will be greater than the supply, and consequently you can expect the price of the stock to be pushed higher, thereby allowing a more propitious selling opportunity.

The major effect of brokerage activities is on buying, not selling, for various reasons. The negative is not as easy to sell as the positive. It is much easier to call clients and state something should be bought because of optimistic prospects, than it is to tell them that a stock they own is not worth owning and should be sold. From the standpoint of the broker, if the client has bought something previously and it is up, them keeping the profitable position (albeit a paper position) reinforces the broker's ability. Conversely, if the broker has placed the client in a position that is losing, it can fit the "long-term" category with no acute realization of loss as long as the position is held. Also, selling might not be emphasized by a brokerage firm because the stock might be that of a corporate client of the brokerage firm. The brokerage firm might either be receiving fees to handle a corporation's offering of new securities or have the corporation as a client through its pension fund and/or managing personnel. In such instances, suggesting selling the corporate client's stock would be an obvious business blunder.

Price decline, therefore, is not usually the result of brokerage firm's direct sell recommendations. The decline in stocks that had been advanced by concentrated sales efforts within brokerage firms can be the result of sales emphasis shifting to another stock (or group), with a corresponding lessening of the sales effort in the previously favored stock (or group). The buying demand is lessened, the selling supply begins to dominate, and down goes the price of the stock.

Our intent is not to make you suspicious of the ethical motivations of brokerage firms or their research. Most brokers are quite ethical and constantly attempt to serve their clientele well: To do otherwise (except for the scummy types who have no intent on long-term broker/client relationships) would effectively hurt the broker's business. However, if a brokerage firm's research is consistently wrong and/or is presented in such a manner (primarily nonspecific in forecasts or untimely) that it cannot be used in market endeavors, it is only reasonable to avoid the research whatever the cause of its inaccuracy or uselessness.

Bad research does not mean the brokerage firm is extracting trading profits through its influence on the buying and selling of clientele. As mentioned previously, many widely accepted theories on market pricing are erroneous and the researcher may believe in such theories. Or the researcher may simply be stupid. The possession of fancy suits, plush offices, academic credentials, and other such status symbols do not make the difference between investment success and failure. The differential is who ends up with the other guy's money.

The trading activities of brokerage firms themselves are difficult to monitor beyond their published research and sales promotions. The degree of such influence varies and as such cannot be incorporated as a constant factor in developing personal strategy. However, the effect of brokerage firms, specifically their advertising, on the buying patterns of their individual and institutional clientele *is* easy to observe; allowing the true professional advantage because of the institution's effect on aggravating short-term pricing. Yet, it is not a consistent factor in developing total strategy.

If an investor is comfortable with a specific investment technique and has firsthand knowledge of the individual analyst employing the technique, significant benefits can be achieved by aligning directly with the brokerage involved. In these arrangements, the client is functioning in direct conjunction with the research on a timely personal basis, not after the fact, which functions to expand profitability. There is no loss of control because the investor knows the investment technique(s) being employed and the individual analyst(s). Such close relationships are generally not possible in large brokerage firms: The large number of different financial instruments sold by such firms tends to inhibit specialization. The optimal application of specific investment techniques is usually confined to relatively small specialty firms, with generally an established clientele whose accounts are under discretionary management and do little or no advertising.

The mention of the existence of specialty firms is not to suggest the investor must seek them out. Indeed, investors who learn to function professionally are specialty firms unto themselves. Brokerage firms can be classified as members or nonmembers. *Member firms* are those that own a seat on a stock exchange, regional or national. *Nonmember firms* do not have an exchange seat and are members of the NASD (National Association of Securities Dealers). Most nonmembers have arrangements with member firms to trade stock on stock exchanges. There is no strict difference as to which better serves its clientele. As long as the accounts are adequately insured, the benefit of any firm to the client depends on the expertise of the brokers/analysts involved, not on the member or nonmember classification.

Nonpublic Exchange Members (Other Than Market Makers)

It is sometimes surprising to the public that not all brokerage firms are exchange members. Even more surprising is that not all exchange members deal with the public. Some exchange members trade solely for themselves or for small groups of investors. (A few trade for brokerage firms on a fee basis.)

An exchange membership is termed a *seat*. Seats on any exchange can be acquired by direct purchase or lease. After a brief orientation, the seat holder can trade directly on the exchange.

Contrary to widespread belief, owning an exchange seat does not guarantee success. Although the advantages are substantial, many exchange members fail. Failures are very common and, as with any type of investing, can be traced directly to an inability to cope with financial and/or psychological stress. However, by a natural selection process, the best exchange members remain and prosper.

This is a relatively small, but important, group of professional short-term traders. By having purchased (or leased) exchange seats, they have the advantage of close proximity to the market (many work directly on the exchange floor) and greatly reduced transaction costs.

The general view of the nonpublic exchange member is a little old man scurrying about the stock exchange trying to eke out a living by gaining a fraction of a point here and there, an insignificant factor in the scheme of things. Not so.

A more realistic picture would be an intelligent individual having seats on several exchanges. Located perhaps thousands of miles away from any one exchange, he or she has direct access to trading floors by means of the telephone and utilizes sophisticated computer equipment to monitor the trading activity on many different exchanges simultaneously. The majority of trades by nonpublic exchange members are very short term (perhaps only minutes). Because of low transaction costs, they are able to profit from price fluctuations as small as $1/8$—and in some instances $1/16$—of a point. They have latitude in where they trade and flexibility in how they trade—and often a great deal of money. In short-term trading, nonpublic members are powerful, important market participants.

There is no accurate way of monitoring this group. They are generally in and out of positions very rapidly and usually extract most of their profits by a continual series of relatively small percentage gains. As such, they are not a potential source of profit for investors using longer-term strategies.

The importance in recognizing this group is to put in proper perspective the competition to be faced by individuals who delude themselves into thinking they are going to be able to become successful as short-term traders through conventional brokerage facilities. Doing so is not feasible for the vast majority. The competition for very short-term profit heavily favors exchange members in all respects—costs accessibility, and so on.

The trading strategies presented in this book concentrate on time durations longer than those usually employed by very short-term oriented nonpublic exchange members and market makers (the next group to be discussed).

In utilizing longer time durations, the advantages of inside (member) groups diminishes significantly. Although the strategies detailed in later chapters involve a few occasions in which positions are held for as little as two weeks, there is a built-in mechanism for avoiding situations in which exchange members have a distinct advantage. In fact, as you shall see, the positioning of exchange members can be incorporated by us as an important ally in extracting profits from other groups.

Market Makers

Each stock listed on a stock exchange is assigned to an exchange member who is responsible for making a market in the stock as well as providing an orderly market. Each transaction in the stock is made under the supervision of the market maker to ensure that trading rules are followed and to provide a real market by posting the market maker's bid or ask price if such bid/ask prices to conduct orderly markets cannot be obtained from other participants.

On national and regional exchanges, market makers are called *specialists*. In over-the-counter stocks the market makers are called dealers. The dealer "system" is not as regulated as the specialist system in that several dealers may "make a market" in a particular over-the-counter stock, whereas on a fully regulated stock exchange each trade can be traced to a particular specialist. Such differentials might appear insignificant, but in practice the differences can be very significant.

Market makers, because of the presumed monopoly in determining stock price, are often portrayed as being the most powerful and consistently profitable group of market participants. Their power is often exaggerated, but their influence is very significant and their activities must be taken into consideration.

Since almost all stock market transactions must be made through market makers, and since market makers often provide the bid and ask prices as well, they are often effectively determining price. Specialists are compensated by fees as well as their own profit (loss) through trading. Dealers' profits or losses are determined solely by trading activities. Market makers, therefore, are in business for themselves as traders. As such, they can be direct competitors against all other investor groups.

The physical position of monitoring the trading of the particular stock issue under the market maker's supervision provides them with opportunities not afforded to any other group. They can see the changes in the supply/demand balance as soon as the changes come from the sell/buy orders placed by other market participants.

This advantage has been slightly diminished (in theory) by efforts to decentralize markets. That is, there may be several specialists (each on a different exchange), as well as over-the counter market makers who trade the same stock.

Superficially, this appears to bring about a more competitive environment and theoretically is of benefit to other investors. However, in actual practice these decentralization efforts have probably done more harm than good. A single market maker usually remains dominant with others just following the lead; by having several markets trading the same issue, real liquidity is impaired.

Market makers can be divided into three basic groups:

1. Major exchange specialists
2. Regional exchange specialists
3. Over-the-counter dealers

1. Specialists on Major Exchanges

The principal U.S. exchanges are the New York and American. The specialist's function in any particular stock is to make a market by establishing a bid and ask price and to add stability to the market price if there is an inordinate imbalance in buying or selling by other participants. Specialists are compensated by fees for making an "orderly" market (basically keeping a record of good-till-cancelled orders and seeing that trading priorities are maintained) and through trading profits. The ordinary fees for a stock that trades actively provide a very significant income, but most earnings are derived through trading.

Specialist positioning (as well as nonspecialist exchange members), buying (long) or selling (short), is reported and followed by major financial publications on a two-week delayed basis. This reported positioning has been shown to be one of the most accurate forecasting measures, since the group tends to profit consistently. If specialists are short selling stock heavily, the probabilities are high that the market will go down. Conversely, if specialists are buying stock, the probabilities are high that the market will advance.

Note that specialist buy/sell data in its published form is not as valuable as it used to be because of highly liquid listed option markets. These markets allow options to function as stock substitutes and/or hedges, which can make the published buy/sell data misleading. This can be overcome by somewhat complete computer systems that monitor block trading. Incorporating such systems, however, is not necessary for the methods described in this writing.

The reasons for the specialists' success are their proximity to their market and their ability to influence price. Buying demand and selling supply are almost never exactly equal. Being physically exactly where the trading is taking place allows the specialist to go with or against (depending on which is more advantageous) the activities of all other groups.

Because of its presumed advantage, the specialist system on the New York Stock Exchange often comes under severe criticism. However, the Exchange rules are such that the trading operates as a free, auction market. Everyone is allowed to bid (announce what they will pay) and ask (announce the price at which they will sell) under strict guidelines of order priority. Those who become disturbed at the specialist's profit are losing sight of the fact that, so far, it is the best market system ever developed. It allows close monitoring of trading and a significant degree of fairness. The gross investor atrocities that have occurred in commodity trading structure and in over-the-counter markets are very rare under the specialist system on major exchanges.

The advantages of being aware of the specialist system are significant. The system's existence should provide warnings for those who wish to employ very short-term trading strategies, which involve direct competition with specialists. In longer-term strategies, the specialist system provides significant advantage in that you can side funds with whatever longer-term position the specialists are taking. That is, buy when there are indications the specialists are buying and sell when there are indications the specialists are selling. This is an important element in the market timing techniques detailed in later chapters.

2. Specialists on Regional Exchanges

Several smaller exchanges (Pacific, Philadelphia, Boston, among others) assume a specialist function in many of the stocks traded on the major exchanges. Although the regional exchanges often attempt to portray themselves as independent, their specialists generally follow the bid and ask prices quoted by the major exchanges. The dominance of the New York exchanges is easily demonstrated when unusual events (bad weather, power outages) stop New York trading. The smaller exchanges usually also close.

Regional exchange specialists can be very competent professional traders who have chosen the smaller exchange because many of the advantages of membership on the major exchanges can be obtained without the higher cost of the major exchange seat. On the other hand, they may be inexperienced, lack adequate knowledge, and be undercapitalized. The point is that, for the majority, the specialist function relative to public service can be only ancillary to the personal trading function.

This group cannot be easily monitored. Nor does it provide a source of profit, simply because they are effectively mimicking the dominant, major exchange specialists. Being aware of this group does, however, reinforce the difficulties associated with individuals attempting to compete with very short-term strategies where specialists of all types have tremendous advantages.

Some brokerage firms will direct orders to regional markets rather than to the principal exchange. Their reasons vary, but often it is because the brokerage firm has a close relationship (perhaps a specialists position itself) with the smaller exchange. Although this practice can be argued as justifiable under the beneficial concepts of decentralization, the fact is that when orders are stopped from going to the largest central market, the central market is losing its liquidity. In doing so it also loses some fairness in that the larger the number of participants in any single market, the more equitable the prices determined.

It is to the investor's advantage to transact orders through brokerage firms that direct orders to the central market.

3. Over-the-Counter Dealers

Over-the-counter market makers are almost entirely controlled by brokerage firms. In over-the-counter stocks that have a large trading volume, many different firms might actively compete in making markets, that is, providing bid and ask prices. However, for the vast majority of OTC stocks, the price will usually be determined by the dominant market maker.

In the over-the-counter dealer system, tracing orders and determining order priority are far more difficult (often impossible) than when dealing with stocks on listed exchanges under the specialist system. This can result in disadvantages to investors because of uncertainties associated with order execution. There is usually no way to really know if the investor has been given the best price.

Knowledge of the dealer system allows the investor to understand, and consequently to avoid, one of the most common fraudulent areas of equity "investing." The schemes generally center on low-priced (penny) stocks where the "market" is controlled by a single market maker and the corporations involved have little justification for existence beyond having their stock "traded." The general pattern is for the broker to entice the client into buying a small dollar amount of a very low-priced stock.

For example, let's say the broker's hype convinces some poor soul to buy $5000 of a stock at 10 cents per share (greedy people like to buy lots of shares). So the investor buys 50,000 shares. The broker then says the shares have gone up to 50 cents, and the client's statement will reflect the paper gain. That is, the client's stock is now presumably worth $25,000 and the client is elated. Surprise! Surprise! The broker has more corporations that look just as promising. The client buys more, and they go up. And so on.

The difficulties evolve when the client wants to sell. No way. There is no real market. The broker (being the only dealer in the stocks) was just making up the prices. The "client" thought he was getting rich when, in fact, the securities purchased never had any real worth. This fraudulent practice is sometimes referred to as the *Roach Motel Scheme*: easy to get in, but no way out.

Corporations

Most of the investing public fail to view corporations as direct market participants. They usually assume that the relationship of a corporation to the trading of its stock is an arm's length situation. The corporation, they reason, is consumed by business activities, and the stock exchange is independently judging the relative merits of the corporation's activities.

Yet corporations and the stock market are intertwined on both a theoretical and practical basis. It is widely presumed, and generally true, that the goals of the corporation's management and the stockholders are identical: to maximize the corporation's profitability and consequently to optimize the value of ownership (that is, the common stock). Corporations are established because of money and the stock market is established because of money.

However, in some instances the objectives of management and stockholders conflict. In these cases, the corporation is both a direct market participant and a direct competitor.

The Dangers of New Issues

Such a conflict is clear, for example, when corporations offer new issues of stock during seller's markets.

The sale of common stock allows access to money without any guarantee it will be returned, and without having to make interest payments. In effect, it is a source of cheap capital. Many corporations, keenly aware of stock market activity, have a genuine desire that their stock command a high market price. The more people are willing to pay for the stock, the higher the (paper) valuation of the entire corporation and the more money available through the sale of new stock.

Thus, when the market is high and a euphoric atmosphere prevails, corporations (both new and established) will come to market to sell new issues of stock. In effect, they are taking advantage of the elevated stock pricing to generate more money through the sale of new stock than would be available if stock prices were lower. In other words, they are selling high—to the corporation's owners!

This type of corporate activity is usually a *clear* warning signal of impending decline. The corporations, by rushing to sell themselves through new stock issues, are effectively advertising that stock prices are too high. Yet few investors heed the warning. On a more elementary basis, the new corporate stock offerings are increasing the supply of stock *and* dissipating buying demand over a larger number of shares. Both factors add to a curtailment of price advance and a consequent lessening of buying demand, with the eventual result of supply outweighing demand, causing prices to decline.

Stock Splits

Corporations might also take advantage of high prices with stock splits. The effect of a stock split is simply to expand the number of outstanding shares. Although attractive to naive investors, the effect of a stock split is usually meaningless to the real value of the stock.

For example, let's say a corporation has 1000 shares outstanding and earns $4000. The earnings per share would be:

$$\frac{\$4000 \text{ earnings}}{1000 \text{ shares}} = \$4 \text{ per share}$$

Now let's say there is a 2-for-1 stock split. The company exchanges two new shares for each old share. The per share earnings change to:

$$\frac{\$4000 \text{ earnings}}{2000 \text{ shares}} = \$2 \text{ per share}$$

The end result is that the investor has twice as much of what is worth half as much. In other words, if the stock was worth $50 per share before the 2-for-1 split, it would be worth $25 per share after the split with twice as much outstanding stock.

Stock Splits Versus Stock Dividends

Many texts and financial publications differentiate between stock splits and stock dividends. There is no real difference. Stock dividends are nothing more than small splits. For example, if a corporation has a 3-percent stock dividend, someone with 100 shares would be issued 3 (or 3 percent) new shares.

Almost all textbooks state the reason for stock splits and stock dividends is so that the stock will be at a lower price level, which makes the stock attractive to a wider range of investors. Because of wider appeal, the assumption is that the stock's price will be more easily supported and consequently will rise more easily. Although this theory might get nods of approval in ivory towers, in the actual market it is not always true. In fact, many stocks literally get smashed after stock splits. This is because of a combination of naive investors bidding up the price too high in anticipation of the split, and professionals shorting in the knowledge that the price is inflated because of irrational buying demand.

The most important realistic aspect of stock splits to corporations is that they increase the number of outstanding shares. The more outstanding shares there are, generally the more trading and eventually the more shareholders. The more shareholders there are, the more difficult their communication with each other and thereby the lower the chance of a concentrated effort by shareholders to oust management. The end result is to make management more secure in its position. This can effectively place the management in a situation of perpetual control, without its ever owning any of the corporation's stock.

Insider Trading and LBOs

New issues and stock splits are the result of overall corporate policy. Competition from corporations can also be from individual officers and directors who have access to information concerning the corporation that has not been made available to the public—an obvious advantage. Those having such positions within a corporation are called *insiders*.

The existence of illegal insider trading abuses is obvious, as demonstrated by publicized arrests and indictments. However, the large majority of corporate insiders (probably) adhere to the law and report their buying and selling to the Securities and Exchange Commission, which is required in an effort to ensure they are not basing their decisions on information not available to the public. These reported trades (often after a significant time lag) are available to the public and provide the basis for a wide range of analytical methods and financial advisory services.

The reasoning behind monitoring reported corporate insider trading is simply that the group's knowledge of corporate events will result in their trading being profitable. Studies indicate that this assumption is basically true. However, the results of these studies of reported insider trading fall well below those considered acceptable by the methods described in this book. Insider theories fail to provide acceptable results apparently because the insiders themselves do not understand the market as well as they should. (The topic of corporate insiders is expanded on in Chap. 6.)

The most notorious abuses of insider information (by both corporate managements and others) involves mergers and acquisitions, primarily leveraged buyouts (LBOs). The term *leveraged buyout* simply means that leverage (or borrowed capital) is used to buy the stock of so many stockholders that the corporation involved is no longer public. Control is transferred to a relatively few individuals who have arranged through borrowing, to purchase the stock. The process is often described as *taking the corporation private.*

Because of the large amounts of money involved, the fees paid to those who construct the LBOs (although usually a small percentage of the total) can be huge with relatively minor risk. The buyers often include members of corporate management, who also stand to profit dramatically with very little risk. The risk is taken by those who put up the borrowed money to effectuate the purchase of the stock.

To entice shareholders to sell their stock to the LBO group, the buyers will offer a price that is at a significant premium above the usual market price. Those involved in the LBO know that a higher price is going to be offered before there is public announcement. In the United States, trading stock with such insider knowledge is illegal. However, a large number of people are involved. Corporate managements, lawyers, bankers, underwriters and their staffs are aware that a higher price is going to be offered, and the temptation to cheat is obviously great. By buying the stock before the announcement of a higher price is made, huge profits can be obtained with minimal risk. As a long list of arrests and convictions, involving hundreds of millions of dollars in illegal profits (most taken from ethical shareholders), clearly demonstrates that such insider trading can be pervasive.

The proponents of LBOs, usually the managements involved and those who are paid fat fees to construct the deals, point out that shareholders benefit by getting to sell their stock at a substantial premium relative to what the stock would be worth if there was not an LBO offer. They also point to somewhat hazy theoretical benefits including (but not limited to) concepts that the nonpublic corporation will be more competitive and thereby benefit the economy as a whole. In addition, they contend that those who provide the financing (usually through junk bonds) are provided higher interest rates than they could otherwise obtain.

Critics of LBOs contend the only true value is to those who construct the deals and the management that takes over the corporation, in that they are provided very large profits with relatively low risk. They maintain that the added debt burden to the corporation detracts from its financial stability, using the high default rate of junk bonds as proof. Their criticism also includes a couple of accusations: For one, the junk bondholders are not properly appraised of the risk involved. Also, when banks are involved in the financing, the taxpayers (because the bank's deposits are insured by the federal government) are subsidizing a process that does nothing except make a select few enormously rich and destabilize the overall economy, as the U.S. savings and loan debacle clearly attests.

Irrespective of the arguments, one aspect is clear. The managements who are buying the stock from stockholders (the owners) are, in effect, competitors thinking they are buying the stock cheap (at least relative to their risk). Otherwise, why would they want the stock all to themselves? Our main point is to demonstrate that the objectives of management and shareholders (for whom management presumably works) can often be divergent and directly competitive.

Corporate Raiders

Corporate acquisitions can take one of two forms: friendly or hostile. In *friendly* arrangements, the buyer and the corporation to be acquired agree on the terms involved and all proceeds (usually) rather smoothly. In *hostile* situations, the management of the corporation resists the buyer's actions. The buyer in such instances is usually termed a *raider*.

For a variety of reasons, including the possibility of loss of employment, managements do not like raiders. They want the raider to go away. To entice the raider to leave, they may offer incentives, such as buying the raider's stock in the corporation at a price significantly above the free market price, providing the raider high paying preferred stock/bonds, or any other enticement that leaves the raider with a profit sufficient enough for him to promise not to return. These payments are called *Greenmail*. In a greenmail arrangement corporate management has paid off the threatening party without the permission of shareholders (or owners). The shareholders have not even been given the choice as to whether they want to take the raider's presumed offer.

Thus, once again, corporate management and shareholder objectives can diverge and, in effect, place management and shareholders in direct competition.

Some raiders have perfected their activities to an art, getting paid off repeatedly without ever really making a serious attempt to takeover the "threatened" corporations. Other raiders have been known to buy stock in a corporation, then announce (or imply) that they might takeover the corporation at a price higher than the current market price. Speculators might rush in and push the stock higher. The raider then "changes his mind" and sells his stock into the buying demand (higher prices) created by the speculation. Such activities turn ethical stomachs. They are mentioned to reinforce the true nature of the market, which includes avoiding the assumption that corporations are automatically investors' friends.

Taking a Corporation Public

In taking a corporation public, instead of management buying stock from the public, it is selling its stock to the public. The sale may take the form of new stock issues, selling stock held previously taken private by means of LBOs, or simply large blocks of stock held by management in corporations already trading publically. Whatever the form, the implication is clear that management is selling because the price of the stock is too high. Again, the managements of corporations so involved have placed themselves in direct competition with other investors.

Avoiding competitive abuses from corporations entirely is not possible. Slimy types have been known to work their way to the top of some of the finest corporations. Once identified as the unethical types that these individuals almost always are, they can be avoided by staying away from the corporations with which they are involved. To reduce the possibility of being victimized by unscrupulous corporate managements, we confine investment interest to the issues that meet the selection criteria discussed in Chap. 2 where shareholders concern plays an important role.

The Media

The market cannot function without information, and there is no shortage of willing providers: radio, television, seminars, print, or any other mechanism that can be devised to attract investor attention.

The most important aspect about those providing information is that they are in business. Whether the surveyor is a sleazy tout sheet or bellowings emitting from an ivory tower, its continued existence requires the attraction and/or retention of customers. Customers are the result of sales. As in almost any business, there can be a wide variance in both the quality of the product and the ethics of the sales effort.

The media can therefore function as friends or foes. They are often the driving force behind prices, and their effect on investors can range from being intentionally misleading to genuine assistance.

Fortunately, the various media sectors are easy to classify and, once understood, play an important role in both risk minimization and profit expansion. The media, as with all other sectors of market participants, involves areas of fierce competition, as well as areas of deep-seated cronyism. The competition/cronyism factors are easy to identify and can be found in each of the four basic media classifications. Because of the flexibility possible in any media sector, there can be (often is) some overlap in the following classifications:

1. Nonadvisory
2. Advisory: nonspecific
3. Advisory: specific
4. Advisory: specific with product variances

1. Nonadvisory

This group includes publications and programs designed to report financial news without providing specific advice. However, because of the structure of the media industry, it is impossible to report financial events/opinions in a truly neutral format.

News reporting, a competitive business, requires the attraction of customers. As with other areas of reporting, customer attraction involves sensationalism. Consequently, in a natural process, the nonadvisory centers attention on the sensational. Yet the sensational (by definition) is the exception, not the rule.

The results of this concentration on the sensational are (1) it aggravates pricing, and (2) has a net effect of misinforming naive investors as to the true nature of the stock market and other investments.

The pricing effect is most clearly demonstrated when the market as a whole or a particular segment is experiencing extremely abnormal price movements. In reporting such events the high/low pricing must be "justified," that is, the media reporting the price event must provide some reasoning as to why the price shift occurred. Without supportive "reasoning," the reporting media can appear stupid.

From the standpoint of real market participation, the most important aspect of media sensationalism is that the sensationalism occurs *after price change*. Indeed, before the price change there was no sensationalism and consequently little or no media attention.

Because most of the media will report "reasons" to justify wild pricing, naive investors will be lured in (if the prices are high) or out (if the prices are low) as a result of following the media's reasoning. This can create extreme price moves, which are unsustainable and form the prelude for dramatic, often very swift, price reversals. The underlying reason for the significant (usually easily predictable) price shifts directly opposite prevailing media sentiment are the result of elemental supply/demand relationships discussed in Chap. 3. When all those who can be convinced to buy have done so, they can no longer influence prices to go higher, and lower prices become inevitable because buying demand is exhausted. Conversely, when all those who have been convinced to sell have done so, prices can easily advance because selling supply is exhausted.

The nonadvisory media's business requirement to concentrate on sensationalism provides a constant flow of misinformation to investors who are unaware that sensational events are the exception. To those so influenced, the market can appear to be dominated by dramatic events, and the usual events (rules) that comprise the vast majority of market activity are ignored or never recognized.

From our perspective, market participation is a rather mundane, repetitive business: acquiring the monies of others consistently in an unemotional environment. This requires that attention remain focused on the normal, unsensational aspects of market structure. It is exceptionally dangerous to fall prey to the delusion that the exceptions have become the rule.

We do not mean to imply that the media's gravitation to sensational exceptions is to be ignored. As you will see in later chapters, media behavior plays an important role in our method of market timing and enhances the process of profit extraction. This requires all aspects of the media to be understood in a realistic context.

The competency of financial media personnel covers the entire spectrum, from the extremely astute to absolute dimwits, from ethical to thieves. The process of differentiation can be accomplished only by reviewing the various suppliers for consistency in providing unbiased, beneficial reporting. Note that the competitive nature of the media business results in rivalries (sometimes bitter) and pockets of cronyism. Also keep in mind that the frequency of reporting the opinion of an individual analyst and/or investment firm is not necessarily a direct function of the ability of those providing the opinion. It can be a direct function of paid advertising or some other relationship that is void of any true concern for the investor the opinion is anticipated to influence.

2. Advisory: Specifically Nonspecific

This, the largest group of "advisory" services, can take any form. Often, they are heavily advertised and provide glossy, detailed descriptions of their "analysis" frequently supported by charts and graphs. Their final conclusion can almost always be summarized as, "The market will go up, or it will go down, unless it remains the same."

Such specific nonspecific advice, of course, is of no practical benefit. However, those providing this "information" place themselves in a position of always being right in their forecasts since they have forecast all possibilities.

Specifically nonspecific advisory services exist (and many prosper) for two reasons. First, all share the ability for selective memory loss. Because they have forecast each of the three pricing possibilities (up, down, even), each correct forecast involves two incorrect forecasts. By conveniently forgetting the incorrect forecasts, the advisory "record" can be presented as perfect. The correct forecast will be vocally recalled (and usually advertised), giving the false impression of ability. Second, memories are short in the market (remember Wallstreetheimer's disease), and there is a continual inflow of new participants. Those so positioned tend to believe what they are told without supportive data. This provides an environment suitable for luring new customers. The new customers are necessary, of course, because the old ones leave in disgust. To continue in existence, this media group must advertise heavily and/or closely align itself with another media segment that accepts selective memory loss in their efforts to acquire new business. The result is an inordinate amount of publicity directed to the specifically nonspecific "advisory" sector.

3. Advisory: Specifically Touting a
Single Investment Product

This group can give the initial appearance that they have surveyed a variety of investments and astutely isolated the "superior" product. The product can be anything: "rare" coins, a specific stock or stock group, certain mutual funds, oil leases, hog brains, and so on. However, the true relative benefits of the investment being touted are never really considered.

These sales techniques amount to nothing more than an attempt to place a totally biased, often illegal, intent under the guise of genuine, unbiased analysis.

The fact is that the relative merit of any investment type changes with condition, the most important change being price. No investment in history has ever *consistently* been the most attractive.

Direct "advisory sales" gimmicks are easy to recognize. In our opinion, such "services" have absolutely no place in the establishment and implementation of an objective investment strategy and should be ignored. They are mentioned simply because they exist, and recognition of their existence provides adequate warning against such lures.

4. Advisory: Specific with Product Variance

In addition to the most astute, true professionals, this group includes totally unethical elements as well as the lunatic fringe. All members of this group share a common bond: They state their investment strategy in specific terms and shift their positioning when they deem necessary. Specific positioning and altering investment types as conditions change are essential in the design and implementation of rational, truly successful investment techniques.

To avoid the dangers and to experience the benefits of this group, it is necessary (as with almost all elements of the financial environment) to recognize that they are in business. This sector's business is to sell advice.

The rational mind can be led to conclude, by a natural selection process, that services whose advice was of little real benefit or resulted in consistent loss would be forced out of business because of a lack of customers. Correspondingly, those remaining and best known can be assumed to provide a superior advisory product. This is not the case.

As with other areas of financial sales, one of the best lures to attract new customers is price change. If prices have risen, the price advance reinforces the belief in the investment's merit, and the assumption that the same price direction (higher prices) will continue. Conversely, if prices have fallen, the price decline reinforces the investment's lack of merit, and the assumption the price direction (lower prices) will continue.

This sales effect results in most advisories simply following price: When prices are up, the advice is bullish, when prices are down, the advice is bearish. By following price, the advisor reaps benefits that go beyond making the sales effort easier by preying upon the psychological preconditioning of new customers. It can give the impression that the entity providing the advice had forecast the price change before it occurred—when, in fact, the price change occurred before the advice was given. In effect, such advisory behavior generally amounts to little more than an exercise in hindsight, packaged in a manner that can easily be misinterpreted as foresight.

Prices shift direction, such shifting being a constant element of the nature of the market. Consequently, advisors that simply follow price *after the price change* are forced to incur losses with each change of price direction. In turn, any specific advice that creates losses for those accepting the advice puts pressure on the advisor in the form of both customer loss and criticism resulting from the publicity associated with the improper advice.

It is statistically impossible to be consistently accurate in determining future pricing. Indeed, market conditions can develop in which data cannot support an acceptable probability for a price change in either direction.

The more ethical elements of the specific advisory group recognize the limitations inherent in price forecasting and provide their clienteles with both an understanding of the analytical methods being employed and full disclosure of all past results. This group is a very small minority.

Many specific advisory services provide products ("advice") that are destined to result in loss when applied to actual market endeavors. These products exist, and many persist, because they are marketed in a method most appealing to greed and/or ignorance and/or information that dominates the thought process of the majority who do not comprehend the true nature of the market.

For whatever reason, ranging from devious sales techniques to ethically motivated miscalculations, services providing specific investment advice will experience periods of relatively poor performance. This can result in both a loss of business and criticism. To offset these unpleasant effects, many advisories demonstrate selective memory loss. They quickly recall and tout those periods during which their advice proved correct, but are seemingly unable to recall periods during which their advice proved incorrect. Some advisories go beyond selective memory loss and simply lie by denying that their advice was faulty.

One way to help reduce the difficulties associated with faulty specific advice is for the advisor to provide the advice under different time frames and be able to change the advice as soon as possible. The most common form is to provide the advice in the format of a regularly scheduled publication and have a telephone "hot line" so that investors can call to see if the advice has changed on a day-to-day, or interday, basis.

By incorporating the hot line, the advisor can be giving advice on a variety of strategies relative to time duration, that is, very short-term trading to very long-term trading. Because of the varying time durations, the same strategy can give opposite projections, such as, short-term down and long-term up. Unless someone has the time and inclination to be on the telephone all day, it is very difficult to evaluate the true merit of the advice so provided.

From the perspective of actual market participation, following hot line advice is not beneficial for the vast majority of investors. Rapid shifting of positioning might look feasible on paper, but not possible in actual market endeavors because the prices specified might not be available in sufficient size to facilitate orders. In addition, such trading brings the investor into more direct competition with professionals who are making the market and who function with greatly reduced transaction costs. Unless trading is a full-time occupation, it is almost impossible to compete effectively against market makers in short-term trading.

Selective memory loss, lying, hot line position shifting and other techniques—all of these can cloud deciphering the benefits (or the lack of them) associated with a specific advisor. This haziness has given rise to entities that attempt to rank advisors. These services are, in effect, specific advisors because they are specifically advising which advisor they found to have the best record.

Superficially, advisor ranking services can appear to fill an important niche in providing specific advisor's results in an unbiased, objective format. However, despite presumed good intentions, most ranking services tend to inject added confusion and can be misleading.

As with most institutions; the results obtained by most specific advisors will, over time, tend to clump together in providing an average return. In other words, the advisor doing better than the others during one time period is very probably going to do poorly relative to the others during the next time period. The end result is that the return is average. Because of this tendency for results to fit a bell-shaped curve (that is, approximately equal results for the majority over time), the advisor providing the rankings can actually provide a disservice by misleading investors to flock to the advisor currently ranked on top. In effect, the advisor ranked on top has gained the position after the fact of results, and chances are that during the next time period of result comparisons the previously top ranked advisor will do relatively worse than the others as the results average. Consequently, investors lured into following the temporarily top-ranked advisor increase their chance for poor performance. Following the results of advisors after they become top-ranked effectively allows ranking of the ranking service. Generally, these results are no better—and are often much worse—than the average of the advisors being ranked.

The existence of the ranking services is interesting because they often create amusing mayhem within the specific advisory industry. It is quite common for an advisor when on top to advertise the high ranking. Then, when the advisor falls to the bottom, tantrums (and lawsuits) often develop as the advisor claims that the ranking service did not properly interpret the bad advice.

The confusion associated with the large variety of specific advisory services is easily eliminated by applying basic logic. For starters, it is not reasonable to entrust one's monies to any advice without having a clear understanding of the abilities of the individual advisor *and* the analytical techniques formulating the advice.

The first thing to avoid is advice touted to utilize proprietary (secret) analytical techniques. The authors of this text have been reviewing investment methods all their adult lives and have yet to see any evidence that market movements are dictated by secret formulas. The market is a structured business. The derivation of probabilities for future price change is a matter of common sense. Applying capital to a technique advertised as proprietary involves inordinate risk. After all, the great "secret" might be a dart.

For most investors who experience loss, the basic cause of their financial discomfiture can usually be directly traced to a misunderstanding of the market environment and/or misdirected emotional behavior. The only rational way to avoid these pitfalls is to have a thorough understanding of the analytical methods directing investment decisions and be psychologically comfortable with the techniques.

Having dismissed the specific advisors that refuse to detail their analytical methods, there is a wide diversity of theories and strategies from which to choose: fundamental, technical, structural, astrological configurations, voodoo, or whatever. Differentiating the absurd methods from the potentially valuable ones is simply a matter of taking the time to understand the techniques involved and verifying the results obtained throughout a variety of market conditions.

When the technique to be employed has been decided on, the selection of the advisor and/or money manager becomes easy: Use the one following the chosen method.

Even if an investor choses not to follow the advice of any particular advisor, making investment decisions with total independence, the small amount of time it takes to separate the logical from the illogical investment methods is invaluable both as to risk minimization and profit expansion. To consciously avoid developing an understanding of the true nature of the stock market (or other investments) under the pretext that the process is too difficult or too time-consuming is, in effect, subjecting one's financial life to unnecessary risk.

Summary

We now have covered the fundamentals necessary to understand the specific investment techniques detailed in the following chapters.

In Part 1 we have effectively isolated and described areas that cause loss, a necessary component for risk minimization. In addition, starting from a very elementary basis, we have established a foundation on which we can construct investment methods that will allow us to expand profitability without added risk.

In effect, we have placed the market in the framework of a professional perspective within the reach of the inexperienced as well as experienced investor. We have:

1. Established a realistic psychological view of the competitive nature of the market.

2. Avoided confusion in stock selection by confining "our market" to a specific list of stocks that we find worthy of investment consideration and that also allows us to formulate an effective timing tool.

3. Directed attention to the basic causes of price change, including the inverse relationship between demand and supply.

4. Isolated and categorized those investors with whom we share the market environment, identifying those from whom profit is to be derived as well as those who will not provide a source of constant profit.

An underlying theme of the past four chapters has been the clear recognition that market participation is basically a predator/prey relationship. Consequently, the probabilities of attaining both profit consistency and a high rate of return are greatly enhanced by understanding the investment methods used by others. In Part 2, Investor Follies, we will take a close look at popular strategies to isolate and identify their weaknesses. The other participant's pain provides our gain.

PART 2

Investor Follies: Recognizing and Taking Advantage of Opportunity

5
Undisciplined Folly

The decision of any investor to buy or sell requires some motivation. The stimulus can stem from an emotional base or from a "logical" investment method devoid of emotion. If the logic is unfounded or the emotion irrational, losses will result. The losses of others can be our gain.

In this chapter we will focus on the recognition of investor errors caused by emotional factors.

Identifying and Measuring Irrational Behavior

Through hindsight it is always easy to show how the specific investor action that created loss was stupid or crazy. The process is simple: Look back, see who lost and the the condition associated with the loss, and call those affected idiots. Masses of investment literature use this technique, but they usually fail to correctly isolate the true cause of loss.

If profit could be derived directly from hindsight, any self-respecting moron would soon discover a way to pay the national debt. Our purpose is to make money through stock trading. Real profit can be obtained only through foresight, the correct anticipation of future buying or selling by other investors.

The correct determination of whether investor behavior is irrational (and whether it provides us profit opportunity) requires some sort of logical measurement. Without such standards, the judgment of other's actions becomes subjective and thereby incorporates the risk of being irrational itself. This is especially true in the stock market where what appears rational today may prove disastrously irrational in the future. Identifying the truly irrational requires objective measurements.

Giant, complex, computer-applied mathematical models have been developed in an attempt to determine the extent to which investor behavior has deviated from reason. Such formulas and equipment may appear intimidating, but the investor should have no fear. To measure investor emotion, you need only a general understanding of some simple relationships.

The seven factors that best help you to monitor irrational investor behavior are:

1. Price/earnings ratios.

2. Dividend yield.

4 Put:call relationships.

5. Surveys of analysts' sentiment.

6. Margin debt.

7. New issues.

1. The Price/Earnings (P/E) Ratio

Elemental logic dictates that true corporate value is a function of both assets and earnings, with earnings generally the most significant force creating price change over time. The most common measurement used to describe the relationship between earnings and market price is the *price/earnings ratio (P/E)*. The P/E ratio is derived by dividing a stock's current market price by the most recent annual earnings per share. Almost all investors are familiar with the measurement, and it may seem too elementary to describe here. However, some basic description is necessary because:

1. It is an essential tool in the evaluation of irrational investor behavior.

2. It plays an important role in market timing strategies presented in later chapters.

3. Many widely believed assumptions as to the value of P/E ratios are erroneous and the cause of loss.

To describe a P/E measurement, let's say a corporation's common stock has a market price of $36 and annual earnings per share of $4. The P/E would be

$$\frac{\$36 \text{ current market price per share}}{\$4 \text{ current earnings per share}} = 9$$

That is, the stock is selling at 9 times earnings: $4 × 9 = $36. With earnings constant, the higher the market price, the higher the P/E will be: the lower the market price, the lower the P/E. Consequently, by monitoring P/E changes we can achieve some insight as to a stock's relative over- or underpricing.

Using this example, let's say the earnings estimate for next year is $5 per share. Since the market appears to be valuing the stock at 9 times earnings, by extrapolation the projected stock price for the next year would be $45 ($5 × 9).

Congratulations! You have just mastered an analytical technique that is taught in MBA programs from coast to coast and forms the basis for the bulk of stock research reports. Unfortunately, such analyses are generally of little benefit in the real world, and those that rely too much on the supposed value of P/E measurements can be battered.

As discussed in Chap. 2, very few corporations have earnings records which provide a basis for consistently accurate projections. Although the analytical community prepares earnings estimates for almost all actively traded corporations and then projects future market prices by extrapolating P/Es, the overall record of such activities is quite poor because of the lack of adequate earnings predictability.

The analytical efforts of pure P/E advocates are further complicated by the fact that P/Es change: They are higher when the overall market becomes elevated and lower when the overall market is depressed. Those who base their investment strategy solely on P/Es tend to become introspective, reclusive, and depressed. The game appears to logical, but remains just out of reach. It is plagued by the dual problems of the vast majority of stocks' failing to provide adequate earnings predictability and P/E levels fluctuating during changing market conditions.

To us, however, P/E measurements are valuable. Thanks to the criteria determining our Master List (Chap. 2), the specific stocks of interest to us are those with a demonstrated record of earnings predictability. This functions to minimize the problems associated with trying to predict the unpredictable.

With earnings predictability controlled, the P/E shifts of the stocks on our Master List act as indicators of the market's being over/undervalued. If the P/E of a stock (or an average of all the stocks on our list) is above normal, the interpretation is that it is overpriced. Conversely, below normal is translated as being underpriced. In our specific analysis, "normal" P/Es are derived by taking an average of the range over the past seven years. Seven years was chosen because such a time period almost always involves a variety of market conditions; up, down, or flat. Our earnings calculations are based on earnings projections for the next 12 months (one year ahead) rather than lagging P/Es (those of the past 12 months) that are listed in the stock quotes of most financial publications. We choose to use projections because it seemed logical that future earnings were much more important as an indication of over- or underpricing than what happened in the past. Although we continue to use projected earnings, over the many years we have monitored P/Es, testing the use of lagging P/Es has provided almost identical results.

To benefit from using P/Es as an indication of the market (or individual stocks) as being too high or low does not require detailed analysis. To gain insight into the market's relative over- or underpricing, all you need to do is casually glance at major financial publications, such as *Barron's*, which list P/Es for individual stocks as well as groups of stocks forming major market averages. Note that P/E measurements of the components of the Dow Jones Industrial Average are of little benefit because the sample size (30 stocks) is too small. The Standard & Poor's 500 Average is far superior. When P/Es are down, the probabilities favor higher future prices. When P/Es are near or at extreme highs, the market is vulnerable to decline. It was an elemental observation during the summer of 1987, when P/Es (both lagging and projected) had become exceptionally high, that the market was due for a splat. This afforded even the most casual investor a clear warning to get out of the market and avoid the discomfiture associated with getting caught in the massive decline that followed.

In effect, extreme P/E levels are a reliable indicator of the degree of irrational investor behavior.

2. Dividend Yield

Dividends are more stable than earnings. Some analysts feel that changes in dividend yields for individual stocks or groups of stocks are a better measurement of irrational behavior than P/Es. The dividend yield is derived by dividing the dividends paid over the past 12 months by the current market price, resulting in a percentage. For example, if a stock paid $2 in dividends over the past year and had a current market price of $50, the dividend yield would be

$$\frac{\$2 \text{ annual dividend}}{\$50 \text{ current market price}} = 4\%$$

The higher the market price, the lower the yield. The lower the market price, the higher the yield.

In our determining over- or undervaluation based on dividend yields, we use a seven-year base to determine the norm. We do not attempt to project dividend changes, that is, we use lagging dividend payments. Accurate projections of dividend changes are impossible within any reasonable degree of accuracy.

As with P/Es, the dividend information is widely published. No great analytical effort is needed to determine if investor behavior has become sufficiently irrational to provide a high probability of a major market move: up if the dividend yield becomes extremely high, down if extremely low. As with P/Es, confining measurements to the stocks on the Master List or to a large stock group (S&P 500) is beneficial. With individual low-quality stocks, the dividend yield measurement can be misleading. The stock might be in so much trouble that it will not be able to make future dividend payments, but the dividend yield measurement is using past payments. When the dividend yield gets so high that it appears too good to be true, chances are that it is not true, and in the future the dividend will likely be reduced or eliminated.

3. Book Value to Stock Price Ratio

Book value per share is a measurement of corporate net worth using standard accounting divided by the number of outstanding shares. To derive a ratio relative to stock price, book value per share is divided by the current market price. For example, if the book value is $10 per share and the stock's market price is $24 per share, the stock would be trading at

$$\frac{\$24 \text{ current market price}}{\$10 \text{ per share book value}} = 2.4 \text{ times book value}$$

With book value constant, the higher the stock price, the higher the times-book multiple; the lower the stock price, the lower the times-book multiple.

Many analysts favor book value versus stock price ratios in deciphering over- or underpricing because book value is often more stable then either P/Es or dividends.

As with P/Es and dividends, book value measurements (at least relative to the component stocks in the major averages) are available in many financial publications, easily discernable by casual observation. In our analysis of book value versus stock price as an indication of irrational behavior, we again use the most recent seven-year period in developing the norm. Lagging book values are used because making consistently accurate projections as to book value change is basically impossible.

Over time, book value measurements have shown to be slightly better than their P/E or dividend equivalents in determining irrational behavioral patterns and the associated benefits in price forecasting.

Note that the popularity of book value measurements among analysts shifts dramatically during varying overall market conditions. During periods of euphoria, such as the late 1960s and late 1980s in which leveraged buyouts, mergers, and acquisitions dominate speculative sentiment, standard book value measurements are routinely considered obsolete with the vogue turning to cash flow relationships. The reasoning among cash flow proponents is that the accounting methods used in determining standard book values are not accurate. The argument is that they overlook aspects such as depreciation and amortization, which are debits in conventional book value accounting but not "really" expenses from a cash flow perspective.

From the standpoint of our many years of experience throughout a variety of market conditions, we can state without reservation that replacing conventional accounting with cash flow beliefs can portend disaster. There can, and have been, huge gains to be realized by cash flow emphasis. However, as clearly demonstrated by the massive common stock declines and junk debt defaults associated with each wave of cash flow popularity, cash flow projections are far less dependable than more conventional measurements. The large, widely publicized gains are more than offset by the forgotten losses using the same analysis. Profit consistency is rendered impossible. The benefits of compounding are negated. Cash flow techniques, over time, are a zero sum game at best. In other words, they can take you for an emotional ride, but when it comes time to total the final result, the majority of players will find themselves lucky to be even.

4. Put:Call Relationships

The advent and expansion of listed option trading, which did not exist during the early printings of some of the author's earlier books, have become an important aspect of market activity and can provide insight into irrational investor behavior.

Despite mounds of literature to the contrary (almost invariably published by those with a vested interest in profiting from the option industry), the author's opinion is that the options markets associated with any investment type (individual stocks, market averages, commodity futures, bonds, and so on.) do nothing but act as a net deterrence to true capital formation and the associated socio/economic benefits from new plant and equipment, expanded employment, and a higher standard of living for the majority. In effect, the option markets are not dissimilar to the "bucket shops" prevalent in the 1920s, when one could walk into a speakeasy and place a bet on the market in the same atmosphere as betting on a horse with a bookie. The monies so applied do nothing for economic development.

In effect, option participation is a simple wager resulting in the gain/loss directed solely to the individual entity that made the bet minus the vig taken by those who maintain the game. There is no question that, in the long term, the allocation of potentially productive capital to nonproductive markets will be deleterious to the overall economy.

(On the other hand, there is no denying that the option markets are an important element of current market structure. The option markets can be used as a source of profit. In later chapters we will detail the characteristics of options and their role in some of our investment methods. At this time, our primary concern is the use of option measurements in determining the degree of irrational investor behavior in the stock market.)

So the purchase of options is basically an outright bet. The buyer of call options is betting that the market (or individual stock) will go up. The buyer of put options is betting on a price decline. The betting represents almost pure speculation. Option activity, therefore, can be very useful in determining the degree of speculative sentiment. If the trading volume of call options increases dramatically and put volume decreases, it is a good indication that there is excessive optimistic speculation and prices are therefore more likely to decline. Conversely, if put volume expands inordinately and call volume declines, it is a good indication that there is excessive pessimistic speculation and prices are likely to advance.

Options, by their structure, can often be assigned an *intrinsic* ("true") *value*. Without going into a lengthy discussion of option valuation methods, the point at this juncture is that the differential the option's trading price and its intrinsic value is called the *premium*. The greater the premium, the greater the differential between the option's market price and its intrinsic value. The expansion of call premiums (that is, high call option prices) is indicative of excessive optimistic sentiment, which is usually a prelude to lower prices. The expansion of put premiums (high put option prices) indicates excessive pessimistic sentiment, usually a precursor of higher prices.

The two option measurements, volume and premium, that can be used as a guide to the degree of irrational investor activity are reported by major financial publications. You do not need to go to great efforts to obtain a measure of option activity. At the time of this writing, *Barron's* weekly had provided summaries of option activity (including a column in each issue) in a consistent format for years. In a matter of a few minutes each week, you can obtain the necessary data to evaluate the current degree of speculative sentiment in the option markets.

5. Surveys of Sentiment Among Analysts

There seems to be a general consensus that, as a group, securities analysts are stupid. Consequently, it is widely assumed the majority of price forecasts made by analysts will be wrong. Ah ha! What better way to be correct on the market than to determine the consensus of a large number of analysts for future pricing—then do the opposite!

With no disrespect for our colleagues intended, fact is fact. When a strong consensus develops among analysts, the consensus usually proves to be in error.

Naturally, a variety of financial services survey analysts and report their findings. As with all other measurements used to develop an understanding of the degree of irrational investor behavior, surveys of analytical sentiment are most valuable at the extremes. When an inordinately high percentage of analysts anticipate higher prices, the market is likely to decline. Conversely, when a large majority of analysts forecast lower prices, there is a high probability the market will advance. In fact, when at extremes, the consensus among analysts is an excellent contrary indicator (that is, the market will do the opposite). This phenomenon should not be interpreted to mean that the analytical community is dominated by dullards. As discussed in earlier chapters (and will be expanded upon later), certain elements inherent in the structure of the securities industry can force some analysts to espouse a position that is the direct opposite of their better judgment.

To elaborate on the possibility of conflicts, let's make up a couple of brief, simple, hypothetical examples:

1. You are the senior analyst for an open-end mutual fund. The market is very high and you know by historical or statistical precedent that lower prices are likely. However, the public wants to participate in the market and are willing buyers for funds that are buying stock. Those buyers pay your salary. Without them, your business will suffer or perhaps falter. You like to have food and shelter. The security of your job and family depends on your business's making sales. Your competitors are spouting euphoria and attracting money. What do you do? Take the money while it is

available? Or do you stand by principle and let the money go elsewhere to experience its inevitable discomfiture of loss?

It becomes easy to rationalize. Not taking the money, you risk loss of employment with no assurance of economic betterment when future pricing proves you were correct. After all, the buyers are willing now. They probably will be gone (through losses) when the real time to buy occurs. If everyone else is taking the money and you do the same, you cannot be singularly criticized for making the "wrong" investment decisions. Such pressures are real and can be immense.

2. You are the senior analyst for a commission-based brokerage firm. The market is down. The public is disgusted and wants to sell. You know that historical or statistical precedent strongly favors higher prices, and selling after prices have declined is now inappropriate. Your brokerage firm wants commissions and its brokers following your analysis depend on commissions for their livelihood. The public that can be easily prodded to sell can take their business elsewhere to fulfill their selling desire, resulting in a direct loss of revenue for you and your co-workers. Although you know a sell recommendation is wrong, what do you do? Again, you rationalize. After all, the others are doing it. You cannot be singled out as being wrong. And you are both helping your business and facilitating the latent wishes of customers. In the face of such real pressure, it's real easy to condescend.

To acquire the results of the most widely recognized surveys of sentiment among analysts, you need not incur the cost of subscribing to the various survey publications. The most recent results are reported by most large financial publications. As with put:call data, *Barron's* presents the survey results in a regular, concise format.

6. Margin Debt

There is no need for great detail on this topic because we discussed it earlier. Suffice it to say that an inordinate expansion margin debt is an indication of excessive anticipation of higher prices and functions as a clear warning that prices will decline. Low levels of margin debt indicate excessive pessimism, with probabilities that the market will advance.

Gross margin data, as well as the degree relative to historical precedent, is available in most major financial publications.

7. New Issues

Initial public offerings (*IPOs*) refers to the first sale of new stock issues, stock that has never before been made available for public trading. IPOs are registered with the Securities and Exchange Commission and published by most major financial publications in the form of a *new offerings calendar*. The calendar lists the corporation selling the IPO, the IPO's characteristics (common stock, preferred stock, debt instruments, warrants attached, and so on.), the number of shares and dollar amount involved, when the IPO is scheduled to be sold, and the lead underwriter. The *underwriter* is the major securities firm involved in selling the IPO.

The sale of stock by corporations to acquire equity financing is a business in itself. The higher the price that "investors" are willing to pay for IPOs, the greater the incentive becomes for corporations to provide new stock. When the market is inordinately high and investor sentiment is euphorically optimistic, the number of IPOs generally expands dramatically. Conversely, if stock prices are low, there is a corresponding reduction in the number of IPOs.

The importance of utilizing IPOs as a measure of irrational investor behavior is quite simple. If the calendar of IPOs is expanding dramatically, it is a strong signal that the market is overvalued because of overly optimistic speculation, which is generally a prelude to sharply lower prices. Conversely, when the calendar becomes very short, it is an indication that the market is underpriced and higher prices will follow.

A great deal of money is to be made by IPO underwriters, as the commissions and fees involved are much larger than the compensation involved in conventional trading in the so-called *secondary markets* (the trading of securities after their sale in the IPO). Consequently, it should come as no surprise that there is often a great deal of media attention (including specialized publications) which touts the benefits available to investors who purchase IPOs. Yet, for most investors, profit consistency (or making any profit at all) is very difficult via IPOs. IPOs are not involved in any of the investment strategies we employ except in very special, rare situations.

The primary difficulties associated with IPO investment are twofold. First, the underwriters determine which individual investors are to be given the first opportunity to buy the IPO. If the IPO is underpriced and has a high probability of rapid appreciation, chances are that the underwriter's best friends or customers will be awarded the low stock price. If the IPO is grossly overpriced, large amounts will be available for anyone dumb enough to buy it. In other words, an all-too-common experience for those lured to IPOs is that, if they are not allowed to buy, the price will go up and, if they are allowed to buy, the price will go down. Secondly, for a short time after an IPO has been sold, the underwriter is allowed to "peg" the IPO's market price. *Pegging* refers to legal manipulation, which generally involves keeping the IPO price up until the total amount of shares involved in the IPO has been sold. While the pegging is in effect, the IPO can create the illusion that the price is stable or appreciating. However, after the pegging effect is lifted, the price can fall substantially. Advisory services that are dedicated to praising the benefits of IPOs can easily quantify the advantages "on paper." However, from a practical perspective, the average investor is usually prohibited from participation in the issues that showed the best gains, and the services that tout IPOs often quit monitoring them after the pegging period.

Seven Is All You Need

Several factors, other than those discussed, can be used to determine the degree of irrational investor behavior. However, these seven topics are sufficient for two basic reasons. First, more data is not necessary to acquire a firm insight into the relative insanity demonstrated by investors. Surveying more data is a waste of time. Second, the seven factors are regularly published by major financial publications in a condensed, consistent format. The current level of lunacy can be determined by a quick glance through *Barron's* once a week.

Irrational behavior can be effectively monitored by taking the differential between the high and the low of each of the discussed measurements over the past seven years and then dividing the differential into quartiles (that is, divide by 4). If the majority of the measurements are in the upper quartile, the market can be considered too high and common stock investment avoided. Conversely, if the majority fall into the lowest quartile, the market can be considered too low and represents a buying opportunity. For example, let's say the P/E factor for the S&P 500 over the past seven years had a high of 20 and a low of 10. The differential between the high and low is 10. The lower quartile would cover the range of 10–12½, the next quartile 12½–15, the next 15–17½ and the highest 17½–20. The P/E in the upper quartile (17½–20) would indicate the market is too high; overly optimistic investors. The P/E in lower quartile (10–12½) would indicate the market is too low, with overly pessimistic investors. If the P/E is in the middle quartiles, it would indicate investors were relatively reasonable.

These measurements of irrational investor behavior should not be used by themselves in determining investment strategy. Far more accurate methods (discussed in later chapters) can be easily applied. However, these measurements help to ensure that the investor is out of the market when prices are exceptionally high and destined to fall, and in the market when prices are low and most likely to rise. In fact, using this simple technique will provide results, over time, superior to those obtained by most advisory publications and the majority of money managers.

The point is that investors' emotions are an important element in stock pricing, with the craziest behavior confined to periods of extreme over- or underpricing, and the degree of irrational activity can be easily quantified.

After-the-Fact Sensationalism

It is widely known that doing the opposite of prevailing emotional sentiment during market extremes will, over time, provide above-average profitability. This fact raises a question. If these pieces of the puzzle for investment success are so well known, why are they routinely ignored? The answer has many facets, including investor ignorance, the structure of the financial/analytical industry, and the structure of the financial media—all of which, in varying degrees, we have previously discussed.

The point is to reinforce the common fact that investors ignore and/or refuse to utilize irrational behavior because they are lured by after-the-fact sensationalism. It is an elemental fact the media stresses the sensational. It has to. It is the media's business. People want to know about sensational events, and providing people what they want is how the media gets paid. When it comes to money, people want to learn how someone, preferably similar to themselves, acquired large amounts of it.

Having "learned," through media sensationalism, how others profited by an investment type, those sufficiently lured will apply their monies to the identical investment under the assumption that the price movement will continue in the same sensational fashion. Yet sensational events, by definition, are the exception; not the rule. Consequently, those enticed to chase the sensational (either on their own initiative or prodded by the sales function of the securities industry) place themselves at risk of misinterpreting the exception to be the rule. For each sensational pricing event there are hundreds of relatively boring, "normal," but more predictable price changes.

The most constant aspect of sensational investment events is that they are temporary. A price reversal takes away the prior euphoria, or a more sensational event occurs, shifting media attention. The crowd moves on to the new area of sensationalism and the chasing game goes on. Because of its temporary aspect, the fact that sensationalism cannot develop until after a major price change, those blindly chasing sensational investment areas incur the risk of embarking on the precise formula for loss: buying high and selling low.

Although the difficulties experienced by those overly influenced by sensationalism are easily documented, there is no question that such irrational behavior will always be present in the stock market and in other investment areas. The reasons go deeper than basic investor misunderstanding and the sales efforts of the securities industry which perpetuates such ignorance. The reasons are basically:

1. Psychological gratification.
2. Short-term illusion.
3. Justified sensationalism.

1. Psychological Gratification

People like to be liked. Being with the crowd is much easier psychologically than being against it. If everyone is doing the same thing, there is a feeling of camaraderie. This bonding, however, reduces clear recognition of the risks inherent in the crowd's behavior. Crowd followers are lemmings. Consistently successful investment is not a team sport.

2. Short-Term Illusion

When a dramatic price event occurs and becomes the center of media attention, seemingly logical reasons to justify the price change accompany the sensationalism. To report and/or analyze a dramatic price change without presenting a reason to justify the change places the reporter/analyst in a position of looking stupid, which is bad for sales.

The reasoning baits the trap. Generally, the major price move has occurred before the sensationalism, the move itself creating the sensationalism. However, when the sensationalism is first reported and the lure sufficient, monies are attracted (through demand/supply) to aggravate the price change. If the price move is up, the sensationalism will attract buyers (demand) and push price higher. If the price move is down, the sensationalism will attract sellers (supply) and push prices lower.

Unless you are a blatant manipulator, to watch price change as a result of one's own actions can create a cruel illusion of profitability. For example, let's take a general case of after-the-fact sensationalism. A stock group goes up dramatically and the price move makes it sensational. Those chasing the sensational buy the stock even though it is well above reasonable value. Their buying pushes the prices higher. They watch the price advance and mark to market. That is, they consider themselves to have profited by the higher price, but they have not actually sold the stock and captured the profit in the form of cash. The sensationalism fades, usually as a result of a sharp price reversal after the sensational effect has run its course, and the stock returns to normal fundamental valuation. Now the buyer wants to sell, but to do so requires taking a loss. The assumed profits were only a paper illusion. The actual result was a cash loss.

Some market participants, most of them using very short-term trading methods that require constant monitoring, jump on the sensationalism early and thereby profit. However, for the vast majority of investors such activity is not practical.

Basic logic dictates that rational investment methods involve predetermined buy/sell points. The major difficulty in chasing sensationalism is lack of any discernible selling point. As long as the sensationalism exists, the buying stimulus remains. Not until the sensationalism has passed, usually as a result of a price reversal, is selling stimulated. Profit optimization becomes impossible and the probability of loss expands. In such instances it can appear that profit capture was just missed because of some "unexpected" event, and the next time it will be easier.

Anyone with experience with the investing public knows that those who get involved with after-the-fact sensationalism tend to repeat their behavior even though they repeatedly lose. With the background we have provided, it becomes easy to understand why such self-destructive actions persist. It is a repetitive scenario. The price goes up, receiving media attention on reasons to justify the higher price even though the price is ridiculous. Following the publicized reasoning, the investor buys. The price goes down simply because it was ridiculously high. The media reports the decline including "new" or "unexpected" reasons for the fall. The investor follows the publicized reasoning and sells at a loss. Each time is "new" because of different "reasons." The repetitive core pattern may never be recognized.

3. Justified Sensationalism

Automatically ignoring (or taking positions directly opposite) prevailing sensationalism can be a mistake. There are times when the sensationalism is correct, the price movement is justified, and the price direction is very likely to continue.

To differentiate between sensationalism that is not justified (creating a very high probability that prices will reverse) and that which is justified (resulting in a high probability that the price direction will continue) is basically a matter of applying common sense. For example, when fraud, mismanagement, and lax government regulations were allowed to combine and force the collapse of the U.S. savings and loan industry, it was no secret that a large number of S&Ls would fail. As the S&L stocks descended and the associated problems were reported by the media, the lower stock prices did not make them all cheap because many were basically worthless and on their way to a value of zero. An example on the upside would be when a stock advances to a crazy level because of a leveraged buyout that is a firm deal. The stock is still going to be bought at nonsensically high prices, even though the corporation is assured to eventually go bankrupt because of the debt load created to buy the high-priced stock.

Adjusting investments because of justified sensationalism is not irrational investor behavior and will be dealt with in more detail in later chapters. In this chapter, our main concern is irrational behavior. Justified sensationalism is mentioned to avoid the premature conclusion that all sensationalism is erroneous.

An extremely important fact is that after-the-fact sensationalism constantly shifts its focus. In an ongoing, repetitive process, one industry group (or individual stocks within the same group) will be in favor (that is, relatively overpriced) while another will be out of favor (or relatively underpriced). The relationships will shift in accordance with shifting sensationalism and associated sentiment. The out-of-favor issue(s) will come into favor and vice versa.

If a control is used to differentiate between justified and unjustified sensationalism, the routine shifting can be used to enhance profitability. The easiest control mechanism is the Master List (Chap. 2) in which one of the selective criteria is earnings predictability. The predictability element makes it relatively easy to identify whether price changes related to the sensationalism are reasonable. As detailed in later chapters dealing with specific investment strategies; simply sitting back and taking advantage of the price shifting can result in returns *more than double* those achieved by popular averages.

Note that strategies that go against prevailing sentiment/sensationalism and have proven to be superior are difficult to employ by most investors because of the psychological pressures associated with going against the crowd.

Hot Stocks and Trend Following

Irrational investor behavior stimulated by nothing other than price change can take forms other than that associated with the after-the-fact sensationalism created by excessive media attention. The media, because of time and/or space constraints, can concentrate on only a few issues/events during a given period. The markets, with thousands of individual items (stocks, bonds, options, commodities, etc.) being traded, are much too large for the media to sensationalize every atypical price shift.

The attraction of "investors" to abnormal price change has not gone unnoticed by the securities industry. To accommodate the behavior investors are willing to exhibit based on nothing other than price deviations, a wide variety of brokerage/analytical "services" provide ongoing publicity to methods that are generally termed *hot stocks* and/or *trend following*. These strategies are based on the ignorant concept that current price direction will continue, for no other reason other than that is the direction prices have been going.

On paper, trend following can be portrayed in such a light as to indicate that it is a viable stock trading technique. This is because attention can always be focused on a particular stock that has advanced dramatically (the hot stock). The stock's price can be graphed to show that large amounts of money "could have" been made had the stock been purchased during the early stages of the advance and not sold.

This, of course, is hindsight. All stocks fluctuate in price, with some showing a higher degree of price change than others. This is nothing more than the inane observation that to go to *any* higher level the stock had to *begin* to go up. In acting on this strategy, trend followers are attracted to buy *after* a price advance has already started and sell after a price decline has begun. This can result in buying high and selling low, the precise ingredients for loss.

The tendency among many people is to think that something is better simply because it is higher priced. In the market, this tendency can be fostered by paranoia that the whole market is fixed. Therefore, when a stock price begins to change significantly for no apparent reason, some investors believe that a secret process has been set into motion that bodes good news (if the price is advancing) or bad news (if the priced is declining). The existence of such a viewpoint is so widespread that it can cause supply/demand imbalances and intensify the magnitude of price change. Many advisory services base their recommendations solely on this concept. In fact, it is the underlying concept of trend following itself.

This paranoid feeling can be acquired by perfectly sane individuals after they have (for any reason) experienced a loss. It is a highly unpleasurable feeling to think you have been outsmarted. In response to loss, there is often a tendency to blame someone else. Trend following will always exist, nurtured by both irrational emotion and a variety of theories that concentrate attention on exceptional situations where it can be shown (by hindsight) that trend following "would have" worked.

Ironically, trend following has a built-in mechanism for self-destruction. The trend followers themselves can cause an imbalance in supply/demand. Thinking they see an upward trend, they concentrate their buying demand (often heavily margined) on the trend. Their buying demand subsides because their interest shifts or they run out of money, and the stock naturally begins to come down. Seeing the downward movement, they interpret that a downtrend has started and rush to sell, thereby increasing the declining price volatility.

The Benefits of Having Trend
Followers in the Market

From our viewpoint, trend following is important because it provides buyers at inflated prices and sellers at low prices.

Often, a stock will decline in price with the same volatility that it advanced. This phenomenon has been recognized by many analysts who have publicized a variety of techniques (measuring angles, logarithmic charting, and "waves"), which purport to correctly forecast future pricing by analyzing past price patterns. The reasoning behind these theories varies. The most popular are biological/psychological forces beyond the understanding of modern science which elicits repetitive behavior, astrological configurations, and a giant conspiracy among market makers whose silent (secret) method of communication is detected by measuring logarithmic angulation.

Genetics, moon beam, conspiracies? We believe that repetitive price shifts have a more reasonable explanation: self-manipulation by various investor types, including trend followers. For example, if trend followers, attracted to a stock, will buy an amount determined by the size of their buying power, and then they see a factor for selling the stock, they will sell the same amount of stock as they had purchased. If supply/demand was in balance before the trend followers' activity, the upward effect of the buying would be equal to the downward effect of the selling. Therefore, the equality of angles, would simply be the result of the actions of an investor type stimulated in mass to buy or sell in equal amounts.

You do not have to go into logarithms or worry about charts. All you need to do is be aware of the relationship. The important thing to remember is that, when prices are falling, the sellers are getting out *and* someone is buying their stock at lower prices. These buyers are not (as their buying against the "trend" indicates) as easily frightened as the sellers. In effect, as prices decline there are usually progressively fewer sellers. The steeper the decline becomes, the more quickly the relatively weak sellers are leaving and the sooner buyers will be able to dominate, that is, prices can then advance.

We have now isolated a factor in market timing that you can use in conjunction with repetitive price shifts among stocks. By selecting quality stocks whose P/Es have descended the most during periods of overall market decline, you have taken a step *both* to select the most undervalued issue *and* to have done so when the sellers are losing their influence.

Buying into declining markets is considered taboo in most market strategies and is termed *bottom fishing*. It is viewed as dangerous by most analysts because, they believe, the amount of the decline cannot be measured. However, this "danger" is greatly minimized by confining interest to quality issues with demonstrated earnings predictability (such as those on your Master List, Chap. 2). As we have just mentioned, the amount of a decline is often directly proportional to the amount of the preceding advance. This relationship gives us a crude framework from which more accurate timing can be developed, which will allow buying only in relatively low (often declining) markets, but greatly minimize risk. And restricting purchases to periods of relatively low prices eliminates the potential hazard of buying at market tops.

Note that not all trend-following techniques are invalid and/or irrational. The irrational aspect dominates when the buy/sell stimulus is based solely on price change. When real fundamental factors are combined with the price change, the "trend" can be justified. If corporate fundamentals are improving, higher-than-normal prices deviations are warranted. Conversely, if fundamentals are deteriorating, lower prices are warranted. In these instances, being aware of the aggravating effects of trend followers can be to our benefit: Buy/sell points can be adjusted for extended price moves before the probable reversal.

Know-It-Alls

It is a natural reaction to initially believe what you read, hear, or see as the truth. We are born rather helpless and to assist in deferring death it is beneficial to avoid harsh disagreement with superiors. Moms, dads, teachers, older siblings, church, state, and others in authority, combine to give us written and oral direction. Irrespective of how inane we recognize any particular directive, the usual outcome is to follow it out of the fear to do otherwise might require a disproportionate hardship—like no food.

As we (hopefully) are allowed to mature, the bombardment of verbal/scribed directives is unrelenting. In age, there can be an attempt to fight back, instilling one's own values. However, it is an elemental fact that from birth to death we are subjected to the attempts of others to have their wills dominate our actions. That's life. That's sales.

With that little biological/psychological background, it should come as no surprise that when entering a new environment it is easy to accept what you are told without question. The market is a business. The business depends upon sales. Those directing sales efforts involve some very competent, ethical people. There are also idiots, liars, and thieves.

The rewards for successful sales efforts can be dramatic. It is only natural, therefore, that the securities industry attracts some very persuasive salespersons, so persuasive that their "advice" is often comfortably accepted without question and/or hesitation. These sales experts can be brokers, analysts, advisors, or financial publications. We are combining them here into one category: know-it-alls.

Surprisingly, there does not seem to be any direct correlation between the ability of a particular know-it-all and the size of its following. This is most easily observed in financial publications whose past advice has been recorded in print and therefore makes it difficult for them to deny that they gave erroneous advice. To determine the validity of such services, all you need to do is check past results throughout a variety of market conditions. Although past results cannot be considered indicative of future performance, it certainly is the only valid measurement of perform- · ance to date.

Whether through lethargy, ignorance, or the emotional appeal of a sales effort, the fact is that a significant number of people are willing to follow the advice of know-it-alls without any reasonable investigation of true merit.

The Importance of Know-It-Alls

From our perspective, the importance of widely followed know-it-alls is an understanding of their effect on our strategy. Some know-it-alls are direct competitors; they will either be buying or selling at the same time as we will be buying or selling. Fortunately, they are in the minority. Most advisory services recommend buying when prices are high and selling when prices are low. The net effect is that they provide us with buyers at high prices and with sellers at low prices. Through their losses, they furnish us with profits.

The reason for their losing behavior can be that know-it-alls do not understand the market. The more probable cause, however, is the difficulties inherent in the sales aspect of the financial industry. The public, the know-it-all's primary customer, is most interested in the market *after* prices have advanced. To facilitate sales, the know-it-all is benefited by being positive *after* price change. This positive image during high markets does two things: (1) It correlates with the mood of potential customers. (2) It can give the *impression* that the know-it-all recommended purchase when prices were lower, when, in fact, the know-it-all did not recommend purchase until after the advance. Conversely, if a service is stressing purchase in low market periods (necessary for profit optimization), it can give the bad *impression* that the service had recommended purchase before the decline, which would hinder sales.

When an individual know-it-all (or a group) generates a great deal of media attention, the publicized advice can have the effect of aggravating pricing. Among heavily advertised analysts (including those with a large subscription base and those on the payroll of major securities firms), there is a constant game analogous to children playing King of the Hill. Someone gets on top of the heap (always temporarily) until knocked off by others who combine their efforts in hope of achieving their temporary fame.

The entire, repetitive process—ascent to splat to ascent to splat—really amounts to nothing other than a media-induced game. Upon careful analysis, the statistical result is generally that those participating provide results no better than those achieved by taking the whole lot and throwing them in a bag and seeing the normal bell-shaped distribution with standard deviations. In other words, the perceived best turns out to be the worst on the next count and the worst then turns out to look (temporarily) like the best. Round and round they go, where they land everybody with any common sense knows: no better or worst than the others.

What is important in this nonsensical circle game is recognition that the temporary king attracts a disproportionate amount of money to follow the advice (after the fact) that led to the hilltop. It is yet another lure to the exception, clouding the rule.

The short-term effects on price are real in that the highly publicized advice will attract buying/selling to push prices in the direction of the advice.

Whenever one acquires something new—dentures, automobile, spouse, or stock—the closest examination and greatest excitement take place immediately after the acquisition. In the purchase of a security, it is only natural for most investors to be very impressed by the first price change. For the naive, this is when hope is highest and interest most keen. If the price immediately advances, it can be cause for self-congratulation. If the price declines, it can be cause for self-doubt. For many, the early price fluctuations will be most memorable, even if the final outcome is destined to be opposite the initial price change.

When a know-it-all generates media attention and a large following, the advice given will immediately be followed by those so influenced. If the advice is to buy, it will stimulate buying demand and create a short-term advance. If the advice is to sell, it will stimulate selling supply and create a short-term depressing effect. By their own behavior, the followers of the know-it-alls are creating the short-term illusion that the advice was correct. True profitability, however, requires a successful outcome when the investment is concluded. Price fluctuations between buy and sell points is of no practical concern. When the king know-it-all's turn comes to be pushed off the mountain (through losses), the followers experience the worst of two worlds. They bought after the advance and sold after the fall—the usual result of irrational behavior.

In our actual portfolio modeling, we generally buy into declining prices and sell into advancing prices. This can be somewhat frightening, especially when strategies are first implemented, because positioning is initiated against prevailing sentiment and there is often some short-term price movement against our original price. This "strain" comes with the turf. The entry and exit points, however, are logically predetermined. Interim price movements are of no concern. As Drach's published portfolio modeling has clearly demonstrated over many years and throughout a variety of market conditions (with 95 percent of individual stock positions concluding profitably), perhaps the heavily publicized know-it-alls don't really know much beyond good salesmanship.

Rumors

A constant irrational threat to logical strategy is the rumor. Rumors often sound something like, "My brother-in-law's sister's cousin knows the secretary to the assistant vice-president and, here's the *real* inside story on the next earnings report."

A trait of rumors is that they are often passed along in low whispers. As a general rule; the more sensational the rumor is, the softer its tone. A characteristic of *any* rumors is that it was once a firsthand secret, but to be a rumor, at least two persons must be involved. So at best a rumor is secondhand by definition.

The primary difficulty with rumors is that they might not be true. The cause of untruthfulness may be an honest mistake or an outright lie. It is not beyond some of the less honorable members of the financial community to start false rumors in the hope of selling their stock at inflated prices to the gullible. This behavior tends to be most prevalent during periods of euphoria, when the more naive are attracted to the market in the hope of finding a stock that will skyrocket in price. Such fraudulent bait and trap schemes are usually confined to low-priced, low-volume stocks where the manipulator can more easily control trading. However, large well-known corporations are not immune when stock market activity is dominated by speculation centering on takeover and leveraged buyout activity. The managements of the corporations involved might have no idea that a false rumor is having an effect on the stock's price.

The mechanics of these schemes need not be discussed because one can largely avoid such abuse by staying with higher-quality issues. It is somewhat analogous to getting mugged: The chances of its happening are greater in a bad neighborhood than in a good one.

A common problem with rumors is that, even when the rumors prove to be true, it might not affect market price. Many an investor who has purchased a stock because of rumored optimistic earnings reports, which subsequently materialize and receive publicity, sees the price of the stock remain unchanged. The reason for this is generally that not enough investors cared whether the earnings were good or not, and the supply/demand balance is not altered. For its price to change in a predictable pattern, a stock must have a following (or have a good chance of developing such). Investors have to be interested enough to put their money in the stock. People determine stock price and volume. If people are not interested, the stock will not be affected by either rumor or actual news. This is another reason to stay with stocks, such as those on our Master List, that have an established investor interest.

The most disappointing result of optimistic rumors is when they come true and make news, only to have the stock immediately decline. This phenomenon is so common that many investors adopt the inane philosophy of buying on bad news and selling on good news. These theories are extrapolations of basic irrational behavior and as such are worthless. The reason for a price decline on good news can be found in the elementary understanding of supply/demand. As a rumor of pending good news proliferates, it creates buying demand, which will tend to advance price. When the rumored event is made official, it creates a selling supply among the group that bought because of the rumor. Their stimulus (the announced good news) for buying or holding the stock is gone. If this selling outweighs the buying in response to the news, the price will go down even though the news was positive.

Rumor utilization goes beyond ethics and price effect. When investors become reliant on rumor, they place their financial fate in the hands of another person. In doing so, investors put themselves into the equivalent of a financial iron lung, relying on the charity of others for sustenance and always in danger that someone will purposely or accidentally pull the plug.

One of our basic investment goals is independence, and that can be gained only by correctly understanding the strategies being used.

In the development of our investment method, the effect of rumor on price change cannot be ignored, but neither can it be satisfactorily measured. Our only reasonable reaction to rumors is to ensure that they work as much in our favor as possible in our development of a market timing technique.

Rumors are almost invariably associated with future events. By using the stocks on our list to aid in determining market timing, we are concentrating on issues with high predictability. Rumors surrounding these stocks are more likely to be unfounded and serve primarily to over- or underprice the specific issues affected, thereby adding to price volatility and our potential profit.

Do not assume that rumors are an insignificant factor in that they affect only a limited number of stocks at any given time. There are conditions during which rumors are the motivating force behind the entire stock market. A recent example is the rumor hysteria associated with leveraged buyouts prior to the crash of 1987. Dramatic price gains were recorded as a result of nothing more than rumors that hundreds of corporations were going to be taken over at ridiculously high prices, encouraging mass speculation. The market, of course, went splat.

Self-Image

The importance of the Master List as our primary tool in market timing now becomes more clear. Since the issues are selected because of earnings predictability (with the emphasis on those having the prospects of higher future earnings), the relative changes in P/E and in price volatility provide some indication as to the degree of irrational investor behavior.

In Chap. 2 it was mentioned that all the stocks need not be followed to approximate similar results. In condensing the list to suit individual needs, it is important to be objective about the types of stocks to be followed. The selection process should not incorporate emotional self-image. Also, the single most important factor in choosing stocks is to make sure several different industry types are included, even if a particular industry includes only one stock issue.

It is very important to be comfortable with the stocks and investment strategy you choose, because it helps you avoid panic and irrational decisions. Nevertheless, keep in mind that price movements are common to all stock types at one time or another. This price movement determines profit and will occur regardless of the self-image that you as an investor might want to project. There is no gain to be achieved by letting your self-image determine what specific stocks are to be followed. Personal preferences or prejudices, when injected into a market strategy, only constrict opportunity. The more areas of the market you survey, the greater the probability of your finding areas of potential benefit.

It is a basic fact that buying and selling interest varies in different market areas at different times. When a specific investment area is favored, prices in that area tend to rise. When investor's interests shift to a new area, the new area tends to rise in price and the previously favored area tends to decline in price. By watching several different areas, you can perceive shifts in investor sentiment.

The emphasis is on observing the sentiment (behavior) of others, not your own. To maximize profit, you cannot allow personal feelings to influence decisions. If you are opposed to smoking and therefore refuse to invest in tobacco stocks when they are exhibiting the most opportunity, you are only punishing yourself financially. To succeed in the market, you must adapt to the market. The market does not respond to individual preferences. You must be concerned with individual investors' values only insofar as they provide you with opportunity.

Market involvement is a business in which the objective is to buy at a low price those stocks people are going to be willing to buy in the future at a higher price. If you were running a shoe store and refused to sell high heels because they may cause damage to feet, customers who demanded high heels will give their business to your competitor. The injection of your personal values into a market situation has a real dollar cost.

Self-image is a more significant factor in the market than you may initially suspect. Much (if not most) of the demand for securities is the direct result of the selling efforts of brokers and portfolio managers. These individuals depend on sales for their income either by commissions or management fees. As salespersons, their role is different from salespersons in other business areas in that the financial product being sold is an intangible. Securities are pieces of paper with valuations placed on theoretical ownership or promises of future payment. As such, emotion plays a much greater role than in the selling of something the buyer can physically see and utilize. To facilitate the sale, emphasizing specific investments that correlate with the investor's self-image can often be the factor that consummates the sale.

Aside from their identification with the physical entity that the security represents, investors are often lured to the market with the idea that stock ownership conveys status. Such a connotation can be an effective sales tool, but those who are influenced by it are effectively severed from a successful investment strategy. The belief that stock ownership carries status is illusory. Those who incorporate the idea of status into their market activities can be placed alongside those who incorporate hope or other illogical factors: None of these reasons change the nature of the market or the predictable (at times predetermined) price changes that will occur.

The most damaging effect of self-image is found in those who have succeeded in their profession and come to the market expecting the same traits that allowed them success in their careers to carry over into success in the market. The rewards of a lifetime of toil can be swiftly dissipated when improperly applied to market endeavors. The occurrence of such loss is not rare.

The cause is not a lack of intelligence, for some intelligence must have been utilized to accumulate the money lost in the market. It could be stubbornness, vanity, or pomposity, but most likely it is a combination of misconceptions concerning the true nature of the market, combined with erroneous self-image. Someone's specialization in a business or a profession can be the cause of dismal failure in the market. After experiencing success in a business or profession, it is easy to assume that the success is the result of personal abilities that can be easily transposed to investing. The market is viewed as a simple environment, easily understood and as easy to succeed in as experienced in other business/professional endeavors. The fact is that market participation involves direct competition with *all* others, including true market professionals who have spent their lives in the market and are generally successful against all other market participants.

The market has an underlying beauty in its fairness. It provides an economic battleground where all can meet. Each participant is given a choice of armament. Those who choose conceit will be bettered by those who choose understanding. Those who assume they are superior have to prove it in direct competition. There is no way to avoid confrontation and still enjoy the benefits of victory, for the maintenance of capital requires investment.

Summary

Self-image, rumors, and sensationalism are all common causes of investor misfortune because of emotion. Recognition of these danger areas is *imperative* in the development of a logical investment strategy. Eliminating the influence of emotionally motivated, irrational factors allows you to focus on the pertinent aspects of price forecasting; it also helps you to instill self-discipline.

Being aware of the emotional aspects of investing can only provide a general framework for our strategy. The magnitude of the effect of emotion in market pricing varies significantly during different periods.

By using stocks that are similar in earnings predictability, *plus* being able to recognize shifting by relative changes in P/E, *plus* watching the volatility of price change, we are able to obtain a general idea as to when prices are excessively high or low. We are therefore positioned to take advantage of irrational behavior when it is present in sufficient magnitude to add to our profit.

Our goal is the development of a consistently profitable strategy. Because of the inconsistencies associated with irrational behavior, the effect of emotional aspects must be relegated to an ancillary role. To meet our objective, we must concentrate our attention on factors that are always present in the market and that function in regular, repetitive, predictable patterns.

Understanding the emotional aspects of market participation allows us advantage during extreme conditions. However, since we are concerned with consistent profit extraction, our primary focus must be on well-established, consistent, disciplined market techniques that are followed by a significant number of full-time market participants. Now, free from the bondage of emotional abstractions, we can examine these disciplined techniques and develop our own disciplined method to take advantage.

6
Disciplined
Folly

Discipline and psychological certainty in themselves do not guarantee success.

However, successful market techniques are basically disciplined, repetitive mechanical processes that regularly produce profit. They are regimented procedures through which the individual places funds with sufficient confidence of success to avoid panic. The differential between the pecuniary benefit or detriment of any method is the difference between the knowledgeable and the inane interpretation of the true nature of the market. The problems experienced in ineffective methodologies can invariably be traced to misconceptions about which factors actually do (and do not) significantly influence stock prices in predictable patterns.

The Search for Systems

Words such as *techniques, methodologies,* and *strategies* can be recognized by any horse player as pinstriped terms for *systems*. The origin and search for systems probably goes back to the first cave dwellers willing to bet their bones on contrary perceptions as to which brontosaurus was the most fleet-footed. Today, in every structured situation in which money is exchanged, the search for systems continues.

In our case, the search is for systems to beat the market! Formulated in an atmosphere of (often tedious) disciplined research, many claim to have discovered rather easy-to-use systems whereby the founder achieves a surefire way to riches. By definition there is an apparent dichotomy in the

attempt to combine an admirable trait, discipline, with a less commend-
able characteristic, lethargy.

However, you must remember the market does not favor moralists.
Nothing in the rules states that those who put forth the greatest effort are
entitled to reap the greatest rewards. In such an environment, it is only
reasonable to take the easiest approach, which is to review the results of
the labors of those who have spent years (often lifetimes) in developing
systems, utilize those aspects that have been shown to be beneficial, and
discard those that are not worthy of consideration. This is a lethargic
scheme, but lethargy has never been noted as a cause of ulcers or heart
failure, and, applied to investment, it allows you more time to spend
enjoying the profit you have attained.

Unfortunately, the search for beneficial systems is not easy. Most stock
market techniques do not come with any reliable consumer warning label.
Even more unfortunate for the naive is the fact that some of the most
publicized and widely accepted methods, although they may superficially
appear logical, do not provide satisfactory results.

Hundreds of disciplined strategies are published and have some following. However, classifying the strategies to isolate their deficiencies and
strengths is not as complex as the raw numbers suggest. Almost all
disciplined strategies can be placed in one of 13 basic categories. The
larger number of published methods generally only have a small difference
(usually insignificant) relative to the core strategies we will discuss.

Random Walk

One of the most widely taught and followed disciplined investment
strategies stipulates that, especially in the short term, stock prices can not
be forecast with any reasonable degree of accuracy; that is, price changes
are random. Fundamental changes that affect stock prices are recognized,
but are considered as unpredictable, with the market prices affected
immediately adjusting for such changes and consequently of no benefit in
accurate forecasting.

The theory that stock pricing is haphazard used to be generally confined
to academic settings. Those who while away their hours in ivory towers
found they could (can) statistically show that price forecasting was (is)
impossible. Their problem was (is) that they did (do) not know what they
were (are) missing in their calculations. The theory has been around for
a long time, continues, and has grown in use in market strategies.

To those not familiar with random walk theories, the initial reaction is
often, "Hey! No analysts are going to get up and say the market is random.

They would look like absolute idiots!" Think about it. Most will state something along the line, "No one can accurately predict the market, but I have something special so give me your money because. . . ."

The belief in random walk can function as a convenient excuse for incompetent money managers and financial academics. If so, so be it. It has been our personal experience, having spent our adult lives in the stock market, that *changes in market prices are sufficiently predictable* to provide a nice livelihood, *and* the overwhelming majority of price changes have always been predictable.

Random walk is fallacious. Drach's published models—without any possibility of hindsight or omission, over many years, and throughout a wide variety of market conditions—have maintained an accuracy rate of over 95 percent as to individual stock positions concluding profitably. The market is far from random. We welcome hard core random walk advocates—as long as we are able to "randomly" take their money in 19 out of every 20 stock positions.

Indexing

Based on the random walk theory, *indexing* is the portfolio strategy that selects stocks similar (or in the exact proportion) to those issues that comprise a popular average. For example, the portfolio may be composed of the same stocks that comprise the Dow Jones Industrials.

Presto! Do we have a method that can never do worse than the "market"? No. It is a method that can never do better than or equal to the "market." Even if exactly parallel to the components, the return will be minus managerial, clerical, and transaction fees. If the capital contribution varies, such as in a mutual fund where purchases and sales can fluctuate, there is the disadvantage of being forced to sell low (when fear dominates) and forced to buy at high prices (when greed dominates).

Why anyone is compensated anything over the minimum wage for monitoring such strategies is questionable. The strategy in itself is an admission that both management and participants have given up hope of outperforming the overall market.

We like Indexing funds because they help provide us with buyers when we want to sell at high prices, and they sell us stock at depressed prices.

Dollar Cost Averaging

Widely utilized, this method contains a type of logic that less imaginative investors can be easily led to believe. It is therefore a popular financial sales tool. It is a hybrid of random walk in that it implies direct attempts at market timing are impossible, but acknowledges that advantage can be taken of price fluctuations.

The dollar costing process is simple. At regularly spaced time intervals an identical dollar amount is applied to a particular investment (usually a specific stock or mutual fund). In doing so, when the price is lower more of the investment will be purchased than when the price is higher. Over time, theoretically, the average price paid will be relatively low.

This technique overlooks some very important realities. First, it is a basic principal of the stock market that what goes up must come down (at least partially), but what goes down does not necessarily go back up. This is a truism painfully learned by investors who have used dollar cost averaging in corporations or funds that collapsed. Second, the technique does not incorporate any value for the time the money is invested. If the issue in a dollar cost averaging program stays flat (no appreciable price change) or is relatively high for extended periods and low for brief periods, the benefit of the averaging effect is minimized. As a result, the monies invested may very well underperform the inadequate return of conventional savings. Third, there is no way of knowing the opportune time to sell, since there is no objective method of judging when the investment is over- or under-priced. The important market benefit of liquidity, as well as the recognition of optimal periods of cash conversion, is lost.

Most important, dollar cost averaging methods can be demonstrated to be truly successful when prices are relatively low and more of the investment was purchased. Applying basic logic, why bother to buy during the periods of higher pricing? If the buying is confined to periods of decline, the results would generally be superior.

Because the method is an easy one to sell, dollar cost averaging will always be present in the market. It is, however, an amateurish application of random walk. From our viewpoint, it is a welcomed technique because it furnishes us with buyers at high prices.

Hedging

A *hedge* is any maneuver that requires a preplanned and in-place factor designed to minimize loss. Of literally hundreds of hedging techniques, all are based on the same or similar reasoning: "I'm going to do something I think is right . . . but I may be real wrong . . . so I'm going to do something that'll make me sort of right if I'm wrong." For example, the stop loss order (Chap. 3) is an example of a supposed hedge. The loss is theoretically minimized, but the gain unlimited.

Another example would be buying a put option on a stock at the same time the stock is purchased. Let's say a stock is purchased at $70 because the investor thinks the stock is going to appreciate. Because he is not too sure, he buys a three-month put option at a strike price of $70 and pays $5 for the put. This means that he has purchased the right, through the put, to sell the stock at $70 anytime within three months. For the right (the put), he has paid $5.

Now, let's say the stock goes up to $90. The investor sells the stock and gains $20 ($90–$70). The put has proved worthless since he was able to sell the stock for more than $70. The cost of the put ($5) has reduced his profit to $15 ($20–$5), a reduction of 25 percent.

Now, let's say the opposite has happened and the stock drops to $50. By exercising the put option, the investor is able to sell the stock at $70. His return on the stock ($70–$70) is even, but less the price paid for the put, $5. Although the amount of the potential loss in the stock was reduced by the hedge, he is still down $5.

Or let's say the stock stays at $70. There is a loss of the cost of the put option ($5) when it expires and no profit or loss on the stock.

The important point is that hedges almost invariably carry a cost and increase the number of separate transactions. Since the commissions associated with hedges are accordingly increased, literature on hedging methods is readily obtainable from most brokerage firms.

There are occasions, such as highly speculative situations or a direct need for capital gains retention, where hedging is advisable. And, a few strategies (discussed in later chapters), hedging plays an important role to meet specific objectives *and* provide profit over time.

In the overwhelming majority of strategies that imply hedging, however, the hedge is generally designed to be a losing factor, that is, it is a cost incurred to minimize loss. But it is also a cost that lessens gain. In these strategies, the underlying question is why investors ever allowed themselves to become involved in situations where hedging became necessary. In a rational investment strategy, where the emphasis should be on profit consistency and risk minimization, the cost of the hedge becomes a detriment to optimizing gain.

Risk is inherent in any investment, and any particular investment has the potential of incurring loss. However, over a large number of investments in a strategy designed for profit consistency, the net effect of the hedge could be to detract significantly from optimal results. In other words, most rational investment strategies produce very consistent results. To absorb the cost of a hedge that appears to minimize risk might provide some psychological satisfaction, but it can easily be a statistical mistake with the costs of the hedge too high.

The techniques to be presented in this text do not incorporate hedging as a *general* prerequisite and in most cases no hedge of any type is utilized.

Growth Stocks: The Life Cycle Concept

Growth stock strategies are the most widely known and followed. The logic is simple: Since earnings determine (theoretically) the value of a stock, select stocks whose earnings appear most likely to increase at a high rate. Then sit back and watch the stocks appreciate in value as the earnings advance.

This elementary logic is easily understood both by those in financial sales and by their clientele. It can easily be demonstrated that today's "blue chip" corporations were once fledgling operations, but had prospects for tremendous earnings growth. If these stocks had been purchased in their early days and the investor held on, he or she would have "obviously" profited handsomely.

One of the basic difficulties associated with growth stock strategies is determining what length of time the investor should "hold on." When growth stock touts are asked the time duration of the investment, the answer is almost invariably, "Growth stocks must be considered 'long-term' investments." *Long term*, however, is a cloudy concept at best. It may give some psychological relief to investors and brokers who buy or recommend a stock for growth and then the stock does not increase in price; they can rationalize that the time has not been long enough. From a practical standpoint, the phrase *long term* is meaningless. The purpose of common stock investment is eventual cash conversion. The investor who does not have a specific time frame in mind could die of old age before the "long-term" benefits are realized.

Another basic oversight of many growth stock theories is that relatively few corporations really do grow and prosper until they are blue chips. For every corporation that has achieved blue chip status, thousands have failed that had fully intended to make it.

Although literature touting growth stock techniques concentrates attention on corporations that grew and prospered, by simple mathematics the odds of selecting a stock in its very early stages that becomes a huge success are small. Even if a large number of stocks are selected to ensure including the big winner, the losses associated with the majority will probably offset the gain. The concept of "picking the small stock now and get rich later" belongs in the realm of speculators. By the term *speculator* we mean someone who advertises a willingness to accept loss. Although some losses will be incurred in any strategy, our goal is to minimize risk.

In our strategy we can, therefore, dismiss a selection process that attempts to isolate small corporations with good growth prospects. To look at it another way, why not let someone else take the speculative risk? The few big winners from the speculative sector (or their heirs) will eventually turn toward capital preservation and come to market with their interest concentrated in large, quality issues. There they will be in our game. Whether they acquired their money by skill or luck, the emphasis was on extrinsic (corporate) factors. However, now they will be entering an area of the market where intrinsic factors are equally important. Chances are they will never fully recognize the importance of the intrinsic side and become easy prey to the true market professionals.

The disadvantages to the long-term growth advocates are therefore both in proper stock selection and timing. Why investors place themselves in such an inopportune situation is questionable, when it is obvious that the market prices even for the best corporations fluctuate significantly. The key to maximum profits requires taking advantage of price fluctuations when probabilities are optimal. Take *any (even the most outstanding)* stock that has been trading over a period of years: If you are able to capture one-half of the annual price fluctuations each year, you will have outperformed the long-term holder (by dramatic proportions) who does not take advantage of price fluctuations.

In the development of our strategy, therefore, we must concentrate on shorter time periods. We know that the time period cannot be too brief because we will run into direct competition with exchange members (including specialists) and/or OTC market makers who have distinct advantages. Neither can the time period be too long because we will lose advantage of catching significant price fluctuations. As described in detail in later chapters, in our published portfolio modeling we have concentrated on holding periods averaging 4 to 6 months, although the holding period for individual positions varies from as short as two weeks to as long as a few years, depending on the market condition. When longer-term holding periods are dictated by predetermined strategy (such as tax considerations), the average holding periods have been $1\frac{1}{4}$ to $1\frac{1}{2}$ years.

At this point, we have further defined our principal timing technique as one based on relatively short-term moves of quality, seasoned stocks.

Understanding the shortfalls of growth stock strategies allows us to better understand why only certain stocks (those on our Master List) are most beneficial both as market timing indicators and as specific investment choices.

In many respects, the stocks of quality corporations follow a cyclical pattern similar to individual consumer products or biological life cycles. *Thousands* of investors, unaware of this characteristic, have been financially shattered after the purchase of well-known corporations that have rightfully achieved an image of quality. The losses suffered in the common stock of these corporations occurred even though the corporate earnings continued to grow.

It is *extremely important* to recognize this phenomenon of stock price decline in conjunction with earnings increases. To gain such understanding, apply the price/earnings ratio (Chap. 5) to a generalized diagram of the life cycle of a quality corporation. As seen in Fig. 6.1, the P/E ascends, levels off and then descends. We can divide these changes into four stages. *Remember*, we are discussing quality corporations whose earnings are constantly increasing. Forget the garbage stocks.

Phase I: Prerecognition

At this time the corporation's growth prospects are sound, but not well known, and the stock is therefore not attractive to a large number of investors. The market price relative to earnings (real or assumed) remains relatively low. In our basic strategy we reject any participation at this stage because of the difficulties associated in discovering which corporations

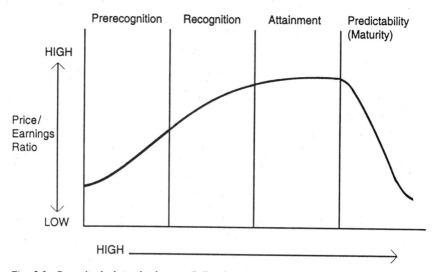

Fig. 6.1. Generalized relationship between P/E and quality stock over time.

will make it to true quality status. In other words, at this stage the corporation is still too speculative.

Phase II: Recognition

The corporation becomes better known. Many investors (and salespersons) begin to recognize the "potential" earnings growth and bid up the "market" price of the stock before the actual earnings increase is experienced. This dramatically elevates the price/earnings ratio because the market price is rising faster than actual earnings.

We reject participation at this stage because it is still a highly speculative situation. Most optimistic earnings expectations are not realized, even though the P/E may be rising. The process of selecting the proper stock at this phase incorporates a risk that does not have to be taken. In other words, this phase is when future earnings projections are most optimistic. If the earnings are not realized or some intrinsic factor begins to dominate, the stock can decline significantly without warning.

Phase III: Attainment

Made it! Anticipated earnings and growth rate are both realized and recognized. The stock has acquired a reputation as a quality "growth" issue. The stock maintains a high P/E because of the reputation achieved and/or continued optimistic expectations. During this phase, many unsophisticated investors can be tempted to buy. When this phase occurs the stock is usually so well known that the media will center attention on it as an example of established growth, with all the accompanying accolades.

This phase may be brief or extended over a long period, but in either event the high P/E will eventually fade. The investor, although having selected a corporation of demonstrated quality, is extremely vulnerable to shifts in earnings anticipation. As a result, the stock is extremely speculative, even though it may be of a quality nature. Because of the risk, we reject any participation in this phase.

Phase IV: Predictability (Maturity)

The transition between Phases III and IV is where severe losses can occur. The stock, having reached the attainment phase, is now well-known and respected. It is widely assumed that the corporation will maintain growth, and its earnings are generally predictable. However, the corporation is now beginning to feel the effects of diseconomy of scale. That is, it is easiest to maintain a high percentage of earnings growth when the earnings are relatively low. As earnings grow, their increase must be in geometrical proportion to maintain the growth rate. Eventually, the company becomes physically too large to do this. In other words, although its overall earnings are increasing year to year, the percentage change is becoming less. This phenomenon is unavoidable, as will be demonstrated in detail later in this chapter.

When a company goes from Phase III to Phase IV, there is a reduction in the price/earnings ratio. Let's say a stock in Phase III is earning $4 per share, and the market price is $100 per share. The P/E would be 25 ($100 ÷ $4), indicating a high expectation of future earnings growth.

Now let's say that the corporation is maturing and the earnings increases 50 percent to $6 per share, but the P/E shifts to 10 because the percentage growth rate is lessening (or any other reason).

The market price would then change to,

$$\frac{\text{Market price}}{\$6} = 10$$

$$\text{Market price} = \$6 \times 10 = \$60$$

The earnings have increased 50 percent from $4 to $6, but the market price of the stock has declined 40 percent from $100 to $60.

This maturation process is a common force affecting the stock price of larger, growth-oriented corporations. It is part of the true nature of the market. By recognizing it, you can avoid an agonizing loss in a situation where the corporation itself does extremely well, but the stock falters.

A problem is determining when the maturation phase begins, that is, when the transition between Phases III and IV starts. No stock goes straight up or down. As a stock matures, the drop in price associated with the shift to lower P/E valuations may occur suddenly or over a prolonged period. The main idea, however, is not to isolate the exact point, but to understand that the process *will occur* and to stay away from the stock until it has happened. Because of the maturation process, many growth stock strategies involving well-known quality issues become as risk-prone as techniques that seek unrecognized, potential growth candidates.

For our purposes, we are interested only in stocks well entrenched in Phase IV as useful tools in developing a market timing technique. By confining interest to these stocks, we have done two important things:

1. We have helped to minimize downside risks associated with swift downward changes in P/E related to cyclical corporate growth patterns.

2. We have generally limited interest to larger, quality corporations (Chap. 2, Master List) that still maintain a growth "image" in the investment community and therefore are attractive to a large number of individual and institutional investors. When common stock becomes appealing as an investment on a large scale, the corporations we are utilizing will have a built-in following because of their reputations. They are considered growth stocks because their earnings are expanding, and they have set a precedent for rapid, dramatic price advance. This rapid advance, however, is usually confined to the past when the corporation's stock was in the recognition phase (II). Growth stock advocates usually fail to see this. They are lured by the stock's past price changes in the anticipatory period, when the P/E increased at a rate greater than actual earnings. The future, however, will be a stock price growth more parallel to earnings.

In market timing, our *general* pattern is to buy when the "matured" issues shift to lower P/Es and sell when these issues shift to higher P/Es. Since individual stocks are our primary investment, not the popularized market averages, it is important to note whether these more seasoned issues tend to lead or lag the market as a whole.

Often, the larger corporations in a stock group lag the smaller ones because of certain aspects of the institutional "sheep syndrome" (Chap. 4). That is, when an industry group begins to get popular, the initial buying is from the speculative sector, which concentrates buying in the smaller corporations. Institutions, seeing the price gains, develop reasons (sometimes real, sometimes imagined) as to why the advancing group is good and turn their buying attention to the larger, more matured corporations in the group. This correlation, however, is not in a sufficiently high probability range to be a primary factor in our strategy. Often, an upward price movement in smaller, lower-quality corporations will quickly falter, and there is no follow-through in price change in larger corporations.

One of our primary interests in watching for downward P/E shifts is that they can provide an indication of a decreasing number of potential sellers, an intrinsic factor. Once the sellers have had their effect (irrespective of overall economic conditions), the buyers can dominate and prices advance. Whether stocks of lesser quality advance sooner, at the same time, or later is of little concern because once the larger corporations begin to change price the rest of the market will generally act similarly.

This will tend to prolong the price movement, especially at turning points in market direction.

It is recognized that our emphasis is not centered on the search for what are commonly considered "lead indicators." A *lead indicator* is generally thought of as a factor that begins to go in a direction *before* the market will follow in a similar direction. Since most factors are considered by the unwary to be "lead" indicators, the market has usually already begun to move (often dramatically) when the indicator is recognized. Our objective is to be properly positioned *before* the anticipated price change.

To maximize profit, we attempt to catch market bottoms as buying opportunities and tops as selling opportunities. Although regularly catching market tops and bottoms is basically impossible, by emphasizing this goal we often come very close to attaining our objective. We are not following a direct lead indicator in the general sense, but we are placing ourselves in a position to become a lead indicator for others. In a theoretical example, let's say a stock is declining, and we believe that sufficient sellers are gone so that further decline is unlikely. We buy, and our buying adds to buying demand. Our buying (because of supply/demand dynamics) can stop the decline and/or tilt the balance so that the price begins to go up. Trend followers and others might see the price advance and apply their buying power, furthering price advance.

Pyramiding: Effects of Compounding

Pyramiding refers to a variety of touted investment strategies, most of which heavily utilize leverage (margin), that can give the impression that tremendous profits can be made through very high annualized returns and consequential compounding.

It is common to see advertising that tremendous profits have been obtained by means of a particular investment type or trading technique. In the world of money managers, a constant source is the results of investing "championships" where the winner made huge gains or publications which specialize in monitoring several advisory services where the current winner has demonstrated a very large percentage return. It does not take much imagination for those lured into the belief that these returns are truly possible on a consistent basis to develop delusions of financial grandeur by simply placing their money as the advertising dictates.

The basic problem with these strategies is simply that they do not work consistently. The results are invariably temporary: What provided a dramatic gain during one time period (generating publicity) will likely generate a dramatic loss the next period (with no publicity because now there is nothing to sell).

The elemental fact is that there is a real relationship between risk and reward. The attainment of extremely large gains incurs inordinately large risk. If one makes 100 percent in an investment and then applies all proceeds hoping to duplicate the process, eventually a large (perhaps total) loss will occur. This wipes out the investor no matter how much money was gained previously.

With their irrational basis, pyramiding patterns are easy to recognize and avoid. Their mention, however, allows us to further formulate our timing and trading strategies.

In functioning in the market as a professional, your participation must be continuous. That is, no risk can be afforded that will put you totally out of business or destroy the capital base so much that it becomes difficult or impossible to expand on the original amount invested.

In general, the greater the percentage gain attempted in any particular investment or with any investment strategy over a specified time period, the greater the risk becomes. A balance, therefore, must be sought in which the annualized percentage gain is maximized without incurring inordinate risk: a combination of profit optimization and capital preservation.

To put capital growth in an understandable context, let's take a look at Table 6.1, which shows the multiplying effect of $1 generating various rates of return over different time periods. This is a basic table that does not continuously compound on a daily basis. The percentage return generated is added at the end of each year rather than at shorter time periods. This table is, however, all that is needed to demonstrate the effect of compounding and provide a reasonable basis of what should be expected from market involvement on a consistent basis.

For example, let's say we place $10,000 where it makes 15 percent a year, and we leave it alone for five years. That is, at the end of each year we leave the money alone so that it continues to generate a return at the same percentage rate. To find the value at the end of the five-year period, we find year 5 in the left-hand column and then move horizontally to the column of numbers under "15%." There we locate the number 2.011. The value of the $10,000 has increased to $20,110 ($10,000 × 2.011) = $20,110.

To ensure that you understand the use of the table, let's take one more example: $10,000 allowed to compound at 20 percent for 18 years. By looking at the table, the multiple is found to be 26.623. The final amount would therefore be $266,230 ($10,000 × 26.623).

Many sensationalized techniques portray gains around 50 percent a year. Let's see how this works out when pyramiding. As can be calculated by using the table, the compounding effect of a $10,000 investment at such

Table 6.1. The Effects of Compounding Growth of $1 at Various Rates over Various Time Periods

Year	10%	15%	20%	25%	50%
1	1.100	1.150	1.200	1.250	1.500
2	1.210	1.323	1.440	1.563	2.250
3	1.331	1.521	1.728	1.953	3.375
4	1.464	1.749	2.074	2.441	5.063
5	1.611	2.011	2.488	3.052	7.594
6	1.772	2.313	2.986	3.815	11.391
7	1.949	2.660	3.583	4.768	17.086
8	2.144	3.059	4.300	5.960	25.629
9	2.358	3.518	5.160	7.451	38.443
10	2.594	4.046	6.192	9.313	57.665
11	2.853	4.652	7.430	11.642	86.498
12	3.138	5.350	8.916	14.552	129.746
13	3.452	6.153	10.699	18.190	194.620
14	3.797	7.076	12.839	22.737	291.929
15	4.177	8.137	15.407	28.422	437.894
16	4.595	9.358	18.488	35.527	656.841
17	5.054	10.761	22.186	44.409	985.261
18	5.560	12.375	26.623	55.511	1,477.892
19	6.116	14.232	31,948	69.389	2,216.838
20	6.727	16.367	38.338	86.736	3,325.257
25	10.835	32.919	95.396	264.698	25,251.168
30	17.449	66.212	237.376	807.794	191,751.059

a rate for a period of 30 years would be $1,917,500,000 (10,000 × 191,750), just shy of $2 billion. Wow! So easy to get super rich!

But wait a minute. The noticeable lack of people having made this amount of money is proof enough of the delusion of most super-percentage-returning pyramiding techniques.

While the table demonstrates that the compounding results of a consistently profitable investment strategy can generate dramatic results over time, *consistency* of profit is the key. As demonstrated in later chapters, we have found that a reasonable expectation for logical, consistent strategies is an annual percentage gain of between 15 percent and 20 percent, depending on the particular technique and objective. The lower end involves the more conservative applications, with the higher levels generally associated with more rapid trading methods (both are discussed in detail in Chap. 9). For the average investor, a 15- to 20-percent annualized return is a reasonable objective.

At first, deluged by advertising that huge gains are consistently possible, the novice might quickly conclude that a strategy providing 20 percent seems too low. However, when considering the risk minimization factor and the compounding benefits as shown in Table 6.1, the results of a compounded 20-percent gain are quite dramatic when compared to what has been documented by *any* unleveraged investment type over an extended period.

Contrary Opinion

These systems incorporate a wide variety of market theories, all based on the concept, "Since the majority lose in the market, success lies in doing what the minority does." Many contrary opinion techniques have demonstrated successful records over time, but most experience difficulty in achieving profit consistency. Those following contrary opinion must, by definition, be in the minority. There are times when the majority does win—significantly. The problems with the contrary opinion advocates is determining precisely what they are contrary to and why.

We have already mentioned the inane reasoning behind any strategy that blindly buys on bad news and sells on good news. We have, however, isolated benefits to be derived from buying into declining markets and selling into advancing markets. This buying relatively low and selling relatively high is fine (that's what makes profits). But both profit consistency and profit optimization must incorporate valid measurements for determining what is really relatively low or high.

If a stock is proceeding downward, it may have very good extrinsic reasons for doing so; it could even be going out of business. Conversely, if a stock is advancing, it may well warrant the price increase. The contrary opinion advocate, going against the majority, may therefore be very wrong. The majority, in fact, are always right (at least temporarily) when they are influencing price moves by their own creation of demand/supply imbalances.

This reaffirms our reasoning for staying with seasoned issues whose fundamental characteristics are well known, those on the Master List. With reasonably predictable fundamentals, the determination of over-/underpricing has a logical base. We can then combine both intrinsic and extrinsic factors to allow us to decide when it is truly time to be contrary.

The decision as to when to act in accordance with contrary opinion is a function of both price and volume. By monitoring historical P/E ratios, you can see when the prices of the stocks you follow are reasonable or ridiculous. In your attempt to catch market tops and bottoms, you need to also attempt to determine when the weight of trading will shift between supply and demand. Simply being aware that prices have advanced or declined does not in itself provide any clear indication as to the duration of the price move before the reversal. Identification of the reversal point is made easier by measuring changes in volume.

If volume increases dramatically and market prices also change dramatically, in either direction, the indication is that (for whatever reason) an inordinate amount of financial force is being applied that cannot continue indefinitely. Most investors attracted to such situations are most influenced by immediate price changes—emotional speculation. They will reverse their opinion if the price direction does not continue. By concentrating their power to disrupt the demand/supply balance in a brief period, they may have quickly exerted their maximum effect on price. With their power having been utilized, a reversal (often quick and dramatic) in price can follow on much lower volume. The more volatile the price change associated with heavy volume, the more those creating the volume are prone to irrational behavior.

Being aware of the importance of volume, we have now taken another step in developing our general framework for timing buy and sell decisions. *To buy*, we look for downward shifts in P/E, *plus* relatively steep price declines in a brief period, *plus* relatively heavy volume. *To sell*, we look for upward shifts in P/E, *plus* relatively steep price advances in a brief time period, *plus* relatively heavy volume.

The Beta (ß) Factor and Relative Strength

Beta Factors

The *beta factor* is a measurement of the price volatility of a specific stock relative to the market average. For example, if the market changed 10 percent and a specific stock's price changed 10 percent, the same amount as the market, the stock would be given a beta of 1.00. If the stock's change was greater than the market, it would be given a beta greater than 1.00, with the amount over 1.00 determined by the degree of relative change. Conversely, if a stock's price change was less than the market average, it would be assigned a beta less than 1.00, with the amount under 1.00 determined by the relative amount of change.

By seeing how individual stocks change in price relative to the market over an extended period, a relative beta can be derived for all stocks traded over the period. Many analysts believe the beta factor can be used (both in strategies that incorporate market timing and that do not) to isolate stocks that will move more or less than the market averages.

Although such use of the beta factor has been shown to have some statistical validity, to make specific stock selections with it is nonsense because it is based on past measurements which are not necessarily applicable to future market activity. A stock with a low beta may suddenly experience relatively volatile price changes and acquire a high beta. Conversely, a stock with a high beta may become relatively dormant in price movement for an extended period and gradually acquire a low beta.

Beta factors also change during the natural life cycle of growth stocks (Fig. 6.1). As stocks mature, their betas tend to decline.

Although invalid as a heavily weighted measurement in sound investment strategy, beta factors are important because of the actions of the believers (including many institutions) who tend to concentrate their buying (and eventual selling) in high-beta issues. By watching these issues, we can get an indication of institutional activity, which is useful to us in market timing. For example, a sharp downmove in high-beta stocks, in conjunction with our other timing tools, would indicate that a significant group of sellers is gone, thereby allowing a better chance for a reversal in the stock's price. We have also isolated an area where the followers of the beta factor will concentrate their next buying.

Betas are provided through a variety of publications, including *Value Line*.

Relative Strength

Relative strength techniques are closely related to the beta factor with the primary difference being that relative strength concentrates on shorter periods to derive the measurement. Relative strength is simply the determination of how strongly or weakly a stock has performed relative to other stocks during recent market activity.

Relative strength methods vary in popularity during different market conditions. During bull markets, when prices have posted a general advance for an extended period, relative strength strategies gain wide popularity. During flat or declining periods, they usually go out of favor because their inherent weaknesses become evident. At the time of this writing, literally billions of institutional dollars function under managements whose analysis is dictated by relative strength measurements.

The concept is simple. When the analyst derives a buy signal, the stocks purchased are those demonstrating the greatest current relative strength, on the presumption that the relative strength will continue. The reliance on relative strength is not confined to strategies incorporating timing. It is popular with managers who are continuously fully invested in the stock market.

Two problems are associated with relative strength strategies: (1) The relative strength shifts between stocks. What was strong yesterday may turn out to be a weakling tomorrow. (2) When relatively "strong" stocks go down, they often do so rapidly and dramatically without conventional warning signs. This can create severe losses and is the reason for the changes in relative strength's popularity during varying market conditions.

From our perspective, the greatest drawback to relative strength techniques is that they do not provide us with the profit-making consistency we consider acceptable. We have never seen a relative strength technique that can come close to our models in providing satisfactory profit consistency. Our buying almost always concentrates in stocks demonstrating current relative weakness with what appears to be satisfactory underlying fundamental value. Risk is consequently minimized, and gains to date have been consistent throughout a variety of market conditions.

Understanding the existence of and fluctuating popularity of relative strength strategies allows us an advantage in identifying buyers for specific stock issues. It also enables us to isolate stocks that will show steep declines during those periods when the relative strength advocates are most likely to get battered.

Historical Repetition

Historical repetition can be divided into two categories: that which is related to intrinsic factors (market structure), and that which is related to extrinsic factors (corporate and other economic events). The intrinsic relationships have continual validity; the extrinsic factors do not. Thus, the only history that really repeats itself in the market is that supply/demand shifts and prices change accordingly. Fortunately, for those who conduct themselves professionally, most strategies that focus on historical repetition concentrate on extrinsic factors.

In market timing and profit extraction, we are concerned with the preconceived notions of large numbers of market participants who believe specific extrinsic factors will affect stock prices. If a significant number of investors believe in a relationship, it will (for a while) become self-fulfilling because of the supply/demand imbalances created by the believers themselves, but will eventually fail.

We do not mean to imply that stock prices function totally independent of extrinsic economic conditions. There are direct relationships. However, the supposed effects of these relationships vary significantly during different market conditions. It is when the presumed relationships become blown out of proportion that opportunities are magnified.

The most popular assumptions are the relationships between common stock valuation versus interest rates and/or gold:

Lower interest rates = Higher stock prices and vice versa

Lower gold prices = Higher stock prices and vice versa

Others include money supply, trade deficits, inflation rates, hemlines, astrological patterns, index arbitrage programs, and anything else that can excite the media and those they influence. The point is that each and every presumed relationship comes and goes in popularity. The purpose is to understand why. As the supposed relationship gains recognition, more and more investors apply their monies in accordance to the presumption. They are reinforced in their behavior by the sales structure of the analytical/media community. It all seems so simple, but rational valuations are becoming correspondingly out of whack. In effect, they begin acting like a herd, thereby creating pricing excesses. When they decide to buy, they will inordinately elevate prices, allowing the professional higher selling prices than would otherwise be available. When they rush out on the sell side, they are providing lowered buy points for the professional.

The presumed historical relationship shifts are popular because each time the believers get crazier the professionals take more advantage. The believers begin to experience losses and they decide it best to quit and start believing in some other presumed extrinsic relationship that is gaining in popularity. The professional adapts, getting into position for the next folly after having taken (and not returned) the monies of those who believed the market "functions" under a strict mantle of extrinsic historical repetition.

As mentioned, some extrinsic factors do affect stock prices. However, the effects vary and as such are not consistently reliable. They can be regarded as an adjunct, adding to the accuracy of market timing, but they cannot be the main element.

Because of the loose correlation of many extrinsic factors to common stock pricing, many methods have been developed to combine several factors to have shown some relationship to the stock market. Yet the tested degree for any particular element is too low to be accurate at an acceptable level in itself. The general thinking behind these methods is that, by combining several different relationships that are "usually" correct, forecasting accuracy can be significantly enhanced when the majority of the factors indicate a particular market direction.

Such combination techniques are well publicized and form the basis of many widely distributed advisory service newsletters, as well as provide the guidelines for many large institutional managers.

Although such methods may seem logical, the effect of combining several factors usually emphasizes not only the benefits of each factor, but the fallacies as well. In practice, therefore, such combinations usually do not produce results any better than concentration on any individual component. If all the components are extrinsic, the accuracy will probably always be inferior to those techniques that incorporate an understanding of the effects of intrinsic factors.

Charting

A prolonged explanation of charting techniques and formations is not needed to show that they cannot be relied on exclusively. Charts and graphs do provide a sometimes helpful format to review historical changes in price, volume, or any other quantifiable measurement. However, as a useful tool in anticipating the future, reliance on using chart patterns alone as an investment guide is extremely dangerous and can result in failure.

Because charting techniques can be presented in a way (basically in the form of *after-the-fact* sensationalism) that makes the methods superficially logical, charting is heavily indulged in by public speculators as well as some more "refined" institutional investors.

Since chartists follow established patterns, it is often possible to predict what they will do in a given circumstance. For example, if our market timing methods indicate that there will be an upward market move, the stocks monitored can be surveyed for those most likely to develop a "break-out" chart pattern. This pattern will give the impression that the stock will move decidedly higher and therefore attract the buying of charting advocates. Knowing they will buy at the "break-out" point is effectively knowing they will buy at a higher level that will provide us expanded profit.

This trapping mechanism can also be applied to mutual fund switching techniques, which gained dramatically in popularity during the middle to late 1980s. These techniques generally follow a trend line (the average of prices over a previous period), buying when the market goes above the trend line and selling when it goes below. These methods have virtually nothing to do with fundamentals or an understanding of market structure, but can greatly (albeit temporarily) influence prices by forcing the mutual funds involved to buy or sell in mass. This activity effectively furnishes us with buyers at higher prices and with sellers at lower prices than would have been otherwise available.

To trap chartists requires focusing on stocks in which a large number of chartists are concentrating interest. To accomplish this, you should make sure that the stock is being followed by major charting services and that the stock's recent price history has shown enough movement to be attractive to those most influenced by swift price change (that is, high relative strength/weakness).

Note that in some very speculative markets, primarily commodities, trapping chartists is an extremely important factor. However, in dealing with stocks and bonds, which is the subject of this writing, trapping chartists is not a very viable strategy in itself. Chart patterns can be of some benefit because of their effect on others. To maximize the benefit, however, they must be used in conjunction with other criteria, as discussed in those chapters dealing with market timing and specific stock selection.

Taking Losses and Letting Profits Ride

These strategies are always popular because they appeal to greed and can be easily employed in financial sales. The underlying concept is to sell (often automatically by means of stop loss orders) those investments performing poorly and retain those investments doing well. This, in theory, provides the chance to participate in that "wonder" stock that shows huge gains and still minimizes risk by limiting the amount of loss by getting out before a downmove becomes too severe. To assist in making sure the winning investments do not suddenly reverse in price direction and turn into losses, many of these techniques stipulate using a *trailing stop loss*; as the investment appreciates keep elevating the price of the underlying stop loss order.

The illogic of any theory that postulates selling losing positions and holding onto winning positions has been discussed in preceding chapters. Some of the major drawbacks are:

1. If a stock maintains all the fundamental, technical, and structural characteristics that made it an acceptable purchase at a higher price, it represents a better value at a lower price.

2. No individual stock maintains superior growth indefinitely. Doing so is basically impossible because of the life cycle aspects of growth stocks.

3. All stocks routinely experience significant price fluctuations, and even the most elementary observation can demonstrate that taking advantage of the fluctuations (buying low and selling high) will outperform buy-and-hold strategies over time.

4. By taking losses and letting profits ride, you have no real assurance that there will ever be any profits, but losses are effectively guaranteed.

The list can be extended, but these points are sufficient to provide an idea as to the difficulties that can be experienced in these strategies.

The implications of "letting profits ride" go far deeper than some mesmerized individual investor willing to take an infinite number of investment "strikes" (including transaction costs) in the hope of hitting a "financial home run." As we shall examine in some detail in Chap. 7, the philosophy plays a significant role in institutional management and has important applications in our strategies.

At this juncture, awareness of the "let profits ride" technique brings up two important points.

1. At important taxing periods, investors are more inclined to take losses. For example, before year end (usually in early to middle December), there will be efforts to offset taxable gains by taking losses. By concentrating our buying emphasis on stocks that have not performed well because of intrinsic factors (such as normal price shifting), lower prices can often be obtained knowing there are willing tax sellers. This same pattern is also commonly present (although usually to a lesser degree than December) before April tax payments are due and investors need to sell to generate cash.

2. In the development of a successful market strategy, it is as important to know when to sell as it is to know when to buy. Letting profits ride does not incorporate rational selling points, which are essential for both risk minimization and profit consistency.

Note also that the general reaction of investors who do have the insight to establish specific, preestablished selling points is to generally look for a particular price. They usually base their decision on a belief in historical repetition of the stock's past prices. This is illogical. The optimal selling price could be well above (or below) past levels. More accurate selling levels can be determined by market *conditions* that are directly opposite the *conditions* that specified buying.

The major importance of the "letting profits ride" philosophy in the development of our strategy is that it provides us with stock for purchase at relatively low levels because of the identification of sellers who are willing to accept lower prices. It also provides us with some insight into seasonal patterns that can affect our buying and selling, as well as the beginning of specific formulation for the length of holding periods that will help ensure our not being trapped by overhanging selling supply. This will become clearer when incorporated into the material in the next chapter. At this point we need only know that the "profit ride" philosophy is a relatively consistent, significant factor in the market.

Following Corporate Insiders and Raiders

Briefly mentioned in preceding chapters, this subject is expanded now in the context of a disciplined technique. To ensure that insiders (corporate officers and directors) are not buying/selling the stock of their corporation based on information not available to the public, insiders are required to inform the Securities and Exchange Commission of their transactions. This information, on a somewhat delayed basis, is made available to the public. It forms the basis for a variety of financial publications and investment techniques. The reasoning of these methods is that the insiders are more familiar with their corporations than anyone else, and the wise investor better do what the insiders are doing, that is, buy or sell in conjunction with the insiders' activities. The underlying assumption, of course, is that the insiders are cheating.

These techniques often have demonstrated statistical validity, but both the rate of return and the degree of profit consistency fall short of our acceptable parameters.

The problems associated with basing market activity on the actions of insiders are twofold. First, the insiders may be buying/selling for reasons other then the future prospects of their corporation. They might by buying in an automatic program unrelated to current corporate events. They might be selling because they need cash for personal needs not associated with the corporation. Second, someone who is really going to cheat is not going to limit the cheating to what is reported to the SEC. In fact, the real cheater could use the SEC reporting to create illusion. For example, let's say an unethical insider knows that others will react to his or her market activity as reported to the SEC. The insider knows that good corporate news is coming. To maximize benefit, the insider sells 1000 shares and reports the sale. The adherents of insider information would take this as an indication that something was wrong with the corporation and sell. The insider, however, buys 10,000 shares in another account, using a camouflaged identity and not reporting to the SEC, perhaps at a lowered price resulting from the news of the reported selling. When good news comes and the stock advances in price, the insider wins on 10,000 shares while giving the impression of having sold at the wrong time and avoiding suspicion of unethical behavior.

The point is that if you assume someone else is being less than honest, it is also logical to assume that the dishonesty may encompass more than readily meets the eye.

Because of the nature of the stocks utilized in our timing technique, as well as the quality of the specific issues we use in actual trading, followers of insider trading often affect prices in our favor. When insider followers are selling, they can create inordinate selling supply and consequently provide lower prices in quality issues. When the insider followers are buying, their actions can help push prices to levels that are inordinately high.

Insider trading techniques are most popular during prolonged flat or downward market movements when investors are discouraged and most prone to paranoia.

During periods of excessive speculation when mergers and acquisitions often become the rage, such as the leveraged buyout craze of the late 1980s, techniques involving following those involved in the activity (corporate raiders) becomes popular. These individuals (many who eventually end up incarcerated and/or broke) will announce they are buying the stock of a corporation, and their followers will exhibit identical behavior in hope that the corporation being purchased by the raider will be taken over at a much higher price.

To the raider's followers, the raider is effectively functioning as an insider except that he is not a direct officer or director of the corporation involved. The greatest difficulty in following the activities of corporate raiders is that the raider may be taking positions to prey on his followers. A typical scenario starts when the raider buys stock and then announces the purchase. The followers jump in, pushing the price higher, and then the raider sells the stock at the inflated prices. During the market smash in 1987 (as well as many other periods of severe, sudden decline), the followers of corporate raiders incurred huge losses. Such strategies have no real place in logical investment methods.

Stock/Nonstock Ratios
(Asset Allocation)

These theories include some of the oldest investment techniques and are of particular importance in institutional management. The underlying concept of these methods is to allocate a percentage of assets to various investment types: stocks, bonds, cash, real estate, gold, commodities, and so on. For our purposes, we are most influenced in stock/bond/cash allocations, which can be classified into either of two groups: constant or variable.

Constant

These strategies maintain a constant percentage ratio as to dollar market value in various investments.

For example, let's say the predetermined balance is 50 percent common stock and 50 percent bonds, and the beginning portfolio is funded with $100,000. The initial ratio would be $50,000 in stocks, $50,000 in bonds. The market prices change so that stocks equal $40,000, bonds $60,000. To maintain the 50-50 ratio, $10,000 worth of bonds would be sold and $10,000 worth of stock would be purchased.

This method looks good (and has some logical base) because it tends to sell the investment type that is relatively high and buy the investment type that is relatively depressed. It is a sort of dollar cost averaging. Over time, this method can be shown to demonstrate validity.

The difficulty is that its end results are less then acceptable. The basic problem stems from the fact that the relationships of the investments are not consistently parallel, but the chosen ratio remains constant.

Referring to our example, interest rate changes directly affect the market prices of debt instruments (bonds), but do not always have a direct effect on stock pricing. Because these methods have a constant percentage allocation, there are periods when stock is being purchased or sold at disadvantageous price levels.

In preying on the advocates of constant stock/nonstock ratios, the important aspect is that they are acting after the fact of price change. By correctly anticipating price change (both in bonds and stock), you also correctly anticipate this group's behavior and as such can expand profitability by having isolated buyers/sellers. That is, more advantageous prices can be obtained knowing that others will buy/sell irrespective of price.

Variable

The constant stock/nonstock ratio followers effectively dismiss many aspects of market timing. In contrast, the variable advocates are, in effect, employing timing by altering the percentage allocation to any specific investment type in any given market condition. The variable techniques

may involve many different investment types, but those of primary importance, to us, vary their allocations among stocks, bonds, and cash.

The most popular variable strategies concentrate on changes in interest
rates combined with a shifting of the stock/bond/cash percentage allocations based on the manager's perception as to the current market condition.

Variable stock/nonstock ratios are logical and are necessary for both
risk minimization and profit optimization. However, the vast majority of
those employing the techniques react after the fact of price change, usually
by means of some sort of "trend"-following technique for stocks combined
with changes in interest rates.

Fortunately, for us, changes in interest rates are almost as easily forecast
as changes in stock prices. We will discuss this forecasting in detail in later
chapters. At this juncture, the important point is that, by being able to
accurately forecast both changes in stock prices *and* interest rates, we can
effectively isolate the future buying/selling behavior of most of those
committed to variable stock/nonstock ratios.

Earnings Projections

Strictly fundamental, this is by far the most popular market strategy,
dominating both institutional buy/sell behavior and individuals through
analytical services. The process is simple. First, have an analyst examine a
corporation to determine future earnings. Then apply these earnings
projections as to what is presumed to be an acceptable P/E ratio, thereby
determining what to buy (good projections) or sell (bad projections).

This method is reasonable and, in theory, the best way to judge the
merits of any individual stock. Such analyses form the bulk of conventional
analytical teachings and investment practice. With such a simple, straightforward methodology available, the question arises as to why those who
adhere to the technique often fare poorly? The answer is fourfold.

1. The evidence is overwhelming that, for most corporations, earnings
   are not predictable within reasonable bounds. The general tendency
   among analysts is excessive optimism. It might seem a bit odd to witness
   seemingly intelligent people spending their lives in an attempt to
   measure what is not measurable, but it is a fact of life in the financial
   world.

2. There is a general tendency among analysts to assume that price (and
   earnings) changes that have occurred in the past will continue in the
   same pattern for the foreseeable future. Such behavior is most evident

in the banking sector where lending in a particularly "hot" area (oil, real estate, or elsewhere) is made on the assumption of ever higher prices until (inevitably) the boom splats. The same is true for equity analysts.

3. Often, investors overreact when there is a publicized change in earnings forecasts. It is not uncommon to see large, sudden price changes in a stock because an analyst up- or downgrades earnings. In effect, those following the analysts (usually a few large institutions) move quickly to follow the analyst's forecast, thereby causing a severe (often very temporary) demand/supply imbalance. Even if the analyst's prediction proves correct (which is usually not the case), the associated price change can be very disproportional. Many an investor has been shocked to follow a change in analytical expectations and quickly see a price reversal after the analyst's effect has run its course.

4. Analysts tend to use a constant P/E related to the projected growth rate of earnings. The higher the earnings growth goes, the greater P/E justified. There is not a direct correlation. Market conditions change, that is, the overall market shifts to higher or lower P/Es, and/or a particular stock's P/E shifts relative to the broadly based market because of changes in the corporation's life cycle. The earnings projections can be perfectly accurate, and the stock price movement can be the direct opposite. This condition can only be avoided by the employment of a logical market timing technique.

The process of taking advantage of those who follow the standard analytical approach of combining earnings and P/E projections is enhanced by our confining interest to the Master List (Chap. 2) and our method of market timing (Chap. 8). We can isolate periods when their earnings projections are wrong and/or when an overreaction to the projections has occurred because of the stability of our list. In addition we have a gauge as to future market direction.

Summary

We have now discussed the major undisciplined and disciplined trading characteristics of most investors. Many specific techniques and behavioral characteristics were not included while others were emphasized. The reason for this is that many factors are of minor importance and do not significantly influence the methods to be discussed.

The stocks we will be utilizing are generally among the largest corporations. The factors bringing about changes in the prices of these issues usually must be significant. That is, a large dollar amount must be involved.

Because of this, some additional focus must be directed to institutional investors, whose actions will most affect the issues in which we confine our interest both in market timing *and* specific issue selection.

To adequately comprehend institutional investment characteristics, it is necessary to go beyond superficial behavioral aspects and the major theories determining their investment strategies. We must look into some structural characteristics of institutions. Then, and only then, will we have acquired sufficient background to understand the specific techniques composing Part 3 of this book.

7

Discretionary Folly

Discretion, in the context of this chapter, refers to any situation in which funds are entrusted to some entity (individual or firm) to make and implement investment decisions. The entity that controls the discretion can take a variety of forms: mutual funds, pension funds, bank trust departments, mutual insurance companies, brokerage firms that accept discretionary accounts, advisory firms, and the like

The funds under discretionary control may be voluntarily generated (such as by mutual fund sales) or involuntarily generated (such as by required contributions to a pension fund). In either event, our concern is how to profit from characteristics of discretionary managers, primarily institutions.

Although our emphasis in this chapter is on institutions and/or individuals with full discretion over the funds they invest, it is important to realize that all investors are to some extent influenced by the discretion of others. The opinion provided by one's broker, the decision of what topic to emphasize by the media, the forecasts of a popular analyst, or any other information generated by sources other than the individual investor involves some element of discretion.

Influences on Institutional Management

We have mentioned many of the difficulties encountered by institutional management in previous chapters. In this discussion our interest is on identifying pressures that often make discretionary managements conduct themselves in predictable, repetitive patterns. There are two basic sources of pressure:

Internal factors, primarily influenced by institutional structure.

External factors, primarily influenced by the actions of clientele who have placed their funds under discretionary management.

Internal

Institutional management, whether the contributions are voluntary or involuntary, incorporates two basic elements: sales and performance. Of the two, sales is more important because if no reason is given for the contributor to entrust monies, the contributor is not going to do so. And with no money to manage, there is no institution. Elementary.

The primary institutional sales tool is image. Astute, presumably educated, well dressed personnel, plush surroundings, organizational names indicating solidarity, and other superficial characteristics are effectively utilized to project an image. Most investors buy the impression.

The average investor neither wants to take the time nor has the inclination to make objective comparison of the relative performance of the many institutions. Often the institution is chosen without any comparison because of a personal friendship with the institutional manager or salesperson, response to advertising, or media hype. For these poorly informed investors, the greatest influence on their choice of discretionary management is paid advertising, which makes the larger (more heavily advertised) institutions appear preferable. We do not intend here to demean sales. Salesmanship is an integral part of all societies; it is involved in politics and religion, as well as in the overall economy. Our point is to emphasize the sales aspect of institutional structure because it is often overlooked by investors, *and* it forms the basis of some predictable institutional market behavior.

While most investors are not keenly aware of the differences in performance among institutions, most institutional managers definitely are. With their firms having costumed and situated themselves in similar surroundings, the managers must do something more to enhance their sales. The obvious factor to emphasize is performance. However, this creates a dilemma since most institutions fare relatively poorly over time. Irrespective of what the institution has really accomplished for clientele, it is obligated (to assure its existence) to make past performance look as good as possible.

For those institutions that publish their holdings, the easiest way to project the *image* of superiority is for the holdings to have appreciated dramatically since the time they were purchased. The accomplishment of this task is within the grasp of any attentive third-grade student: sell holdings that are losing and retain those that have appreciated. Then—ah ha—when the institution's holdings are published, it will provide the *image* that the institution has a fantastic ability to achieve superior results. To add to the image, right before the holdings are to be published, the manager determines which stocks have gone up the most and are receiving the most positive media attention, and then buys some irrespective of the current high price. The end result is a published portfolio that is stuffed with winners and the "hottest" current stocks. The impression is that the institution has both a history of winning and continues to be "on top of the market" by having positions in those stocks currently in vogue.

This process of adjusting portfolio for the sake of appearance—window dressing—is most pronounced when the majority of institutions publish their quarterly portfolios, on or near the last day of March, June, September, and December. As might be expected, the window dressing effect is most dramatic during December when it is combined with selling by the public and others for tax reasons.

The problem with window dressing is, of course, that it not only involves the precise formula for loss (buying high and selling low), but also precludes optimal profit capture by retaining positions that are too high and destined to fall.

To those who conduct themselves professionally, being aware of the influence of window dressing adds to the benefits obtained by normal shifting in relative strength. In effect, window dressing aggravates pricing, making prices too high/low than they would be without the effect. As you will see in Chap. 9, being aware of the window dressing pressures in combination with normal rotational shifts in relative strength can, *in itself,* more than double the return available from the market as a whole as measured by the popular averages.

The risks associated with portfolio modification for the sake of appearance are magnified in management techniques stressing "growth" stocks. Retaining a position simply because it has attained an exceptionally large gain could involve the stock's being in the attainment phase of the life cycle concept discussed in Chap. 6. In this phase quality stocks are most vulnerable to steep, often sudden price declines.

The reason for some institution's refusal to sell their positions that have appreciated dramatically (and that are most vulnerable to decline) can be deeper than the impression desired by publishing the positions. Management's compensation is usually a set percentage of the market value of the assets managed. If a profitable position is sold, the gain may be subject to taxation and paid out to clientele as a capital gains distribution. This effectively reduces the amount of money being managed and the associated fees.

The problems associated with selling positions that have profited most can be particularly acute in small mutual growth funds that have followed the practice of "taking losses and letting profits ride" for an extended period. The result is that their portfolio consists of only a few issues. By having locked themselves into holding a few profitable stocks, the fund's value becomes a function of the value of the rigid holdings and has nothing to do with the overall ability of management.

Keep in mind that money managers are human beings with basic needs such as food and shelter, which require employment. Also recognize that, especially in the larger institutions, clientele are not aware of the identity of the individual analyst making the investment decisions. This anonymity is often strictly enforced and a prerequisite for employment.

In this environment, the individual analyst (whether a genius or an idiot) is under pressure to conform to the crowd (the sheep syndrome, as described in Chap. 3). To be too good or too bad relative to one's peers involves risks of criticism or resentment with the associated occupational hazards. This effect is obvious to anyone familiar with the financial media. When an analyst (usually independent) becomes popular because of accurate forecasting and then stumbles, the mistake (even though the overall return over time has been far superior) is pounced on. On the other hand, a spokesperson for a large institutional analytical service that has consistently been wrong, but that is one of the crowd, attracts media attention when making forecasts without criticism of past mistakes.

Understanding the structural aspects of institutional investing practices and employment pressures, you would logically conclude that the average institution would underperform the market, with the underperformance magnified by the fees involved. Yup.

External

Aside from the difficulties associated with internal structure and characteristics, institutions have the added problem of dealing with their clientele. Discretionary clientele who do not properly understand the stock market, although they have entrusted their investment decisions to someone else, *often have a tendency to self-destruct.* This is particularly evident in mutual funds, whose investors are continually adding or withdrawing (redemptions) money. People tend to add money when the market is high and the mood optimistic. Redemptions tend to dominate when the market is low and the mood pessimistic.

The institutions are forced to invest the money—that is what they are being paid to do. Therefore, with more money coming in when the market is high, the institutions so affected are forced to buy at relatively high levels. Conversely, when redemptions dominate and the market is low, the institutions are forced to sell at depressed prices to fulfill the investor's demand for cash.

From the professional standpoint, the process is marvelous. We know we have buyers at high prices and sellers at low prices because of the demands of discretionary clientele creating a supply/demand imbalance. When they are doing their forced buying, it creates underlying buying demand and we can raise our prices. When they are forced to sell, we know there is "overhanging supply," and we can lower our purchase prices.

This buy-high/sell-low behavior (required to fulfill clientele's wishes) is not limited to mutual funds. It can affect any funds that can redeem or add capital according to their client's emotions: bank trust departments, pension funds, and the like. An important exception is closed-end mutual funds where the capital base is fixed and the investor must buy/sell shares in the open market rather than affecting the funds' specific holdings.

The market is a business. The purpose of the business is to acquire the monies of others through the process of buying low and selling high. Because of the anonymous nature of trading structure, it is very difficult to specifically identify the individual to whom you are selling or from whom you are buying. Consequently, physical coercion to create losing behavior among fellow market participants cannot be applied. People do not enter the market to lose. However, they must be placed in a situation in which they will willingly part with their money. The only way to elicit losing behavior is psychological pressure. The most effective tool for applying the pressure is a change in *market price*. Faced with "paper" losses, those vulnerable to the emotion associated with "apparent" losses will capitulate, accepting the loss in the form of *cash* to relieve the psychological strain.

The discretionary manager is subjected to the same emotional pressures as all other market participants. It is not uncommon for discretionary managers to buckle under the pressure and sell low in direct conflict with historical or statistical precedent to alleviate pressures both self- and clientele-imposed. Conversely, when prices are too high, the emotional lure of greed can stimulate buying when prices are most vulnerable to severe decline. Those who conduct themselves professionally are acutely aware of the psychological effects of price on institutional managers and take advantage. Such advantage is possible only by strict adherence to a methodology that prevents being lured into the irrational (emotional) behavior of the crowd. This is easily accomplished by having *predetermined buy/sell points dependent upon market condition*, not price in itself.

The forced behavior of institutions provides one of the most important profit centers for the true professional.

Justification Problems

In addition to the more obvious (external and internal) problems of institutional management, there are relatively subtle influences on their investment decision making.

Whenever a constraint is introduced into logical investment strategy, the imposition of the restriction can only function to induce behavior that will detract from profit optimization.

To avoid criticism, and in many cases to meet legal requirements, many institutions must (or feel they must) be able to justify each investment decision. These justification problems can be divided into three basic classifications, each of which, when understood, helps to enhance profit for the professional. They relate to:

1. Regulatory agencies.
2. Clientele.
3. Image.

1. Justification to Satisfy Regulatory Agencies

Often, by law, institutions are restricted to limiting their investments to specific types, usually issues considered to be of high quality. Such legislation is rightfully designed to help protect those who have entrusted funds. Often, such legislation is simply stupid and can detract significantly from the return the institution could achieve without incurring greater risk.

From a professional perspective, the most important aspect is that the institutions so affected must concentrate their investments. This concentration can add to demand/supply imbalances, as well as isolate where institutional involvement will occur. Profit extraction is made easier by knowing both the likely direction of the buy/sell balance and the stocks that are most likely to be involved.

2. Justification to Satisfy Clientele

Related to the sales aspect of institutional management, the institution might be influenced to concentrate investment in areas (and methods) that fit the client's perspective of which factors influence stock prices. It is obviously much easier to convince a client that a buy/sell decision was made because of something in which the client believes, even though the belief is erroneous and the investment method destined to fail.

In such circumstances, the institution is really not providing a discretionary service. Clients could do the same thing themselves and save the cost of the management fee.

The advantages of such institutional justification to the professional is that the institution is making itself vulnerable to all the erroneous concepts discussed in the previous two chapters.

3. Justification to Satisfy Image

One of the most rational approaches for any investor toward investment is to follow several theories and/or advisory services over time. That is, they may test the various theories and/or services in a reasonable, statistically accurate manner to determine what would have been the result had the advice been followed.

This is a simple process whereby the various investment techniques can be both back-tested and monitored for current performance. The result is a valid comparison of abilities over the period monitored, with the comparisons increasingly valid as the time period increases in length. As a rule of thumb, seven years is adequate because usually within any seven-year period a wide variety of market conditions (up, down, flat) have been experienced.

Investment selection and portfolio management are professional techniques; they involve both art and science. Unlike other professions, in which objective comparisons of individual abilities are difficult or impossible, the ability of the investment advisory (research) profession is easy to monitor. At varying levels and with varying degrees of risk, money has either been made or lost.

In following this comparative procedure, the investor can isolate the services that have provided the best results in the past. *Absolute* certainty of the future is, of course, impossible, but past results do provide the most logical basis of results to date. If an advisory service or any other entity has demonstrated satisfactory results during a variety of market conditions and over an extended time period, the investor might be best served by being attentive to the advice provided by that service (or theory) in future investment endeavors.

Financial institutions generally have sufficient staff and facilities to monitor several investment methods in a statistically accurate manner to isolate the best, and some institutions do follow this process. A great many, however, concentrate their research on their own investment selection, refusing to acknowledge and/or take advantage of the work of other analysts.

Institutions that fail to carefully monitor and utilize the beneficial aspects of other research staffs are subjecting their clientele to two inadequacies: the advice of talent possibly better than their own research staff is being overlooked, and there is no statistical basis for measuring the relative ability of the institution's own staff.

The reason for the lack of such rational comparison can often be traced to image preservation. An institution with its own research staff that is discovered to be following the advice of other research services is subject to shortsighted, sarcastic criticism. The institution, while projecting an astute, knowledgeable image and then is discovered relying heavily on others, can be viewed on first reaction as carrying a taint of hypocrisy. In other words, if the institution does not create the image that it is conducting its own investment research and providing a unique product, there is a risk of losing clientele to the originator of the accurate analysis.

From a professional trading standpoint, institutions that rely totally on their own research staffs or do very little statistically accurate monitoring of comparative abilities are welcomed. The end result adds to pressures associated with the sheep syndrome. It also helps to propagate belief in those investment techniques (Chap. 6), which are well-known and widely accepted, but which provide unsatisfactory results. The institution overly concerned with image can be a repetitive source of profit opportunity for the professional.

Measuring Money Managers

To determine the ability (or lack of it) of any money manager and/or investment technique, the most reasonable approach is to evaluate past performance.

In previous discussions we have mentioned selective memory loss, blatant lying, poorly defined forecasts, and other devious techniques to mask poor results that are used by less than ethical elements of the financial community. This group, because there is no objective way to measure ability, should be ignored entirely and are not a subject of this section.

Because of the large number of money managers and/or investment techniques that have published results, as well as the large number of entities whose purported documented results are actually fallacious, a wide array of "services" have been developed to assist investors in deciphering which investment technique and/or individual manager is truly superior. These ranking services come in a variety of forms. There are widely distributed and heavily advertised rating services. And then there are very private organizations that slither about secretively to ferret out the very best managers for a small group of clients.

There is nothing wrong with measuring the relative benefits of investment techniques or individual managers. In fact, it is the only reasonable method which you can develop and understand an investment strategy with any reasonable assurance that the strategy will meet your individual needs. However, as with many areas of finance that look straightforward and simple, the simplicity can be superficial. Ranking services can (and often do) provide more problems for their followers than they solve. To derive true benefit from ranking services, it is necessary to recognize and understand the dangers, which can be divided into three areas.

1. Those who derive compensation for deciphering the merits (or their lack) of techniques and/or advisors are in *business*. And, as with most other businesses, there is a *great deal of ethical variance*. The person providing the rating comparisons might just be pushing funds toward the control of his brain dead brother-in-law or some other entity with a mutual financial interest. Direct kickbacks, although usually illegal, are not unheard of. There are also more subtle methods of cooperation such as cross advertising, in which the highest-ranked analyst advertises the name of the organization by which he was ranked while the ranking organization is touting the analyst. It is also interesting to note the lack of ranking attention given to analytical services that do not advertise or that have voiced criticism of the ranking service. The "buyer beware" warning applies both to specific techniques/analysts and to those who purport to provide objective, unbiased, statistically accurate comparisons.

2. The most common drawback to ranking services is that *they do not really know what they are measuring*. This fault is most evident in ranking services that attempt to monitor several popular financial publications and then develop model portfolios based on the publication's advice. Whichever publication does the best in the time period utilized is then the highest ranked. The difficulty is that most such publications (probably by design) are so ambiguous or so complex that it is really not possible to

create an objectively accurate portfolio model. The results become as nonsensical as the original task.

Despite the shortcomings of such ranking services, they are popular with the public. The reason for this is a matter of conjecture, but we suspect it is because it is entertaining. These elements of the advisory community tend to behave like actors in a soap opera with endless love-hate relationships. When an analyst is on top, he or she and the ranking service are mutually complimentary. Let the analyst be ranked as having faltered and it becomes hate time until the ranking reverses and love returns. All the while, both sides are generating (often free) publicity.

Even when you move away from technique/advisor tabloids and into the world of specific, well documented results; there are problems with providing accurate, useful comparisons. The most common difficulty has to do with management changes. Investment decisions must be made by individuals. If mutual fund X is well managed and outperforms mutual fund Z, which has been run by idiots or crooks, and then the management switches, the investor jumping into fund X because of its past record, is going to be subjected to all the difficulties associated with the old management of fund Z.

The problems associated with providing objective comparisons in a world of constantly shifting managers is obviously immense, and, as discussed in the next section, is a major structural flaw of institutions that is often far from accidental.

3. As we have repeatedly discussed (this point cannot be overemphasized), emotion plays a very important role in market pricing, and any given emotion (greed, fear, boredom) is temporary. The majority of investors, guided by emotionalism, will be most attentive to whatever is currently the most sensational. Naturally, the ranking services (being in the business) know this and will gravitate to whatever area provides the most interest and associated sales. Consequently, most ranking services concentrate on *short-term time horizons.*

What evolves is a myriad of "investing championships," usually covering time spans from as short as a few days to a year. To see the dangers involved in being influenced by such comparisons, all you need do is have a basic understanding of risk/reward relationships. The more risk there is, the more possible the (short-term) reward. The wilder the investment strategy is, therefore, the greater chance for being the "champion" for the brief time frame. This is precisely what happens.

Advisor A makes it to the top with all the associated hoop-da-la during one time period and then falls to the bottom. But the fall does not seriously affect wildly speculative advisor A. All the attention has shifted to advisor B, now taking a brief turn on the top with the public now forgetting (temporarily) advisor A until the next turn on the top. And so on . . . and so on.

The investor lured into following the "champ" under such circumstances is likely destined to fail. When the speculative (statistically required) nature of the "champ's" technique hits its rough spot, it might result in total loss. The "champ" gets to play again, but the investor so lured has been financially retired.

To avoid the pitfalls associated with following the short-term champion, all you need to do is concentrate on long-term results and understand the necessity to retain base capital (that is, risk reduction).

Another way to eliminate the lure of "following the short-term champion" is to paper-trade with the current champ. This is accomplished simply by seeing who is the current champion and then taking (on paper) the champ's current positions. Then, when a new champ arrives, sell the old champ's positions and take the positions of the new champ. Most following this theoretical investing will be surprised at how quickly they go broke. This exercise of "paper-trading with the champions" can be extrapolated to ranking the ranking services which, by their own design, cannot perform better than their exchamps.

The fact is that the truly superior investment techniques will likely never be ranked as a short-term champ. Real, attainable, long-term money growth requires maintaining a capital base (risk reduction) and achieving profit consistency to maximize the benefits of compounding. Overly speculative strategies simply will not provide acceptable results over time. Such strategies are popular because of the emotional gratification during winning periods, but when the inevitable losses occur the capital base is so depleted that the strategy results in loss. In other words, truly successful strategies must both acquire profits and retain the profitability.

Selecting a Money Manager

Although the emphasis of this book is to assist individuals in developing and implementing their own investment strategies, we do not mean to imply that all money managers should be avoided. There are many competent managers.

Yet the selection of a manager cannot be taken lightly. The fate of the monies entrusted is most likely sealed at the time the manager is selected. It is no time to blindly follow friendships, media hype, or personal emotion. Almost all of the difficulties associated with the selection process can be eliminated by following three simple guidelines.

1. Familiarity with the Investment Technique

Money is a tangible: Either you have it or you don't. Generating money from money is a very specific process: Specific investments, must be chosen and the investments managed under specific techniques. Irrespective of how money is applied (even hidden in a mattress), there is an element of risk. To place the element of risk in a context suitable to individual resources, needs, and goals, it is *mandatory* that investors understand the specific investment techniques determining how monies are invested.

Obviously, avoid managers who stipulate techniques that have not produced suitable results when back-tested over a *long* period or who stipulate that their methods are proprietary (secret to all but themselves). Despite the glaring dangers, people seem to be attracted to proprietary "systems," the bait probably associated with greed. The fact is that the markets have been around for a long time. There is little that is not known and has not been adequately tested. In other words, would you entrust your life to a brain surgeon whose operational procedure was his own little secret? Suffice it to say that, within the financial community, there is ongoing communication among the ethical elements to provide clientele with superior products.

In effect, the investment method being utilized by the manager should be the same method you would personally use had you not decided to entrust the day-to-day investment routine to the expertise of others.

2. Familiarity with the Individual Analyst

Little known to the investing public, there has been a prolonged and ongoing battle within the financial community over full disclosure to clientele as to the specific identity of individual analysts managing the clientele's money in larger institutions.

Institutional management generally favors anonymity, stating that specific investment decisions (unless very bad and some underling is selected for blame) are a "team effort," and no one individual should be singled out as being better or worse than the team.

Many analysts counter that the "team" argument is a joke. It allows the institution to maintain fat salaries for dead wood ("good old boys") while inhibiting the advancement of truly superior individual analysts—sort of a slave labor relationship. These analysts further contend that the institution's desire for anonymity is to keep monies under institutional management. If the better analyst, known to clientele, were to leave the institution, the clientele would also leave to keep their funds with the superior analyst.

To us the bottom line is simple. You should know the specific analyst who is involved with your money and have some means of individual communication. It is your money and you have a right to know both the investment methods being used and the individual making the investment decisions.

In the world of investment techniques, the originators of the methods often manage money using those techniques. In effect, the investor often has access to the source. If the source is not in the money management business, he or she will probably be willing to direct the investor to a manager who has demonstrated a familiarity with the originator's work. If the originator is dead or out of business someone else will likely emerge as the best known analyst following the technique who can personally provide (or personally recommend another for) appropriate discretionary management. If you want the best, nothing can be lost by seeking it.

3. Familiarity with the Institution

Beyond knowing the specific investment techniques being employed and the specific analyst(s) involved; it is important to be properly treated by the institution itself. The better analysts who have achieved some notoriety will generally have many accounts and many millions of dollars to supervise. As such, it may be impractical (or physically impossible) for the analyst to be in continuous, personal contact with all clientele. Support personnel are necessary and investor's communication with the analyst's aides should be in a familiar, congenial atmosphere.

Support personnel can provide warning signs. If there is rapid turnover, terse responses, or any other form of discontent, it could indicate that there are problems with upper management's abilities to conduct themselves properly with employee's or clientele's needs.

Other warning signs can be the behavior of the specific analyst(s). It is *virtually impossible* to properly manage money while repeatedly crisscrossing the country for interviews, constantly appearing in "dog and pony" shows (speech/seminar circuits), or being available for any media event that provides a chance for the analyst (or the organization represented) to get a picture or quote in the news. Proper money management takes time—lots of time involving continuous access to changing data that affect clients' goals and needs. Inordinate amounts of time spent on publicity tours can only detract from personal account supervision. It also raises a question: If the analyst is so well-known and so good, why spend so much personal time advertising?

As mentioned, it may be physically impossible for the manager to personally convey the logic for each investment decision to each client. However, the client should be aware of the manger's current basic reasoning. After all, maybe the manager went to that proprietary brain surgeon.

Most analysts whose client base is too large to allow individual verbal communication will provide regular written correspondence regarding the reasoning behind portfolio positioning. If a manager does not provide such regular written or verbal communication, it could be a sign of laziness or pomposity, neither of which are characteristic of prudent account management.

The rewards, or the lack of them, associated with the selection of discretionary management are not limited to those who have personal control of their own funds and therefore have personal control of their own financial fate. Billions of dollars are taken from the earnings of people (employees, estates, trusts, and others) and turned over to discretionary management, over which the individual contributors exert little or no control. The abuses that can result from involuntary "contributions" (fat fees, funding the personal projects of managers, ludicrous costs paid to families and friends, kickbacks, and the like) are well-known. These abuses would stop if those making the involuntary contributions stood up and demanded their right to the three "familiarity" points just discussed. Such action would make a lot of nasty people angry, but would certainly provide a lot of nice people the money they deserve.

Summary

We have now come to the point where sufficient background has been provided to discuss the specifics of market timing, methods of stock (and other investment) selection, and actual portfolio modeling.

Our portrayal of the market so far might seem intimidating to some, but it is important to emphasize the competitive aspects. All investment is competitive, including real estate and insured savings accounts where the competing effects of inflation, deflation, and taxation can destroy principal if capital growth cannot be maintained.

The competitive aspects of markets provide opportunity. Because of the various industries and the ability to profit from both advances and declines (through short selling), the stock market probably provides more consistent opportunity than any other single investment area. Understanding the stock market can also provide the foundation for success in other investment types.

We live in a relatively free society, but personal freedom largely depends on financial freedom. The stock market has its place in providing this freedom. It must, however, be understood in a realistic manner.

Throughout the first seven chapters, we have attempted to take the reader on a step-by-step journey into the market and describe the various factors that comprise the environment. Although the market is manmade and functions within physical rules, it is also heavily influenced by the emotions of the inhabitants. As in any natural setting, the most successful species is that which best adapts to surroundings. In our adaptation process, we have rejected many widely held theories and accepted others, while constantly emphasizing that the dominant underlying forces of the market are the simple relationships between demand and supply.

Through hindsight it is easy to identify periods in which the market was "overbought" (too high, followed by a significant decline) or "oversold" (too low, followed by a significant advance).

Hundreds of financial texts are devoted to exercises in hindsight. The process is fairly simple: Test any number of "systems" to see which one "would have" worked best, and then state that's the way to do it. For those so inclined, there are computer programs designed to do that. Plug in any data and the computer will search day and night for the best strategy. The difficulty with such programs is that the "selected methods" usually turn out to be nothing more than points at the long end of standard deviations associated with any bell-shaped curve. In other words, for those not statistically inclined, they are worthless.

Hindsight has its place, but does not provide true profit. Success can be achieved only through foresight. The material in the following chapters is not an exercise in hindsight. The methods described are those that have been, and continue to be, utilized by the authors in actual market endeavors.

The results to be discussed are real.

PART 3

The Actual Processes:

Market Timing
Investment Selection
Portfolio Modeling

$$8$$

Basic Market Timing
and Specific
Stock Selection

The attainment of profit consistency (and the associated benefits of compounding) is basically the systematic reduction of the risk of loss. A helpful aid in this process is to have a fairly good idea of which way the overall market is going. When the popular market averages advance or decline, usually (not always!) the majority of stocks will go in the direction of the average.

Not all stocks will perform in direct proportion to changes in the popular averages. In dealing with specific stocks, it is necessary to develop objective criteria designed to provide both a high probability of profitability and risk minimization.

Successful market participation, therefore, involves the blending of two separate processes: market timing and specific investment selection. We call this process *Time Overlay*, that is, a model for market timing is combined (overlaid) with a model to determine the specific investment(s) chosen.

Market Timing: The Determination
of Satisfactory Accuracy

Because of practical factors including commission costs, direct competition with market makers, and time considerations, a timing technique for very short-term market moves is impractical for most investors. In this text, the timing technique is designed to be within the practical grasp of all serious investors.

Our basic timing method requires comparing current market conditions with conditions at some past period. The farther spaced the periods compared, the more time between the buy and sell indications. To establish a method for documenting the accuracy of the technique, as well as for placing the technique within a reasonable time frame, it was decided to use comparisons separated by four weeks and make the comparisons on a weekly basis. That is, each week the market is compared to its position four weeks ago. It was anticipated the average specific investment position would result in a holding period of between four and six months using this comparative time frame. And depending on the specific technique for stock selection used (described later in this chapter), the results on average fell into the expected four- to six-month period. As will be discussed, this period can be altered, but for the published demonstration of our basic timing method, the four-week comparison was the only time period utilized.

There is nothing magical about the four-week comparison period we chose to utilize in our published portfolio modeling. Any comparative time period can be used, and the buy/sell points derived for the specific holdings will very likely average four to six times the comparison period. For example, if a one-day comparison was used, the buy/sell points would average every four to six days. If three-month comparisons were used, the buy/sell points would average twelve to eighteen months, and so on.

As will be seen in Chap. 9, we can interject significant bias in determining the specific stock (or closed-end fund) selected for investment. That is, when there is a buy indication concerning the market as a whole, we are not selecting specific investments at random and blindly hoping the investments go with the market. It is our intent to have the specific investments significantly outperform the market as a whole.

The techniques to be described are not utilized on a theoretical basis. They form the basis for actual buying and selling. Unless we are dealing with stock index futures, *we cannot buy the entire market, nor would we want to*. We must buy and sell specific stocks (or closed-end funds). The issues chosen will presumably be selected because of inherent merits that will allow them a significant chance of outperforming the market average. In other words, we do not need to be as accurate in predicting overall changes in market averages to attain the same degree of accuracy in predicting the price changes of the actual specific issues selected for investment.

To understand this clearly, See Fig. 8.1. In this figure we have graphed a generalized relationship between the number of opportunities available

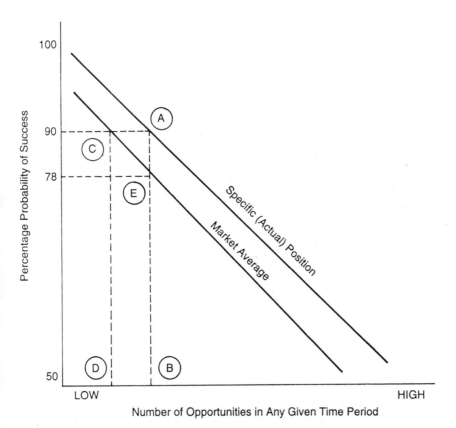

Figure 8.1. Relationship between the opportunities and the percentage probability of success.

and the percentage probability for success. If graphs and lines confuse you, don't get discouraged; go ahead and skip this explanation of the figure.

At this time, our objective is profit consistency. It is necessary to develop a method of consistent profit before we can expand the size of the gain. As can be seen, the number of opportunities available, whether for the market averages or for specific investments, varies with the percentage chance for success. That is, the higher the probability of success goes, the fewer times market conditions will be in place to provide the higher probability. The closer we get to 100-percent accuracy, the fewer opportunities there are for investment.* To ensure a reasonable number of investment opportunities, we have chosen in this example a 90-percent

---

*One-hundred-percent certainty can never be attained because the line is actually curvilinear and approaches (but never actually reaches) 100 percent.

level of success; that is, 9 out of 10 positions will be profitable, a reasonable degree of profit consistency.

We can then draw a line from the 90 percent level to the sloped line for "specific (actual) positions." From the point where these two lines meet (point A), we can then draw a line to the horizontal axis to see the relative number of opportunities available (point B). Looking back at the line drawn from the 90-percent level to point A, it can be seen that the line goes through the sloped "market average" line at point C. We can then draw a line from point C to the horizontal axis (point D).

The importance of all this is the space between points B and D. At a 90-percent accuracy level, there are more opportunities for actual market positions to be successful than if we waited for the market averages in themselves to give us the 90-percent level of success in any given investment.

To get a little complicated, we can draw another line from where line AB crosses the "market average" line (point E) to the vertical axis. The location of this line on the vertical axis is approximately at the 78-percent level. So, to achieve a 90-percent accuracy of success for a specific stock, we only need to have a 78-percent accuracy in predicting the change in the market average.

In other words, anytime we achieve a 78-percent accuracy in predicting a change in the market average, we would have a 90-percent chance of success in a chosen investment.

In actual practice we should achieve (and have achieved to date) results in excess of 78 percent for the market and 90 percent for specific issues because these are the minimum levels. Although most conditions are near the minimum levels, when probabilities are above the minimum levels, they are also considered acceptable. We will, of course, utilize higher probability levels when available. In effect, this means we would have a buy indication anytime the probabilities that the broadly based "averages" will advance are 78 percent or higher.

As we shall see, in the actual published Time Overlay common stock portfolio modeling (covering 16 years and a wide variety of market conditions), the accuracy rate of specific stock positions concluding profitably has been a little over 95 percent.

Market Timing: Determining
Buy and Sell Points

Our determination of buy/sell points is based on a logical understanding of the structure of the market and of the behavioral patterns of fellow market participants. We are not concerned with waves, angles, astrological configurations, or other such data, which by some magical force are presumed to be satisfactory indicators of future prices.

The purpose of our timing technique is to help facilitate our objective—to take the monies of others in a repetitive, consistent fashion that minimizes risk in actual market endeavors. We have no interest in theoretical abstractions in that time so spent can only detract from fulfilling our objective. At this point, we are attempting only to ensure acceptable accuracy in forecasting changes in the major market averages. The final goal is to develop profit consistency for our stock positions at the percentage level we have chosen (90 percent minimal) within the average holding period we have decided to use (four to six months).

Because of the upward bias in the specific stocks we utilize (on the Master List created in Chap. 2), we do not need the probabilities for accurate timing of the popular averages to be as high as those associated with the specific stocks. As discussed in the previous sections, our 95-percent accuracy rate with individual stock issues needs only around a 78-percent or better accuracy probability relative to the popular averages.

In actual market participation, decisions must be made quickly and without emotion. Our timing technique, therefore, must not be influenced by emotional "subjectivity," and it must be easily and quickly calculated to avoid time lags that would take away from maximizing the number of available opportunities.

Market timing is nothing more than reviewing statistically valid data to derive probabilities for future price moves. Consequently, because of the probability variances at any given time, *not all buy/sell points are created equally.*

As you will see in the next chapter, the relative strength of any buy/sell point can be compensated for by altering the "investment level," that is, by varying the percentage allocation between stocks and cash.

At this juncture, our objective is to develop buy/sell points that meet our *minimum* requirements related to the purchase or sale of specific common stocks. Application to options, index futures and more speculative trading strategies (discussed in Chap. 9) require adjusting our timing probabilities upward from those that are the focus of this discussion.

Our discussion of the technique, *at this time*, is designed for the process of buying specific stocks, then selling. The basic elements are buy indications that increase the percentage of funds allocated to common stock investment (that is, increasing the investment level), a holding period, and then sell indications that would result in selling specific positions to adjust to a lower investment level.

This buy-to-sell aspect is stressed because you cannot assume the process can be automatically reversed. That is, the same criteria cannot be used in reverse for short selling with the same degree of accuracy in specific positions—selling short on sell indications and covering (buying back the short positions) on buy indications. The reason it cannot be reversed automatically is because of the upward bias in the stocks we utilize. For accurate short sale techniques, alterations (to be discussed) are necessary to eliminate this upward bias.

In this discussion, we are going to fully describe the criteria that we actually use. Some of the criteria might appear rather complex, and the information to implement exact duplication might be difficult for many investors to obtain. However, after such detailed descriptions, *greatly simplified methods within reach of almost all investors* will be described. In fact, the basic timing method can be compacted so it takes less than one hour each week without any need for complicated equipment. Nothing is necessary beyond the ability to read.

The factors we use to determine buy/sell points are of two types: essential (or primary) and ancillary. There is only one essential factor, and it *must* be present for any buy/sell indication. There are twelve ancillary factors; any six (or more) must coincide with the essential factor to have a buy/sell indication.

Essential (Primary) Criterion

The Master List (Chap. 2), whether all the issues are being monitored or only the minimal acceptable number, forms the core of the indication. These stocks, with their relatively high degree of earnings predictability, we use both to gauge forces within the market and to make specific investments.

In effect, we are functioning in a market within a market. We want to buy low and sell high. By confining interest to specific stock issues that have demonstrated fundamental superiority, we have chosen stocks that have an upward bias relative to the market as a whole. This bias in itself, however, is far from enough to meet our goals. We are very much interested in the relationships between demand and supply. We want to purchase when there are strong signs that selling supply might be exhausted. In other words, we want to buy soon before or in conjunction with the last period in which the sellers are dominant. Once the selling dominance has been eliminated, buyers can dominate and prices can advance. Conversely, we want to sell soon before or in conjunction with the last period in which buyers are dominant. When the buyers have exhausted their influence, sellers can dominate and prices can decline.

The best indication of seller dominance is a downward shift in market price relative to earnings (the price/earnings ratio). Lower P/Es both provide stock at lower prices relative to earnings and indicate that sellers are using up their influence. Therefore:

- For a *buy* indication, it is *essential* that the P/Es of the stocks monitored are falling.

- For a *sell* indication, the P/E condition must be the reverse of that for a buy: It is *essential* that P/Es are rising to have a sell indication.

Since by the design of Drach's published Time Overlay portfolio modeling we are looking at the market weekly and comparing it to four weeks before to see the relative change, we are looking for upward or downward moves in P/E relative to the P/Es four weeks ago. The minimal acceptable level is that 75 percent of the stocks monitored have moved down or up in P/E from their level of four weeks before. If the percentage is less than 75 percent, there is *no* indication. To repeat:

- The *essential factor for a buy indication* is that 75 percent or more of the stocks monitored have declined in P/E from their level four weeks before.

- The *essential factor for a sell indication* is that 75 percent or more of the stocks monitored have advanced in P/E from their level four weeks before.

In the calculation of P/E ratios, both price and earnings are variables, that is, both change over time. In most financial publications, the P/Es listed are "lagging P/Es." That is, they are calculated by taking the corporation's earnings over the last four quarters (one year) and dividing the earnings into the current market price. Because earnings change and because one of the criteria for stocks to qualify for our Master List is earnings predictability, it is reasonable to assume that calculating P/Es using earnings projections covering the *next* four quarters (the next year) would be a more accurate gauge of the P/E shift, indicating that the stock was becoming (or is) under- or overpriced.

In Drach's publication, as well as in actual account management under the author's supervision, P/Es are calculated using *earnings projections*. Also note that the authors' P/E calculations are to two decimal points since this significantly expands the number of buy/sell points.

When we developed our investment methods, we assumed that using P/Es based on projections rather than lagging P/Es would create a significant difference in results. Over the many years that this basic portfolio modeling has been published and applied in actual market endeavors (covering a wide range of market conditions and thousands of individual stock positions), to our surprise, that the results obtained by using earnings projections in P/E calculations has not (to date) resulted in significantly better results than using lagging P/Es. In other words, although the authors use projections in their analysis, lagging P/Es so far have provided almost identical results. Whether earnings projections or lagging P/Es are utilized, taking the calculations to two decimal points is necessary to maximize the number of buy/sell points.

Since P/E is a function of price, we must consider whether price (a much easier measurement, the week's closing price) can be substituted. The answer is *yes*, but there will be some (to date quite minor) loss of accuracy. For example, if a stock's earnings suddenly declined dramatically and the stock's market price also declined, the decline in market price might not be directly proportional to the decline in earnings. The price would go down, but the P/E (price now divided by lower earnings) might go up because the earnings drop was proportionately greater than the price drop. Watching for changes in price, without paying attention to earnings changes as well, will prevent your gaining a refined perspective of true supply/demand.

If you choose to substitute price change for P/E change, the accuracy differential can (in most cases) be compensated for by raising the required percentage of issues that must be down or up in price to 80 percent. There will be fewer buy/sell points derived by using price rather than P/E, but (to date) the price method would have identified all *major* buy/sell points. Consequently, the essential elements for an indication are:

BUY: 75 percent of the P/Es or 80 percent of the prices of the stocks monitored must be down.

SELL: 75 percent of the P/Es or 80 percent of the prices of the stocks monitored must be up.

A question is now raised: Would it not be easier just to see if the market averages had gone lower and take that (or the P/E of the Dow or some other average) as an indication? The answer is *no*. The averages can be misleading. They can be significantly influenced by dramatic price moves in stocks and stock groups that do not warrant consideration (that is, stocks not on the Master List) as an indicator of investment. An attempt to gauge market conditions by the average of a conglomeration of unrelated stocks brings in extrinsic factors that are unpredictable. Our stock selection (Chap. 2) is designed to make the most important extrinsic factor (earnings) predictable.

To attempt to incorporate past changes in market averages as forecasting tools for future changes can be done, but it requires extensive calculations, including degree of price change in relation to volume change for each stock involved. It results in lower levels of accuracy than achieved by our technique. In our method, the design is not only to achieve superior results; it is also designed to be as simple as possible. In our method to get a signal from our *primary* indicator, the degree of decline (what percentage decline in P/E or price occurred) is not a necessary measurement. For example, if 80 percent of the stocks monitored declined in price only 1/8 of a point from their previous price level, the essential criterion for a buy indication would be met. The ancillary criteria are designed to filter for the magnitude of the primary criterion.

Why (for the basic portfolio modeling techniques) do we not consider it essential to wait for some upward price movement to occur to ensure that the effect of selling pressure is gone? Conversely, why not wait for some downward price movement to occur to ensure that buying demand is gone? The reasons are twofold.

First, often when price reversals occur, they are very rapid, and a significant portion (sometimes almost all) of the anticipated price change can occur before positions can be taken.

Second, the authors are in the business of stock trading on a scale that involves many millions of dollars. We are not engaged in theoretical observations that include the naive belief that infinite amounts of stock can be bought or sold at the prices quoted. Stated flatly, for us to acquire stock in large amounts at appropriate prices, it is necessary to have adequate sellers; to sell stock in large amounts at appropriate prices, it is necessary to have adequate buyers. Real people and real money are involved. Stock purchased at acceptable prices is available only when sufficient sellers at the acceptable prices are in place; which is usually as prices are declining, *not after* the price decline. Selling stock at acceptable prices can be accomplished only when there are adequate willing buyers, which is usually as prices are advancing, not after the advance.

Ancillary Criteria

The primary criterion, be it P/E or price, will not always give a buy/sell indication. In fact, most of the time (and sometimes for very long periods) the primary criterion will not meet the parameters to form the preliminary basis for a change in basic portfolio modeling. The primary criterion (depending on which method—projected earnings, lagging P/Es, or price—is chosen) is by far the most time consuming aspect of our timing technique.

The ancillary criteria are designed to confirm or reject the primary indication. The ancillary criteria (aside from a few rare exceptions) will always be issuing a buy or sell bias. Without an indication from the primary criterion, there is no need to be concerned with the ancillary facets in basic portfolio modeling because there can be no change.

There are twelve ancillary criteria, which might at first seem too burdensome to calculate. However, most (if not all) can be determined by a casual glance at major financial publications (*Barron's* or *The Wall Street Journal*). A weekly review of the ancillary criteria can probably be attained within 10 minutes after the sources are identified.

For the ancillary criteria to confirm the primary criterion, a minimum of six ancillary criteria must be in place.

1. Institutional Cash Reserves

If all markets involve predator/prey relationships, to acquire the cash of others requires that the others actually have cash from which they can be parted. Because of the specific stocks we utilize, as well as the growing dominance of institutions in day-to-day trading patterns, those institutions against whom we compete are important sources of profit.

The term *institutional cash reserves* refers to the ratio of institutional holding of cash (or cash equivalents) to common stock. The higher the institutional cash reserves, the more money they have available for the purchase of stock. The lower the cash reserves, the lower the institution's ability to buy stock irrespective of sentiment. To emphasize the importance of this institutional cash:noncash ratio, it was all you needed to understand to avoid the crash of 1987. At the time, the institutions were so lured into the stock market and their cash reserves became so depleted, they could not support stock prices. It was an *inevitable* splat time because of the depletion of possible buying demand.

Institutional cash reserves are tabulated regularly by a variety of surveys that scan mutual funds and/or pensions (Lipper, Herzfeld, a wide variety of brokerage firms, and the like) and the results regularly published in major financial publications.

For our purposes, all we need to know is the change in the cash:noncash ratio relative to where it was four weeks ago (or the next nearest reporting period depending on the source utilized).

BUY: The cash amount has increased. We have isolated potential buying demand that can be lured into the market to push prices higher.

SELL: The cash amount has decreased. The institutions are depleting their buying power, making themselves increasingly weak (perhaps helpless) in providing price support and thereby allowing selling supply to more easily dominate and depress prices.

2. Public Cash Reserves

Because of the rapid growth of institution's dominating trading activity, it has become popular to dismiss the public as an important market factor. However, as we have discussed in detail in previous chapters, the public is a very important factor, not only because of the predictable behavioral patterns of individuals, but because of the effects these patterns have on the institutions in which the public has entrusted funds.

We monitor this group's cash status by the weekly reporting of the total assets of money market funds. Money market fund assets include monies from groups other than the public, but for our purposes the changes in money market fund assets is all that is necessary for this criterion.

The weekly money market fund asset figures are reported in all major financial publications. Our comparison period is four weeks.

BUY: The amount (gross, no ratio needed) has increased. This isolates potential buyers (buying demand) and the associated potential for higher stock prices.

SELL: The amount has decreased. The amount of potential buying demand is lessening, and selling supply can more easily become dominant to depress stock prices.

3. Money Supply

The two previous factors were designed to isolate specific participants and their ability to effectuate future behavior because of their cash/noncash position. The amount of money in the overall economy is also important and is influenced by the actions of the Federal Reserve.

The figures relating to available money supply are provided weekly by the Federal Reserve and reported by all major financial publications. The money supply calculations include various categories (M-1, M-2, and M-3 being the most popular in gross form). Because of the various components of the money supply categories and changes in the economy, there is an ongoing debate within the financial community as to which measurement (with a myriad of adjustments) is the most accurate. For the purposes of our basic market timing, time and brain cells need not be wasted in agonizing as to which "M" (money supply measure) is chosen. One need only be concerned with sticking with the M originally chosen. We use M-1, which is basically the amount of cash in circulation.

As a criterion in our basic timing method, we compare the gross (not ratio) amount of M-1 to its level four weeks before.

BUY: The amount is increasing. More money is coming into the system, a portion of which can be lured into the stock market in the form of buying demand. In addition, the increased amount of available money helps the overall economy to expand.

SELL: The amount is decreasing. The withdrawal of money from the overall economy creates cash needs, on which investors draw against their stock holdings (because of the liquidity) before selling most other assets. This selling supply can function to depress prices. And the lessened money supply is often a good indication of a coming constriction in the broadly based economy.

4. Gold Price

The stock market, as with any other market, is constantly in competition with other investments. Gold, because of its history and physical nature relative to paper money, is a good indicator of relative popularity. Real estate, collectibles, and other "hard" commodities could probably be substituted for our gold criterion; but we have selected gold for its liquidity (with the metal being actively traded in markets throughout the world).

Again using a four-week comparison, we simply look at the net change in price for our indication. We use spot prices, but futures can be substituted as long as the same contract month is being compared.

BUY: Gold is up in price. This can be a good indication that stocks have become unpopular and undervalued. When the gold price declines and the metal disappoints investors, their buying demand can more easily shift to the stock market.

SELL: Gold is down in price. This can indicate stocks have become overvalued and can precede a reversal in investor sentiment, creating increased selling supply in the stock market.

5. Bonds

There is an inverse relationship between bond prices and interest rates. Higher bond prices mean lower interest rates, and lower bond prices equal higher interest rates.

There is also generally a very strong, direct correlation between stock and bond prices. Higher bond prices are usually accompanied by higher stock prices, lower bond prices by lower stock prices. The bond/stock price relationship is logical. Higher interest rates (lower bond prices) increase corporate costs borrowing and as such function to reduce earnings. Higher interest rates, because of the increased cost of capital, tend to slow the overall economy which can adversely affect corporate sales and consequently have a negative effect on corporate profitability. Within market structure, higher rates increase the cost of margin buying, which reduces buying demand.

Periods during which stock and bond prices diverge usually involve high levels of investor emotionalism. If sentiment is extremely pessimistic, high-quality bonds become viewed as safe havens and buying demand increases, adding price support for bonds while stocks falter. Conversely, during periods of extreme euphoria, bonds can become viewed as providing returns too low relative to stocks, creating selling supply in the bond market; this lowers bond prices while stock prices are advancing.

Our concern with the bond market in our timing model is the most common, direct price relationship. Using a four-week comparison period, our indication for this criterion is the next change in bond price down or up—we are not concerned with the magnitude of the differential. We use long-term U.S. Treasury bonds.

BUY: Bond prices are down. Interest rates have moved higher, probably depressing stock prices and making a price reversal more likely.

SELL: Bond prices are up. Interest rates have moved lower, possibly having an unsustainable elevating effect on stock prices and increasing the chance for a reversal.

6. Volume and Price Relationships

Our previous criteria were designed to get a general idea as to our opponent's ability to participate in the market (cash or the lack of it), as well as some insight into the effect of alternative investment types.

We will now turn our attention to what is actually happening within the stock market. The two most important variables are price and volume. If *volume* is increasing as prices are advancing, it is indicative of an expanding number of buyers coming into the market. This can also indicate that the buyers are depleting their power and will eventually no longer be able to maintain price support. Conversely, if volume is expanding as stock prices are declining, it indicates that those selling out will eventually lose their force (depleting selling supply), which can allow prices to reverse.

In calculating this criterion, we want to know if the cumulative volume over the last 20 trading days is greater or less than the cumulative trading volume of the preceding 20 trading days. This is accomplished by adding up the total volume on the New York Stock Exchange over the last 20 trading days and comparing the total with the volume the preceding 20 days. Forty days of data are needed. Calculating this criterion takes only a couple of minutes: adding the newest day and deleting the latest in an ongoing total. For most indications all you need to do is look at a chart of recent volume (available in most major financial publications) by which significant changes in volume can be quickly and easily identified.

For this criterion to be given any consideration, volume must have *increased*. The amount of the increase is of no concern. If the volume has decreased, this criterion is not considered to have given any indication.

For the *price* component of this criterion, the net change (plus or minus) of a popular average will suffice. The amount of the change is of no concern, just the direction. Using a four-week comparison period, we use the New York Stock Exchange Index because of the large number of issues forming the measurement. The Standard & Poors 500, Dow Jones Industrials, or other popular averages could be substituted.

BUY: Volume is increasing as prices have declined—an indication that selling supply is being depleted.

SELL: Volume is increasing as prices are advancing—an indication that buying demand is being depleted.

NO INDICATION: Volume has decreased.

7. Volatility

The faster prices are going down, the faster sellers are getting out, and the higher the probability that the excess selling supply will soon diminish and allow buying demand (higher prices) to dominate. The faster prices are going up, the faster buyers are using up their money supply, and the higher the probability that selling supply can soon dominate to push prices lower.

In the past, we have incorporated beta measurements as one of our volatility criterion, but these calculations were time-consuming and difficult for many investors. We are now substituting a very simple measure of volatility rather than the more time-consuming beta comparisons. The simplified method can be applied without any loss of accuracy.

Remember that, by confining specific investment interest to the stocks that qualify for our Master List (Chap. 2), we are effectively participating in a market within a market. When purchasing stocks, we would prefer to invest in those that will outperform the market. When selling, we want to get out when the chances are that our stocks will go down at a faster pace than the overall market. Consequently, it is to our benefit to have some idea as to how the stocks we follow are doing relative to the broadly based market. If our stocks are relatively depressed, to us they represent better values. If our stocks are relatively overvalued, they would appear more vulnerable to decline.

To determine the relative over- or underpricing, we compare the percentage price change of the stocks we monitor to the percentage price change of the NYSE Composite Average. Any other broadly based market "average" could be substituted for the NYSE Composite.

Using a four-week comparison, the percentage of advance/decline of the popular average selected is calculated and compared with the average percentage advance/decline of the stocks we follow. Whether this ancillary criteria develops a buy or sell indication depends on what direction the popular average being followed has taken.

If the NYSE Composite has *declined*.

BUY: If the stocks we follow have declined more than the Composite average.

NO INDICATION: If our stocks advanced or declined less than the Composite.

If the NYSE Composite has *advanced*.

SELL: If the stocks we follow have advanced more than the Composite average.

NO INDICATION: If our stocks declined or advanced less than the Composite.

8. Trend Analysis

Technical analysis in its pure form measures price and/or volume without consideration of anything else, such as the standard charts and graphs which are often complicated by moving averages, angles, or anything else the technician can think to impose. We have already explained why most technical analysis is basically useless because it does not take into consideration what actually caused the price or volume change. Even in those relatively rare instances when chart "patterns" could be shown to have some validity in future price forecasting, the associated probability levels were far too low to meet our standard. At the risk of repeating ourselves, suffice to say that (with a few exceptions to be discussed) pure technical analysis is largely nonsense.

Despite its shortcomings, technical analysis is extremely popular. "Don't fight the trend," is a standard saying among some of the most heavily advertised gurus. The "trend" no matter how complicated (or simple) its derivation, is almost invariably nothing other than an observation of recent price direction and an assumption that the same price direction will continue.

To question the credibility of "trend analysis," all you need to do is notice the lack of results in a format of full disclosure among the "trend followers." Understanding the disproportion between the popularity of trend analysis and the results attained by it, allows an insight into the causative agents of price change and how seemingly logical, mature adults can be induced to exhibit behavior akin to being financially brain dead.

The true nature of market structure and associated pricing mechanisms is basically a simple, mundane, repetitive business. Throughout the U.S. market's 200-year history, repetitive pricing and behavioral patterns have occurred in sufficient magnitude to derive probability distributions. In other words, there are huge mounds of data to which you can easily refer to see what has most repeatedly occurred in the past. To us, logical strategy is nothing other than applying historical/statistical data to current market endeavors. However, this easily attainable data is (and always will be) routinely ignored by the majority.

As with any business, the securities industry depends on sales. To consummate the sale, the buyer must be convinced to buy out of presumed logic and/or emotionalism. In selling someone a stock, it is much easier to tout an issue that has advanced (in an "up trend") than one that is depressed. The elevated price, *in itself*, functions as "proof" of the investment's merit: "Look—it *has* gone up." In addition, the previous advance stimulates greed in that it can be shown that money could have been made; of course, the fact that the "could" element is history is not stressed. Conversely, if a stock is depressed, the emotionalism and associated "logic" are pessimistic and the customer can be more easily enticed to sell. The broker gets commissions both ways, and the customer's "logic" and emotional needs are fulfilled.

This buy-high-and-sell-low behavior happens to be the precise formula for loss, but it will always persist for reasons other than sales.

The financial media is also in business and to attract attention (again sales) it must report whatever is of most interest to clientele. People want to hear about the sensational. The sensational events, by definition, are the exception. By concentrating on the exception, it becomes easy to become ignorant of the rule. The more dramatic the exception(s), the greater the lure to forget the rule(s). This characteristic runs throughout the entire history of all ongoing, liquid markets.

Whether a stock goes to the moon or goes splat, it can be shown by its "trend" that one could have profited by seeing the trend's direction and behaving with the trend. What this ignores is that, by chasing the exceptions, the rules (most stocks failing to maintain a "trend") are rejected. Stated simply, it is far easier to extract money from the market by isolating conditions conducive to trend reversals than by believing that the "trend" will continue.

With this background, it becomes easy to identify some common gimmickry utilized by some analysts and financial writers.

1. Whether a stock goes to the moon or goes bankrupt, the "trend" analyst can claim success—success in identifying a sensational event and conjuring up the deepest fear/greed emotions. In effect, the analyst has bought relative strength and sold (or shorted) relative weakness, and thus made (by definition) the "big hit." The problem with actually following this course in the market is that so many hundreds of positions do not maintain their trend and usually result in so many repetitive losses that the "big hit" is relatively meaningless in offsetting the losses. This "trick" forms the basis of some hedge funds (long and short stocks at the same time), which can be made to look good on paper but fail in application.

2. A favorite among some "advisory" publications is to overview the market and recommend stocks demonstrating relative strength (those that are up the most relative to the others), and sell demonstrating relative weakness (down the most relative to others). This can give the *impression* that the "advice" was correct when *in fact* it was *after the price change*. The results of those lured into the market following this (often heavily advertised) logic can be disastrous. These publications can effectively "forget" their many losses and hype their very few wins. In actual practice, the losses can be so severe that the follower is put out of the game. In fact, many such publicized methods will invariably lead to eventual loss. As previously discussed, many aspects of institutional window dressing are similar attempts to replace fact with fiction.

We do not mean to discredit all "trend following" and other methods of pure technical analysis. Some have validity. However, the majority we have tested are of no practical value beyond their negative effect on the unsuspecting.

The easiest way to avoid being victimized by trend-following "tricks" is to avoid the analysts/publications that fail to provide full disclosure of their results using the method over an extended time period. At least seven years of disclosure is needed because the seven-year parameter will almost always involve a wide variety of market conditions—up, down and flat.

Another warning signal is constant, widespread commercialized advertising. Most analytical methods are subject to "diseconomics of scale." The market is a competitive environment. Using any analytical technique, the amount of money to be extracted from competitors is finite. The shorter the time period a position is held, the less the amount that is likely to available for extraction from competitors.

If a publication has an inordinately large number of subscribers or if a money manager has an inordinately large amount of money applied to a technique, the large amount of people/monies following the technique can render the technique useless in practical application. This "finite" reality raises a question: Why so much commercialized advertising? The answer might be that the publication or manager is in constant search for "new blood" to survive. That is, clientele get wiped out and quit because of their dissatisfaction and need to be replaced.

Note: Watch out for a "mirage effect," in which an advisory can "document" results that are impossible to attain in actual market endeavors. For example, let's say a publication touts a low-price, low-volume stock (we'll call it Mirage Corp.) that is selling at 3. The subscribers follow the advice and buy the stock at market, and their buying demand pushes the stock to 6. They didn't buy at 3; they got it at 6 because they bought at the "market price." Now the publication says sell at 6 and records a 100-percent gain on its recommendation. The publication's followers sell, but their selling supply takes the price back to 3. The publication wins big time, but the followers lose big time.

Now let's place Mirage Corp. in the context of a pick by a money manager who bids the price up by his own buying demand and gloats in the gains. The position is really impossible to sell without taking a loss, but makes everything look wonderful (temporarily) on paper.

It may appear that it is easy to shrug off these hypocrisies by simply avoiding penny stocks where the most easily identifiable examples concentrate. This is not the case. Artificial pricing can grow to massive scales, as the collapse of the junk bond markets and the savings & loan debacle provide clear evidence.

Seeing "paper empires" crumble, we can more easily understand the Achilles' heel so prevalent in almost all markets: the differentiation between assumed (paper) profitability and actual profit capture in the form of cash. To the majority, this differential can easily appear to be so subtle as to be meaningless. Understanding the difference is, in fact, a primary factor between success and failure. "Never count it until you cash it" is valid advice, which in principle defies standard trend analysis.

The deficiencies and popularity of trend analysis (weighted against its sometimes benefits) are sufficient for us to include it as an ancillary criteria at the distrain of many.

There is no need to be very complicated in determining which "trend" we use as a base in that almost any trend measurement can be incorporated as a comparison. We use a simple 20-day moving average (another four-week comparison) of the NYSE Composite.

BUY: The moving average is going down.

SELL: The moving average is going up.

9. Put:Call Ratios
(Premium and Volume)

It is always helpful to know the mindset of the competition: the crazier they become, the easier the task of separating them from their money.

In the old days, the best measurements of the speculative public sector's behavior were odd lot ratios and cumbersome calculations associated with price/volume shifts in low-priced stocks. Thanks to the advent and popularity of listed option markets, we can now use put:call ratios as an easily observed substitute, taking only the time to flip to the proper page of *Barron's* to get an insight into this sector's current behavior. The purchase of call options is an indication that the buyer anticipates higher prices. Conversely, the purchase of put options indicates that the buyer forecasts lower prices.

Because of a lack of knowledge, the reluctance to sell short, or whatever, the volume of call buying generally exceeds the volume of put buying. Therefore, the two opposing elements cannot be considered equal in their volume: Calls are more popular. Consequently, it is the change in the ratio of put:call volume that is important to us as a measure of nonprofessional sentiment. Whether you use the volume of listed options associated with specific stocks, or those associated with market indices, or a combination, you should get the same results as long as the measurement is consistent. We use the total volume associated with individual common stocks *plus* the listed options on market indices (averages).

A somewhat more refined analysis involves the changes in option premiums, that is, the amount that the option's market price is above its intrinsic value.

Whether volume, premium or a combination is used is of little concern because the results are almost invariably parallel.

In determining this ancillary criterion we use a very simple comparison of the current ratio (and/or premium) with that of four weeks ago.

BUY: Put volume (and/or premium) has increased disproportionately to calls. This can be indicative of excessive pessimism, reducing overhead supply and allowing prices to advance more easily.

SELL: Call volume (and/or premium) has increased disproportionately to puts. This can indicate excessive optimism, making the market more vulnerable to decline.

10. Advisory Sentiment

We consider put:call relationships as measures of the sentiment of the public speculative sector. To gain a measure of the feelings within the analytical community and the effect on the institutional sector, a variety of services survey analysts and report their findings. These services vary in their clarity, most dividing analytical sentiment into three categories: bulls, bears, and neutral (or "correctionist").

Many an analyst's outlook is ambiguous: "If the market fails to advance or decline, it will stay even, and so on, and so on . . ." This is of no use in practicality, but it does help in job retention because the analyst cannot be wrong.) Most surveys also incorporate a great deal of subjectivity in their results. In addition, the surveys can be biased by a lack of adequate sample size, an overweighting (lack of randomness) of investment techniques utilized by the analysts selected for the survey, and a lack of method for compensating for changes in the analyst's forecasts between surveys.

Despite these shortcomings, the surveys (especially during extreme conditions) can be useful. If overly optimistic they have likely followed their emotions and have bought, possibly exhausting their buying demand and allowing prices to descend more easily. Conversely, when pessimism prevails, the analysts have likely sold, thereby reducing overhead supply which can allow prices to more easily advance.

The selection of the survey to be utilized is not important because, when dealing with adequate sample size, their results are generally parallel. Several are followed by *Barron's* weekly, you need to do to see the survey's results is flip to the appropriate page. The survey selected should be consistent, that is, use the same survey for each weekly comparison.

As previously mentioned, these surveys divided the analyst's sentiment between the percentage of bulls, bears, and "other." We only look at the percentage of bulls, comparing the current reading to that of four weeks ago.

BUY: The percentage of bulls has decreased. This can be an indication of pessimism and a reduction in overhead supply, making an advance more likely.

SELL: The percentage of bulls has increased. This can indicate that increasing optimism is depleting buying power and making the market more vulnerable to decline.

11. The Media

By its very nature, the business of reporting is to describe events after they have occurred. This is fine. However, when applied to financial markets, descriptions do very little to enhance profitability which requires being properly positioned *before* the price change occurs. As a business, reporting depends on sales, which are made to customers attracted to the product being sold. That attraction is a direct function of sensationalism: the more sensational the news event, the greater the attraction. When it comes to the stock market, the most sensational event is dramatic price change *after the fact that the price change occurred.*

Price change occurs because of demand/supply imbalances created by the conscious buy/sell decisions made by market participants, the majority of whom have a long, well documented record of the being wrong during pricing extremes. They are engaged in either panic selling or emotionally induced euphoric buying. In reporting the sensational pricing extremes, most reporters find themselves forced to justify the pricing: high prices "justified" by some positive event, and low prices "justified" by some negative event. To do otherwise entails the risk of looking stupid. After all, if you saw a reporter who said prices have risen dramatically because of bad news (or conversely prices have fallen because of good news), your natural reaction might be to categorize the reporter as a fool. Even if the reporter knows that pricing extremes are at nutland levels and very likely to soon reverse, job preservation can take precedent over reason.

Now, let's combine the media's after the fact reporting of price sensationalism with the sales aspect of the securities industry and its effect on a typical misguided investor, Mrs. Shnook. She is greedy, and she and her hubby have some bucks. Mrs. Shnook sees, reads, or hears about sensational price gains in the stock market and seemingly logical reasons given to justify the gains. When hubby comes home, she shows him the news and their greedy brains consummate as one. The phone rings; it's Joe

Broker, letting them know about the news. They already know why it is all wonderful, having seen it themselves through the media. Joe has little problem selling a customer who is already preconditioned to buy. In go Mrs. Shnook and hubby's money, and they are *happy* to be there. Watching their stock purchases go up on paper, they have no intention to sell as the ride looks as though it can never end, and they can count up how much their worth has appreciated. Glee.

But, then, as with every period of excessive overpricing in the market's history, a decline eventually ensues. When the downmove occurs, the glee associated with counting paper profits turns into discomfort as the paper profits change to paper loss. As the decline becomes sensational, the Shnooks turn to the news, which reports negative rationalizations after the fact of price change. Their greed turns to fear and they call Joe to whine. Joe replies, "Well, you saw the bad news. Gosh, what a surprise!" With little coaxing, they sell at a loss, happy to relieve themselves of the pressure of watching their presumed wealth fade. Joe gets another commission.

As with every overly discounted condition throughout the history of the market, prices eventually advance. The Shnooks, of course, don't like the market after taking a loss. However, chances are that they will be back the next time sensationally high prices occur, fully believing the news rationalizations. They will think the market is "different," get their greed juices flowing, and plunk down their bucks again. Heh. Heh.

Mr. and Mrs. Shnook went for an emotional ride along the road to loss (buying high and selling low)—and chances are that they will do it again! In this simplified example, it is helpful to reinforce three points.

1. The buy/sell decision process was the result of a chain reaction: media sensationalism after the fact of price change, with accompanying "justifications" for the change, followed by emotional preconditioning, followed by the sales pitch of the securities industry.

2. The victims liked it. They didn't like the end result of loss, but they enjoyed feeling the greed when they bought and relieving tensions associated with fear when they sold. After all, as adults they made the conscious buy/sell decisions.

3. They will likely do it again because the next wave of sensationalism stimulating their greed will be accompanied by different reasons for price "justification." The market will appear to have changed, creating the same lure and providing the same end result. History clearly attests that every time the stock market has become exceptionally over- or underpriced, with the associated sensationalism, the pricing reversed direction—often quickly and dramatically.

So the media are among our closest allies in eliciting irrational behavior among our opponents. The criteria are simple.

BUY: A leading nonfinancial newspaper (or network evening news program) finds the stock market so sensationally bad that it makes the front page of the paper (or the lead story on TV).

SELL: The same publications (or program) find the market so sensationally wonderful that it makes the front page (or the lead TV story).

12. New Offerings

You need not be paranoid to grasp the concept that the market is composed of a diversity of people, each of whom would take great delight in acquiring the monies of all others. What is sometimes overlooked is that individuals are not the only ones involved. The corporations, whose stock is being traded, are also active participants.

Greed being the dominant factor, the corporations themselves as well as individual corporate "insiders," (officers, and directors who are required to report their trading activities to the SEC) are very likely to be willing to buy when prices are low and sell when prices are high. This group, better than anyone else because of their proximity to the corporations involved, are positioned to utilize their greed factor far differently than the other naive emotional/sensational market participants. This "corporate insider" group knows firsthand the fundamental status of the corporations involved.

The data is firm that blindly following this corporate insider group's buy/sell behavior is not the panacea that it might appear. Intrinsic, structural forces within the market can influence corporate insiders to make the wrong decision. However, the behavior of this group is sufficient to make it one of our ancillary criteria.

This insider selling can be in two basic forms:

1. *Initial public offerings (IPOs)*, which represent stock in corporations that has never previously been offered to the public.

2. *Secondary distributions*, which basically represent stock of corporations that is already being traded.

Several publications (*Barron's* is a good source) list the "New Offerings." A casual glance at the listings is all that is necessary to determine this criterion. Looking at the list, either add up the total dollars involved in new offerings or just add up the number without bothering with the dollar amount of each specific new offering. This criteria uses a four week comparison.

BUY: The number of new offerings (by dollar amount or number count) is decreasing. This indicates that fewer insiders find the available prices attractive because they consider the market too low.

SELL: The new offerings (by dollar amount or simple count) are increasing. This indicates that the corporate insiders sense overpricing and are willing to sell their own corporations.

Other Ancillary Considerations

We did not limit the number of ancillary criteria to 12 because these are the only valid measurements. Many factors have established credibility as aids in deciphering future pricing. The reason for our limitation is that we want the timing method to be simple and rapid. Once the data sources have been located, the 12 ancillary criteria can easily be calculated within one hour each week, without the need for complicated mathematical formulas.

Note that all the ancillary factors are basically intrinsic, that is, they are not concerned with individual corporate events and/or fundamental valuations. The emphasis is on cash/stock flow patterns among different market participants and/or among various investment types, which are structural factors as well as sentiment (psychological) influences.

Many fundamental measurements, such as stock price versus book value and relative dividend yield, have good records indicating over- or underpricing. We did not include these because the primary criterion (shifts in price/earnings ratios) is totally fundamental and the other measurements are usually parallel. In addition, confining interest to the Master List (Chap. 2) is a strong fundamental parameter.

Also note that corporate insider transactions, which are followed by many publications in detail, are not included as an ancillary criteria (substituting the new offerings count). The detailed insider transactions are of greatest benefit when associated with individual corporations. Our interest is only in a basic timing method, not the buy/sell selection of individual corporations. This individual data is often reported somewhat late and is of less use in the overall market timing technique than the simple new offering count.

Another important factor, the activities of trading professionals (exchange members, including specialists) which is often discussed in the weekly report that forms the basis of this book, has been excluded because of the time constraints involved in making the appropriate calculations. The buy/sell activity of this group is reported each week on a two-week delayed basis. Before the advent of listed option trading, this data was very easy to interpret: They simply were net sellers or net buyers. The advent and popularity of listed options has provided a large, very liquid market, allowing hedging which can function to make the reported raw data misleading. It is still possible to decipher this group's positioning, but accurate interpretation requires a somewhat complex, computerized program which goes well beyond the time constraint and simplicity of this timing technique. This professional trading group will almost always be on the same side of the market as our timing method.

Actual Buy/Sell Points

The application of the technique discussed in this book is not an exercise in hindsight. It has been published on a weekly basis since January 1, 1977, following the close of the market on the last trading day of the week (Fridays unless Friday was a holiday and then published following Thursday's close). The Report is mailed following the last trading day of each week. In a very specific, straightforward format and mailed prior to the beginning of trading the following week, the published buy/sell indications are presented in a manner that makes hindsight or omission impossible.

Appendix A lists the date of each publication during which the primary criterion qualified for a buy or sell indication. The primary criterion is not supported by all the ancillary criteria on all dates. The dates when the primary and ancillary criteria were in agreement are indicated by an asterisk.

At this juncture we are concerned with the basic derivation of buy/sell points in a general context. As you will see in the next chapter, not all buy/sell points are created equal. Those during which only the primary criterion qualified would not create any change in the associated portfolio modeling. Those that involved both primary and ancillary agreement have a wide variance in relative strength, that is, some indications are far more important than others.

Specific Stock Selection

Keep in mind that our stock market participation is limited to the very select group of stocks on our Master List (Chap. 2). In effect, we are dealing in our market within the overall market.

At any given time, each stock on the Master List will vary as to its relative over- or underpricing when compared to the others. When a buy indication occurs, we do not want to buy the entire list. We want to choose from the list the specific issues that appear to provide the highest probabilities for appreciation.

To accomplish this objective, as well as to demonstrate valid factors that can be utilized in specific stock selection, three separate methods (earnings, yield, price) are incorporated into our portfolio modeling and each method is followed in detail in the published weekly Report.

Earnings

The most fundamental value of most corporations is earnings, which can be measured relative to stock pricing by the price/earnings ratio. The higher the P/E is, the higher the relative pricing. Conversely, the lower the P/E, the lower the relative stock pricing will be.

Lagging P/E ratios (the current stock price divided by the last full year of reported earnings) are provided in the daily stock quotations published in most major newspapers.

The problems associated with using the published P/Es are twofold.

1. The earnings of most corporations are erratic and basically unpredictable. What looks like an attractive low P/E could suddenly skyrocket with lower earnings. To overcome this, one of the conditions for inclusion on the Master List is an established record of earnings predictability. Only by confining interest to stocks with demonstrated earnings predictability can the P/E selection method be viable.

2. The published P/Es are associated with past earnings and earnings change. This is why we use earnings projections that are somewhat time-consuming to generate. To repeat, although we continue to use earnings projections in our P/E selection technique, over the many years of this technique's publication there is not a significant difference in the results obtained using either lagging earnings or projections.

Having made a reasonable attempt to overcome the obstacles associated with P/E valuations, our objective during buy indications is to purchase issues that are trading at the most attractive (lower) P/Es. Each stock on our Master List has a history of P/Es; that is, the past P/Es are available, and you can see the high and low P/Es (the P/E range) that the stock has experienced. We go back seven years in determining the range.

Not all stocks or stock groups trade in the same range. Stocks that are viewed as having superior growth will trade in a higher range than those viewed as stodgy.

During a buy indication, we want to purchase issues that are trading in the lower portion of their P/E range, thereby providing higher probabilities for appreciation than those that are trading in the upper portion of their range.

In the published portfolio model concentrating on the P/E method, generally, during buy indications, a wide variety of stocks with different P/E ranges are selling at a similar low level. Since only a very limited number of stocks are selected, a mechanical technique to determine which issues are selected from among those in similar P/E ranges is employed. You simply select those with the lowest P/E, irrespective of the range. Consequently, as you will see in detail in Chap. 9, this selection method tends to concentrate in low-P/E stocks. In addition to the selected stocks being in the lower portion of their P/E range, they must also be selling below their price four months ago.

Yield

There is a widespread belief that a corporation's growth is enhanced by a low dividend payout, based on the logic that the money not paid out in dividends can be reinvested in the corporation thereby facilitating its expansion. This is logical and essentially true, but is not as important as many believe. As we will clearly demonstrate in a later discussion of actual results, the total return (capital appreciation plus dividends) of the stocks on our Master List is about the same irrespective of perceived growth rates.

We like money in any form, and if it happens to come from dividends, that's just fine. In fact, it is so fine that dividend yield can be valid stock selection factor all by itself.

The problem with selecting stock simply on the basis of the highest dividend yield is that dividends (as with earnings) are not constant. A fat dividend yield could suddenly go poof if the dividend is lowered or omitted. This risk is reduced by the construction of the Master List, which attempts to confine interest to issues of demonstrated superior fundamental quality, affording both above average dividend protection and dividend growth.

In employing this method of stock selection, all you need to do is, at the time of a buy indication, review the Master List and select the issues that have the highest dividend yield *and* that have experienced a price decline over the chosen comparison time period. In the publication of this type of portfolio modeling, the Report uses a four-week price comparison to match that associated with the primary criterion and several of the ancillary criteria. As previously discussed, the actual time periods compared depend on individual preference.

Price

Although most elements of the financial media and analytical community are quick to dream up reasons to justify any price change, the fact is that many price shifts have no fundamental basis and are simply natural imbalances in demand/supply. Since our objective is to buy low and sell high, it seems logical to review the Master List at the time of a buy indication and select the issues that have experienced the sharpest percentage price decline over the chosen comparison period. This percentage price shift is so significant that price change in itself can be considered a valid method of stock selection.

In the published portfolio modeling, again using a four-week comparison period, at the time of a buy indication the issues on the Master List are reviewed to isolate those that have experienced the greatest percentage decline. Those issues that are down the most are chosen for purchase.

Again, the importance of the Master List comes into play. If a corporation turns into garbage, its stock is going to go down. If a corporation reaps fantastic profits, its stock is going to go up. In such instances, the price changes are the result of not a basic demand/supply price dislocation creating over/under valuation; the price shift is based on true underlying fundamentals. The Master List's design is to confine interest only to those issues of demonstrated superior fundamental quality, thereby allowing clearer focus on price changes that are not related by true underlying fundamental change. In other words, the Master List is a conscious attempt to isolate stocks that become more attractive as their prices drop.

Oversimplification?

The initial reaction to determining specific stock selection by these three methods might be that it is too simple to really be valid. No complex mathematical formulas are involved. There is no need for computer assistance. Neither is there a need for a staff of analysts or heeding the predictions of puffed-up gurus. And there is not even any need to pay much attention to the financial media beyond acquiring the necessary data to determine if a buy/sell point has been established as well as the specific stocks involved.

The fact of the matter is that we have found the market to be quite simple. It is often presented, and consequently perceived, as complex, but we have found its core to be nothing other than a straightforward, repetitive, man-made business.

Recognizing this basic, underlying simplicity and comparing it to the rantings of many analysts and media sensationalism, you can gain insight as to why the simplicity is widely overlooked by the majority and always will be. The majority within the analytical community will always attempt to present a reason to justify any price change, after it occurs, in the context of the reasoning being most easily accepted by clientele. Because of the assumed, widespread belief that all price changes are based on fundamental change, the consensus among analysts repeatedly ignores structural and/or psychological pressures that can create prices that are extremely divergent from underlying fundamental norms.

To understand how an erroneous consensus can develop, place yourself in the position of an institutional analyst, keeping in mind that job preservation provides some nice things, such as food and shelter. Now let's say the market makes a significant move because of psychological and/or structural pressures that move prices well away from underlying fundamentals. You are asked to explain why. If you say you don't know, you look stupid to clientele (after all, you are being paid to know everything), and you risk loss of employment. Your image, as well as your future, might very well depend on providing an answer that is most easily accepted by your clientele, which have been conditioned by you and/or other analysts to believe that every price change is justified by a purely fundamental factor. Looking about at what the other analysts say is the cause of the price change, you simply repeat what they are saying and join the consensus. You are one of the group. Even if absolutely wrong, your retaining employment is enhanced because you are in full agreement with your peers (they can't fire everybody).

The sentiment among analysts is reinforced by most elements of the financial media which (in its attempt to generate sales) stresses uncommon events.

The sales structure of the securities industry is also a powerful force that is bolstered by the consensus among analysts and concentrated media attention. It is elementary logic that a sale is made easiest when the customer is predispositioned to making a decision.

The consensus among analysts *plus* media concentration *plus* the sales structure of the securities industry combine to create tremendous pressures that can *make the exception appear to be the rule.* Consequently, chasing price after the fact of price change creates a lure that ignores the market's underlying simplicity. It also ignores the basic logic that profitability requires being properly positioned before the fact of price change.

Summary

In this chapter we have been able to blend the elements of previous chapters into a framework that allows easily discernible buy/sell points, as well as the selection of specific common stocks.

The determination to buy or sell or do nothing can be quickly calculated. All you need is an easily calculated primary criterion (P/E or price shift), supported by at least six of twelve ancillary criteria (institutional cash reserves, public cash reserves, money supply, gold price, bond pricing, volume and price relationships, volatility, trend analysis, put:call ratios, advisory sentiment, the media, and new offerings).

Using any of three different methods (earnings, yield, or price), you can also easily and rapidly determine specific stock selection during buy indications.

At this juncture, a constant underlying theme of this text becomes more clearly focused: The stock market is a simple business. Yet the inherent simplicity is (and always will be) overlooked by most investors because of the tremendous pressures created by a combination of factors: erroneous rationalizations formulating a consensus among analysts, media sensationalism, and the sales structure of the securities industry, which can make the exception appear to be the rule.

With this background, we can now apply what we have discussed to actual market participation. After all, the proof of the pudding is in the eating.

9

Time for
Real Time

Everyone wants a system, and there are hundreds of analysts who clamor for attention as they lay claim to having found the fail safe road to riches.

Mastering the market through hindsight is easy. Just look back at what has occurred, copy the consensus, or make up your own reasons why the price changes occurred, and, presto, you have a foolproof system. The process of developing "the great system" is therefore fairly simple. Sift through the mounds of data the market has accumulated throughout its 200-year history and see what would have worked. Then, going back over the data, tabulate the results and claim that, because this is what happened in the past, it will surely repeat in the future. You can then claim to have achieved the past results.

This is a very common practice among system seekers, and in some cases the underlying analytical search is valid. However, in most cases the discovered system is nothing other than what would be a normal bell-shaped curve created by random results. In other words, something can be derived that looks wonderful, but it is really only a random variable that has no real validity in future investments. Another thing about this group's "discoveries" is that they almost invariably point to results obtained in hindsight. They are concerned in proving their merit by listing what could have happened after the "system" was discovered. They did not acquire their results through real time foresight by making their forecasts known and presenting them in a format prohibiting any form of hindsight or omission.

This lack of foresight is extremely clear when you take a careful look at the hundreds of entities (ranging from independent analysts to brokerage firms, to pension funds, to mutual funds, to anybody else wanting to manage others' money). They all claim they can do it better because they have the best system, when actually their results are a function of hindsight or tainted by selective memory loss.

The line of system sellers is dramatically shortened when confined to those who have documented results that eliminate any possibility of hindsight or omission. Some entities (such as mutual funds) are forced into full disclosure (and by their results most would probably prefer otherwise), but most system sellers have not really presented their work in a credible format requiring documented foresight.

Our concern is with reality, not hindsight or hypocrisy.

The Time Overlay Concept

Keep our objective in mind: to extract profit from the stock market through the buying and selling of common stocks. Although risk can never be eliminated from stock market participation, the goal of profit consistency requires that a conscious, rational effort be made for risk minimization.

Beyond developing a realistic understanding of the nature of the market, our risk minimization involves two distinct, specific elements. (1) We want to confine investment interest to stocks that are of superior fundamental quality and that therefore are less likely to present any nasty fundamental surprises. (2) We would prefer to have the overall movement of the market on our side by means of a market timing technique.

By confining our interest to the Master List (Chap. 2), it is helpful to reinforce the concept that we are dealing with a market within a market. At any given time, each individual stock we monitor will vary as to its over- or underpricing with the others in the group. At the time of a buy indication, we only want to invest in the issues on the Master List that appear relatively discounted to the others. In effect, by being so selective we are employing an aspect of market timing through our selection process.

Relative to overall market timing, we will not buy or sell in the published portfolio modeling unless the primary and ancillary criteria are in agreement. Although the stocks on our Master List generally parallel the major market averages, because of the small number of issues we monitor, it is possible that our list will not always be directly aligned with the popularized averages.

Our method of participation involving market timing involves two distinct and separate analytical elements: specific stock selection and market timing. We term this combination Time Overlay: one analysis combined (or overlaid) with another analysis.

The Importance of Diversity

Two types of diversity are important in portfolio modeling: issue and time.

At the time of this writing, over the 16 years that the Time Overlay models have been published, 1065 specific stock positions have been concluded of which 1016 have been profitable. Although we consider this 95-percent accuracy rate to be acceptable (as we shall see later, it can be improved), some losses have occurred. Even though the probability is very low that an individual stock position will fail to be profitable, the possibility does exist that, if a portfolio consists of only a few stocks, they could turn out to be the losers and the method would result in loss.

Because of this, albeit very low, chance of loss, it is reasonable to reduce this loss possibility to a minimum by having several different issues in the portfolio. In actual market endeavors, over many years of employing the Time Overlay technique, we have never seen an account actually lose money that strictly adhered to the method. However, because the possibility exists, it is only prudent to consider issue diversity.

Of greater importance is time diversity. As you can see in Appendix A, listing the published buy/sell points, several buy indications are generally followed by several sell indications, and so on—an ongoing cyclical process. This inclusion of more than one buy or sell in sequence is by design. We are not primarily concerned with picking exact tops and bottoms in the popularized averages, with our emphasis being on the specific stocks we follow. Our concern with movements in the popularized averages is that these movements will enhance our profit extraction through the buying and selling of specific stocks.

As previous mentioned, there is a constant change in the relative attractiveness of the issues on our Master List. There is no reason for us to buy or sell everything at once. We want to enter the market gradually, expanding our exposure (investment level) over a series of buy indications, providing us time diversity as well as a better chance for issue diversity. When selling, our desire is the same, to gradually reduce our exposure. In other words, since the stocks we are involved with will not all hit their low or high points at the same time, it would be stupid for us to buy or sell everything at the same time.

When buying stock that qualifies for inclusion on our Master List, the lower the price is, the better. Since accumulation (buying) is designed to occur over a series of buy signals, it is possible that a stock can be bought repeatedly as its price descends, and this has occurred. The diversity in this case is by time: same issue, different prices.

In most cycles, the time duration between buy indications automatically provides issue diversity because different stocks will be relatively low-priced during different buying periods. During those buying periods in which stocks tended to duplicate—that is, the same stock was purchased during each buy indication—it might seem reasonable to conclude that the duplication increased risk. The actual results to date contradict this assumption, with the time and issue diversities of equal importance. The same stock purchased at increasingly lower prices reduced risk to the same degree as selecting several different issues.

The results of this technique, to date, also firmly indicate that the amount of diversity necessary to approach median return need not be very great. Only five to six individual positions, diversified by either issue or time, have been shown to almost invariably provide returns ± 5% of the median. This allows the technique to be employed by relatively small accounts.

Because of the careful selection technique of individual stocks, the results to date have repeatedly shown that time diversity is more important than issue diversity. It is more prudent to apply monies to a few stocks at different times than to many stocks at any one time. In fact, overdiversification as to the number of stocks can often be a severe disadvantage in optimizing return.

The important point is recognizing that both time and issue diversity are built into our investment technique. The time diversity aspect is automatic because of spacing the buy/sell points. The issue aspect is also (usually) automatic because the different stock issues appearing to have the best profit potential will generally vary between different buy indications.

Testing the Models: Controls and Elimination of Bias

As background to this technique, remember one of the criteria for stock selection is institutional involvement. The issues utilized, therefore, are suitable for investment consideration by at least some institutions.

This allows us a valid comparison: matching the results obtained by our methods with those obtained by institutional management over the same time period. Similar comparisons can be made by measuring the market performance that was (or could have been) obtained by following the recommendations of any broker or advisor as well as providing a valid comparison with popular market averages.

The reason for this is not to identify relative competence, but to eliminate a possible bias. If the techniques employed used little known stocks or information not widely distributed, it would detract from the validity of the results. That is, to enhance the validity of the techniques, the methods must incorporate data available to other investors during the same time period.

The timing techniques being employed use no special or inside information. All stocks utilized are well-known and widely followed. The information used in determining specific stock selection was (is) easily available.

Another aspect incorporated to eliminate bias is that the stocks utilized are usually higher-priced with relatively high trading volumes. This adds to the validity of the results. Methods using low-priced, low-volume stocks can be biased to the point of total invalidation. For example, low-priced, low-volume stocks could be easily changed in price by the action of a few individuals who through their own activities create price changes and the illusion that they have acquired actual profits. This illusion of actual price change has been used in fraudulent schemes where the investor is talked into buying a low-priced, low-volume stock from a crook who "makes a market" in the stock. The investor is unaware that the elevated price was made up at the discretion of the crook since no one else is interested in the stock. Seeing the appreciation, the crook sells the investor another stock with the same result, etc, . . . until the day comes that the investor wants to sell and there is no real market.

Crooks aside, percentage price fluctuations in low-priced stocks can often be dramatic on very low volume. Because of this, parallel (or even close to parallel) returns in actual practice would be impossible. Note that, because of this effect, many published advisory "services" that tout low price/low-volume stocks can be extremely misleading. For example, they could recommend a stock and then their followers proceed to bid up the price by their own buying. The service then identifies the price advance as an indication of the service's "ability" and may recommend sale at the higher price. The followers sell, thereby forcing price down in the same magnitude that their selling had advanced the price. The "service" looks good, but the followers could never obtain prices parallel to the service's recommendation because the appropriate prices were never really available. In other words, the followers bought high and sold low, while the service created the impression of success.

A malady shared by many analysts is selective memory loss. When they are correct, they become vocal to attract attention to their ability. When they are wrong, they shut up, and the error is forgotten. Another manifestation of selective memory loss is the "cover all your bases babble," in which market forecasts go something like, "If the market does not remain unchanged, it will advance unless a decline occurs." Such yappings are extremely common, but absolutely worthless to anyone except the analyst who, after employing selective memory loss, can point to any market outcome as proof of forecasting ability.

We, the authors, are in the market in real time. Our livelihoods are dependent on accurate price forecasting. There is no place for selective memory loss and associated nonsense. The results of our decisions are clear and crisp: Either we have acquired the money of fellow market participants or lost. Period.

In demonstrating the basic Time Overlay investment technique, we developed a format involving several controls making hindsight or omission virtually impossible and allowing the method to be easily used in actual market endeavors.

1. The specific application of the Time Overlay method is followed in a weekly Report which has been published continuously since January 1, 1977 by Drach Market Research.

The Report is prepared following the close of the last trading day of the week (Friday, unless a holiday when preparation is conducted on Thursday).

The Report is always mailed before trading begins the following week. This preparation and mailing sequence prohibits any possibility of waiting until the next week begins before presenting the forecast for that week.

2. The Report is very specific—no "if's." It states clearly and specifically to BUY, or SELL, or DO NOTHING. The text is devoted to an explanation of current positioning and outlook.

The Report uses only the week's closing prices. There are no qualifications to buy or sell if this or that happens. When a buy or sell decision is made, it is firm using the week's closing price. Period. No buy or sell decisions are contingent on anything that happens between publications of the weekly Report.

It can easily be seen that this strict adherence to only making buy or sell decisions once a week introduces a significant constraint: Better prices may be available during the week rather than confining the buying or selling to only one price during that week, the week's closing price. However, this is how the Report is structured. In effect, it is only looking at the market once a week at the week's closing prices to determine if any changes are warranted in portfolio modeling.

Obviously, this constraint is not necessary in actual market endeavors. In a later section involving how to expand return, we will address how this constraint can be easily overcome.

3. The Report follows three different portfolio models based on the three previously discussed methods of stock selection: earnings, yield, and price. Each model functions independently of the others, even though they are basically interrelated by the technique's design.

As mentioned previously, not all buy/sell indications are of equal strength. These differentials will be discussed later in this chapter. At this juncture, our concern is describing basic format structure.

Whenever there is a buy indication, five stocks are selected for purchase in each category (earnings, yield, price) using the simple stock selection techniques discussed in Chap. 8. The price (the week's closing price) is listed with each stock specified for purchase.

Between the time specified for purchase and the time specified for sale, the stocks are listed in the Report as "Open Positions" and the date specified for purchase. No position can be forgotten.

When a sell indication occurs, those positions selected for sale are listed with each position detailing the percentage profit/loss and time the position was held. The positions sold are then deleted from the Open Positions, and the results are incorporated into an ongoing summary of results published in each weekly Report.

Using this rigid format, each stock position is followed continuously from the time of purchase through the time of sale. With no possibility of hindsight or omission, the technique's validity is carefully documented.

4. The results summaries (discussed in detail later in this chapter) do not include dividend payments. The results are accordingly understated.

5. The percentage profit/loss calculations for each specific stock position take into account transaction costs in the following manner.

Inherent in the Time Overlay techniques because of the timing criteria, stocks are almost invariably purchased during declining markets and sold during advancing markets. This is by design. As such, there has always been some price decline after purchase and some price advance after sale. In other words, because of the published format's construction, stocks have never (to date) been specified for purchase at their exact low price and have never been specified for sale at their exact high price. The minimum price differential is quite specific and is incorporated into the

Report to more than offset reasonable transaction costs as follows (providing 1/8th increments for each $12.50 of stock price):

Specified minimum amount (at 99% probability level). Stock: Stock should trade under specified purchase. Price: Price or over specified selling price.	
Less than 12⅝	⅛
12⅝ to 25	¼
25⅛ to 37½	⅜
37⅝ to 50	½
50⅛ to 62½	⅝
62⅝ to 75	¾
75⅛ to 87½	⅞
87⅝ to 100	1
100⅛ to 112½	1⅛
etc. . . .	

For example, if the Report specified a stock for purchase at 35, by design the stock should trade at least ⅜ less, 34⅝. If the stock went to 40 and selling was indicated in the Report; by design the stock should sell at least ½ higher, 40½.

In this example, the result recorded by the Report would be to purchase at 35 and sell at 40. By using the differential, the actual result would have been to purchase at 34⅝ and sell at 40½.

This pricing differential is another constraint that need not be experienced in actual market endeavors.

6. The published portfolio modeling, is purely mechanical, totally objective, and void of any subjectivity. The published modeling will only alter model portfolio structure (buy or sell) when the primary and ancillary criteria are in agreement on a timing signal. The buy/sell signals are therefore predetermined by market conditions. Because of the modeling's design, under no circumstances will there be any change in portfolio structure unless the predetermined conditions for a buy/sell signal are given. In other words, the models have absolutely no concern about events between the predetermined buy/sell points.

It is mandatory that the published models function on a purely mechanical design. The injection of subjectivity would function to invalidate the published results.

This is a very significant constraint which, as we will see later in this chapter, can be easily overcome in actual market participation.

The Investment Level

Having constructed a rigid framework by which the investment techniques can be demonstrated, we can now turn to a more detailed discussion of the specific portfolio modeling.

As mentioned, our primary concern is extracting money from our fellow market participants through the buying and selling of specific common stocks. We are not concerned with pinpointing highs and lows in the popular averages because the components of these averages are not an exact duplication of the issues in our trading universe (the Master List). We do, however, prefer the broadly based market to be on our side, being heavily invested during market lows and reducing (or eliminating) exposure during market highs.

We previously discussed that, because of ongoing shifting in relative over- or undervaluations between the stocks we utilize, it is not prudent to become fully invested or divested at any one time: Accumulation (buying) and distribution (selling) should be a somewhat gradual process to enhance profitability.

The degree of exposure to common stocks is followed in the weekly Report for each stock selection method, with the percentage of funds allocated to common stock investment termed the *investment level*. If virtually no common stock investment is warranted, the investment level would be 0 percent (no stock, 100 percent cash). Conversely, if full common stock investment is warranted, the investment level would be 100 percent (no cash, all monies applied to stock).

Optimally, in theory, the market would warrant either warrant full (100-percent) investment or no involvement (0 percent). Except in relatively rare conditions, the market is not so well defined. The usual situation is that the market warrants involvement at levels between the extremes. This is because most of the time not all stocks (or stock groups) are similarly over/under priced at any given time. There is usually some stratification. That is, stocks of similar fundamental quality are experiencing significant pricing divergences from their peers. Such stratification warrants investment in some issues (groups) at the same time that other issues (groups) should be avoided.

In designing the models, it was decided that the mechanical structure's basic movement would be to go from the 0-percent investment level to 100 percent invested over four successive buy indications. That is, on the first indication, go from 0 percent to 25 percent invested in stocks. On the next three indications, increase exposure to 50 percent, then to 75 percent, and then to full (100 percent) investment. Then, when sell indications occurred, review the holdings and in a mechanical process reduce exposure.

Appendix B lists the investment levels for each stock selection method (earnings, yield, price), as well as a composite, which blends the three categories associated with each buy/sell indication since initiation of the Report's publication. As you can see, the movement between extremes has generally been gradual, as was the intent of the method's mechanical design.

Also note that the investment levels for each of the three selection methods are usually similar, but with significant differences in some periods. This is because each method functions independently, as well as the mechanical aspects of the buy/sell process.

During any buy indication, five stocks are selected in each method of stock selection in the simple manner discussed in Chap. 8. That is all there is to it: moving the investment level toward 100 percent by means of four separate buy indications.

During sell indications, the entire Master List is reviewed to see what percentage of the stocks are trading over or under their average measurement relative to each method over the past 52 weeks. For the earnings category, price/earnings ratios are used. For the yield category, dividend yields are used. For the price category, market prices are used. Then a similar comparison is made on a four-week range (that is, the percentage over/under their average) because that is the time span chosen for the determination of the published modeling's primary and ancillary criteria used to determine buy/sell points.

This process might initially appear complex, but is very simple and easy to calculate. The data (P/E, Yield, Price) is published in all major financial publications.

For example, let's say we have four consecutive buy indications, taking the investment level in each category up to 100 percent. Then we have a sell indication. We look at the stocks on the Master List and see what percentage are selling at P/Es under their 52-week average and find that 85 percent are below the average. Then, we look at the four-week comparison and find that 75 percent are below the average. We average the two calculations: 75 + 85 = 160/2 = 80 percent. Using this calculation, 80 percent of the stocks on our Master List are down. We therefore want to reduce our earnings (P/E) model to the 80 percent investment level from the 100 percent investment level. For the yield model, we use the identical process, incorporating dividend yields. For the price category, we use price changes. The mathematical process is identical for each category.

In this example, our four consecutive buy indications took the investment level from 0 percent to 100 percent, with five stocks selected during each buy signal, resulting in the model portfolio holding 20 stock positions. A reduction in the investment level from 100 percent to 80 percent would require the elimination (sale) of four positions.

The mechanical selection of the four to be eliminated would be those that had moved the most in their respective method of selection from their level at the time of purchase. In the earnings category, those sold would be the ones that have experienced the greatest upward movement in P/E. In the yield method, those sold would be the ones that have shown the greatest reduction in dividend yield (the yield has an inverse relation to price). The price method would simply sell those whose price had advanced most from the time of purchase.

Now, we can clearly see the reason the technique has demonstrated such a high rate of profit consistency over many years and throughout a wide variety of market conditions, including the 1987 crash. Only stocks of superior fundamental quality are considered for purchase, and purchase is confined to periods during which they are relatively discounted (low priced). Selling is only considered when they stocks appear to be relatively overpriced. The buy/sell points are predetermined by a mechanical formula, as is specific stock selection. There is absolutely no subjectivity or the possibility of emotion to sway the method of participation.

The weekly Report that forms the basis of this book enjoys a worldwide subscription base. To give credit where credit is due, many subscribers have pointed out that *going through the screening process to determine the investment level reduction and then applying the reduction level to specific holdings is not necessary.* They have pointed out that almost exactly the same annualized returns can be achieved simply by selling those positions that are profitable at the time of a sell indication and retaining those that have not yet demonstrated profitability. This is a very rapid process that takes only a few minutes or less. They add that not only does this simple method of selling determination usually parallel the published model's results in percentage return, it also increases profit consistency. In effect, they say, "Just take the money and don't waste time on the investment level scan."

There is no question, at least to date, that the subscribers are correct in their observation and that the scanning process is not necessary to come close to matching the published modeling's results.

The weekly Report, however, continues to use the more time-consuming method to determine the investment level for three reasons.

1. The models were designed to be purely mechanical in a very strict predesigned structure, which has never been altered since initiation of the Report's publication. This consistency in methodology will never change because any change could function to invalidate future results. That is, if the method is changed, its results would also have to begin anew.

2. As discussed later in this chapter, there are ways to expand return beyond that of the published modeling by both the removal of con-

straints and other methods which require the longer investment level calculations.

3. The investment level can be important in timing overall market movements and the application of stock and index options.

Losses

At the time of this writing, over the history of the Report's publication there have ben 1065 concluded positions of which 1016 (95 percent) have been profitable. This accuracy rate is higher than any other method of which we are aware that has been published in a full disclosure format with virtually no possibility of hindsight or omission over the same time period and with a large sample size.

However, there have been some losses, and it is important to understand why they have occurred. The mechanical modeling can be forced into accepting a loss in two ways:

1. The investment level leads in determining the number of positions to be sold during a sell indication. That is, the percentage change in calculating the investment level reduction is done first, and then the proportionate number of stock positions being held is deleted (sold). Under some conditions, there is a directive to reduce the investment level, and the specific positions being held are still relatively discounted. Consequently, a situation can develop during which the mechanical structure of the Report can dictate a sale (investment level reduction), even when the specific positions being held are low and have extremely high probabilities for future appreciation. In effect, selling is forced because of the strict mechanical design.

2. As the Master List changes over time, sometimes a stock that is being held as an open position in the models has been deleted from the list. In this event, irrespective of current price, the mechanical structure of the Report will sell the deleted issue to equate to the new investment level before considering the sale of any other open positions.

Now, given these two conditions, it becomes clear why some of the Report's subscribers have found it easy to identify a method both of achieving greater profit consistency and of saving time in making sale calculations, while coming very close to the Report's annualized returns. In effect, the mechanical aspects of the publishing modeling can, and have, forced unnecessary losses.

However, as we shall see, their observation is shortsighted. There are ways to significantly increase return over the published models in both accuracy and percentage gains, which depend on the more refined investment level calculations.

Margin

By the design of its construction, the published Time Overlay portfolio modeling is extremely conservative. It confines investment interest to issues scanned in an attempt to isolate fundamental quality, and then purchasing selected issues only when they appear overly discounted. The use of margin (borrowing) to purchase stock is discouraged by the Report's mechanical design. However, in rare circumstances in which the discounting is severe by historical standards, the mechanical structure allows for the use of leverage. These periods are very infrequent and generally quite brief. As seen in Appendix B, there have only been six such occasions during the entire history of the weekly Report, and they were very brief. The incorporation of margin is not necessary—and, in fact, is strongly discouraged in most managed account programs—to achieve the published portfolio's results.

The mechanical aspect of the margin periods is quite simple. If after four consecutive buy indications, there is another or more buy indications, the margin aspect will kick in as long as the stocks on our Master List are at the 90—percent investment level and in their lower 52-week quartile for P/Es *plus* yield *plus* price. All three specific investment selection methods must indicate that the stocks we follow are exceptionally discounted.

In actual market endeavors, most people have difficulty with the psychological strains associated with the most basic successful strategies. Margin can add to the strain, and the majority of investors probably should ignore the use of margin. Its use on those rare occasions when the published modeling incorporates leverage does very little to alter the results. Almost identical results can be obtained without ever considering or implementing the use of margin. Margin is mentioned because it is designed into the mechanical structure of the published models.

We have now come to the point where we have established sufficient background to move into a discussion of the actual results of the published modeling.

Time Overlay

This basic timing and stock selection method is the focus of both this book and the weekly Report. As mentioned, this modeling is divided into three portfolio types (earnings, yield, price), which share the same buy/sell points, but which function independently as to stock selection and invest- ment level. The results of each stock selection are listed in Appendix C ("Time Overlay Earnings"), Appendix D ("Time Overlay Yield"), and Appendix E ("Time Overlay Price"). Table 9.1 summarizes the results to date of the itemized positions in the appendices incorporating every concluded position from the time of the Report's initial publication on January 1, 1977 to the date of this writing.

It is reasonable to assume that over time stock pricing is a logical representation of a corporation's value. For almost all ongoing corpora- tions, the primary value lies in current and future earnings. As such, the Time Overlay Earnings model (which is based on changes in price/earn- ings ratios) is most sensitive to the earnings factor and could be expected to be the most accurate. The Time Overlay Yield model could reasonably be expected to follow in the degree of accuracy because the earnings aspect is not the primary concern. The price category, reacting to nothing other than gross price change and having no fundamental basis beyond the stocks qualifying for the Master List, could be anticipated to be the most speculative and least accurate. As you can see, this is how the results as to the percentage of positions concluding profitable have been so far: earnings 98.03 percent, yield 94.65 percent, and price 93.52 percent.

The percentage profitability of the average position could be expected to be a function of the volatility of the specific stocks emphasized in each selection method. The price method is the wildest and could be expected to show the largest price swings, followed by the earnings method, with the lower beta (low volatility) and the yield-sensitive method experiencing the least volatility. As you can see by looking at the percentage profitability of the average position for each method in Table 9.1, this is how the results to date have come in.

Table 9.1. Time Overlay Results

	Earnings		Yield		Price	
Total positions	355		355		355	
Profit	348	98.03%	336	94.65%	332	93.52%
Loss	7	1.97%	19	5.35%	23	6.48%
Even	0	0.00%	0	0.00%	0	0.00%
Average positions						
Percentage	+	6.08%	+	4.52%	+	6.97%
Weeks held		21.14		20.24		24.82
Annualized	+	14.96%	+	11.61%	+	14.60%

Of course, the most important result is the annualized return. In the result summaries, the earnings method has had the best return (14.96 percent), followed by price (14.60 percent), and yield (11.61 percent). These differentials, however, are misleading when total return is considered because *they do not include dividends.* The dividend yield for the stocks selected in the yield method has averaged around 7 percent, the earnings method around 4 percent, and the price method around 4 percent. When the total return (capital gains plus dividends) is calculated, the return achieved by each method is almost identical, around 19 percent.

With a sample size of over 1000 individual stock positions taken over an extended time period involving a wide variety of market conditions, and without any possibility of hindsight or omission, *our objective has been accomplished.* The conservative technique has provided us a high level of profit consistency (around 95 percent) and an annualized return of approximately 19 percent. And, because of the simplicity of the method, the results were obtained without having to do much analytical work.

With these results in hand, it is interesting to note they were obtained by means of a method that in many ways directly contradicts many widely believed investment theories. It is generally assumed safety is best achieved by buying stocks that are advancing (demonstrating relative strength) rather than those declining (demonstrating relative weakness). The reason for this belief is the "price is proof mentality." If a stock is going down, the price activity can be interpreted as "proof" that something is wrong. If the stock is going up, the price activity can function as "proof" that something is good. We buy them going down and sell them going up and in doing so have profited around 95 percent of the time against those who have lured themselves into the "price is proof" belief. The price is proof mentality is the basis for the widely believed adage, "Cut your losses and let your profits run."

Our objective is to capture profits in the form of cash and run before losses occur. Yet the price is proof mentality will always persist because, in extreme conditions (where stocks go to zippo or show phenomenal gains), it can be seen that by following the price action (getting out of those going down and into those going up) the discomfiture of splats can be avoided and maximum gains captured. This behavior is actually an attempt to capture the exceptions—the few stocks that have created the most sensationalism (after-the-fact of price change). The underlying reason that we can buy into relative weakness with confidence is the strict criterion that the stocks be the Master List (Chap. 2).

A review of the individual Time Overlay positions in the appendices shows that there is a great deal of variance in the time duration for which positions are held. Some are sold quickly and others retained for extended periods because of the mechanical selling process. For example, let's say there is a buy indication during which all stock groups are depressed and a diversity of issues by industry type are purchased. Then, let's say an inverse price stratification occurs, during which the oil sector experiences pricing directly opposite the broadly based market. That is, when the oil stocks are up, the rest of the market is down; when the oil stocks are down, the rest of the market is up. Our portfolio contains all stock groups including oils. Now, let's say the market goes up (except for the oils) and we get a sell indication reducing the investment level, but not taking it to zero. The position(s) retained are the oils because they are most discounted relative to the others. Thus it could happen (and has) that, during repeated sell indications, the issues being retained are the same for long periods. As we will discuss in the next section, this is easily overcome.

Also note that, although each of the three stock selection methods functions independently, the same stock sometimes qualifies in more than one method during a buy indication. In such circumstances it can appear reasonable to conclude that, because the stock was selected more than once, it is "better" than the other stocks purchased during the buy indication. However, the actual results to date do not confirm this logic. That is, each stock has an equal chance for success no matter how many methods it qualifies for.

A wide variety of "systems"—managed account programs, mutual funds, and the like—provide their description of results. These groups tend to present themselves in the most favorable manner. With past results, the easiest way to do this is to select the results obtained over the best time period. For example, most equity mutual funds will show their performance from a market low, thereby showing the most dramatic gains possible and perhaps conveniently forgetting their preceding smash. In our results there is no such latitude. The publication of the models began on January 1, 1977. At the time publication was initiated, the Dow Jones Industrial Average was 1004. At the time of this writing, the popularized Dow is 3200. This represents a compound annualized return of around 8 percent. If the Dow had been able to advance 10 percent annually during this time period it would now be around 4500; a 15-percent annual rate would result in an approximate 8000 level, and at 20 percent the Dow would now be near 15,000. Consistency and compounding can sure be dramatic!

Enhancing Time Overlay Return

Although we find the basic Time Overlay method satisfactory in achieving our objectives of profit consistency and return, several factors can significantly increase return in actual market endeavors.

1. Rotation.   The published models are very strict. They will only change positions during outright buy/sell points that can only occur on the Report's publication date. *The models completely disregard price movements between the predetermined, published mechanical buy/sell periods.* Almost invariably, better prices are available at times other than the instant of a published buy/sell indication.

We know, by the results derived over the many years of the modeling's publication, what the average percentage return per position is by strictly adhering to the published buy/sell points. We also know that each stock selected has an equal chance of concluding profitably irrespective of price fluctuations between the predetermined buy/sell points. If we can get equal or better prices than those of the published models between buy/sell points, there is no reason not to capture gains before an outright sell signal.

Knowing that prices fluctuate, we can attempt to take advantage of the intervening price movements by rotating our positions. For example, let's say there is a buy indication and two stocks (A and B) appear equally suitable for purchase, and both are selling at 20. We purchase stock A. Rather than wait for a sell signal, we decide that we will take our profit if we realize a 10-percent gain. The 10-percent profit would capture a return greater than that averaged by the published models for individual positions. (Any parameter can be used, it is a matter of personal preference). Now, let's say that our stock (A) advances to 22, meeting our 10-percent objective, and that stock B has stayed at 20. We do not want to reduce our investment level because there has not been a sell indication. We sell stock A, taking the profit and move to stock B. Then, let's say stock B goes to 22 providing us our 10-percent profit, and stock A has fallen back to 20. We sell stock B and rotate back to stock A, and so on, until there is an indication to sell out entirely and/or reduce the investment level.

In actual managed accounts, the rotational process is utilized and, to date, *without exception* accounts incorporating rotation have outperformed the published Time Overlay models. During exceptionally volatile periods, the incorporation of rotation can create very active trading. However, during such periods and/or during extended market cycles, the use of rotation can dramatically improve results.

2. Optimizing Rotational Selections.   In the previous rotation example, the rotational selections were made from stocks selected at the time of buy indications without consideration of the other issues on the Master List.

This is an unnecessary constraint. It is possible that, at the time a purchase is warranted because of a rotational sale, there might be a stock on the Master List that is a better bargain than any of those selected at the time of a buy indication. In actual rotational trading, we move to whatever stock appears most undervalued from all those on the Master List, irrespective of whether they are being held as open positions in the published modeling. This wider selection generally expands return.

3. Delaying Buying.   The published modeling is designed to be early. That is, lower prices are available after buy indications and higher prices are available after sell indications. As discussed, this is necessary to assure that compensation has been made for transaction costs and to provide sufficient price latitude so that the method can be duplicated in actual trading.

At the time of a buy indication, each specific stock selected has an equal chance of concluding profitably. Price fluctuations between the predetermined buy/sell points are of no concern to the strict models because nothing is going to happen between the buy/sell points.

Price fluctuations (both up and down) between the predetermined buy/sell points can be significant and, since each position has an equal chance of concluding profitably, there can often be some advantage in waiting until after a buy signal and then selecting issues that are demonstrating relative discounting. For example, let's say that there is a buy signal and two stocks (A and B) are selected, each at a price of $20. Instead of buying one immediately, we wait and see that stock A is remaining at $20 and stock B has declined to $18. We then buy B because it is relatively discounted, having an equal chance of being above its initial published purchase price as does stock A when specified to be sold.

In our real time application of the Time Overlay portfolio modeling, we do not wait until after a buy indication to begin expanding the investment level. Although better prices become available after the buy indication, we usually get them anyway because of the rotational aspects. In fact, because of the rotational advantages, we are often a bit more aggressive in our investment level than the Report. However, for those wishing to avoid the sometimes rapid trading associated with rotation and/or the added analytical time, delaying buying and emphasizing the most discounted issues can often significantly increase return.

4. Watching for Ex-Dividend Dates.   Dividend payments, which are not considered in the published results, are an important source of income.

It is a general assumption that, when a stock goes ex-dividend (the day after those who hold the stock are entitled to the next dividend payment), the value of stock is reduced by the amount of the dividend. For example, if a stock's price is $40 and it pays a dividend of $1, at the time of the ex-dividend date the inherent value of the stock is reduced by the dividend amount $40 − 1 = $39.

This reduction in the stock's market price is logical. In our example, the corporation paid out $1 of its value and the corporation's worth is reduced accordingly. This is even accounted for in stock quotations. As in our example, if the stock closed at $40 the day before the ex-dividend date and closed the next day at $39, its day-to-day price change would be printed as no change.

Our experience with the stocks we monitor has been that, in depressed conditions (when we often are doing our buying), the market price of the stock does not always descend by the amount of the dividend payment. Our reasoning as to why this occurs is purely theoretical. We suppose that, because of the superior quality of the issues on the Master List, during depressed market conditions when many people are frightened, there is a "flight to safety," which can function to prop up our stocks. In other words, buying demand picks up in our stocks relative to the broadly based market because of their image of safety created by their demonstrated fundamental quality.

For whatever reason, when two stocks appear equally attractive for purchase, some advantage in total return can often be achieved by selecting the one with the nearest ex-dividend date.

5. Combining the Time Overlay Models. The three methods of specific stock selection (earnings, yield, price) function independently. One of the reasons for this is academic—to demonstrate that each method by itself is valid in determining stock selection.

In the actual implementation of the Time Overlay modeling, we have found that better results can be obtained by concentrating purchase on stocks that qualify best in all three categories. For example, a stock may qualify very well for the yield method, but may be well down the priority list in the price method. In combining the methods we do not take the average of a stock's rank in each category, which might appear to be the most logical approach. The reason is that there is too much weighting to the earnings and yield selections which often overlap. What we do is rank each stock for each method and then take the lowest rank for each issue. Then, we concentrate on the stocks with the highest low rank. To date, we have found that this combining can add to both profit consistency and expanded return.

6. Loss Reduction. As previously discussed, the weekly Report, which applies the Time Overlay portfolio modeling to current market conditions, functions in a purely mechanical format. There is no allowance for subjectivity because it could function only to invalidate the results.

The losses, which at the time of this writing comprise only around 4 percent of the concluded positions, are often forced because of the mechanical structure, and we have found that this losing percentage can be significantly reduced.

Keeping in mind that the Report's structure only allows for changing positions in the model portfolios during outright buy/sell indications, recall that losses occur for two reasons.

At the time of a sell indication:

1. The specific stocks selected for sale to reduce investment level appear the most overvalued relative to the stock selection method but still might return high probabilities for future appreciation.

2. The stocks have been deleted from the Master List, which causes them to be sold first irrespective of their ranking when compared to the other holdings.

When incorporating rotation, quite often when a stock has been deleted from the Master List, it will have already been sold profitably between the predetermined buy/sell points in the published portfolio models. In other words, the published models are holding the position because an outright sale indication has not occurred, but the rotational application has sold the position profitably and now will not repurchase the stock because of its elimination from the Master List.

The Master List is extremely selective, and sometimes a stock is deleted because of only a very minor change in underlying fundamental quality. In fact, in some instances a stock can be kicked off the list briefly for a closer look at its condition and then be reinstated, in a sort of probationary period as its quarterly Report is reviewed. Under these circumstances, there is no reason to abandon the stock even though the Report's mechanical modeling will automatically kick it out. In actual theory, we will retain the stock as a holding (but not purchase any more of it) when it is close to qualifying for the list and compare it to the others when selling as though it still qualified for the list. This is significant in eliminating the forced sale effect.

We will not, however, wait forever for a stock to remain in a probationary phase. If the stock has not requalified for the list after two consecutive quarterly Reports, we will sell it.

Note that, of the very few positions the mechanical structure of the Report sold at a loss, 75 percent have so far subsequently doubled in value after being sold from the Report's selling price. In our own experience in actual Time Overlay portfolio management, which has involved many times the number of individual stock positions in the published models, at the time of this writing we have experienced only 12 losses, and most of those have been minimal (less than three points).

Continuous Full Investment

Many people firmly believed that market timing is impossible, and it is theoretically possible that our documented Time Overlay results are not a function of timing. The sample size and many years involving a wide variety of market conditions eliminate any statistical chance that the results were obtained by luck. However, it could be reasoned that our performance is a result of the strict criteria for the stocks we utilize (those on the Master List). That is, because the stocks we trade are of such high fundamental quality, they would have provided superior results irrespective of market timing.

To demonstrate that the timing aspect is valid, the weekly Report also follows Continuous Full Investment portfolio models for each stock selection method: earnings, yield, price. These models are always fully invested in common stock (no cash balance) and use the same stock selection technique that is used in Time Overlay modeling.

As with all the published portfolio models, the Continuous Full Investment models are purely mechanical to avoid any possibility of subjectivity. At the end of the first week after each quarter (March, June, September, December), the stocks on the Master List are reviewed as though there was a buy indication. The top ten specific stocks are selected for each selection method. Consequently, each selection method in Continuous Full Investment models always has ten specific stock positions. Model portfolio changes are made when any of the stocks being held from the previous quarter no longer qualifies for a top ten position: Those stocks no longer qualifying are deleted (sold) and replaced by those who have made it to the top ten.

The decision to make changes (if any) at the beginning of each quarter was not arbitrary. The end of the quarter often involves strong institutional window dressing pressure. In doing so, they will generally buy into stocks that are up (showing relative strength) and receiving positive media attention. By having these stocks in their portfolio, even if they bought them after the price gains, they can create the *impression* that they bought them properly and having the stocks demonstrates superior ability. Conversely, they will often sell those stocks that are low (demonstrating relative weakness) and receiving negative media attention. By eliminating the losers from their published holdings they have a chance to create the *impression* that the positions never existed and elude as any associated criticism. This institutional behavior is effectively buying high and selling low, not quite the formula for profit. Going opposite this action probably helps our Continuous Full Investment modeling.

The summaries of the Continuous models use the same format as Time Overlay, and are presented in Table 9.2. The results do not include dividends, which would accordingly add to return.

A comparison between the Continuous Full Investment results and those of the Time Overlay method (Table 9.1) demonstrates clearly that *our objectives have been realized.* The application of market timing significantly increases both the percentage of positions concluding profitably and annualized return.

The Continuous Full Investment section was originally included in the published portfolio modeling as a control section, that is, to provide a quantitative comparison showing the advantages of market timing. However, these models, in addition to their basic function, also allow insight into both theoretical and practical aspects of common stock investment.

Going back to the beginning of the Dow Jones Industrial Average, the yearly compounded growth rate has been 5½ percent. The average dividend yield has been around 4½ percent. Combing the two sources of return, the market on average over many years has provided around 10 percent. The Continuous Full Investment model's published results *do not include dividends.* By using a very simple, mechanical process, the Continuous Models have about doubled the historical growth rate for stocks as measured by the popularized Dow.

Not counting dividends which add an average of 3–4 percent in annualized return, the Continuous models have provided an annualized return of around 10 percent. Academicians can nod in agreement that around 10

Table 9.2. Continuous Full Investment Results

	Earnings		Yield		Price	
Total Positions	218		152		553	
Profit	135	61.93%	100	65.79%	304	54.98%
Loss	82	37.61%	52	34.21%	234	42.31%
Even	1	0.46%	0	0.00%	15	2.71%
Average positions						
Percentage	+	8.36%	+	7.37%	+	2.99%
Weeks held		35.17		50.79		14.80
Annualized	+	12.36%	+	7.55%	+	10.51%

percent is the average return (capital appreciation plus dividends) for stocks over an extended time period. However, the average return really depends on when you start counting. The 10-percent figure is no comfort to those who bought during market highs and who have experienced lower probability or losses. In our modeling, there is no flexibility in choosing when to begin the count. The models began their publication in 1977, period. Since then, if the Dow had kept pace with the Continuous Full Investment models, the Dow would now be around 4500. In other words, the boring Continuous ("control") modeling has managed to outpace the Dow by around 40 percent. This, we believe, is not by accident, and the basic Continuous modeling is actively incorporated in some types of managed account programs.

It is a widespread belief that market price is "proof" of a stock's merit or lack of it: Up is good, down is bad. Consequently, there is a natural tendency among the naive to buy stocks that have advanced and sell those that have declined. In other words, buy relative strength and sell relative weakness. The fact is that, although the worst may never go back up, even the very best experience periods of significant decline.

By design, the Continuous models almost always concentrate on those issues on the Master List that are demonstrating relative weakness and have, to date, significantly outperformed the popularized averages, which include stocks exhibiting a wide range of relative strength and weakness. As the results clearly attest, when the counting is done, purchasing the stocks we follow when they are demonstrating relative price weakness significantly outperforms those demonstrating relative strength.

In our modeling, the principal reason for this is the strict guidelines for inclusion on the Master List. In effect, after making a reasonable attempt to avoid the garbage that should go lower, the cheaper the price is, the better. One of the inherent problems faced by relative strength advocates is that they do not have discernible selling points until there has been some price erosion, which could be sudden and traumatic. For the broadly based market, the arguments as to the advantages/disadvantages of buying relative strength/weakness will likely go on forever because the underlying data is extremely mixed. Let them argue. We have settled the matter for ourselves by confining investment interest to stocks of superior fundamental quality, and by having very clear predetermined sell points, which do not necessarily involve price sacrifice.

It is no secret that the average managed account program (be it mutual funds, pensions, or whatever) does no better than the popular averages *minus* management fees and transaction costs. A manager's ability is often gauged by his/her performance to beat the popular averages. Consequently, a wide variety of investment methods are attempted to beat the averages, and the results obtained during any given time period can be extremely divergent as to over- or underperformance. However, to repeat, when all is said and done, almost all gravitate to a median return near the popular averages minus the costs.

Some investors allocate a fixed percentage of assets to stocks irrespective of market conditions. Many, in an attempt to avoid underperforming the overall market, have decided to construct their portfolio exactly as some popular "average" and let it be. Their return (minus management/administration fees and transaction costs) is going to be whatever the chosen average returns. This is called *indexing* and many millions of dollars are devoted to this practice.

There is no question that indexing suits these "investors'" purpose. However, with our Continuous Full Investment model results in hand, we can look at indexing and state without any reservation that it is basically stupid. The logic of our observation is elementary. The popular averages comprise a large number of stocks with a wide variance in fundamental quality. It makes no sense to us to initiate an investment in a stock that has shown itself to be fundamental junk, be it in the averages or not. The results clearly demonstrate that there is no reason to. We manage "index" funds, but rather than use the components of an average that includes stocks of dubious fundamental merit, our index is the Master List. So far, there has never been any problem with easily outperforming the popular averages, and we attribute this success to the concentration on fundamental quality. So, the return can be enhanced by concentrating on issues on the Master List that are most discounted.

When continuously fully invested, there is no way to avoid the effects of wide, broadly based swings (up or down) in market pricing. The agonies associated with being invested in depressed market conditions cannot be avoided, and there is little real consolation in having lost less than the popular averages.

In managed account programs requiring Continuous Full Investment, we have found that pricing volatility can be significantly smoothed by hedging by writing (selling short) index call options against the market valuation of the stocks being held. This is a little tricky in exceptionally volatile market conditions, and it will not be dealt with in great detail. However, the basic advantage derives from the option's premium. In flat markets, the capture of the premium adds to total return. In strongly advancing markets, the total return will be reduced from what it would be without the option hedge because of the option's appreciation, but the premium will shrink. In strongly declining markets, the downmove in the stock portfolio can be significantly reduced (often eliminated) by the reduction in the value of the short options.

This Continuous Full Investment (with hedging through the writing of index options) technique does not take all the volatility out of shifts in portfolio valuation, but it has so far evened out results. On average, the stocks involved have returned around 13 percent (dividends plus capital gains), and options have increased the return by about 3 percent for a total return of around 16 percent irrespective of market conditions. The only downside we have experienced so far in employing this technique is that the return is limited to this level. If the stocks go down, the options make up for the loss bringing the end annualized return to around the 16-percent mark. If the stocks go up, the short calls contain the return to around the 16-percent level. In any event, the returns using the hedging aspect have, to date, been overwhelmingly superior to standard index funds over extended time periods.

In Chap. 6, "Disciplined Folly," we discussed that most hedging techniques were unacceptable because they incorporated the acceptance of loss by means of the "hedge" and that losses should be avoided. In our application of the hedge, through index call writing, the *hedge itself is profitable over time* because of the option premiums.

Over the time the Continuous models have been published, to match the hedging results (dividends *not* included), the Dow Industrial Average would be around 5000, well above the 3200 level at the time of this writing.

The Continuous Full Investment (with hedging) technique can provide other advantages for some investors. For many, the psychological pressures associated with stock investment are so intense that they elicit irrational behavior. In other words, it can make some folks financially deranged. For those at risk of losing their sanity, the reduction in the volatility of portfolio valuation, while still maintaining a relatively high rate of return, can be comforting. Hedging also provides latitude as to the time the investment method is terminated. In Time Overlay modeling, as well as in Continuous modeling without hedging, the optimal time for terminating a program is at the conclusion of a market cycle: that is, after the criteria for a sell indication have fallen into place and the Time Overlay models are getting out of stocks. Because the Continuous modeling with hedging allows a more consistent rate of return, participation using this modeling can usually be terminated without much profit sacrifice at any time. This can be especially important for those who only want to participate in the market for a specified period irrespective of cyclical price changes.

Long-Term

When the publication of our portfolio modeling began, there were significant tax advantages for long-term capital gains. The Time Overlay portfolio modeling is therefore designed for maximum adaptation of any given market condition and has no concern for taxation aspects. To provide for the long-term tax advantage, mechanical models were included that concentrated on longer holding periods. These models buy exactly the same stocks as the Time Overlay selections, but do not sell until the first sell indication after the positions have been held a minimum of 53 weeks.

The tax laws have changed, eliminating the advantage in holding positions for an extended period. However, the Long-Term models are still published along with the others to both maintain the statistical base for comparisons and to be in place should the tax advantage return.

The result summaries for the Long-Term models, using the same format as with Time Overlay and Continuous Full Investment, are listed in Table 9.3. As with other models, dividends, which would accordingly add to return, are not included in the results.

Unlike the Continuous models, which do not utilize any direct market timing, the Long-Term models incorporate timing (only buying and selling in conjunction with appropriate signals) with a very significant time constraint.

Comparing the Long-Term results with those of Time Overlay and Continuous Full Investment, the profit consistency and associated compounding results are as anticipated. The best obtained by Time Overlay, which attempts to maximize the timing aspect, followed by the Long-Term, which uses timing modified by a time constraint, and the Continuous models, which do not incorporate timing, coming in last.

Without the tax advantage, the Long-Term models are of little practical significance, with their only current function being a control to demon-

Table 9.3. Long-Term Results

	Earnings		Yield		Price	
Total positions	355		355		355	
Profit	262	73.80%	254	71.55%	240	67.61%
Loss	88	24.79%	94	26.48%	114	32.11%
Even	5	1.41%	7	1.97%	1	.28%
Average positions						
Percentage	+	22.15%	+	13.51%	+	18.02%
Weeks held		61.30		60.43		61.63
Annualized	+	18.83%	+	11.63%	+	15.20%

strate the timing advantages. They are included because they are published in the Report along with the others and provide quantitatively the disadvantages in accurancy of profit consistency associated with the introduction of a time constraint.

Other Applications

One of the most common mistakes investors make is to understand one market and automatically extrapolate the theory and application to another market. All free, liquid, ongoing markets share identical characteristics as to greed and fear, but each functions under its own fundamental guidelines and the man-made structure of its trading mechanisms.

One reaction to our method might be that it is all well and fine, but it appears to be exceptionally conservative. That's right; it is very conservative by its design. The intent is to provide profit consistency and the associated benefits of compounding, as well as to minimize psychological strain.

Seeing the consistency of results, greedy eyes might sparkle at the thought of forgetting direct stock investment, and going to the listed options market. There the purchase of options allows huge leverage and predefined risk with the possibility of achieving fantastic returns.

Keep in mind that the focus of this text is profit extraction through the use of specific common stocks and, although options are a common stock derivative, each market functions somewhat differently. Our modeling has no great concern as to how long any stock position is held. As can be seen in the appendices, some positions have been held for only a few weeks while others have been held for years. The option buyer has to overcome time and premium disadvantages, which can result in being correct on the stock, but losing because of the time and/or premium erosion. There are option applications, but they are beyond the scope of this text and will likely be a more closely examined topic in the future. We do not publish option portfolio modeling and do not manage option accounts except for the application to Continuous Full Investment hedging.

Options, in addition to the complexities involved in deciphering the shifts in premium and time, also create tremendous psychological pressures for most investors and require very astute capital base management. In reviewing the specific positions of Time Overlay in the appendices, it is obvious that the best results, to date, would be the purchases associated with buy indications resulting in a very high investment level. This is true, but it is still a tricky business, which involves excessive risk for those inadequately prepared. This does not imply that the option markets cannot be beaten; they can, on both the buy and the write sides. However, a thorough description would require a text about as thick as this one. Without a strong background, we would strongly suggest that the option markets be avoided despite their lure.

There is a strong correlation between stock pricing and interest rates: Lower rates generally boost stock prices, and higher rates generally depress stock prices. This is why interest-rate-sensitive data is involved in many of our ancillary criteria (Chap. 8) in determining buy and sell points. Because of this, there is a correlation between shifts in bond pricing and our stock portfolio modeling. This correlation is especially applicable to our Time Overlay Yield models which, by definition, is interest-rate-sensitive.

Although the bond portfolio modeling is not published, we manage large bond portfolios, not by the direct purchase of specific individual bonds, but by purchase/sale of closed-end bond funds; discussed in Chap. 10.

The Time Overlay stock selection methods (earnings, yield, price) each function independently, resulting in different investment levels for each category (Appendix B). Only the Yield category is appropriate for the bond portfolio modeling.

When the probabilities for lower interest rates are greatest, you should be more heavily exposed to long-term bonds, which will experience the greatest capital appreciation should rates decline. Conversely, when higher rates are anticipated, the long-term sector, which will show the most price erosion as rates go up, should be avoided with monies applied to very short-term instruments that will not experience the downward price shift.

Aside from the determination as to which bond fund to select (discussed in the next chapter), the application is simple. The percentage of monies applied to the long-term bonds match the Time Overlay Yield investment level, with the remainder applied to the short-term maturities. For example, if the investment level is 23 percent, then 23 percent of the account's worth would be in long-term funds, with 77 percent in short-term cash equivalents. At extremes, if the investment level was 100 percent, we would be all long term, if 0 percent, all short term, with the differences between reflecting shifts in probabilities.

Mutual fund switching has grown in popularity with a variety of no-load (no sales charges) funds allowing investors to buy and sell the fund quite easily. One of the reasons for the popularity of such funds, beyond the fact that sales charges are eliminated (which is a real benefit), is that they give the impression that the investor can enter and exit the market for free. This perception, of course, is nonsense. Although the sales charge has been eliminated, the no-load funds are paying transaction costs when they buy or sell and have management and administrative fees.

Although most investors would probably be better served to manage their own funds, the availability of no-load mutual funds that switches into and out of the market very quickly and easily does offer some timing advantages. Most popular no-load mutual fund switching techniques are nothing other than trend following. The problem is not in the timing, but in selecting the most advantageous fund. The authors do not publish no-load mutual fund switching methods or manage such accounts, simply because the results are not as good as they are often portrayed. We have found it far more beneficial to utilize closed-end funds because of the discount advantage (Chap. 10).

Keep in mind that our market timing technique is centered around our objective of profit extraction through the buying and selling of the stocks that qualify for the Master List (Chap. 2). Although this small universe of stocks will usually advance/decline as a group in conjunction with the popular averages, they sometimes significantly diverge. Consequently, it cannot be assumed that our buy/sell points will match the popular averages.

Because of the leverage involved, it can be tempting to use the methods discussed in this book in the trading of stock index and bond futures. However, as with options, such assumed extrapolations can be very dangerous.

The focus of this writing is profit extraction by the use of specific stocks (or closed-end funds), with broadly based market movements incorporated as an aid rather than as a means pinpointing exact tops and bottoms in the popularized averages. Stated differently, our first concern is with specific stock selection from our narrow universe of stocks; movements in the averages take a secondary (but very important) role.

In trading stock index or bond futures (or for any type of ongoing liquid futures market, such as gold, soybeans, pork bellies, and the like), much better timing techniques are available. The best involve what is termed *level and subset betting* (note the the word *betting* is substituted for *investment*), which is relatively complex and forms the basis for another text. If you are going to get involved in the futures markets, there is no reason not to use the best, most specific methods available rather than trying to quickly extrapolate one market to another.

Futures trading is far more complex than often portrayed. The primary reason is the leverage involved, which requires very careful capital base management, that is, not being forced out because of a lack of capital when implementing and retaining positions. For those lured into the futures markets without adequate, specific preparation, it might be helpful to note that several studies show that around 85 percent of those who "invest" in futures lose and about 85 percent of the trading methods attempt to be trend following. The best methods we have found are those designed to isolate significant trend reversals. To explain this adequately is not within the scope of this book. In other words, learn one game at a time and learn it well.

All the specific stock selection methods we have described involve a buy-to-sell process. They do not incorporate short selling, and it might be automatically assumed that the process can be reversed to profit at the same rate using the sell to buy process. Not so. To understand why, recall material from earlier chapters. First, the stocks utilized were generally selected because the earnings were both predictable and forecast to be increasing. This rigid selection criterion has allowed our stocks to have an upward bias relative to the overall market, as clearly demonstrated in the Continuous Full Investment results. Second, the stock selection process attempted to identify issues in the maturity stage (Chap. 6) of corporate life cycles. This helps ensure that market price will be influenced by earnings gains more than downward shifts in P/E.

Without presenting charts and resorting to lengthy discussion, let it just be said that the methods cannot be automatically reversed to accommodate short selling. If you are going to do short selling, it is only reasonable to avoid stocks that have a demonstrated upward bias because of superior fundamentals.

To offset the upward bias of the specific stocks utilized in the Time Overlay models, it might seem reasonable to simply substitute stocks with terrible fundamentals and incorporate them into a short selling method. The task, however, is far from simple for four reasons.

1. Stocks with terrible fundamentals are often highly unpredictable. For example, a corporation whose earnings appear to be heading toward bankruptcy can often have assets that have a real value well in excess of book value, making the company worth more than the earnings fundamentals indicate. The corporation may have properties or licenses that have been written down over time on their financial statements, but are actually quite valuable. To sift through the corporation's statements to ensure that such assets are not present is extremely difficult and time-consuming.

2. Corporations in bad financial shape have generally already achieved low price and/or volume characteristics, which make professional participation difficult.

3. Shaky stocks generally do not have institutional involvement, which detracts from our profit potential and makes the issues more vulnerable to manipulation.

4. To short, you must borrow the stock. If it becomes obvious that a corporation is going to belly up, the stock might not be made available for borrowing by you; having been taken by trading insiders.

We do not mean to imply that short selling is not viable because it certainly can be profitable. However, we have found that the best targets are not stocks that everyone already knows are rotten. Short selling candidates are the "hot stocks" that, when the overall market is overpriced, do not have the fundamentals to support ongoing elevated P/Es. During euphoric speculative periods something is always well overpriced depending on the cycle: casinos, biotech, computers, oils, and so on. They all have their turn and, as anyone with experience in the market knows, when they lose the favor of the speculative crowd, they go splat.

We are not going into a detailed description of selecting stocks to sell short because it is too lengthy and would take away from this book's central themes. We mention going after the "high flyers" during overpriced (low investment level) market conditions because in doing so the previously mentioned four difficulties are often overcome.

Specific methods involving short selling are discussed in Chap. 10.

Summary

We have isolated and discussed all the elements of a basic, total investment strategy.

We have developed an understanding of the nature of the market including the various market participants and trading mechanisms. We have eliminated confusion by concentrating attention on our objective of extracting profit through common stock trading by developing a logical, easily implemented, step-by-step process. This process provides predetermined buy/sell points involving a method of market timing coupled with a variety of methods for specific stock selection. And we have tested the techniques over a lengthy period in a format that makes hindsight or omission impossible.

We can now leave Drach's work and concentrate on Herzfeld's, applying the basic concepts of the first eight chapters to a specialized investment area: closed-end funds.

10

Closed-End Funds

In preceding chapters, one of the points emphasized was that it can be extremely dangerous to automatically assume that the characteristics of one market (or a section of it) can be easily transposed to another. All freely traded liquid markets share common traits related to psychological pressures (fear and greed), but each differs as to fundamental relationships, trading mechanisms, and structural factors. Each market's individual characteristics must be understood. Once this understanding has been achieved, proper evaluation of similarities or differences, as well as interrelated pricing effects, with other markets can be accomplished.

One market that allows easy application of Drach's common stock analysis is closed-end funds, also known as *publicly traded funds* or *closed-end investment trusts* (*CEITs*). In this chapter we are going to discuss the basic characteristics of closed-end funds and the specific application of Drach's timing and selection techniques to them.

Background

Although one of the oldest forms of investment, closed-end funds are among the most misunderstood and consequently often overlooked investment areas. Their origin can be traced back to the establishment of a Belgian fund in 1822; thereafter they flourished, particularly among English and Scottish investors in the latter 1800s. The first U.S. fund was formed in 1893 and, until the time of the stock market crash of 1929, closed-end funds were the dominant form of publically owned investment companies.

The dominance of closed-end funds ended with the arrival of mass appeal open-end investment companies. There are currently almost 4000 open-end funds with assets well over $1\frac{1}{2}$ trillion dollars, far surpassing the number of publicly traded closed-end funds (almost 400) with assets approaching $150 billion.

Net Asset Value (NAV)

Both closed- and open-end funds share the same fundamental purpose. They are both investment companies; that is, they are companies whose business it is to invest in the securities markets, primarily stocks and bonds. The investor (stockholder) in either type of fund owns a proportionate share of the assets of the investment company.

To determine the value of each share of an investment company (open-end or closed-end) is usually an easy process. Add up the assets at their current market value and divide by the number of outstanding shares.

For example, let's say the market value of the assets (stocks, bonds, cash, and the like) of a fund is $15,000,000 and there are 1,000,000 shares outstanding. The *net asset value (NAV)* would be:

$$\frac{\$15,000,000}{1,000,000 \text{ shares}} = \$15/\text{share}$$

With the number of shares constant, the net asset value will fluctuate with changes in the market value of the assets that the fund holds.

Capitalization

The major difference between open-end and closed-end funds is the method by which they are capitalized.

In *open capitalization*, when an investor purchases shares, the fund issues new shares, thereby increasing the number of shares outstanding. Conversely, when the investor sells shares, the fund purchases (redeems) the shares, paying the investor the proportional amount of the fund's assets and reducing the number of outstanding shares. The capitalization is variable. That is, the amount of assets under the fund's management changes as a result of the net purchases or sales (redemptions) of shares.

In *closed capitalization*, the investment company has a fixed amount of shares just like an industrial corporation. The shares trade in the open market. As investors buy and sell the shares, the number of outstanding shares remains constant. The capitalization is fixed. That is, the amount of assets under the fund's management does not change as the result of the shares being traded.

These methods of capitalization might at first seem insignificant. After all, if a fund is going to do well or poorly in its chosen investments, it might be logical to assume that the value of the shares will appreciate or depreciate accordingly. This is *not* the case. To understand why, we must examine differentials in pricing mechanisms.

Pricing

When buying or selling either an open-end or closed-end fund, an investor usually knows the current value of the fund's assets per share (NAV).

For example, to buy an open-end fund with a NAV of $15, an investor pays $15 per share. The fund simply issues new shares to the investor at the current NAV. The assets the fund manages have increased, but the value per share remains the same because the new shares have exactly the same value as the other shares. If the investor sells, he or she is paid the NAV. The amount of assets the fund manages has been reduced, but the NAV of outstanding shares has not changed because the shares redeemed were equal in value to all others.

With closed-end funds, the shares are traded in the open market and are consequently subject to demand/supply imbalances. They may trade at a price greater than their NAV (termed a *premium*) or at a price below the NAV (termed a *discount*).

For example, if the NAV is $15 and the closed-end fund's stock is selling at 16½ ($1.50 above the NAV), the fund would be trading at a 10-percent *premium*. That is, the stock price is 10 percent greater than the NAV. Conversely, if the closed-end fund's stock is selling at 13½ with a NAV of 15, the shares would have a 10-percent discount. That is, they would be trading at 10 percent below the NAV.

With the exception of some dual-purpose funds and a few specialty funds, almost *all* closed-end funds have at some time sold at discounts to NAV. The weekly listing of closed-end funds in many major financial publications often includes the percentage differential (premium or discount) between the closed-end fund's current market price and NAV. Such data is easily accessible.

We can now begin to see why closed-end funds can provide advantages. When selling at a discount, the investor is able to purchase assets below their portfolio's underlying market valuation. In addition, the premium/discount can vary with changing market conditions and shifts in investor sentiment. When the market is overpriced and optimism prevails, premiums tend to increase and discounts narrow. When the market is depressed and pessimism dominates, premiums tend to fall and discounts widen.

Costs

Both open- and closed-end funds have both management and administrative fees. They also bear transaction costs associated with the fund's buying and selling of securities.

Fund expenses aside, the investor also has some costs. Open-end funds may require a sales charge (termed the *load*), which the investor must pay when buying shares in the fund, or they may not have a sales charge (termed a *no-load*). In addition, open-end funds may charge the investor a redemption fee, that is, a charge when the shares are sold. Some open-end funds also have a *12b-1 charge*, which is basically an advertising expense. A "pure" no-load fund has no sales, redemption, or 12b-1 charges.

Closed-end funds have no special purchase or redemption costs. The transaction costs (commissions, markups, markdowns) the investor pays are the same as when buying any other stock on listed exchanges or over-the-counter.

Many studies involving large sample sizes have shown that (by group) there is no significant difference in NAV performance between closed-end, load open-end, or no-load open-end funds over long periods, although closed-end funds have an edge. From this, it can appear reasonable that the fund investor should confine interest to pure no-load open-end funds, thereby eliminating sales charges, redemption fees, 12b-1 costs, and commissions, or markups/downs involved in CEIT purchases. The costs reductions add to return by allowing more principal to work.

Everything else being equal, there is no question that pure no-load funds would be preferable. However, *all is not equal!*

Premium/Discount Functions

Since almost all closed-end funds tend to sell at a discount, it can appear obvious that there is no reason to purchase closed-end funds when they are selling at a premium. Sometimes a special feature, for example, a closed-end fund having a private placement in its portfolio which is about to go public as a hot issue, may justify purchase at a premium. Otherwise, it is difficult to make a case for paying a price higher than NAV.

Central to the advantages of closed-end funds is the discount; both as to dividends and as to pricing variances.

Relative to *dividends*, purchasing a fund selling at a wide discount effectively provides leverage at no cost. This is especially important in bond funds and funds specializing in high-yielding stocks. Let's say the fund is purchased when it is selling at a 20-percent discount. The investor is effectively paying 80 cents for each $1 of assets. As a consequence, the investor is receiving dividends from $1 worth of investments, having paid only 80 cents.

The amount of the discount can vary dramatically with the greatest changes usually occurring during extreme market conditions. In depressed markets, discounts in the double digits are common. When investors become overly optimistic, discounts can be significantly reduced or even change to premiums. By properly incorporating market timing, closed-end funds can significantly outperform their open-end counterparts.

For example, let's say the NAV of both a closed-end fund and an open-end fund is $10, and the dominant sentiment is that the market stinks. Because of prevailing pessimism, the closed-end fund is selling at a 20-percent discount, a market price of $8. The open-end fund would be selling at its NAV of $10.

Now let's say that the market advances 10 percent and optimism returns. The NAV of both the open- and closed-end fund has appreciated to $11. As is usually the case then, investors become optimistic because of elevated prices. Let's say the discount on the closed-end fund has narrowed: in our example from 20 to 10 percent.

The price gain on the open-end fund has been $1 ($10 to $11, the 10 percent increase in NAV). The price gain of the closed-end fund is $1\frac{7}{8}$ (from 8 to $9\frac{7}{8}$, a combination of both the change in NAV and the narrowed discount). The change in NAV for the open- and closed-end fund has been equal, but the closed-end fund's share price has gained 23 percent while the open-end shares appreciated 10 percent. The closed-end fund more than doubled the return available from the open-end fund.

Of course, if the closed-end fund was purchased in an untimely fashion, the closed-end fund would perform worse (perhaps dramatically) than the comparable open-end fund.

Why Discounts Exist

A primary reason for discounts is a lack of sponsorship. If a securities salesperson (dependent on commissions) has a choice of selling someone an existing closed-end fund (say at a regular stock commission of around 1 percent) or a load mutual fund with a sales charge (that can be as much as 8 percent), the incentive is to direct "investors" to the open-end fund.

The incentives associated with higher sales charges can be easily observed when new closed-end funds are issued. In new issues, compensation is by underwriting fees. A typical fee is 7 to 8 percent. If a fund was coming public at $10 per share, an 8-percent underwriting fee would be 80 cents per share.

The buyer does not see a commission and the naive might think that, by buying a new issue, a transaction cost is being avoided. The cost in our example (8 percent) is far higher than a standard commission on a stock trade. Although the buyer is paying $10 per share, the new closed-end fund is only being capitalized at $9.20 per share after paying the underwriter's fee. The net asset value is $9.20. In effect, the buyer is paying a premium from the onset.

As previously discussed, almost all closed-end funds eventually trade at a discount to NAV. From this, it is easy to conclude that the buyer in our example has incurred the risks involved in paying a premium for an investment that is likely destined to develop a discount. This conclusion is absolutely correct. Yet the securities industry was not deterred from selling billions of dollars of new closed-end funds in the 1980s at the same time that established closed-end funds could be purchased at substantial discounts.

Discounts can occur for reasons other than a lack of sponsorship: poor yield, subpar performance, a heavy supply of competitive issues, high expense ratios, illiquid portfolios, and potential capital gains tax liabilities. Of course, all these negative factors also affect open-end funds, which will trade at NAV despite inefficiencies.

Note that some closed-end funds can be converted to open-end funds. In these instances, if the closed-end fund is selling at a discount, the price will appreciate to the NAV at the time of conversion.

Management Pressures

Management's income is usually based on a percentage of the market value of the securities in the fund. The larger the asset base is, the greater the income. Both open- and closed-end fund managers are (at least theoretically) compensated to provide superior investment performance. If the value of the assets being managed grows, the management fees expand proportionately. In addition to pressures associated with performance, the open-end fund manager is faced with problems that can arise form variable capitalization.

Statistically, there is virtually no question that the popularity of both closed-end and open-end funds varies with market conditions. When the market is high, especially during periods of excessive speculation, open-end mutual fund sales increase (sometimes very dramatically), and there is an increase in the number of new closed-end funds. When the market is depressed, open-end sales decline (sometimes redemptions dominate), and there are few new closed-end funds formed.

Generally, someone who purchases a mutual fund does so with the presumption that the fund's management will invest the money in whatever investment the fund was designed for: stocks, bonds, or the like. Even the open-end fund manager who knows that the market is overpriced and destined to falter can be pressured to buy stocks because of the demands of stockholders. Conversely, if prices are depressed and shareholders want to sell (redeem), the open-end fund manager can be forced to sell at depressed prices to raise the cash necessary to pay for redemptions. In effect, the open-end fund management can be forced into the precise formula for loss (buying high and selling low) by following the demands of clientele.

The closed-end fund manager has the benefit of fixed capitalization. If shareholders do not like the management and/or market conditions, they can sell their shares in the open market. The closed-end fund's capitalization is therefore not affected.

Some critics contend that the fixed capitalization of closed-end funds can create lethargic management because the asset base is not exposed to the risk of being sold by discontent shareholders, as they are in open-end funds. The previously mentioned close average performance by various fund types negates this criticism.

Most managers would obviously prefer fixed capitalization, avoiding both the risk of losing assets resulting from shareholder sales and being forced into investment decisions by shareholder demands. Investors obviously prefer variable capitalization, avoiding the discount discomfitures, as evidenced by the far larger number of open-end funds than closed-end.

Measuring Discounts/Premiums

In determining which specific closed-end fund provides the best buying opportunity, it might appear that the process is exceptionally simple: Just see which one is selling at the widest discount and buy it.

Unfortunately, the process is a bit more complicated. As previously discussed, there are valid reasons for discounts. There is also a wide variety of fund types: equity (stocks in general or in industrial sectors), bonds (different types, such as municipal, corporate, foreign, or U.S. government; all with varying maturities), convertible bonds (combining both bond and stock characteristics), specialty (confining interest to a specific country, a very narrow industry sector, venture capital, or specific private placements), dual-purpose (where the fund seeks both capital gains and income), or anything else that can generate public interest and enough sales to capitalize the fund.

One way to simplify the process of deciding which funds to buy is to determine an "average" premium/discount over an extended period and then determine the degree of discounting at any given time by comparing the current discount to the average discount.

For example, let's say we are looking at two funds. Fund A is selling at a 10-percent discount and its average discount is also 10 percent. Fund B is selling at an 8-percent discount, but its average is 4 percent. The gross discount of Fund A is greater than Fund B (10 percent versus 8 percent). Fund B, however, would represent the better purchase based on its past because it is 4 percent below its average discount, while Fund A is not below the past average discount. All other factors being equal, Fund B would be preferable because normalization to the average discount would involve capital appreciation, whereas Fund A is already normalized to its past average.

The length of time utilized to determine the average past discount depends on investor preference. We use a rather lengthy time period (usually four years for funds that have been in existence that long), using discounts on a weekly basis. That is, the discount at the end of each week for the past 208 weeks is added up and then divided by 208, thereby deriving the average. When the next week's discount is added, the oldest past week is subtracted, as in any other moving average.

The average discount calculation need not be as lengthy as the one we use. Yet an extended period is generally helpful because many funds come to market when there is a speculative binge and the fund's structure (investment types) appeals to emotionalism. This effect was clearly evident during the rage in the late 1980s for single-country funds. Once sold to the public, the funds often traded at very high premiums before settling to discounts. Using a short time period to determine the average discount could give the initial impression that these funds would always sell at a premium when, in fact, after they were "seasoned," the premiums went poof.

We have attempted to provide only a very general outline of closed-end fund characteristics, just enough to apply our analytical techniques to closed-end funds. A very thorough discussion of closed-end funds can be found in *Herzfeld's Guide to Closed-End Funds*, by Thomas Herzfeld (McGraw-Hill, 1993).

Applying Specific Market Timing and Selection Techniques to Closed-End Funds

The ease of adapting Drach's methods to closed-end funds is based on the similarity of scanning for relative discounting. The essence of the timing technique is to attempt to expand common stock investment when the overall market is relatively low, confining investment interest to stocks that qualify for the Master List (Chap. 2), which appear relatively discounted to the others.

Scanning for the most appropriate closed-end fund based on discounts has the same objective: isolating the cheapest. In Drach's objectives, he is searching for specific stocks that are overly discounted. In Herzfeld's closed-end fund analysis, he is searching for the most discounted fund. The focus of both techniques is to isolate excessive discounts relative to historical/statistical norms.

A significant differential between Drach's concentration on specific stock and Herzfeld's concentration on specific funds is that the funds, by their structure, involve diversity in the number of different positions.

As can be seen in Appendixes C, D, and E, listing Drach's published results, he has been successful in approximately 49 of every 50 stock positions. Although the probabilities are quite low, it is possible for a portfolio lacking diversity to be overly exposed in the few losing positions. Also, as the results demonstrate, there is a wide variance in the degree of profitability in individual stock positions. A portfolio lacking full diversity could by chance be weighted in the lower spectrum of profitability or by the same chance far outperform Drach's published modeling by being weighted in the more profitable trades.

In almost all closed-end equity funds, some positions fail to qualify for Drach's Master List and consequently carry the probability of underperforming the Master List issues. In other words, the diversity of holdings in a closed-end fund can make the fund underperform Drach's specific stock selections, but can smooth returns. Stated differently, the pricing volatility inherent in Drach's head-on, rigid approach to specific common stocks is reduced in closed-end fund application.

The decision to utilize specified stocks or closed-end funds in our techniques depends on the individual investor's goals, needs, and resources, as on well as the ability to withstand psychological pressures.

The investment techniques described in this text can be divided into five basic trading strategies:

1. Time Overlay
2. Bonds

3. Continuous Full Investment without hedging

4. Continuous Full Investment with hedging

5. Long-Term

1. Time Overlay

The application of the timing method to closed-end funds is straightforward. As you can see in Appendix B, the degree of exposure to common stocks (investment level) varies with buy/sell indications. Using the Composite investment level as a guide, the percentage of monies allocated to closed-end funds versus the percentage retained in cash equivalents parallels the composite figure.

The Composite investment level is based on factors affecting the pricing of common stocks. Consequently, the closed-end funds surveyed for possible purchase are those heavily weighted in equity investment (stocks or, in some instances, convertible bond funds). Funds that can quickly and dramatically alter their asset allocations (percentage changes in stocks, bonds, and cash) are less suitable than those that maintain heavy equity exposure because the fund's allocation changes run the risk of mismatching our investment level.

The selection of specific funds is the result of surveying the discount differentials, with those funds demonstrating the greatest discounts relative to their historical norms generally preferable.

For example, if you had purchased Morgan Greenfell SMALLCap Fund, Inc. in February 1990, when Drach issued a buy recommendation, you would have been buying the fund at a 14-percent discount to net asset value, at $8½. Beginning in May 1990, when Drach announced his sell recommendation, and through July 1990, you could have sold the fund as it narrowed to a 3-percent discount from net asset value at 11 to 11½, a gain of approximately 35 percent.

Throughout the August and September 1990 buy signals, you could have purchased H&Q Healthcare Investors, Inc. at a wide 21-percent discount, trading at 8⅞. When investment level was reduced in February, March, and April 1991, the fund had narrowed to 3- to 5-percent discounts, and the price had increased to 13.

2. Bond Funds

In both the primary and many of the ancillary criteria that determine buy/sell signals, interest rate projections play an important role. When stocks are priced at reasonable or discounted levels relative to historical fundamental norms, lowering interest rates can have a strong positive effect. Conversely, especially when stocks are overvalued relative to fundamentals, higher interest rates can be shown to have a very negative effect on stock pricing.

The effect on bonds (and bond funds) resulting from interest rate changes are more straightforward than stock pricing relationships because the effect on stocks at any given time depends on stock price levels. The effect on bonds is direct: Lower rates create higher bond prices, and higher rates result in lower bond prices. The effect of rate changes on bond prices can be more dramatic than many investors realize, with the greater price shifts associated with longer maturities.

For example, using a base interest rate of 8 percent with the bond trading at par, let's say interest rates go down 1 percentage point to 7 percent. A 2½ year bond would generally appreciate 2 percent, a 10-year maturity would gain about 7 percent. And, a 20-year bond would appreciate around 11 percent. If the change was 2 percentage points (rates dropping from 8 percent to 6 percent), the 2½-year maturity would gain about 5 percent, the 10-year would go up about 15 percent, and the 20-year would appreciate around 23 percent.

Now let's take a look at the opposite effect, and say rates increased 1 percentage point from 8 percent to 9 percent. The 2½-year maturity would decline about 2 percent, the 10-year about 7 percent, and the 20-year nearly 9 percent. A 2-percentage point increase (from 8 to 10 percent) would drop the value of the 2½-year bond about 2 percent, the 10-year down around 13 percent, and the 20-year would incur a loss of approximately 17 percent.

These gains/losses associated with changing interest rates demonstrate two points. First, and most important, the market value of bonds of all qualities can change dramatically with changes in interest rates. Second, although in our example we were starting with an 8-percent bond selling at par value, there is not an identical correlation between plus/minus interest rate changes and bond value. This is because of potential capital gains/losses associated with bonds selling below/above par and held to maturity.

Because of the large potential swings in the market price of outstanding bonds, a timing technique providing a reasonable forecast of rate changes is extremely valuable in both reducing risk and expanding return, In Appendix B, there is an investment level associated with yield-sensitive stocks, those most affected by changes in interest rates. In the closed-end fund application, the attempt is simply to match the yield investment level. When the yield investment level is high, purchase bond funds, and then accordingly sell them when the yield investment level is reduced. The specific bond funds chosen for purchase would usually be those exhibiting the greatest discount relative to historical discount norms, concentrating on funds with longer maturities, which provide the largest potential capital gains.

A good example can be found with one of the Putnam family of closed-end funds, Putnam Premier Income Trust. When Drach went to 125 percent investment at the end of April 1990, the fund was trading at a 15-percent discount to net asset value, at 6⅝ per share. In fact, I wrote an article in *Barron's* about this Putnam fund, and some similar Putnam issues ("Pummeled, Promising: Why a Pro Favors Four Putnam Closed-Ends") *Barron's*, May, 14, 1990. We began to sell the position at the end of May 1990, when Drach issued a sell indication as the discount narrowed to 8 percent and continued to sell around 7¼. When Drach went to 100-percent investment in late August/early September, 1990 we again became a buyer of the fund at a 21-percent discount at the $6⅛ level, and held it until Drach's investment level was reduced to 37 percent in March, 1991. During the six months we held this conservative bond fund (35% investment in U.S. governments, at the time) it had gained 24 percent to 7⅝ and was trading at a 4-percent discount to net asset value.

3. Continuous Full Investment Without Hedging

In the published common stock portfolio modeling the Continuous Full Investment portfolio models were included to function as a control to allow objective comparisons with the market timing models.

Although intended as a control, allowing demonstration of the validity of the timing technique, the Continuous Models have significantly outperformed the broadly based popularized market averages. The reasons for this superior performance are twofold. First, the rigid requirements for stocks to qualify for the Master List (Chap. 2) results in the stocks comprising the Continuous Models to be of usually superior fundamental quality, thereby giving the group an upward bias relative to the overall market. Second, the Continuous Models change positions in a gradual, relatively slow process in which new positions are selected that are among the most discounted (low-priced relative to the others) on the list. In effect, a rotational process adds those that have become more discounted and deletes those less discounted.

In applying this concept to closed-end funds, the search for relative discounting is the same. Purchases are confined to the issues demonstrating the largest current discount relative to historical norms and selling those whose discount has lessened.

There is a very significant difference between the published Continuous modeling that is confined to stocks on the Master List and the basic modeling when applied to closed-end funds. The stock modeling, by definition, is confined to stocks. The wide variety of different types of closed-end funds allows many more choices when searching for those specific funds demonstrating the most potentially advantageous discounts. For example, four single-country funds invest primarily in German companies. In January 1991, you could have sold The Germany Fund at an 18-percent premium to net asset value and in the same month moved into The New Germany Fund, then trading at a 20-percent discount. A month later New Germany Fund was trading at its net asset value, while The Future Germany Fund was an obvious switch at a 17-percent discount. The Future Germany Fund's discount narrowed to the 1-percent range by October, although The Emerging Germany Fund's discount still stood at 10 percent from net asset value. Just a month later, The Emerging Germany Fund's discount had narrowed to 3 percent, while The New Germany Fund's discount had widened to 20 percent.

The convertible funds also provide a good example of this technique. TCW Convertible Fund was trading at a 10-percent discount at $8\frac{1}{8}$ in February 1991. At the same time, Castle Convertible Fund was trading at a 15-percent discount at $16\frac{3}{4}$. By March of that year, Castle Convertible Fund's share price had gained 14 percent to $19 per share, moving it to about a 10-percent discount, while TCW Convertible Fund had moved to an 8-percent discount, its share price declining 12 percent to $7\frac{1}{8}$—an 8-percent discount to net asset value. If you had been a buyer of TCW Convertible Fund at that time and sold it six months later, when it was trading at a 13-percent premium at $8\frac{7}{8}$, you would have pocketed a 24-percent gain plus six months' worth of dividends. When you sold, you could have switched into another convertible fund, Lincoln National Convertible Fund, then at a 15-percent discount at a share price of $14\frac{3}{8}$, which over the next two months increased in price by 8 percent to $15\frac{1}{2}$. Thus, it is possible to continually rotate within the same group of funds, buying the one(s) with the widest discount(s).

4. Continuous Full Investment with Hedging

In the common stock investment techniques, the most obvious hedging strategy might be to be long the stocks that are relatively discounted and sell short those that appear most overpriced. However, the process is not so simple.

Because of the composition of the Master List, the stocks as a group tend to do significantly better than the market as a whole. Consequently, although the long positions have significantly outperformed the broadly based market, the short positions, if sold, will likely provide lesser returns than the overall market.

It is because of the Master List's positive bias that in hedging accounts Drach utilizes writing index call options as a substitute for the short side. This substitution both eliminates the effect of the Master List's upside bias that would be experienced in attempting to short Master List stocks and provides added profitability for the short side because of premium capture. As discussed in Chap. 9, the method of going long the selected Master List issues and proportionately shorting (selling) index call options is a lethargic process, which has so far produced a constant annualized return of about 15 percent irrespective of overall market conditions.

The hedging limitations resulting from investment considerations confined to the Master List and index call writing can be overcome with closed-end funds because of both the diversity in fund types and the discount function.

A very large number of hedging strategies have been developed by imaginative closed-end fund traders. In this writing we will limit our discussion to the six most popular and easily understood.

1. Buy a closed-end fund selling at an excessive discount, at the same time sell a closed-end fund that is priced at a premium. If a down market carries the first fund's shares still lower, it will almost surely do greater damage to the premium-priced fund, enabling the short side to cover at a profit that more than offsets the long side's loss. On the other hand, should the market advance, the excessively discounted fund will likely appreciate more than the fund selling at a premium.

For example, in February 1991 Gabelli Equity Trust was trading at an 8-percent premium to net asset value at $12\frac{3}{8}$, while another diversified equity fund, General American Investors, was at a 13-percent discount, at a price of $20\frac{3}{4}$.

By November 4, 1991, Gabelli Equity Trust had declined 21 percent to $9\frac{3}{4}$ and was trading at a discount of 12 percent to net asset value, while General American had increased by 30 percent to $27 per share and its discount had narrowed to 8 percent.

2. Buy a closed-end fund at an excessive discount, and meanwhile go short on an equivalent proportional amount of individual stocks in the same fund's portfolio. During a rally, the NAV will rise in direct proportion to the rise in the short positions. However, the long position in the fund will probably outperform the rise in the fund's stocks as the discount

narrows. Should the market fall, because the fund was purchased at an excessive discount, the decline will likely be less than the fall of the individual stocks shorted.

For example, in September 1991 you could have purchased H&Q Healthcare Fund at $16\frac{5}{8}$ at an 11-percent discount to net asset value and sold short its largest positions at the prices indicated in Table 10.1.

On November 1, 1991 you could have sold the H&Q Healthcare position at a 14-percent premium to net asset value at a price of $23\frac{3}{4}$, a gain of approximately 45 percent, while the short positions created a loss of approximately 6 percent, thereby leaving a net gain of 39 percent.

3. Buy a closed-end bond fund at an excessive discount; sell short U.S. Treasury bond futures, or a combination of U.S. Treasury and corporate bonds. If the bond market rallies and the excessive discount of the bond fund narrows, the long position will generally become more profitable than the short positions. The loss in the shorts will mirror the performance of the overall bond market. But, because of the leverage factor in buying the closed-end bond fund at an excessive discount, it will usually produce a larger profit than the loss on the short position. If the bond market declines, the losses on the short positions will usually be greater than the loss in the bond funds because of the excessive discount at the time of purchase; that is, the discount is not likely to widen.

A typical closed-end bond fund hedge involving Treasury bond futures would have looked something like this on December 2, 1977, with the Dow Jones Bond Average at 91.91 The following long positions could have been established: 2000 shares of John Hancock Income Securities (JHS) with a net asset value of 20.29, a discount of 18.7 percent, and a per-share price of $16\frac{1}{2}$ for a cost of $34,650; 2100 Drexel Bond Fund (DBF) with a net asset value of 20.29, a discount of 18.7 percent, and a per-share price of $16\frac{1}{2}$ for a cost of $34,650; and 2300

Table 10.1.

	Short sale price	Purchase price
Medco Container Services	60	70
Bristol Myers	$85\frac{7}{8}$	$86\frac{5}{8}$
Elan	$40\frac{3}{4}$	$46\frac{1}{2}$
Genzyme	47	$49\frac{3}{4}$
Immunex	$44\frac{7}{8}$	47
U.S. Healthcare	$27\frac{3}{4}$	$31\frac{3}{4}$
St. Jude Medical	$50\frac{3}{4}$	47
Total loss on short positions of approximately 6%.		

shares of Pacific American Income Shares (PAI) with a net asset value of 15.73, a discount of 13.4 percent, and a per-share price of 16⅝ for a cost of $31,377.50. The combination of these purchases amounted to a long position investment of $99,737.50.

Two things must be kept in mind when establishing a long position in this kind of hedge. First, since Treasury bond futures contracts represent face value of $100,000 worth of Treasury bonds, the investor will want to go long approximately $100,000 worth of closed-end bond funds. When it comes to trading closed-end bond funds, I do not recommend buying more than 2000 or 3000 shares of a single fund for a short-term trade. That is why we would go long several different closed-end funds, representing positions of from $31,000 to $34,000 and amounting to approximately $100,000. That $100,000 long position offset the short position of 1 September U.S. Treasury bond futures contract at 100.18, priced at a 7.943 yield.

On February 10, 1978, with the Dow Jones Bond Average down to 89.79, two significant changes had taken place since we established our theoretical long and short positions: (1) The long positions in the bond funds had become profitable, and (2) so had the short position in the Treasury bond futures contract. For example, JHS was selling at 17⅜, up from 16⅞; DBF was up to 16⅝ from 16½; and PAI had gone from 13⅝ to 13¾. The net asset values of all three funds had declined but the discounts, as predicted, narrowed more than the decline in net asset values, resulting in the profits.

The proceeds from the sale of the long positions on February 10 would have been $101,287.50, resulting in a gain of $1550. Covering the short position in the Treasury bond futures contract would have been at 96.12, resulting in a profit of $5187.50 and a total gain on the long and short transactions of $6737.50.

The type of hedge just described is primarily directed to the institutional investor. At the same time, it is designed to demonstrate to all investors some of the key advantages obtainable in trading bond funds as opposed to dealing strictly in straight corporate bonds.

4. Buy a closed-end fund that is going to be open-ended or liquidated and that is selling at a discount; sell short the stocks in the fund's portfolio. This is an almost riskless arbitrage. As the closed-end fund approaches the date that it is to become an open-end fund, the discount will narrow. As an open-end fund it will not sell at any discount (redeemable at NAV). The trader is locking in the amount of the discount as a profit, with the shorts eliminating risks of changing market prices that might occur before the fund is open-ended.

For example, Schafer Value Trust announced plans to liquidate in April 1990. If you would have purchased the fund shortly after that news, you would have paid $10 per share, which represented a 5-percent discount from its net asset value. At the same time you could have sold short the five largest positions of the fund at the prices indicated in Table 10.2. The fund paid liquidating distributions totalling $10.675, of which 96 percent was paid within three months, representing a gain of 6.75 percent, while the short positions created a loss of 2.96 percent. This is an overall gain of 3.79 percent, with much of the risk eliminated from the transaction.

5. Buy an equity closed-end fund at an excessive discount; sell naked call options against the fund's portfolio positions. If the stock market declines, the diminishing time factor of the option, plus the probable erosion of the price of the underlying stock, exerts pressure on the excessive premiums of the options. This probably would result in a greater gain on the short option positions than the resulting loss in the long position in the excessively discounted closed-end fund. If the market rises, in-the-money options will tend to lose their rich premiums and will probably not rise as fast as their underlying stocks. In addition, the diminishing time factor is working against the option. At the same time that the underlying stocks rise, the net asset value of the fund should increase, combined with the probable narrowing of its discount possibly causing it to become more profitable than the loss developing in the options. The hedge may also be benefited by dividends being received on the long positions in the fund.

For example, in June 1977, U.S. & Foreign Securities (UFO) was selling at an excessive discount of 26.7 percent. Its net asset value was 20.97, and the fund was selling at $15\frac{3}{8}$. The Dow Jones Industrial Average was at 912. A purchase of 4100 shares of UFO at $15\frac{3}{8}$ would have cost $63,375.

Had one of each of the following naked calls been sold on the major positions of UFO, the proceeds from the sale would have been $3718.75: IBM October 260s, selling at $6\frac{1}{4}$, Amerada-Hess November 30s at $5\frac{1}{4}$, Digital Equipment October 40s at $4\frac{1}{2}$, American Telephone & Telegraph

Table 10.2.

	Short sale price	Purchase price
Fruit of the Loom, Inc.	$14\frac{1}{8}$	$12\frac{1}{8}$
Philip Morris	$41\frac{1}{4}$	$49\frac{1}{4}$
BAT Industries PLC-ADR	$12\frac{13}{16}$	$11\frac{1}{2}$
Archer Daniels Midland Co.	$23\frac{7}{8}$	26
Atlantic Richfield Co.	$116\frac{5}{8}$	$115\frac{3}{4}$

October 60s at 4, General Electric October 55s at 2, Texaco October 25s at $2\frac{1}{16}$, Corning Glassworks December 30s at $1\frac{7}{8}$.

By September 24, 1977, the discount on UFO had narrowed to 20.7 percent. The price of the stock had risen to $16\frac{5}{8}$, in spite of a down market (the Dow Jones was at 839). Yet UFO's net asset value, after rising in August and September, was exactly where it had been in June—20.97. At that juncture the hedge could have been closed.

Proceeds from the sale of 4100 UFO shares at $16\frac{5}{8}$ would have amounted to $68,162.50, the cost to cover the short positions in the calls would have been $2622.25. This would have meant a gain from the long position of $4787.50 and on the short position of $1096.50, for a total gain of $5844.

6. Sell short a closed-end fund selling at a premium; write naked put options against the fund's portfolio positions. This is effectively the reverse of hedging method 5, that is, taking advantage of the fund's excessive premium rather than an excessive discount.

5. Long-Term

Long-Term portfolio modeling utilizing closed-end funds is the same as that incorporating specific common stock (Chap. 9), with the closed-end funds being selected by scanning for those with the most attractive discounts.

This method incorporates market timing directly with the Time Overlay in determining entry (buy) points, but constrains selling by requiring all positions to be held at least one year.

The results of this modeling incorporating closed-end funds has, to date, paralleled the published specific common stock modeling detailed in the preceding chapter. However, the imposition of the holding time requirement detracts form profit consistency. Without long-term positions receiving beneficial tax treatment, there is no reason to impose the time constraint.

For example, in February 1990 when Drach announced he had increased investment level to 100 percent, Putnam High Income Convertible and Bond Fund was trading at a wide 12-percent discount from net asset value at a price of $6\frac{3}{8}$. After holding the position for one year, Drach's prescribed investment level had been reduced to 23 percent in April 1991. At that time the discount of Putnam High Income Convertible and Bond Fund had evaporated and the fund was trading at 7, a 33-percent gain; plus we had been paid the monthly dividend of 7.1¢ during our holding period.

Summary

We have now discussed the theories and specific trading strategies that provide the foundation for our basic investment techniques. With this information established, we can turn our attention to examining some other characteristics of the securities industry which, when properly understood, can be of benefit in actual market participation.

11
Functioning as a Professional

Our definition of a *professional* in the stock market is anyone who can consistently extract profit at a satisfactory rate of return.

While many different investment methods have demonstrated merit in actual market endeavors, we have made a concentrated effort to fully describe a few investment techniques that are inherently conservative and quite easy to apply.

Every investor has individual needs, goals, and resources. At varying degrees, all investment methodologies involve risk. We have developed and implemented our techniques because they meet our financial objectives and our conservative nature. The methods are not suitable for everyone.

Suitable or not, the results of these methods are firm over an extended period, including a wide variety of market conditions: strong rallies, flat periods, and severe declines. As such, we believe that these results provide a benchmark from which investors can compare their own results over the same time period.

For those who have the personal ability to direct the placement of their funds, by making their own specific investment decisions or by selecting their own money manager (mutual fund, bank trust department, or other agent), or for those who do not have a personal choice (such as employee pension programs with the money control dictated by others), the results comparisons can be easily made and subsequently judged.

Too Easy?

It is reasonable to assume that the average stock investor's return is parallel to the popular averages minus transaction costs and any applicable management or administrative fees. After all, if there is a set number of stocks with a set number of shares outstanding and somebody has to own it at all times, the return should match the broadly based averages.

Actually, it is more than likely that the average investor fares more poorly than the popular averages (minus associated costs) because new stock is generally offered in greater quantity to the public and institutional sectors when the market is at highs. Sometimes, such as during the 1987 peaks (prior to the crash) and when the markets were making all-time highs in 1992, the amount of new offerings has been massive. In addition, companies that are obviously on their way to bankruptcy are often conveniently deleted as components from some of the averages and replaced with financially healthier issues. This imbalance in the availability of new issues and changes in the "averages" components aside, the popularized averages can reasonably be considered as a rough measure of approximate median return.

Our results have significantly outperformed the "averages" without the necessity of time-consuming and/or complicated mathematical models, secretive data, or relying on the advice of others.

The initial reaction to our methods is often, "It cannot be that easy," or "If it is that easy, then why don't more people do it?"

While the simplicity of the methods in this text and the associated results clearly demonstrate their ease, we are convinced the techniques will never appeal to the majority.

In early editions of this book, we had some concern that describing our methods could make them too well-known and popular, incurring the risk of reducing our profitability. However, after experiencing worldwide distribution of our writings and investment methods, we have not noticed any sacrifice in profitability and have come to the conclusion that, because of the structure of the market, it is basically impossible for our methods to become overly popular.

Our methodologies are totally objective, making decisions on fundamental and/or structural analysis that are totally devoid of emotion. *The stock market also happens to be a brain game,* involving tremendous psychological pressures, which our methods virtually ignore. In our techniques, we make a concentrated effort to avoid buying unless prices are relatively depressed. For prices to become so depressed, it is generally necessary for the majority to dislike the investment: that's why it became depressed in the first place. In other words, by the method's design, we must usually have to be in the minority to initiate or terminate a position.

Our methods also directly conflict with media sensationalism and the sales structure of the securities industry. For example, if a stock on our Master List goes down and receives media attention, the media's comments must be negative to justify the lower price. If the media makes positive comments when a price declined, the comments would appear stupid. A broker in the business of selling for commissions (or an advisor charging fees) would generally have difficulty getting customers to buy a stock that is experiencing negative publicity. "Hey, mister, want to buy XYZ Inc? Did you read in the paper how horrible it is and its price is going down the tube?" Such reasoning doesn't help make the customer inclined to buy or stay. It is far easier to get customers to sell the stock using the negative media attention as support for making the sell decision. In other words, the easiest commission/fee generation is by suggesting to clientele to do what they are already predisposed to doing because of media influence.

Even if commissions/fees were not involved, the broker or money manager who follows media sensationalism is (at least initially) deriving some protection form criticism, which can help enhance job preservation. If a stock's price is extremely high, the positive media attention can be used to justify purchase. When the same stock goes splat because of the overvaluation and then receives negative attention in the media, selling at a loss is not the broker's or portfolio manager's fault because the media will support the decision in justifying the lower pricing, usually attributed to some "surprise" event.

This interrelationship between media sensationalism and the structure of the securities business is extremely strong and is constant. It obviously can result in the precise formula for loss (buying high and selling low), but will never end. Thankfully, for us, these pressures are an integral part of the *business* of the market.

People react to sensationalism. There is a giant financial media industry devoted to creating such reaction. Sensationalism is how most elements of the media generate sales. The exception is stressed, not the rule. After all, people want to hear what is wild and different.

Sensationalism is fine with us; we often prey upon it. However, for many the exception becomes the rule, creating illogical investment behavior. Suppose a stock begins to decline and then keeps going into bankruptcy and to zero, or suppose a stock experiences a huge upmove. The "after-the-price-change" media attention and associated behavior among brokers and portfolio managers functions to show them to have been correct, as well as to have captured huge price changes. The problem is that the exception is rare by definition and the investor can be destroyed by the rule (price reversals generally occur) as the exception is chased.

The lure of the exception is also used by some advisory publications and portfolio managers who make wild forecasts or embark on extremely risky strategies in the hope of showing dramatic gains when they are correct, thereby generating sales: irrespective of the statistical fact that the exception's gains will be more than wiped out by the losses incurred by going against the rules.

Sticking with the Plan

There is no sensationalism in our techniques. They are designed to grind out what they consider to be an acceptable profit, largely at the expense of those chasing the sensational.

In our methods, the buy/sell points are predetermined by the primary and ancillary criteria. Price differentials between the buy/sell points are of no concern because the price swings are not going to make any difference in the final outcome. In effect, our portfolio modeling is quite rigid and is not concerned with media hype or any other emotional aspect between the predetermined buy/sell points.

People tend to watch the market price of their holdings: finding great delight when they are appearing to win and becoming worried when they appear to be losing. This practice of marking to market has absolutely nothing to do with our objective of marking someone else's money to our pocket in the form of cash at the time a stock position is concluded. To us, marking to market does nothing to alter the final outcome and has no purpose except to inject unnecessary emotion (fear and greed) between buy/sell points. Our absolute lack of concern for marking-to-market exercises or other emotional aspects is basically the absorption of what can often be tremendous psychological pressures. Aside from plain stupidity, capitulation to emotional strains created by price gyrations and/or unfounded media sensationalism is the greatest cause for investor disappointment. Neither stupidity nor emotionally dictated investment decisions have any place in a logical strategy.

It has been our experience that the primary difficulty people have in implementing our strategies is that the methods are devoid of emotion and will not alter positions because of psychological pressures. At market extremes, it is invariably the consensus of the majority that the "market has changed this time." The price-is-proof mentality is shared by the crowd. As our results to date attest, we have never experienced a change in market structure, and we doubt there has ever been a significant change in the lure of misguided emotions. We have found the market to be nothing other than a repetitive, ongoing, man-made business designed to transfer the monies of many to a knowledgeable few. Most people cannot accept this simplicity. Finally, it has been our experience that investors can concentrate on a single stock out of a portfolio of many issues. For example, they buy a stock and then sell it at the predetermined sell point, after which the stock skyrockets. "Gosh!" the reaction goes, "I could have stayed in and made a fortune!" They concentrate on the one that made exceptional gains with no rational concern as to the many others that were sold profitably at their predetermined points and subsequently declined. When added up for total profitability, staying with all of the issues would have resulted in far less return, irrespective of the dramatic gains associated with the exception.

A more common investor reaction occurs when an account has achieved a very high percentage of profitable trades and an acceptable rate of return but in the process has experienced a losing position. Although the account is fat with profits from the large number of successful transactions, focus becomes concentrated on the real or potential loss. Attention shifts from the basic overall strategy to a minor facet. In effect, to eliminate the loss, the basic strategy is altered, and in doing so the large number of profits (which make the loss insignificant in the context of overall return) is sacrificed.

The psychological pressures to alter any logical investment strategy before the method has been allowed to run its predetermined course can be tremendous, even when the statistical data is clear that such alteration can be disastrous.

In the application of our timing method, we do not expect to profit in every individual stock position. We are well satisfied with our results to date, profiting in 95 percent of our Time Overlay positions.

Even if the investor is able to absorb the psychological strains, other pressures are created by wide variances in trading activity. When the investment level is high, the trading can be active, especially if rotation is utilized, as the profits are locked in. Then, when the investment level is significantly reduced, the trading can literally stop for extended periods.

After experiencing a string of profits, most people do not want to stop because it was so much fun. It becomes easy to emotionally justify continued participation because you are "playing" with profits, thereby reducing the probability of loss of initial capital. This psychological lure to stay in when our modeling avoids stock market participation can be very strong. We have watched accounts that have profited handsomely while our methods were utilized shift to some other method after we have sold with the thought of returning to our methods the next time we initiate buying. When they return, they often have been battered because of their decision to abandon statistical logic in exchange for short term psychological gratification.

In effect, our methods are designed for adaptation to the market rather than expecting the market to adapt to personal preference or emotional whim. We simply go into the market when the probabilities for profit appear acceptable and leave when they are not acceptable. Capturing profit in the form of cash is our objective and, if probabilities do not favor that objective, we will not participate.

Statistically, we have found our methods to be very easy: psychologically, they are very tough.

Understanding Brokers' Services

If an individual is not going to personally place his or her buy/sell orders, a personal relationship with a broker is required. The broker is compensated by commission charges and/or markups and markdowns when dealing with over-the-counter issues. Although the cost is a one-time event per transaction, it covers three distinct functions:

1. Retail brokerage service
2. Order execution
3. Clearing

The Retail Brokerage Service

The retail broker initiates (takes) customers' orders and (perhaps) advises clients on the merits (or lack thereof) of any particular investment.

Whether the broker is relied on for advice or is used only as an order taker, the client-broker relationship should be open and cordial. If a mistake should occur (in some firms they are common), a friendly relationship with the broker can help assure that the problem will be promptly resolved.

Disliking or not knowing your retail broker can have more subtle effects. The relationship can create an underlying psychological uncertainty that can permeate investment decisions and possibly destroy a logical strategy. A reasonable rule of thumb is that, if you feel any uneasiness in calling your broker, look for a new one. This feeling may be present from the beginning of the relationship or develop as the relationship progresses. It is not uncommon for some brokers (the hard-core sales variety) to attempt to sell something every time they talk to a client. This can become increasingly annoying, and it could be indicative of the broker's method of receiving compensation through commissions generated by sales pitches rather than servicing established accounts.

The brokerage profession is a service. The client has a right to be treated as an individual rather than a number. Whatever the commission schedule, this individualized attention is of primary importance. A neglected account in a brokerage firm providing reduced commissions can be more costly to you in the long run than a properly serviced account in a firm with higher commissions. There is not, however, a direct relationship between commission structures and brokers' abilities. Individual investors must find brokers most suitable to their needs and preferences.

Brokerage firms with the higher commission schedules often advertise heavily, offer a diversity of financial services, have many offices, and include highly salaried midmanagement positions, all of which add to overhead expense. This overhead, much of which may be of little or no personal benefit to the investor, might necessitate the higher commission charges.

Many of the larger, more costly commission firms maintain research staffs to aid their retail brokers. These firms often attribute their higher commission charges to the expense of research personnel. Judgment as to the merit of any research is relatively simple. If it is logically based and makes money throughout a variety of market conditions, it is desirable. If it produces haphazard results or loss, it is not. For investors making their own investment decisions, there is no point in supporting (through higher commissions) a research staff that is not utilized.

If you desire research, realize that there is no automatic correlation between the size of a research department and the quality of its service. Determining the relative quality is not an easy task. It is not reasonable to expect a brokerage firm to recommend the research of a competitor. A prudent method is to check into the writings (if any) of the senior research staff. There is also some benefit to be gained by asking various firms for research material, and then watching to see how profitable it would have been if the research were followed, preferably through different market conditions to eliminate the effect of luck. Another practice is to ask other investors about their experience with a firm's research. Whatever method you employ, do not be surprised if you find exceptionally poor quality among well-known firms.

It is always helpful in human relationships to give some thought as to the reasons for the association: mutual gain or one-sided manipulation. We have attempted to reinforce that the market is a business and the participants are in the business in their own niche. To help assure their survival, some elements may compromise themselves. This goes far deeper than a broker soliciting a sale that the broker knows is wrong for the investor. It can transcend to the research being provided. For example, if a brokerage firm has a large sales staff, the salespersons (brokers) are in constant need of something to sell. Consequently, the research department is pressured to suggest something to buy irrespective of any dangers involved with the overall market condition.

Among those whose livelihood depends on constantly getting clientele to buy something, it is common for them to state that market timing is impossible and common stock investment should be made for the long term. Beware of such verbiage. In the long term the only thing assured is death, and, as the results we have achieved clearly demonstrate, market timing is alive and well.

The Order Execution Service

When an order is entered by a retail broker, someone has to see to it that the order is handled as the retail broker has specified. It is very important to have prompt, efficient order execution, and it is preferable that the brokerage firm selected have the most modern equipment. In the author's firm, confirmations that an order has been executed can take only a few seconds—faster than a telephone call. For very large orders (block trades), orders often need special handling and are called in to a specialized *block trading desk*. For those stocks listed on the major exchanges, computer linkage allowing extremely rapid order execution has (in most firms) replaced more time-consuming methods.

You can know an order's status at any given time as the orders are given a priority determined by set rules when they are entered. Usually the priority criterion is time, meaning that, for instance, the first limit order received at a specified price will be the first filled when that price becomes available. For market orders, they should be filled as soon as the order is received. These rules, and the ability to check a limit order's status, make the larger listed exchanges very fair trading centers.

The over-the-counter market is not so fair because of the lack of a central meeting place for all buyers and sellers. The OTC market is composed of many scattered brokers/dealers without clear priority given to orders. OTC market makers might not execute an order unless they are able to obtain a better price for themselves, and *then* execute the customer's order with a markup or markdown. For example, let's say we want to buy a stock at a limit price of 20. The stock might be shown to be trading at 20. Our order, however, is not filled unless the OTC market maker is able to buy the stock at $19\frac{3}{4}$ and then sell it to us at $20, thereby allowing the market maker a $\frac{1}{4}$-point (markup) profit. There is nothing you can do about this. It is the way the over-the-counter market is structured.

The retail broker usually has no control over the efficiency of order executions. However, with modern communications available, there is no reason to be subjected to delays in order processing.

The Clearing Service

When a transaction occurs on a listed exchange, it is done in the name of an exchange member (usually a clearing corporation). This exchange member is responsible for the payment due or funds to be collected, as well as the acceptance or delivery of stock certificates that result from trading. The clearing firm is also responsible for issuing statements to retail customers, providing insurance coverage, and the registration and shipment of stock certificates. In effect, the clearing corporation handles the paperwork.

Most larger brokerage firms have their own clearing firms, which often provide clearing services for smaller brokerage firms as well as for the larger firm's clientele.

Some firms appear to have chronic paperwork problems, while others appear to run smoothly. The only way to find out if a clearing service is efficient is by experience. Mistakes can (and do) occur. If they are frequent or if inordinate time passes before they are corrected, you may assume that something is wrong with the clearing service. Paperwork errors can be extremely irritating and sometimes detract dramatically from the effectiveness of strategy. In such an event it is reasonable to seek a brokerage firm using a different clearing firm. While your natural reaction to paperwork errors may be anger at the retail broker, you should keep in mind that in larger firms the retail broker usually has little or no personal relationship with the clearing firm and to yell at the retail broker does little to solve the problem. Such complaints are probably best served when directed to the manager of the retail office.

What Do You Want to Pay for?

The value, then, of a brokerage service is threefold: the correct initiation of orders and (possibly) advice of the retail service; efficiency in the order execution service; and accuracy and speed of processing paperwork by the clearing service. The relative ability in each of these functions determines the justification of transaction charges.

Most investors have contact only with their retail broker and as such have little awareness of the other services. As a result, you might utilize a more costly commission structure because you feel secure with a well-known (perhaps heavily advertised) brokerage firm. Yet you might be able to obtain *exactly the same* clearing service, including insurance protection and better order executions, at a lesser known discount firm.

The process of choosing a brokerage firm is a balance between the client-broker personal relationship, the quality of services rendered, and cost. The mixture most suitable depends on individual circumstances.

Fortunately, there is not necessarily a direct correlation between the quality of the services provided and the associated costs. Adequate service that parallels (or exceeds) that of full commission firms can often be found in some discount firms. Unfortunately, comparison is difficult. To gain some insight into the relative merits, it is reasonable to ask the firm itself about its commission structure, methods of order placement and execution, and clearing facilities. There is no reason to feel intimidated about making such inquiry. It is your money, and you should know how it is going to be handled and whether it is going to be properly serviced. You should expect some rebuffs when making such inquiries. However, such reaction is a valid reason to scratch a firm from consideration. If a firm is secretive or hazy in defining its commission structure and/or services, there must be a reason, and it is probably not worth your time to figure out the reason.

When dealing with a specialized investment type or technique, it may be beneficial to search for a specialty firm that concentrates on that particular investment area or method. Such firms often have excellent research in their particular specialty and remain small enough (with reduced overhead) to offer attractive discounts. Because of their speciality, they probably have the most efficient order execution system and clearing services to precisely fit the specialized investment type or methods. Such firms are often difficult to locate, but, once found, they can be of great benefit for specific investment needs.

Seeking and Identifying
Professional Assistance

Irrespective of how much knowledge you acquire of the securities industry, successful participation requires both time and a solid psychological base adaptable to the market environment. As stressed throughout this book, the market is not as easy as many would like the public to believe. It is very competitive and inhabited by true professionals. If you are under time constraints and/or do not have the temperament to do your own trading, it might be beneficial to place funds under the management of a true professional.

The difficulty, of course, is finding the true professional. To do so, it is *mandatory* that you have a firm idea as to what investment type and trading techniques you wish to employ. *It is folly to entrust funds to someone else's decision making without having a very clear understanding of the decision-making process.* Whether the relationship is discretionary or the professional only suggests investment moves, the best protection you have is to understand the strategy being employed.

Whatever means are utilized to locate the professional (writings, lectures, formal or informal inquiries), there is absolutely nothing wrong in feeling free to question the professional's knowledge. The true professional will know the intricacies of the business and has no reason to conceal knowledge. If answers are ambiguous or the "professional" relies heavily on others for advice and support, it might be prudent to contact the "others" and forget the supposed professional.

As with any profession, portfolio management involves competition among many individuals who vary in their ability and ethical standards. Although there is no reason to become paranoid, it can be helpful to employ some common sense.

The stock market has been around in the United States for 200 years and has demonstrated a variety of investment methods that have been successful at varying levels of risk. Having spent our adult lives as analysts, we have yet to see any great secret system. Yet many money managers stipulate that their methods are proprietary and the only way the investor can profit from the great secret is to blindly entrust funds. It is absolutely insane for anyone to entrust funds to an investment technique that is unknown to the investor. Any manager should fully disclose to clientele the investment method being utilized.

Money managers are compensated by commissions and/or fees that might not be as straightforward as they first appear. For example, a manager might stipulate a management fee and the investor considers this the total cost. Then "administrative" costs are added. The management and administrative fees are usually disclosed, but often in a manner that makes it difficult for investors to easily comprehend what they are paying. The easiest way for an unethical manager to inject excessive added costs is to fully disclose management and administrative fees and omit transaction (commissions, markup/markdowns) costs. Their logic is that they are not being compensated through transaction costs and such costs are consequently of no concern. For unsavory types, this can obviously open up some unethical and/or illegal relationships between the broker and the money manager.

In a kickback arrangement between the manager and the broker, the commission charges might be higher than if the relationship was not in effect, or the number of transactions could be unnecessarily increased.

Simply providing the investor the commission charges and to whom they were paid does not cover costs associated with markups or markdowns in over-the-counter trading, which can be high, especially with bonds. In addition, with new offerings there is no commission or markup/markdown charges because the broker's profit is in underwriting fees. Full disclosure of costs should include everything the client pays whether directly to the money manager or not: management fees, administrative fees, and all transaction costs (commission, markups/markdowns, and underwriter fees). This full disclosure of costs should be substantiated by the portfolio manager's clients having direct access to the transaction confirmations.

For individuals whose accounts function independently under a money manager, confirmations of specific transactions allowing full disclosure of costs should be provided as a matter of course. For those whose funds are commingled, such as mutual funds or pension funds where the monies of many are pooled, such detailed cost information (both dollar amount and to whom paid) is generally not made easily available, but there is no reason why it should be withheld.

Because transaction costs can vary with market activity dictated by changing market conditions, projecting total costs by the money manager can be logically presented as being impossible. Because of this, it is reasonable and acceptable that the manager place a maximum cap of total charges during any given time period. This allows latitude in trading activity that could benefit the investor while providing a limit to total costs.

Specific investment decisions must be made by an individual or a group of individuals. When entrusting funds to others, the investor should be made fully aware of the identities of the individual(s) involved and their background. Risk cannot be eliminated, and investments can significantly underperform expectations. However, this should not preclude specifically identifying the decision maker(s). This identification injects pressures on the manager(s) which they may dislike. However, honesty dictates that a manager's ability includes both successes and disappointments. Only by this full disclosure of identities can a manager's true ability be adequately known.

To avoid individual criticism, some managers will have decisions made by a committee consensus. Then, if something goes wrong, they blame the decision on underlings and fire them, giving the impression that the "error" will not be repeated. The praise or blame should actually center on the senior committee member who is most influential in making the specific investment decisions.

Identification includes not only the individual involved, but also the investment technique the individual employs. Anyone can be *portrayed* as a "star" by advertising and other commercialized media attention. Real reputation is a combination of demonstrated knowledge, experience in actual market endeavors, and recognized expertise in noncommercialized sectors of the financial community. Again, it is a matter of unbiased full disclosure.

To provide at least the image that the best money managers are being utilized, many pensions and other entities select "outside" managers. That is, rather than personally managing the funds under their discretion, they screen others and allocate a portion of their funds to other managers. Many brokerage firms do the same by providing clients a list of outside managers to choose from, with the brokerage firm monitoring the managers for performance. The brokerage firm is compensated by commissions that are generated by the trading of the chosen outside manager.

This outside manager selection process, if properly applied, is reasonable in that it acknowledges expertise exists outside a single organization and the investor is benefited by access to a wide spectrum of recognized professionals. For example, if a large pension fund both manages funds directly ("in house") and apportions other funds to other managers, the in-house manager offers a true picture of his or her ability when compared with others. However, as with other aspects of the industry, easy loopholes are available for the unethical. A portfolio manager who has a kickback scheme with an outside money manager could automatically reject consideration of a superior manager to keep the "friendly" relationship in good light. Or, if a brokerage firm gets more business from one manager than another (or a superior manager will not do business with the brokerage firm), an inferior manager might be portrayed beyond his or her real abilities. The only protection against such abuses is full disclosure of the outside managers being compared fully and fairly with in-house managers.

In fact, the bottom line to all investors who place their monies at the discretion of others and who prefer to avoid being abused is remembering six words: FULL DISCLOSURE. IF NOT, WHY NOT?

While you should be aware of the sleazy elements and their practices, as well as being able to identify them, our experience has been that these elements are in the minority. They can generally be easily identified with some practical knowledge, and most (not all) are purged from the industry before they do widespread harm.

We can now turn our attention to the ethical elements of the professional money management industry, and discuss the limitations on what any professional can provide. You should be aware of what not to expect as well as what to expect.

The securities business, like all professions, has become increasingly specialized. Any individual in the business can spend only so much time developing and implementing an expertise in an area of investment. Because the time and effort of the expert are concentrated in one area, other areas cannot be equally emphasized.,

To understand professional common stock portfolio managers, view the situation from their perspective, keeping in mind that their time is best spent when devoted to their particular expertise. If the manager is in a traditional broker position, clients commonly expect the broker to direct decisions in the area of expertise as well as buy and sell securities outside the area of the broker's speciality. For example, you may start with a broker in a specialized stock trading program for which the broker has unique abilities. You may then decide to buy stocks outside the original strategy and naturally you expect the broker to watch these stocks too. This can increase the broker's workload and detract from the effectiveness of your original strategy. Unfortunately, this is a common occurrence, with many brokers taking orders outside their areas of expertise because of the commissions and/or to keep a friendly relationship with the client. With many clients doing the same thing, brokers can soon become overwhelmed by attending to matters outside their specialized area. Brokers can become an order taker, simply writing orders as directed by clientele, rather than devoting proper attention to the implementation of logical, controlled strategies.

The condition is similar for money managers outside the traditional client/retail broker relationship. Because fees are involved, managers might overstate their abilities in areas other than their specialty in an attempt to keep the relationship with the client.

You, as an investor, must know as precisely as possible what you want before utilizing the services of brokers or advisors. Because of their specialization, there is only a theoretical possibility (nothing practical) that they will be exceptionally proficient in a wide variety of investment types. There is simply not enough time.

Credible brokers/advisors will tell you whether your desires are attainable, as well as the specific services they are personally able to provide in an attempt to meet your goals. If they stipulate that they have access to specialized personnel for specialized investment functions outside the expertise, you should be directed to the specialized personnel rather than relying on communications through the brokers advisors.

In whatever specialized area you seek assistance, there is absolutely no reason not to search for very best broker/advisor available. The costs involved will be fully disclosed by the true professional, and they might be far lower than those of imitators.

True professionals will address the broker/advisor's abilities and the client's ability to achieve his objectives. If the brokers/advisors cannot meet your goals, they will direct you to someone (if such knowledge is available) who can better meet your requirements, or simply tell you that it is doubtful that your objectives can be attained. The true professional money manager knows full well that the most beneficial client relationships are those that are long lasting. A complete understanding at the onset of the relationship is extremely important.

You may even successfully seek out a professional, and the professional will not accept you as an account. There is no hippocratic oath in the broker/advisor business, and a money manager may reject a client simply because the manager doesn't like the potential client. More often, an investor is rejected because there is not a mutuality of the investor's desires and the manager's ability. Although the investor may feel angry, it is much better to be rejected than to be accepted by a money manager who cannot properly serve the investor's needs. It is unlikely that any individual broker/advisor can properly serve a wide range of investor types because of their differing objectives and the associated areas of specialization.

Stock market participation can involve tremendous mental (and sometimes financial) stress, which can result in emotionally induced decisions and destroy logical strategy. To reduce, or eliminate, the potentially dangerous psychological pressures, the money manager and the client must have open, ongoing communication. The easiest way to accomplish this is for the money manager to provide regularly scheduled written correspondence, specifically stating the manager's outlook and associated investment positioning.

Regularly scheduled written correspondence is beneficial to both the client and the manager. The client is afforded a timely, ongoing explanation of the logic dictating portfolio management. The manager, although he or she should always be personally available for questions/comments from established clientele, is benefited by the written correspondence, minimizing the time necessary for duplicated verbal communication and thereby maximizing the time available for research and analysis.

The written correspondence also helps assure the client that the original investment strategy is being adhered to. Without such communication, the client could be at risk. Perhaps the manager went crazy, or is shifting strategy to techniques that are not suitable for the client. Or perhaps the individual the client trusted is replaced by a stranger. In addition, ongoing written correspondence assures clients that they are receiving equal treatment with other accounts under the manager's direction. It is not uncommon for pompous personalities or larger accounts to want preferential treatment. By providing all clientele with a duplicated publication discussing outlook and portfolio positioning, clients are better assured that the manager's behavior is ethical in that all accounts are being treated equally.

An important factor in professional portfolio management is whether the funds to be managed involve a fixed or variable-based capitalization. That is, are funds to be added or withdrawn at predetermined intervals or randomly? Proper market involvement and portfolio analysis is an art as well as a science in which it is extremely important for the manager to make projections. Optimization of projections requires advance knowledge of the amount of funds that are to be applied to a strategy, as well as if and when the amount is to be varied.

In portfolio modeling incorporating hedging, it generally makes little difference as to the time funds are added or withdrawn because the return is relatively constant. However, in those techniques incorporating market timing, the haphazard addition or withdrawal of funds can detract from, perhaps destroy, the profit potential of the technique. In any technique involving timing, if funds are unexpectedly added or withdrawn at inappropriate times, or if the investor decides to alter the predetermined strategy, profit optimization may be sacrificed and losses may occur that would otherwise have been avoided.

The knowledgeable professional will inform you of the benefits of fixed capitalization with a predetermined schedule for additions or withdrawals. It is very difficult (if not impossible) to develop a viable timing trading strategy with a variable capital base. You should suspect the credibility of any money manager who does not stress this aspect.

It is common for professional money managers to specify a minimum amount of money to be utilized in a particular strategy. This is not necessarily prejudicial against the small investor. There is a real advantage to both issue and time diversity. If there are insufficient funds to diversify, a manager might consider it too great a disadvantage (or simply not want small accounts) and dissuade market participation. Other managers will adapt strategies so that the methods are more suitable to the smaller investor. Whatever the situation, the true professional will know and relate to the client the importance of diversity.

Some Closing Comments

Throughout this text we have reinforced our basic theme that self-reliance through realistic understanding is the investor's best protection against loss and abuse.

We have presented the stock market from the perspective of two professionals whose livelihood heavily depends upon consistent, accurate price forecasting.

It may seem that the market is a brutal place with professionals preying on the ignorant. This is partially true, as any honest, knowledgeable appraisal would recognize. This aspect, however, is not unique to the stock market; parallel situations can be found in any competitive environment. We have portrayed the market environment as we have found it and have explained how we have adapted in order to function profitably. It is worth mentioning some things we have not found but are widely believed to be true.

We have never seen any grand design by specialists or other market makers to control pricing. The belief by some that the whole market is crooked and/or fixed has no basis in our experience. We have never detected any great conspiracy. The market, especially the major exchanges, is open to all who qualify for participation. Trading is conducted in an orderly, fair manner. Most participants compete on approximately equal terms. It is true that specialists and other market makers have an advantage because of location. This advantage, however, is generally limited to very short-term price fluctuations, which are not of great concern to the vast majority of investors who (unless they employ a professional trader) should not attempt very short-term trading because of the location disadvantage.

There is no question that some market participants have demonstrated repeated profitability at the expense of others. However, this does not mean the stock market is fixed. To us, it is simply the natural result of differences in knowledge and the ability to withstand psychological pressures.

We have also found erroneous the belief that the market is a place where corporate insiders regularly take advantage of the naive public. There are cases of the abuse of inside information, but they are rare exceptions when considered in terms of the total trading volume. You can usually (but not always!) avoid the risk of being involved in such manipulative situations by staying with quality corporations where reliable information is more readily available. Methods devoted to following corporate insider trading activity have, in our experience, produced results well below those achieved by the methods presented in this text.

Index arbitrage programs were blamed by many to be a cause of the 1987 crash and other sharp downmoves. We consider such complaints to be groundless, with the arbitrage programs injecting some volatility, but a zero sum game as to long-term effects. That is, the demand/supply sides are equal: Each stock bought in such programs must be sold in equal portion. We welcome the increased price volatility because it can be used to enhance profitability. If there were complaints about index arbitrage programs driving prices down, they were noticeably absent when the same programs pushed prices higher than they would otherwise have been.

We have also found the "doom and gloom" scenarios, which are occasionally fashionable in financial writings, to be unfounded. Those who warn of the collapse of the U.S. corporate structure are usually in the business of selling "rare" coins or dehydrated survival foods. To the chagrin of those who transferred their monies to nonincome-producing investments and moved into their cellars to subsist on dried oats, the collapse has never come. The securities industry and corporate structure have repeatedly demonstrated their resilience to deflation and inflation, as well as to political and social change. It is the most productive economic system ever designed. To base your investment strategy on a total collapse (or anything else that has never occurred) is shortsighted and potentially dangerous.

It is easy to understand why conspiracy or doom and gloom theories exist. In common stock, as in any investment type, there are winners and losers. It is much more comfortable for the losers to feel that they have been cheated or that the sky is falling than to realize that they have been outsmarted or that they acted irrationally.

Risk can never be totally eliminated. Even the most rational, documented strategies with superior success records can experience some difficulties. However, almost all investor disappointment can be traced to losses that resulted from the investor's ignorance, fear, or greed.

The stock market is an environment with definite characteristics. It will not adapt to individual preferences; the individual must adapt to the market. The recognition of opportunity requires understanding common stock trading in a realistic context. That, we believe, is the key to success.

In this writing we have discussed very specialized investment methods. Other investment types or entirely different markets can be more suitable to individual preferences and/or circumstances.

Whatever investment type is chosen, the investor must be aware that each type is an environment unto itself and that success depends on understanding the environment and adapting to it. Success in any investment type requires the knowledge of (and blending of) four analytical methods:

1. *Fundamental*: The economic merit relative to price.

2. *Structural*: The trading mechanisms and entities involved.

3. *Technical*: Volume, price, and other relationships that indicate over- or underpricing.

4. *Psychological*: Emotional pressures that create aberrant behavior.

In effect, know all you can about whatever market you chose.

All markets can be considered in the context of a large number of people with a wide range of abilities pooling their money in a big investment pot. They all hope that, when they pull money out of the pot, they will leave with a disproportionate share. It is our firm belief that it is only through self-reliance instilled by developing a realistic knowledge of the market chosen that will determine, when the pot is divided, who will take it or leave it.

■ ■ ■

We welcome questions and comments about the methodology presented in this book and its practical application.

Inquiries concerning the Master List, market timing, and stock selection chapters may be directed to:

Robert F. Drach
Drach Market Research
P. O. Box 490092
Key Biscayne, FL 33149
Tel. (305) 361-5461

Inquiries concerning closed-end fund chapters may be directed to:

Thomas J. Herzfeld, President
Thomas J. Herzfeld & Co., Inc.
The Herzfeld Building
P. O. Box 161465
Miami , FL 33116
Tel. (305) 271-1900
Fax. (305) 270-1040

Buy/Sell Indications

Buy/Sell indications from initiation of the Report's publication (1/1/77) to date of this writing.

This list includes all indications that meet the primary criteria. Those indications that are supported by the ancillary criteria are noted with an asterisk(*).

B=BUY   S=SELL

Ind.		Date	Ind.		Date	Ind.		Date
B		1/28/77	B	*	11/10/78	S		3/20/81
B	*	2/04/77	S	*	1/19/79	S		4/03/81
B	*	2/11/77	S	*	1/26/79	B		7/24/81
B	*	2/18/77	B		2/23/79	B	*	8/28/81
B	*	4/01/77	B	*	3/02/79	B	*	9/04/81
B	*	4/07/77	S	*	3/23/79	B	*	9/11/81
B	*	4/29/77	S	*	3/30/79	B	*	9/18/81
B	*	5/13/77	S	*	7/11/79	B	*	9/25/81
S	*	6/24/77	S	*	8/10/79	S	*	10/23/81
S	*	7/01/77	S	*	8/17/79	B		1/15/82
B		10/14/77	S	*	8/24/79	B	*	1/22/82
B	*	11/04/77	S		8/31/79	S	*	4/08/82
S	*	11/18/77	B		10/12/79	S	*	4/16/82
S	*	11/25/77	B	*	10/19/79	S	*	4/23/82
S		12/02/77	B	*	10/26/79	B		6/04/82
B		12/23/77	B	*	11/02/79	B	*	6/11/82
B	*	1/06/78	S	*	12/07/79	B	*	6/18/82

Ind.		Date	Ind.		Date	Ind.		Date
B	*	1/13/78	B		2/29/80	S	*	8/27/82
B	*	1/20/78	B	*	3/07/80	S	*	9/03/82
B	*	1/27/78	B	*	3/14/80	S		9/10/82
S	*	4/14/78	B	*	3/21/80	S	*	9/17/82
S	*	4/21/78	B	*	3/28/80	S	*	9/24/82
S	*	4/28/78	S	*	5/16/80	S	*	10/01/82
S	*	5/05/78	S	*	5/23/80	S	*	10/08/82
S	*	5/12/78	S	*	5/30/80	S	*	10/15/82
S	*	5/19/78	S		6/06/80	S	*	10/22/82
B		7/07/78	S		6/13/80	S	*	10/29/82
S	*	7/28/78	S	*	7/11/80	S		11/05/82
S	*	8/04/78	S	*	7/18/80	S	*	11/12/82
S		8/11/78	S		7/25/80	S	*	3/04/83
S		8/18/78	S		8/01/80	S	*	4/15/83
S		8/25/78	S		8/08/80	S	*	4/22/83
B		9/22/78	S		8/15/80	S	*	4/29/83
B	*	10/06/78	S		8/22/80	S		5/06/83
B	*	10/20/78	B		12/12/80	S	*	9/23/83
B	*	10/27/78	B	*	12/19/80	B		11/04/83
B	*	11/03/78	S	*	3/13/81	B	*	2/10/84
B	*	2/17/84	S		1/30/87	S	*	5/19/89
B	*	2/24/84	S		2/06/87	S		5/26/89
B	*	5/25/84	S		2/20/87	S		6/02/89
S	*	8/03/84	S	*	2/27/87	S	*	6/09/89
S	*	8/10/84	S		3/13/87	S	*	7/28/89
S	*	8/17/84	B		4/16/87	S	*	8/04/89
S	*	8/24/84	B	*	4/24/87	S		8/11/89
S	*	9/14/84	B	*	5/01/87	S		8/18/89
S	*	1/18/85	S	*	6/19/87	B		10/27/89
S		1/25/85	S		6/26/87	B	*	11/03/89
S		2/01/85	S		7/02/87	B	*	1/26/90
S	*	2/08/85	S	*	8/14/87	B	*	2/02/90
S		2/15/85	S		8/21/87	B		2/09/90
S		3/01/85	B		9/11/87	B	*	2/16/90
S		5/17/85	B	*	9/18/87	B	*	4/27/90
S		5/31/85	B	*	10/16/87	S	*	5/18/90
S		6/07/85	B	*	10/23/87	S	*	5/25/90
B		8/09/85	B	*	10/30/87	S		6/01/90
B	*	8/16/85	B	*	11/06/87	S		6/08/90
B	*	9/20/85	B	*	11/13/87	B		8/03/90

Ind.		Date	Ind.		Date	Ind.		Date
B	*	9/27/85	B	*	12/04/87	B	*	8/10/90
S	*	10/25/85	B	*	12/11/87	B	*	8/17/90
S	*	11/01/85	S	*	12/31/87	B	*	8/24/90
S	*	11/08/85	S	*	1/08/88	B	*	8/31/90
S	*	11/15/85	S	*	1/29/88	B	*	9/07/90
S		11/22/85	S	*	2/05/88	B	*	9/28/90
S	*	11/29/85	S	*	2/12/88	B	*	10/12/90
S		12/06/85	S	*	2/19/88	S	*	11/23/90
S		12/13/85	S	*	3/18/88	S	*	11/30/90
S		2/07/86	B		4/15/88	S	*	12/07/90
S		2/14/86	B	*	5/06/88	S	*	12/14/90
S		2/21/86	B	*	5/13/88	S	*	12/21/90
S		2/28/86	B	*	5/20/88	S		12/28/90
S	*	3/07/86	B	*	5/27/88	S	*	2/01/91
S		3/14/86	S	*	6/10/88	S	*	2/08/91
S		3/21/86	S		6/17/88	S	*	2/15/91
S		3/28/86	S		6/24/88	S	*	2/22/91
S		4/18/86	S	*	9/16/88	S	*	3/01/91
S		5/30/86	S	*	9/23/88	S		3/08/91
S		6/13/86	S		9/30/88	S		4/12/91
B		8/01/86	S	*	10/07/88	S	*	4/19/91
S		8/29/86	S		10/21/88	S		11/08/91
B		9/12/86	B		11/18/88	S	*	12/27/91
B	*	9/19/86	B	*	11/25/88	S		1/03/92
B	*	9/26/86	S	*	1/27/89	S		1/10/92
B	*	10/03/86	S		2/03/89	S	*	1/17/92
S	*	10/17/86	S		4/14/89	S	*	11/06/92
S	*	1/09/87	S	*	4/21/89	S	*	11/13/92
S		1/16/87	S		4/28/89	S	*	11/20/92
S		1/23/87	S	*	5/12/89	S	*	11/27/92

Appendix B

Investment Levels for Each Selection Method

Complete record of all Time Overlay Buy/Sell indications and associated changes in investment level since initiation of publication 1/1/77.

B = BUY	S = SELL	A = Adjustment for stock deleted by takeover. Investment level change not associated with an outright Buy or Sell indication

Ind.	Date	E	Y	P	C	Ind.	Date	E	Y	P	C
B	2/04/77	25	25	25	25	S	8/24/79	4	5	22	12
B	2/11/77	50	50	50	50	B	10/19/79	28	37	42	34
B	2/18/77	75	75	75	75	B	10/26/79	52	69	61	56
B	4/01/77	100	100	100	100	B	11/02/79	76	75	81	78
B	4/07/77	125	125	125	125	S	12/07/79	33	19	27	26
B	4/29/77	150	150	150	150	B	3/07/80	50	39	45	45
B	5/13/77	175	175	175	175	B	3/14/80	67	59	63	63
S	6/24/77	20	5	110	45	B	3/21/80	84	80	82	82
S	7/01/77	20	5	100	42	B	3/28/80	100	100	100	100
B	11/04/77	40	29	105	57	S	5/16/80	44	13	33	29
S	11/18/77	18	5	59	27	S	5/23/80	18	4	13	16
S	11/25/77	18	5	46	23	S	5/30/80	14	4	11	14
B	1/06/78	39	29	60	42	S	7/11/80	11	4	11	13

Ind.	Date	E	Y	P	C	Ind.	Date	E	Y	P	C
B	1/13/78	59	53	73	61	S	7/18/80	7	4	11	12
B	1/20/78	80	77	84	81	B	12/19/80	30	28	33	34
B	1/27/78	100	100	100	100	S	3/13/81	4	5	12	9
S	4/14/78	21	5	48	28	B	8/28/81	28	29	34	32
S	4/21/78	17	5	42	24	B	9/04/81	52	53	56	55
S	4/28/78	13	5	39	21	B	9/11/81	76	77	78	78
S	5/05/78	13	0	36	18	B	9/18/81	100	100	100	100
S	5/12/78	13	0	33	17	B	9/25/81	125	125	125	125
S	5/19/78	13	0	30	16	S	10/23/81	63	48	65	59
S	7/28/78	13	0	27	15	B	1/22/82	72	61	74	69
S	8/04/78	13	0	17	11	S	4/08/82	68	53	63	61
B	10/06/78	35	25	38	33	S	4/16/82	68	49	52	56
B	10/20/78	57	50	59	55	S	4/23/82	68	45	48	53
B	10/27/78	79	75	80	78	B	6/11/82	76	59	61	60
B	11/03/78	100	100	100	100	B	6/18/82	84	73	74	73
B	11/10/78	125	125	125	125	S	8/27/82	59	49	45	48
S	1/19/79	63	50	46	53	S	9/03/82	47	46	35	40
S	1/26/79	36	20	42	33	S	9/17/82	41	39	35	36
B	3/02/79	52	40	57	50	S	9/24/82	41	35	35	35
S	3/23/79	20	22	34	26	S	10/01/82	35	35	35	33
S	3/30/79	20	18	34	25	S	10/08/82	35	32	35	32
S	7/11/79	20	14	34	24	S	10/15/82	32	28	25	27
S	8/10/79	4	9	30	16	S	10/22/82	32	28	25	26
S	8/17/79	4	5	26	13	S	10/29/82	32	28	22	26
S	11/12/82	29	25	22	24	S	3/18/88	54	50	42	49
S	3/04/83	19	25	16	19	B	5/06/88	66	62	57	62
S	4/15/83	13	7	13	11	B	5/13/88	77	75	71	75
S	4/22/83	7	4	13	8	B	5/20/88	89	88	86	88
S	4/29/83	4	0	10	5	B	5/27/88	100	100	100	100
S	9/23/83	4	0	7	4	S	6/10/88	35	33	34	34
B	2/10/84	28	25	30	28	S	9/16/88	35	30	31	32
B	2/17/84	52	50	53	52	S	9/23/88	35	30	28	31
B	2/24/84	76	75	77	76	S	10/07/88	32	30	21	28
B	5/25/84	100	100	100	100	B	11/25/88	49	48	41	46
S	8/03/84	67	60	21	52	S	1/27/89	36	38	22	30
S	8/10/84	53	50	21	46	S	4/21/89	29	38	22	28
S	8/17/84	48	50	21	43	S	5/12/89	26	31	22	25
S	8/24/84	48	45	21	41	S	5/19/89	10	10	18	12
S	9/14/84	43	45	21	39	S	6/09/89	7	7	14	9
S	1/18/85	10	5	12	11	S	7/28/89	4	4	11	6

Ind.	Date	E	Y	P	C	Ind.	Date	E	Y	P	C
S	2/08/85	5	0	12	8	S	8/04/89	4	4	7	5
B	8/16/85	29	25	34	31	B	11/03/89	28	28	30	29
B	9/20/85	53	50	56	54	B	1/26/90	52	52	53	53
B	9/27/85	77	75	78	77	B	2/02/90	76	76	77	77
S	10/25/85	34	20	33	29	B	2/16/90	100	100	100	100
S	11/01/85	19	10	29	20	B	4/27/90	125	125	125	125
S	11/08/85	19	5	29	18	S	5/18/90	53	96	69	73
S	11/15/85	10	0	25	12	S	5/25/90	43	67	32	48
S	11/29/85	5	0	25	11	B	8/10/90	62	77	49	61
S	3/07/86	5	0	17	8	B	8/17/90	75	87	66	74
B	9/19/86	29	25	38	31	B	8/24/90	88	97	83	87
B	9/26/86	53	50	59	54	B	8/31/90	100	107	100	100
B	10/03/86	77	75	80	77	B	9/07/90	125	130	125	125
S	10/17/86	39	45	25	35	B	9/28/90	150	153	150	150
S	1/09/87	0	0	8	3	B	10/12/90	175	177	175	175
S	2/27/87	0	0	4	2	S	11/23/90	123	112	142	124
B	4/24/87	25	25	28	26	S	11/30/90	119	101	138	117
B	5/01/87	50	50	52	51	S	12/07/90	91	99	117	100
A	5/22/87	50	50	47	49	S	12/14/90	87	99	104	95
S	6/19/87	10	5	9	8	S	12/21/90	79	99	100	91
S	8/14/87	5	0	9	5	S	2/01/91	59	99	62	73
B	9/18/87	29	25	32	29	S	2/08/91	55	92	58	68
B	10/16/87	53	50	55	53	S	2/15/91	47	85	54	62
B	10/23/87	77	75	78	77	S	2/22/91	31	44	46	40
B	10/30/87	100	100	100	100	S	3/01/91	27	44	42	37
B	11/06/87	125	125	125	125	S	4/19/91	12	33	25	23
B	11/13/87	150	150	150	150	S	11/08/91	12	26	25	20
B	12/04/87	175	175	175	175	S	12/27/91	12	15	21	15
B	12/11/87	200	200	200	200	S	1/17/92	12	15	13	13
S	12/31/87	132	145	119	132	S	11/06/92	0	0	0	0
S	1/08/88	98	120	95	104						
S	1/29/88	64	55	62	60						
S	2/05/88	59	55	62	58						
S	2/12/88	54	50	57	53						
S	2/19/88	54	50	52	51						

Appendix **C**
Time Overlay: Earnings

Purchase Date	Selling Date	Company	Purchase Price	Selling Price	Percentage Profit (+) Loss (–)	Holding Period Weeks
2/4/77	6/24/77	Labatt (John) Ltd. CV A	17	19⅛	+12.50	20
2/4/77	6/24/77	Mobil	66⅞	68¾	+ 2.80	20
2/4/77	6/24/77	Texaco Canada	26½	29	+ 9.43	20
2/4/77	4/26/78	Standard Oil (California)	42½	43⅜	+ 2.06	64
2/4/77	6/24/77	Searle (G.D.)	11⅞	12⅞	+ 8.42	20
2/11/77	6/24/77	Labatt (John) Ltd. CV A	16⅝	19⅛	+15.04	19
2/11/77	6/24/77	Mobil	63⅞	68¾	+ 7.63	19
2/11/77	6/24/77	Standard Oil (California)	39⅝	42⅜	+ 6.94	19
2/11/77	6/24/77	Searle (G.D.)	11⅞	12⅞	+ 8.42	19
2/11/77	8/10/79	*Shell Oil	39	40	+ 2.56	130
2/18/77	6/24/77	Labatt (John) Ltd. CV A	16⅝	19⅛	+15.04	18
2/18/77	6/24/77	Mobil	64⅝	68¾	+ 6.38	18
2/18/77	8/10/79	*Shell Oil	37⅝	40	+ 6.31	129
2/18/77	6/24/77	Searle (G.D.)	11½	12⅞	+11.96	18
2/18/77	6/24/77	Standard Oil (California)	40⅛	42⅜	+ 5.61	18
4/1/77	6/24/77	Labatt (John) Ltd. CV A	17¾	19⅛	+ 7.75	12
4/1/77	6/24/77	Mobil	67¾	68¾	+ 1.48	12
4/1/77	6/24/77	Shell Oil	70	70¾	+ 1.07	12
4/1/77	6/24/77	Standard Oil (California)	39⅞	42⅜	+ 6.27	12
4/1/77	6/24/77	Mercantile Stores	39¾	40¼	+ 1.26	12
4/7/77	6/24/77	Labatt (John) Ltd. CV A	17⅜	19 ⅛	+10.07	11
4/7/77	6/24/77	Mobil	65⅞	68¾	+ 4.36	11
4/7/77	3/23/79	*Shell Oil	35⅞	36½	+ 1.74	102
4/7/77	6/24/77	Texas Utilities	19⅛	21¾	+13.73	11
4/7/77	6/24/77	Standard Oil (California)	39⅝	42⅜	+ 6.94	11
4/29/77	6/24/77	DEKALB AgResearch	26½	27	+ 1.89	8
4/29/77	6/24/77	Labatt (John) Ltd. CV A	16⅝	19⅛	+15.04	8
4/29/77	6/24/77	Mobil	66¼	68¾	+ 3.77	8

Purchase Date	Selling Date	Company	Purchase Price	Selling Price	Percentage Profit (+) Loss (−)	Holding Period Weeks
4/29/77	6/24/77	Standard Oil (California)	40½	42⅜	+ 4.63	8
4/29/77	6/24/77	Texaco Canada	28⅜	29	+ 2.20	8
5/13/77	6/24/77	Beatrice Foods	24⅝	25¼	+ 2.54	6
5/13/77	6/24/77	Labatt (John) Ltd. CV A	17½	19⅛	+ 9.29	6
5/13/77	6/24/77	Mobil	66⅜	68¾	+ 3.58	6
5/13/77	6/24/77	Shell Oil	67½	70¾	+ 4.81	6
5/13/77	6/24/77	Texaco Canada	27½	29	+ 5.45	6
11/4/77	11/18/77	Labatt (John) Ltd. CV A	18	18¼	+ 1.39	2
11/4/77	11/18/77	Standard Oil (California)	38¼	39¼	+ 2.61	2
11/4/77	11/18/77	DEKALB AgResearch	20	20¾	+ 3.75	2
11/4/77	11/18/77	Mobil	61⅜	63¾	+ 3.87	2
11/4/77	11/18/77	Standard Oil (Indiana)	46	47⅝	+ 3.53	2
1/6/78	4/14/78	Standard Oil (California)	37	40	+ 8.11	14
1/6/78	4/14/78	Labatt (John) Ltd. CV A	20¼	21¼	+ 4.94	14
1/6/78	4/21/78	DEKALB AgResearch	18½	18¾	+ 1.35	15
1/6/78	4/14/78	Shell Oil	30⅞	31⅞	+ 3.24	14
1/6/78	4/14/78	Mobil	60⅝	62⅞	+ 3.71	14
1/13/78	4/14/78	Standard Oil (California)	35⅜	40	+13.07	13
1/13/78	4/14/78	Labatt (John) Ltd. CV A	19⅝	21¼	+ 8.28	13
1/13/78	4/14/78	Shell Oil	28¾	31⅞	+10.87	13
1/13/78	4/14/78	Mobil	59⅞	62⅞	+ 5.01	13
1/13/78	4/14/78	Reynolds (R.J.) Industries	55⅜	58¼	+ 5.19	13
1/20/78	4/14/78	Standard Oil (California)	35¼	40	+13.48	12
1/20/78	4/14/78	Labatt (John) Ltd. CV A	19¼	21¼	+10.39	12
1/20/78	4/14/78	Shell Oil	28⅞	31⅞	+10.39	12
1/20/78	4/14/78	Mobil	59⅞	62⅞	+ 5.01	12
1/20/78	4/14/78	Reynolds (R.J.) Industries	54⅜	58¼	+ 7.13	12
1/27/78	4/14/78	Labatt (John) Ltd. CV A	19⅛	21¼	+11.11	11

Purchase Date	Selling Date	Company	Purchase Price	Selling Price	Percentage Profit (+) Loss (–)	Holding Period Weeks
1/27/78	4/14/78	Mobil	59¾	62⅞	+ 5.23	11
1/27/78	4/14/78	Standard Oil (California)	35⅝	40	+12.28	11
1/27/78	4/14/78	Shell Oil	29⅜	31⅞	+ 8.51	11
1/27/78	4/14/78	Reynolds (R.J.) Industries	52½	58¼	+10.95	11
10/6/78	1/26/79	Mobil	71⅝	72½	+ 1.22	16
10/6/78	8/10/79	Labatt (John) Ltd. CV A	22½	23⅝	+ 5.00	44
10/6/78	3/23/79	Shell Oil	36⅛	36½	+ 1.04	24
10/6/78	4/09/82	Texas Utilities	20¼	21¾	+ 7.41	183
10/6/78	1/26/79	American Tel. & Tel.	63⅜	64	+ .99	16
10/20/78	1/19/79	Labatt (John) Ltd. CV A	20½	21⅞	+ 6.71	13
10/20/78	3/23/79	Shell Oil	33⅜	36½	+ 9.36	23
10/20/78	1/19/79	Mobil	67⅜	70⅛	+ 4.08	13
10/20/78	1/19/79	Standard Oil (Indiana)	50⅞	56¾	+11.55	13
10/20/78	1/19/79	DEKALB AgResearch	20	26	+30.00	13
10/27/78	1/19/79	Mobil	65⅜	70⅛	+ 7.27	12
10/27/78	1/19/79	Labatt (John) Ltd. CV A	20⅜	21⅞	+ 7.36	12
10/27/78	3/23/79	Shell Oil	33⅞	36½	+ 7.75	22
10/27/78	1/19/79	Texas Utilities	18½	19⅝	+ 6.08	12
10/27/78	1/26/79	Reynolds (R.J.) Industries	57½	58	+ .87	13
11/3/78	1/19/79	Labatt (John) Ltd. CV A	20	21⅞	+ 9.38	11
11/3/78	1/19/79	Shell Oil	31¾	32	+ .79	11
11/3/78	1/19/79	Texas Utilities	18¾	19⅝	+ 4.67	11
11/3/78	1/19/79	Mobil	68¾	70⅛	+ 2.01	11
11/3/78	1/26/79	Reynolds (R.J.) Industries	57½	58	+ .87	12
11/10/78	1/19/79	Mobil	66⅞	70⅛	+ 4.86	10
11/10/78	1/19/79	Labatt (John) Ltd. CV A	19¾	21⅞	+10.76	10
11/10/78	1/26/79	Shell Oil	32½	32⅝	+ .38	11
11/10/78	1/19/79	Texas Utilities	19¼	19⅝	+ 1.95	10

Purchase Date	Selling Date	Company	Purchase Price	Selling Price	Percentage Profit (+) Loss (–)	Holding Period Weeks
11/10/78	1/26/79	Reynolds (R.J.) Industries	56¾	58	+ 2.20	11
3/02/79	3/23/79	Reynolds (R.J.) Industries	55⅞	58⅝	+ 4.92	3
3/02/79	3/23/79	Bendix	38½	39	+ 1.30	3
3/02/79	3/23/79	Standard Oil (California)	34⅛	36½	+ 6.96	3
3/02/79	3/23/79	Mobil	72¼	75	+ 3.81	3
3/02/79	8/10/79	Universal Leaf Tobacco	18⅞	23⅛	+22.52	23
10/19/79	5/23/80	Labatt (John) Ltd. CV A	22½	23¼	+ 3.33	31
10/19/79	12/07/79	Walter (Jim)	28¾	32⅝	+13.48	7
10/19/79	12/07/79	Mallinckrodt	28¾	31½	+ 9.57	7
10/19/79	3/31/81	Borden	26	27½	+ 5.77	73
10/19/79	12/07/79	Sears Roebuck & Co.	18¼	18⅜	+ .68	7
10/26/79	12/07/79	Labatt (John) Ltd. CV A	21⅜	21⅞	+ 2.34	6
10/26/79	12/07/79	Walter (Jim)	28⅜	32⅝	+14.98	6
10/26/79	5/23/80	Bendix	39⅝	42	+ 5.99	30
10/26/79	12/07/79	Sears Roebuck & Co	18⅛	18¼	+ .69	6
10/26/79	7/11/80	Borden	25⅝	25¾	+ .49	37
11/2/79	5/23/80	Labatt (John) Ltd. CV A	22¾	23¼	+ 2.20	29
11/2/79	12/7/79	Walter (Jim)	29⅛	32⅝	+12.02	5
11/2/79	12/7/79	Borden	24¾	25⅜	+ 2.53	5
11/2/79	12/7/79	Colgate-Palmolive	14	14⅝	+ 4.46	5
11/2/79	5/23/80	Bendix	41	42	+ 2.44	28
3/7/80	7/18/80	Dana Corp.	23½	24½	+ 4.26	18
3/7/80	5/23/80	Gordon Jewelry Cl A	22⅛	23	+ 3.95	11
3/7/80	5/16/80	International Multifoods	15¼	16¼	+ 6.56	10
3/7/80	5/16/80	Walter (Jim)	25¼	30⅜	+20.30	10
3/7/80	5/16/80	May Department Stores	20⅞	22⅝	+ 8.38	10
3/14/80	5/23/80	Gordon Jewelry Cl A	21¾	23	+ 5.75	10
3/14/80	5/16/80	Wetterau	11¼	11⅞	+ 5.56	9

Purchase Date	Selling Date	Company	Purchase Price	Selling Price	Percentage Profit (+) Loss (−)	Holding Period Weeks
3/14/80	5/16/80	Colgate-Palmolive	12⅝	15	+18.81	9
3/14/80	5/16/80	International Multifoods	15⅛	16¼	+ 7.44	9
3/14/80	5/16/80	Pay'n Save	19⅜	21¼	+ 9.68	9
3/21/80	5/23/80	Gordon Jewelry Cl A	21⅝	23	+ 6.36	9
3/21/80	5/16/80	Wetterau	11	11⅞	+ 7.95	8
3/21/80	5/16/80	International Multifoods	15⅛	16¼	+ 7.44	8
3/21/80	5/16/80	Pay'n Save	20	21¼	+ 6.25	8
3/21/80	5/16/80	May Department Stores	19¾	22⅝	+14.56	8
3/28/80	5/30/80	Dana Corp.	20⅝	21⅝	+ 4.85	9
3/28/80	5/16/80	Gordon Jewelry Cl A	18⅛	20¼	+11.72	7
3/28/80	5/16/80	Wetterau	10⅜	11⅞	+14.46	7
3/28/80	5/16/80	International Multifoods	13¾	16¼	+18.18	7
3/28/80	5/16/80	May Department Stores	18⅞	22⅝	+19.87	7
12/19/80	3/13/81	Niagara Frontier Services	17½	21	+20.00	12
12/19/80	3/13/81	Gordon Jewelry	19½	22	+12.82	12
12/19/80	3/13/81	Allied Stores	19	23½	+23.68	12
12/19/80	3/13/81	Borden	24½	27½	+12.24	12
12/19/80	3/13/81	Federated Department Strs.	27	35⅜	+31.02	12
8/28/81	10/1/82	Bendix	61⅞	73¼	+18.38	57
8/28/81	10/23/81	Bell Telephone of Canada	14½	14¾	+ 1.72	8
8/28/81	4/22/83	Exxon	33	33⅛	+ .38	85
8/28/81	10/23/81	International Multifoods	19⅛	20½	+ 7.19	8
8/28/81	3/4/83	Mobil	28¾	29⅝	+ 3.04	79
9/4/81	9/3/82	Bendix	57⅝	58½	+ 1.52	52
9/4/81	4/15/83	Exxon	32⅛	33	+ 2.72	84
9/4/81	10/23/81	International Multifoods	18⅝	20½	+10.07	7
9/4/81	3/4/83	Mobil	27¾	29⅝	+ 6.76	78
9/4/81	4/22/83	Canadian Pacific	38½	38¾	+ .65	86

Purchase Date	Selling Date	Company	Purchase Price	Selling Price	Percentage Profit (+) Loss (–)	Holding Period Weeks
9/11/81	10/1/82	Bendix	59¾	73¼	+22.59	55
9/11/81	3/4/83	Mobil	28¼	29⅝	+ 4.87	77
9/11/81	4/29/83	Exxon	33⅝	35¼	+ 4.83	85
9/11/81	10/23/81	International Multifoods	18¾	20½	+ 9.33	6
9/11/81	10/23/81	Standard Oil (California)	41⅝	42⅜	+ 1.80	6
9/18/81	9/3/82	Bendix	56⅛	58½	+ 4.23	50
9/18/81	10/23/81	Bell Telephone of Canada	14⅜	14¾	+ 2.61	5
9/18/81	4/15/83	Exxon	31¼	33	+ 5.60	83
9/18/81	10/23/81	International Multifoods	18⅝	20½	+10.07	5
9/18/81	10/23/81	Mobil	26⅝	27	+ 1.41	5
9/25/81	10/23/81	Bendix	54	55	+ 1.85	4
9/25/81	10/23/81	Exxon	29⅞	30⅛	+ .84	4
9/25/81	10/23/81	Mobil	24⅞	27	+ 8.54	4
9/25/81	10/23/81	Kidde Inc.	36¾	43¾	+19.05	4
9/25/81	10/23/81	International Multifoods	17¾	20½	+15.49	4
1/22/82	9/3/82	Bendix	54¾	58½	+ 6.85	32
1/22/82	10/15/82	Exxon	29⅞	30¾	+ 2.93	38
1/22/82	8/27/82	NBDBancorp	22⅜	23⅛	+ 3.35	31
1/22/82	8/27/82	Mobil	22¾	23⅛	+ 1.65	31
1/22/82	11/12/82	Irving Bank	45¾	45⅞	+ .27	42
6/11/82	8/27/82	Irving Bank	36½	38	+ 4.11	11
6/11/82	9/17/82	Manufacturers Hanover	28¾	30½	+ 6.09	14
6/11/82	8/27/82	Sperry	23⅛	24	+ 3.78	11
6/11/82	8/27/82	Texas Gas Transmission	24¾	25¾	+ 4.04	11
6/11/82	8/3/84	Continental Illinois	26½	4 ¼	–83.96	112
6/18/82	9/17/82	Manufacturers Hanover	27¾	30½	+ 9.91	13
6/18/82	8/27/82	AmSouth Bancorp	17¼	19	+10.14	10
6/18/82	8/27/82	Irving Bank	36¾	38	+ 3.40	10

Purchase Date	Selling Date	Company	Purchase Price	Selling Price	Percentage Profit (+) Loss (–)	Holding Period Weeks
6/18/82	9/3/82	Panhandle Eastern	25¾	26⅜	+ 2.43	11
6/18/82	8/27/82	Sperry	22¼	24	+ 7.87	10
2/10/84	1/18/85	Manufacturers Hanover	38¼	38⅜	+ .33	49
2/10/84	1/18/85	Mellon National	43½	46¾	+ 7.47	49
2/10/84	1/18/85	Pacific Lighting	34⅜	40⅛	+16.73	49
2/10/84	1/9/87	Mercantile Texas (M Corp)	25⅛	11	–56.22	153
2/10/84	9/14/84	Citicorp	36¾	38	+ 3.40	31
2/17/84	2/8/85	Manufacturers Hanover	39½	41¼	+ 4.43	51
2/17/84	8/3/84	Consolidated Edison	23	26⅜	+14.67	24
2/17/84	1/18/85	Mellon National	43⅜	46¾	+ 7.78	48
2/17/84	8/3/84	American Water Works	29½	35½	+20.34	24
2/17/84	1/18/85	New England Electric Sys.	37⅝	38	+ 1.00	48
2/24/84	1/18/85	Manufacturers Hanover	38⅛	38⅜	+ .66	47
2/24/84	8/3/84	American Water Works	29	35½	+22.41	23
2/24/84	8/10/84	Citicorp	34¼	35⅛	+ 2.55	24
2/24/84	8/3/84	Consolidated Edison	23	26⅜	+14.67	23
2/24/84	1/18/84	Mellon National	42	46¾	+11.31	47
5/25/84	8/10/84	Manufacturers Hanover	28¼	28⅝	+ 1.33	11
5/25/84	8/3/84	Citicorp	30	32⅞	+ 9.58	10
5/25/84	8/10/84	Mellon National	37⅞	40¼	+ 6.27	11
5/25/84	8/3/84	First Bank Systems	21¾	24¼	+11.49	10
5/25/84	8/17/84	MercantileTexas	20¾	21⅞	+ 5.42	12
8/16/85	11/1/85	Bank of Boston	49⅝	53¼	+ 7.30	11
8/16/85	11/1/85	SecurityPacific	27⅜	27½	+ .46	11
8/16/85	11/15/85	Texas Utilities	28⅞	29⅝	+ 2.60	13
8/16/85	10/25/85	Central & South West	24½	25½	+ 4.08	10
8/16/85	11/1/85	New England Electric Sys.	43½	43⅞	+ .86	11
9/20/85	10/25/85	Bank of Boston	46½	49½	+ 6.45	5

Purchase Date	Selling Date	Company	Purchase Price	Selling Price	Percentage Profit (+) Loss (–)	Holding Period Weeks
9/20/85	10/25/85	Texas Utilities	26⅝	27⅞	+ 4.69	5
9/20/85	10/25/85	New England Electric Sys.	41½	43¼	+ 4.22	5
9/20/85	11/15/85	M Corp	19⅞	20	+ .63	8
9/20/85	10/25/85	Citicorp	41⅛	41¾	+ 1.52	5
9/27/85	10/25/85	Bank of Boston	45⅝	49½	+ 8.49	4
9/27/85	10/25/85	Texas Utilities	26⅛	27⅞	+ 6.70	4
9/27/85	10/25/85	New England Electric Sys.	41	43¼	+ 5.49	4
9/27/85	11/28/85	M Corp	20	20⅛	+ .63	9
9/27/85	10/25/85	Citicorp	40¾	41¾	+ 2.45	4
9/19/86	10/17/86	Chemical New York	43⅜	44¼	+ 2.02	4
9/19/86	10/17/86	Texas Utilities	33⅛	33½	+ 1.13	4
9/19/86	10/17/86	Central & South West	32⅝	33¾	+ 3.45	4
9/19/86	1/9/87	Mellon Bank	55	56¾	+ 3.18	17
9/19/86	1/9/87	Citicorp	51	56¼	+10.29	17
9/26/86	1/9/87	Chemical New York	44¾	45¾	+ 2.23	16
9/26/86	10/17/86	Security Pacific	34⅛	35⅞	+ 5.13	3
9/26/86	10/17/86	Texas Utilities	32⅝	33½	+ 2.68	3
9/26/86	1/9/87	Mellon Bank	54⅜	56¾	+ 4.37	16
9/26/86	1/9/87	Citicorp	50½	56¼	+11.39	16
10/3/86	10/17/86	Chemical New York	43¼	44¼	+ 2.31	2
10/3/86	1/9/87	Citicorp	49	56¼	+14.80	15
10/3/86	10/17/86	Security Pacific	34⅛	35⅞	+ 5.13	2
10/3/86	10/17/86	Texas Utilities	33¼	33½	+ .75	2
10/3/86	1/9/87	Mellon Bank	54¾	56¾	+ 3.65	15
4/24/87	6/19/87	Chemical New York	41¼	46½	+12.73	8
4/24/87	6/19/87	Capital Holding	29½	32	+ 8.47	8
4/24/87	6/19/87	Texas Utilities	31⅛	33¼	+ 6.83	8
4/24/87	6/19/87	Citicorp	51⅞	63⅝	+22.65	8

Purchase Date	Selling Date	Company	Purchase Price	Selling Price	Percentage Profit (+) Loss (–)	Holding Period Weeks
4/24/87	2/1/91	Rockwell International	28¼	28⅜	+ .44	197
5/1/87	6/19/87	Chemical New York	42¾	46½	+ 8.77	7
5/1/87	6/19/87	Capital Holding	30	32	+ 6.67	7
5/1/87	6/19/87	Texas Utilities	31⅝	33¼	+ 5.14	7
5/1/87	8/14/87	Central & South West	32	33¾	+ 5.47	15
5/1/87	6/19/87	Bank of New York	40¾	42⅞	+ 5.21	7
9/18/87	7/28/89	Texas Utilities	31¼	33¼	+ 6.40	97
9/18/87	5/19/89	New England Electric Sys.	25	25½	+ 2.00	87
9/18/87	1/29/88	Central & South West	30⅝	34⅝	+13.06	19
9/18/87	4/21/89	Capital Holding	33⅞	36⅛	+ 6.64	82
9/18/87	2/5/88	Bell Canada Enterprises	30⅞	30	– 2.83	20
10/16/87	6/9/89	Texas Utilities	30⅞	31¼	+ 1.21	86
10/16/87	5/19/89	New England Electric Sys.	24⅝	25½	+ 3.55	83
10/16/87	10/7/88	Capital Holding	33¼	33⅝	+ 1.13	51
10/16/87	2/12/88	Chemed	33⅛	35½	+ 7.17	16
10/16/87	5/19/89	AmSouth Banocorp	26¼	26⅞	+ 2.38	83
10/23/87	1/29/88	Texas Utilities	29	30	+ 3.45	14
10/23/87	5/19/89	New England Electric Sys.	24¼	25½	+ 5.15	82
10/23/87	1/29/88	Central & South West	31¼	34⅝	+10.80	14
10/23/87	1/8/88	AmSouth Bancorp	23½	25	+ 6.38	11
10/23/87	1/29/88	Capital Holding	29⅜	29¾	+ 1.28	14
10/30/87	1/29/88	Texas Utilities	28¼	30	+ 6.19	13
10/30/87	5/12/89	New England Electric Sys.	24	24¼	+ 1.04	80
10/30/87	12/31/87	Chemed	27½	33¼	+20.91	9
10/30/87	1/8/88	AmSouth Bancorp	23⅞	25	+ 4.71	10
10/30/87	1/8/88	NCNB Corp.	18⅜	19⅜	+ 5.44	10
11/6/87	1/29/88	Texas Utilities	29¾	30	+ .84	12
11/6/87	12/31/87	Chemed	28	33¼	+18.75	8

Purchase Date	Selling Date	Company	Purchase Price	Selling Price	Percentage Profit (+) Loss (–)	Holding Period Weeks
11/6/87	1/8/88	NCNB Corp.	18¾	19⅜	+ 3.33	9
11/6/87	1/8/88	AmSouth Bancorp	23½	25	+ 6.38	9
11/6/87	12/31/87	Capital Holding	26	27	+ 3.85	8
11/13/87	1/29/88	Texas Utilities	28¼	30	+ 6.19	11
11/13/87	12/31/87	Chemed	30¼	33¼	+ 9.92	7
11/13/87	1/8/88	AmSouth Bancorp	23⅛	25	+ 8.11	8
11/13/87	12/31/87	Capital Holding	26⅝	27	+ 1.41	7
11/13/87	5/19/89	New England Electric Sys.	24¼	25½	+ 5.15	79
12/4/87	12/31/87	Texas Utilities	26¾	27	+ .93	4
12/4/87	12/31/87	AmSouth Bancorp	22	23⅛	+ 5.11	4
12/4/87	12/31/87	Affiliated Publications	41¼	57	+38.18	4
12/4/87	12/31/87	New England Electric Sys.	22¼	22⅜	+ .56	4
12/4/87	12/31/87	Central & South West	28¾	29½	+ 2.61	4
12/11/87	12/31/87	Texas Utilities	25¾	27	+ 4.85	3
12/11/87	12/31/87	Affiliated Publications	44¾	57	+27.37	3
12/11/87	12/31/87	New England Electric Sys.	22⅛	22⅜	+ 1.13	3
12/11/87	12/31/87	Central & South West	28⅞	29½	+ 2.16	3
12/11/87	1/8/88	NCNB Corp.	17½	19⅜	+10.71	4
5/6/88	6/10/88	Texas Utilities	25½	25⅝	+ .49	5
5/6/88	6/10/88	New England Electric Sys.	20⅝	23⅜	+13.33	5
5/6/88	6/10/88	Rockwell International	18⅝	20	+ 7.38	5
5/6/88	6/10/88	Central & South West	31	33	+ 6.45	5
5/6/88	6/10/88	Wisconsin Energy	24¾	26⅜	+ 6.57	5
5/13/88	6/10/88	Texas Utilities	25½	25⅝	+ .49	4
5/13/88	6/10/88	New England Electric Sys.	20½	23⅜	+14.02	4
5/13/88	6/10/88	Rockwell International	18¼	20	+ 9.59	4
5/13/88	6/10/88	Capital Holding	27¼	31⅛	+14.22	4
5/13/88	6/10/88	First Virginia Banks	23¼	24⅝	+ 5.91	4

Purchase Date	Selling Date	Company	Purchase Price	Selling Price	Percentage Profit (+) Loss (–)	Holding Period Weeks
5/20/88	6/10/88	Texas Utilities	25⅛	25⅝	+ 1.99	3
5/20/88	6/10/88	Rockwell International	18½	20	+ 8.11	3
5/20/88	6/10/88	Central & South West	30⅞	33	+ 6.88	3
5/20/88	6/10/88	United Jersey Banks	19⅜	21¼	+ 9.68	3
5/20/88	6/10/88	Capital Holding	27¾	31⅛	+12.16	3
5/27/88	6/10/88	United Jersey Banks	19⅞	21¼	+ 6.92	2
5/27/88	6/10/88	American Water Works	15	15⅞	+ 5.83	2
5/27/88	6/10/88	Consolidated Edison	42¾	44¼	+ 3.51	2
5/27/88	6/10/88	First Virginia Banks	23⅝	24⅝	+ 4.23	2
5/27/88	6/10/88	UVV Corp.	29⅜	29⅝	+ .85	2
11/25/88	1/27/89	Rockwell International	19⅜	21⅝	+11.61	9
11/25/88	1/27/89	Texas Utilities	28¾	29⅛	+ 1.30	9
11/25/88	1/27/89	Citytrust Bancorp	38¼	40⅛	+ 4.90	9
11/25/88	1/27/89	Central & South West	30⅝	32¼	+ 5.31	9
11/25/88	4/21/89	United Jersey Banks	21⅝	23⅞	+10.40	20
11/3/89	2/22/91	Fleet/Norstar Financial	27½	14⅝	–46.82	83
11/3/89	5/25/90	Barnett Banks Inc.	34½	35⅝	+ 3.26	29
11/3/89	5/18/90	Rockwell International	23¼	26	+11.83	28
11/3/89	2/15/91	American Water Works	17⅞	18⅜	+ 2.80	67
11/3/89	5/18/90	PPG Industries	39	47¾	+22.44	28
1/26/90	11/6/92	UJB Financial	17⅞	18¼	+ 2.10	145
1/26/90	2/22/91	Fleet/Norstar Financial	24½	14⅝	–40.31	56
1/26/90	5/18/90	SunTrust Banks	20⅝	23¼	+12.73	16
1/26/90	5/18/90	Barnett Banks Inc.	31⅜	32⅞	+ 4.78	16
1/26/90	5/18/90	Rockwell International	22	26	+18.18	16
2/2/90	11/6/92	UJB Financial	19	18¼	– 3.95	144
2/2/90	2/22/91	Fleet/Norstar Financial	24⅛	14⅝	–39.38	55
2/2/90	5/18/90	First Virginia Bankshares	26½	28⅛	+ 6.13	15

Purchase Date	Selling Date	Company	Purchase Price	Selling Price	Percentage Profit (+) Loss (–)	Holding Period Weeks
2/2/90	5/18/90	SunTrust Banks	20⅞	23¼	+11.38	15
2/2/90	5/18/90	Barnett Banks Inc.	31¼	32⅞	+ 5.20	15
2/16/90	11/6/92	UJB Financial	18	18¼	+ 1.39	142
2/16/90	2/22/91	Fleet/Norstar Financial	24⅛	14⅝	–39.38	53
2/16/90	5/25/90	Barnett Banks Inc.	33	35⅝	+ 7.95	14
2/16/90	5/18/90	Rockwell International	21⅝	26	+20.23	13
2/16/90	5/18/90	SunTrust Banks	21⅝	23¼	+ 7.51	13
4/27/90	5/18/90	UJB Financial	14	16¾	+19.64	3
4/27/90	5/18/90	Fleet/Norstar Financial	19	22⅛	+16.45	3
4/27/90	5/18/90	Capital Holding	42¼	45⅞	+ 8.58	3
4/27/90	5/18/90	SunTrust Banks	20⅜	23¼	+14.11	3
4/27/90	5/18/90	Raytheon Co.	62⅞	64¾	+ 2.98	3
8/10/90	4/19/91	UJB Financial	11½	12⅝	+ 9.78	36
8/10/90	12/14/90	First Virginia Banks	23⅛	23¼	+ .54	18
8/10/90	2/1/91	*First of America Bank	21¾	23⅝	+ 8.62	25
8/10/90	11/23/90	SunTrust Banks	20⅛	21⅛	+ 4.97	15
8/10/90	2/1/91	Universal Corp.	23⅞	27½	+15.18	25
8/17/90	4/19/91	UJB Financial	11½	12⅝	+ 9.78	35
8/17/90	12/7/90	First Virginia Banks	21¼	23	+ 8.24	16
8/17/90	2/1/90	First of America Bank	21⅝	23⅝	+ 9.25	24
8/17/90	11/23/90	Raytheon	60	67¾	+12.92	14
8/17/90	2/1/90	Universal Corp.	23⅞	27½	+15.18	24
8/24/90	4/19/91	UJB Financial	10⅞	12⅝	+16.09	34
8/24/90	12/7/90	First Virginia Banks	21	23	+ 9.52	15
8/24/90	12/7/91	*First of America Bank	20³⁄₁₆	20½	+ 1.55	15
8/24/90	11/23/91	Universal Corp.	23½	23¾	+ 1.06	13
8/24/90	2/15/91	Barrnett Banks	24⅜	24⅝	+ 1.03	25
8/31/90	12/7/90	First Virginia Banks	22	23	+ 4.55	14

Purchase Date	Selling Date	Company	Purchase Price	Selling Price	Percentage Profit (+) Loss (−)	Holding Period Weeks
8/31/90	12/21/90	*First of America Bank	$20\frac{3}{4}$	$21\frac{7}{8}$	+ 3.01	16
8/31/90	11/23/90	SunTrust Banks	$19\frac{7}{8}$	$21\frac{1}{8}$	+ 6.29	12
8/31/90	11/23/90	Universal Corp.	$23\frac{1}{4}$	$23\frac{3}{4}$	+ 2.15	12
8/31/90	3/1/91	Barnett Banks	25	$25\frac{1}{2}$	+ 2.00	26
9/7/90	12/7/90	First Virginia Banks	$22\frac{1}{2}$	23	+ 2.22	13
9/7/90	12/21/90	*First of America Bank	$20\frac{11}{16}$	$21\frac{3}{8}$	+ 3.23	15
9/7/90	11/23/90	SunTrust Banks	$19\frac{3}{8}$	$21\frac{1}{8}$	+ 9.03	11
9/7/90	4/19/91	Barnett Banks Inc.	$24\frac{5}{8}$	$27\frac{7}{8}$	+11.17	32
9/7/90	12/7/90	Mercantile Stores	$29\frac{7}{8}$	$30\frac{1}{4}$	+ 1.26	13
9/28/90	2/8/91	UJB Financial	$9\frac{1}{8}$	$9\frac{1}{2}$	+ 4.11	19
9/28/90	11/23/90	Barnett Banks Inc.	$17\frac{7}{8}$	$18\frac{1}{2}$	+ 3.50	8
9/28/90	11/23/90	First Virginia Banks	$18\frac{1}{8}$	$19\frac{1}{4}$	+ 6.21	8
9/28/90	11/30/90	VF Corp.	$15\frac{1}{2}$	$15\frac{3}{4}$	+ 1.61	9
9/28/90	12/7/90	First of America Bank	$18\frac{15}{16}$	$20\frac{1}{2}$	+ 8.25	10
10/12/90	11/23/90	UJB Financial	$8\frac{1}{8}$	$8\frac{5}{8}$	+ 6.15	6
10/12/90	11/23/90	Barnett Banks	15	$18\frac{1}{2}$	+23.33	6
10/12/90	11/23/90	First Virginia Banks	$18\frac{3}{8}$	$19\frac{1}{4}$	+ 4.76	6
10/12/90	11/23/90	First of America Bank	$15\frac{13}{16}$	$18\frac{1}{4}$	+15.42	6
10/12/90	11/23/90	Capital Holding	29	$33\frac{7}{8}$	+16.81	6

The following purchase prices were adjusted for stock splits as follows:

2/11/77	Shell Oil	2:1	8/24/90	First of America Bank	2:1
2/18/77	Shell Oil	2:1	8/31/90	First of America Bank	2:1
4/7/77	Shell Oil	2:1	9/7/90	First of America Bank	2:1
8/10/90	First of America Bank	2:1	9/28/90	First of America Bank	2:1
8/17/90	First of America Bank	2:1			

Time Overlay: Yield

Purchase Date	Selling Date	Company	Purchase Price	Selling Price	Percentage Profit (+) Loss (–)	Holding Period Weeks
2/4/77	6/24/77	American Brands	$44\frac{1}{2}$	$47\frac{7}{8}$	+ 7.58	20
2/4/77	6/24/77	Texas Utilities	$21\frac{1}{8}$	$21\frac{3}{4}$	+ 2.96	20
2/4/77	6/24/77	Reynolds (R.J.) Indus.	64	67	+ 4.69	20
2/4/77	5/5/78	Sterling Drugs	$15\frac{3}{8}$	$15\frac{7}{8}$	+ 3.25	65
2/4/77	6/24/77	Saerle (G.D.)	$11\frac{7}{8}$	$12\frac{7}{8}$	+ 8.42	20
2/11/77	6/24/77	American Brands	$43\frac{3}{4}$	$47\frac{7}{8}$	+ 9.43	19
2/11/77	6/24/77	Labatt (John) Ltd. Cv A	$16\frac{5}{8}$	$19\frac{1}{8}$	+15.04	18
2/11/77	6/24/77	Texas Utilities	$20\frac{7}{8}$	$21\frac{3}{4}$	+ 4.19	19
2/11/77	6/24/77	Standard Oil (California)	$39\frac{5}{8}$	$42\frac{3}{8}$	+ 6.94	19
2/11/77	6/24/77	Reynolds (R.J.) Indus.	$64\frac{1}{8}$	67	+ 4.48	19
2/18/77	6/24/77	American Brands	44	$47\frac{7}{8}$	+ 8.81	18
2/18/77	6/24/77	Texas Utilities	$20\frac{1}{4}$	$21\frac{3}{4}$	+ 7.41	18
2/18/77	6/24/77	Labatt (John) Ltd. Cv A	$16\frac{5}{8}$	$19\frac{1}{8}$	+15.04	18
2/18/77	6/24/77	Tampax	$35\frac{1}{4}$	$37\frac{1}{2}$	+ 6.38	18
2/18/77	6/24/77	Standard Oil (California)	$40\frac{1}{8}$	$42\frac{3}{8}$	+ 5.61	18
4/1/77	6/24/77	Exxon	51	$52\frac{1}{4}$	+ 2.45	12
4/1/77	6/24/77	Standard Oil (California)	$39\frac{7}{8}$	$42\frac{3}{8}$	+ 6.27	12
4/1/77	6/24/77	Reynolds (R.J.) Indus.	64	67	+ 4.69	12
4/1/77	6/24/77	Standard Oil (Indiana)	$52\frac{1}{4}$	$54\frac{1}{4}$	+ 3.83	12
4/1/77	6/24/77	Texas Utilities	$19\frac{3}{4}$	$21\frac{3}{4}$	+10.13	12
4/7/77	6/24/77	Texas Utilities	$19\frac{1}{8}$	$21\frac{3}{4}$	+13.73	11
4/7/77	6/24/77	Tampax	$33\frac{1}{2}$	$37\frac{1}{2}$	+11.94	11
4/7/77	6/24/77	Exxon	$50\frac{3}{4}$	$52\frac{1}{4}$	+ 2.96	11
4/7/77	6/24/77	Mobil	$65\frac{7}{8}$	$68\frac{3}{4}$	+ 4.36	11
4/7/77	6/24/77	Standard Oil (California)	$39\frac{5}{8}$	$42\frac{3}{8}$	+ 6.94	11
4/29/77	6/24/77	Texas Utilities	$19\frac{1}{4}$	$21\frac{3}{4}$	+12.99	8
4/29/77	6/24/77	American Tel. & Tel.	63	$63\frac{5}{8}$	+ .99	8
4/29/77	6/24/77	Labatt (John) Ltd. Cv A	$16\frac{5}{8}$	$19\frac{1}{8}$	+15.04	8

Purchase Date	Selling Date	Company	Purchase Price	Selling Price	Percentage Profit (+) Loss (–)	Holding Period Weeks
4/29/77	6/24/77	Mobil	66¼	68¾	+ 3.77	8
4/29/77	6/24/77	Heublein	23½	26	+10.64	8
5/13/77	6/24/77	Texas Utilities	19½	21¾	+11.54	6
5/13/77	6/24/77	Labatt (John) Ltd. Cv A	17½	19⅛	+ 9.29	6
5/13/77	6/24/77	Exxon	51⅜	52¼	+ 1.70	6
5/13/77	6/24/77	Mobil	66⅜	68¾	+ 3.58	6
5/13/77	6/24/77	Sterling Drug	13⅞	14⅞	+ 7.21	6
1/4/77	11/18/77	American Tel. & Tel.	59⅛	60⅞	+ 2.96	2
1/4/77	11/18/77	Texas Utilities	20⅛	21¼	+ 5.59	2
1/4/77	11/18/77	Mobil	61⅜	63¾	+ 3.87	2
1/4/77	11/18/77	Tampax	30	34¼	+14.17	2
1/4/77	11/18/77	Exxon	47	47¾	+ 1.60	2
1/6/78	4/14/78	Mobil	60⅝	62⅞	+ 3.71	14
1/6/78	4/14/78	Tampax	33¼	36½	+ 9.77	14
1/6/78	4/14/78	Exxon	45⅝	46¾	+ 2.47	14
1/6/78	4/14/78	Standard Oil (California)	37	40	+ 8.11	14
1/6/78	4/14/78	Reynolds (R.J.) Indus.	55¾	58¼	+ 4.48	14
1/13/78	4/14/78	American Tel. & Tel.	59	62	+ 5.08	13
1/13/78	4/14/78	Texas Utilities	19⅞	20¼	+ 1.89	13
1/13/78	4/14/78	Mobil	59⅞	62⅞	+ 5.01	13
1/13/78	4/14/78	Standard Oil (California)	35⅝	40	+13.07	13
1/13/78	4/14/78	Exxon	44½	46¾	+ 5.06	13
1/20/78	4/14/78	American Tel. & Tel.	57¾	62	+ 7.36	12
1/20/78	4/14/78	Texas Utilities	19¾	20¼	+ 2.53	12
1/20/78	4/14/78	Mobil	59⅞	62⅞	+ 5.01	12
1/20/78	4/14/78	Standard Oil (California)	35¼	40	+13.48	12
1/20/78	4/14/78	Exxon	43⅞	46¾	+ 6.55	12
1/27/78	4/14/78	American Tel. & Tel.	57⅛	62	+ 8.53	11

Purchase Date	Selling Date	Company	Purchase Price	Selling Price	Percentage Profit (+) Loss (–)	Holding Period Weeks
1/27/78	4/14/78	Exxon	$43\frac{3}{4}$	$46\frac{3}{4}$	+ 6.86	11
1/27/78	4/14/78	Texas Utilities	$19\frac{3}{4}$	$20\frac{1}{4}$	+ 2.53	11
1/27/78	4/14/78	Mobil	$59\frac{3}{4}$	$62\frac{7}{8}$	+ 5.23	11
1/27/78	4/14/78	Standard Oil (California)	$35\frac{5}{8}$	40	+12.28	11
10/6/78	4/8/82	Texas Utilities	$20\frac{1}{4}$	$21\frac{3}{4}$	+ 7.41	183
10/6/78	1/19/79	Tampax	29	33	+13.79	15
10/6/78	1/26/79	Standard Brands	$25\frac{3}{4}$	$26\frac{1}{4}$	+ 1.94	16
10/6/78	8/17/79	Lucky Stores	$16\frac{3}{8}$	$16\frac{3}{4}$	+ 2.29	45
10/6/78	8/10/79	Universal Leaf Tobacco	$20\frac{1}{8}$	$23\frac{1}{8}$	+14.91	44
10/20/78	1/19/79	Tampax	$26\frac{1}{4}$	33	+25.71	13
10/20/78	1/19/79	Texas Utilities	$19\frac{3}{8}$	$19\frac{5}{8}$	+ 1.29	13
10/20/78	1/26/79	Exxon	50	$51\frac{1}{4}$	+ 2.50	14
10/20/78	1/19/79	Mobil	$67\frac{1}{2}$	$70\frac{1}{8}$	+ 3.89	13
10/20/78	3/30/79	Reynolds (R.J.) Indus.	$58\frac{5}{8}$	$58\frac{3}{4}$	+ .21	23
10/27/78	1/19/79	Texas Utilities	$18\frac{5}{8}$	$19\frac{5}{8}$	+ 5.37	12
10/27/78	1/19/79	Tampax	$27\frac{1}{2}$	33	+20.00	12
10/27/78	1/19/79	American Tel. & Tel.	61	$61\frac{1}{8}$	+ .20	12
10/27/78	1/19/79	Exxon	49	$49\frac{1}{8}$	+ .26	12
10/27/78	1/26/79	Reynolds (R.J.) Indus.	$57\frac{1}{2}$	58	+ .87	13
11/3/78	1/19/79	Tampax	25	33	+32.00	11
11/3/78	1/19/79	Texas Utilities	$18\frac{3}{4}$	$19\frac{5}{8}$	+ 4.67	11
11/3/78	1/19/79	American Tel. & Tel.	61	$61\frac{1}{8}$	+ .20	11
11/3/78	1/26/79	Reynolds (R.J.) Indus.	$57\frac{1}{8}$	58	+ 1.53	12
11/3/78	1/19/79	Mobil	$68\frac{3}{4}$	$70\frac{1}{8}$	+ 2.00	11
11/10/78	1/19/79	Texas Utilities	$19\frac{1}{4}$	$19\frac{5}{8}$	+ 1.95	10
11/10/78	1/19/79	American Tel. & Tel.	$60\frac{5}{8}$	$61\frac{1}{8}$	+ .82	10
11/10/78	1/19/79	Mobil	$66\frac{7}{8}$	$70\frac{1}{8}$	+ 4.86	10
11/10/78	1/26/79	Exxon	$49\frac{7}{8}$	$51\frac{1}{4}$	+ 2.76	11

Purchase Date	Selling Date	Company	Purchase Price	Selling Price	Percentage Profit (+) Loss (–)	Holding Period Weeks
11/10/78	1/26/79	Reynolds (R.J.) Indus.	56¾	58	+ 2.20	11
3/2/79	3/23/79	American Tel. & Tel.	61½	61⅝	+ .20	3
3/2/79	3/23/79	Exxon	50	52¼	+ 4.50	64
3/2/79	5/23/80	Tampax	31¼	33	+ 5.60	64
3/2/79	3/23/79	Reynolds (R.J.) Indus.	55⅞	58⅝	+ 4.92	3
3/2/79	3/23/79	Kellogg	17¾	18½	+ 4.23	3
10/19/79	12/7/79	American Tel. & Tel.	52¼	54	+ 3.35	7
10/19/79	12/7/79	Texas Utilities	17½	18¾	+ 7.14	7
10/19/79	5/16/80	Exxon	57⅜	60⅜	+ 5.23	31
10/19/79	12/7/79	Kellogg	18⅛	19	+ 4.83	7
10/19/79	12/7/79	Sears Roebuck & Co	18¼	18⅜	+ .68	7
10/26/79	12/7/79	American Tel. & Tel.	52⅞	54	+ 2.13	6
10/26/79	12/7/79	Texas Utilities	17¾	18¾	+ 5.63	6
10/26/79	12/7/79	Exxon	56¼	56⅞	+ 1.11	6
10/26/79	12/7/79	Kellogg	17⅝	19	+ 7.80	6
10/26/79	7/11/80	Borden	25⅝	25¾	+ .49	37
11/2/79	12/7/79	American Tel. & Tel.	53½	54	+ .93	5
11/2/79	12/7/79	Texas Utilities	17⅞	18¾	+ 4.90	5
11/2/79	12/7/79	Kellogg	18¼	19	+ 4.11	5
11/2/79	12/7/79	Colgate-Palmolive	14	14⅝	+ 4.46	5
11/2/79	5/23/80	Bendix	41	42	+ 2.44	29
3/7/80	5/16/80	Texas Utilities	15½	18⅜	+18.55	10
3/7/80	5/16/80	American Tel. & Tel.	45⅛	52⅞	+17.17	10
3/7/80	5/16/80	Central Tel. & Utilities	21⅝	24⅛	+11.56	10
3/7/80	5/16/80	Sears Roebuck & Co	15½	18	+16.13	10
3/7/80	5/16/80	Colgate-Palmolive	12¼	15	+22.45	10
3/14/80	5/16/80	American Tel. & Tel.	47⅜	52⅞	+11.61	9
3/14/80	5/16/80	Central Tel. & Utilities	22⅝	24⅛	+ 6.63	9

Purchase Date	Selling Date	Company	Purchase Price	Selling Price	Percentage Profit (+) Loss (–)	Holding Period Weeks
3/14/80	5/16/80	Sears Roebuck & Co	15⅞	18	+13.39	9
3/14/80	5/16/80	Colgate-Palmolive	12⅝	15	+18.81	9
3/14/80	5/16/80	Borden	21⅝	23¼	+ 7.51	9
3/21/80	5/16/80	American Tel. & Tel.	47⅛	52⅞	+12.20	8
3/21/80	5/16/80	Sears Roebuck & Co	15	18	+20.00	8
3/21/80	5/16/80	Borden	21⅜	23¼	+ 8.77	8
3/21/80	5/16/80	Kellogg	15⅞	18¼	+14.96	8
3/21/80	5/16/80	Exxon	58½	60⅜	+ 3.21	8
3/28/80	5/16/80	American Tel. & Tel.	48½	52⅞	+ 9.02	7
3/28/80	5/16/80	Sears Roebuck & Co	16	18	+12.50	7
3/28/80	5/16/80	Central Tel. & Utilities	22⅜	24⅛	+ 7.82	7
3/28/80	5/16/80	Borden	20⅜	23¼	+14.11	7
3/28/80	5/16/80	Kellogg	16⅜	18¼	+11.45	7
12/19/80	3/13/81	Allied Stores	19	23½	+23.68	12
12/19/80	3/13/81	Borden	24½	27½	+12.24	12
12/19/80	3/13/81	Luckey Stores	14⅜	16⅛	+12.17	12
12/19/80	3/13/81	International Multifoods	17¾	19½	+ 9.86	12
12/19/80	3/13/81	Kellogg	18⅜	23½	+27.89	12
8/28/81	10/23/81	Bell Telephone of Canada	14½	14¾	+ 1.72	8
8/28/81	10/23/81	American Tel. & Tel.	55¾	57⅞	+ 3.81	8
8/28/81	4/22/83	Exxon	33	33⅛	+ .38	84
8/28/81	10/23/81	International Multifoods	19⅛	20½	+ 7.19	8
8/28/81	4/9/82	Borden	28¼	33	+16.81	32
9/4/81	10/23/81	American Tel. & Tel.	54¾	57⅞	+ 5.71	7
9/4/81	4/15/83	Exxon	32⅛	33	+ 2.72	84
9/4/81	10/23/81	United Telecom.	19¾	20½	+ 3.80	7
9/4/81	10/23/81	International Multifoods	18⅝	20½	+10.07	7
9/4/81	10/8/82	Texas Eastern	49½	53¼	+ 7.58	57

Purchase Date	Selling Date	Company	Purchase Price	Selling Price	Percentage Profit (+) Loss (–)	Holding Period Weeks
9/11/81	10/23/81	American Tel. & Tel.	$56\frac{5}{8}$	$57\frac{7}{8}$	+ 2.21	6
9/11/81	4/29/83	Exxon	$33\frac{5}{8}$	$35\frac{1}{4}$	+ 4.83	85
9/11/81	10/23/81	United Telecom.	$19\frac{5}{8}$	$20\frac{1}{2}$	+ 4.46	6
9/11/81	4/15/83	Genstar	$21\frac{5}{8}$	$21\frac{1}{8}$	– 2.31	83
9/11/81	10/23/81	International Multifoods	$18\frac{3}{4}$	$20\frac{1}{2}$	+ 9.33	6
9/18/81	10/23/81	Bell Telephone of Canada	$14\frac{3}{8}$	$14\frac{3}{4}$	+ 2.61	5
9/18/81	10/23/81	American Tel. & Tel.	$55\frac{7}{8}$	$57\frac{7}{8}$	+ 3.58	5
9/18/81	4/15/83	Exxon	$31\frac{1}{4}$	33	+ 5.60	82
9/18/81	10/23/81	United Telecom.	$19\frac{5}{8}$	$20\frac{1}{2}$	+ 4.46	5
9/18/81	4/15/83	Genstar	$22\frac{1}{2}$	$21\frac{1}{8}$	– 6.11	82
9/25/81	10/23/81	Exxon	$29\frac{7}{8}$	$30\frac{1}{8}$	+ .83	[illegible]
9/25/81	10/23/81	United Telecom.	$19\frac{5}{8}$	$20\frac{1}{2}$	+ 4.46	4
9/25/81	4/15/83	Genstar	21	$21\frac{1}{8}$	+ .60	81
9/25/81	10/23/81	International Multifoods	$17\frac{3}{4}$	$20\frac{1}{2}$	+15.49	4
9/25/81	10/23/81	Texas Eastern	$45\frac{3}{4}$	$48\frac{1}{2}$	+ 6.01	4
1/22/82	4/16/82	Bell Telephone of Canada	$15\frac{3}{8}$	$15\frac{1}{2}$	+ .81	12
1/22/82	10/15/82	Exxon	$29\frac{7}{8}$	$30\frac{3}{4}$	+ 2.93	38
1/22/82	11/12/82	Genstar	$18\frac{1}{8}$	$19\frac{1}{2}$	+ 7.59	42
1/22/82	9/24/82	Tenneco	$29\frac{7}{8}$	$30\frac{1}{4}$	+ 1.26	35
1/22/82	4/23/82	United Telecom.	$20\frac{1}{8}$	$20\frac{1}{4}$	+ .62	13
6/11/82	9/3/82	Amstead Industries	$21\frac{3}{8}$	$22\frac{3}{4}$	+ 6.43	12
6/11/82	8/27/82	Exxon	$28\frac{1}{8}$	$28\frac{3}{8}$	+ .89	11
6/11/82	9/17/82	Manufacturers Hanover	$28\frac{3}{4}$	$30\frac{1}{2}$	+ 6.09	14
6/11/82	8/27/82	American Tel. & Tel.	$52\frac{1}{8}$	$55\frac{3}{8}$	+ 6.24	11
6/11/82	8/27/82	Tenneco	25	27	+ 8.00	11
6/18/82	8/27/82	Amstead Industries	$21\frac{1}{8}$	$21\frac{1}{4}$	+ .59	10
6/18/82	8/27/82	Exxon	$27\frac{1}{4}$	$28\frac{3}{8}$	+ 4.13	10
6/18/82	8/27/82	Tenneco	$23\frac{7}{8}$	27	+13.09	10

Purchase Date	Selling Date	Company	Purchase Price	Selling Price	Percentage Profit (+) Loss (−)	Holding Period Weeks
6/18/82	8/27/82	American Tel. & Tel.	50⅝	55⅜	+ 9.38	10
6/18/82	9/17/82	Manufacturers Hanover	27¾	30½	+ 9.91	13
2/10/84	1/18/85	Pacific Lighting	34⅜	40⅛	+16.73	49
2/10/84	1/18/85	United Telecom.	20¾	23⅛	+11.45	49
2/10/84	1/18/85	Manufacturers Hanover	38¼	38⅜	+ .33	49
2/10/84	8/10/84	GTE	40¼	42¼	+ 4.97	26
2/10/84	8/24/84	Tenneco	38⅝	39½	+ 2.27	28
2/17/84	8/3/84	GTE	37	40⅛	+ 8.45	24
2/17/84	1/18/85	United Telecom.	20½	23⅛	+12.80	48
2/17/84	8/3/84	Consolidated Edison	23	26⅜	+14.67	24
2/17/84	1/18/85	New England Electric Sys.	37⅝	38	+ 1.00	48
2/17/84	2/8/85	Manufacturers Hanover	39½	41¼	+ 4.43	51
2/24/84	8/3/84	Consolidated Edison	23	26⅜	+14.67	23
2/24/84	1/18/85	United Telecom.	20	23⅛	+15.63	47
2/24/84	1/18/85	New England Electric Sys.	35⅜	38	+ 7.42	47
2/24/84	8/3/84	GTE	37⅜	40⅛	+ 7.36	23
2/24/84	1/18/85	Manufacturers Hanover	38⅛	38⅜	+ .66	47
5/25/84	8/3/84	United Telecom.	17¾	19¼	+ 8.45	10
5/25/84	8/10/84	Manufacturers Hanover	28¼	28⅝	+ 1.33	11
5/25/84	8/3/84	GTE	36⅜	40⅛	+10.31	10
5/25/84	8/3/84	Bell Canada Enterprises	22⅜	26	+16.20	10
5/25/84	8/3/84	Centel	33½	36¾	+ 9.70	10
8/16/85	11/15/85	Texas Utilities	28⅞	29½	+ 2.16	13
8/16/85	10/25/85	Central & South West	24½	25½	+ 4.08	10
8/16/85	11/1/85	New England Electric Sys.	43½	43⅞	+ .86	11
8/16/85	11/8/85	National Fuel Gas	26¼	27¼	+ 3.81	12
8/16/85	10/25/85	GTE	39	39¾	+ 1.92	10
9/20/85	10/25/85	Texas Utilities	26⅝	27⅞	+ 4.69	5

Purchase Date	Selling Date	Company	Purchase Price	Selling Price	Percentage Profit (+) Loss (−)	Holding Period Weeks
9/20/85	10/25/85	New England Electric Sys.	41½	43¼	+ 4.22	5
9/20/85	10/25/85	Central & South West	24	25½	+ 6.25	5
9/20/85	10/25/85	Tucson Electric Power	38	39⅛	+ 2.96	5
9/20/85	11/1/85	National Fuel Gas	26	26¼	+ .96	6
9/27/85	10/25/85	Texas Utilities	26⅛	27⅞	+ 6.70	4
9/27/85	10/25/85	New England Electric Sys.	41	43¼	+ 5.49	4
9/27/85	10/25/85	Central & South West	24½	25½	+ 4.08	4
9/27/85	10/25/85	GTE	38½	39¾	+ 3.25	4
9/27/85	10/25/85	National Fuel Gas	25⅝	25¾	+ .49	4
9/19/86	10/17/86	Texas Utilities	33⅛	33½	+ 1.13	4
9/19/86	1/9/87	Pacific Lighting	47⅛	51¾	+ 9.81	17
9/19/86	10/17/86	New England Electric Sys.	28¼	28⅞	+ 2.21	4
9/19/86	10/17/86	Central & South West	32⅝	33¾	+ 3.45	4
9/19/86	1/9/87	Bell Canada Enterprises	26⅞	28⅜	+ 5.58	17
9/26/86	10/17/86	Texas Utilities	32⅝	33½	+ 2.68	3
9/26/86	1/9/87	Pacific Lighting	48⅞	51¾	+ 5.88	16
9/26/86	1/9/87	New England Electric Sys.	29⅜	31⅛	+ 5.96	16
9/26/86	1/9/87	Central & South West	33¾	36½	+ 8.15	16
9/26/86	1/9/87	Bell Canada Enterprises	27	28⅜	+ 5.09	16
10/3/86	10/17/86	Texas Utilities	33¼	33½	+ .75	2
10/3/86	1/9/87	Pacific Lighting	48¼	51¾	+ 7.25	15
10/3/86	1/9/87	New England Electric Sys.	28⅞	31⅛	+ 7.79	15
10/3/86	10/17/86	Central & South West	33½	33¾	+ .75	2
10/3/86	1/9/87	Bell Canada Enterprises	27	28⅜	+ 5.09	15
4/24/87	6/19/87	Texas Utilities	31⅛	33¼	+ 6.83	8
4/24/87	6/19/87	Central & South West	31⅛	31¾	+ 2.01	8
4/24/87	6/19/87	New England Electric Sys.	27½	27⅞	+ 1.36	8
4/24/87	6/19/87	Consolidated Edison	42	44½	+ 5.95	8

Purchase Date	Selling Date	Company	Purchase Price	Selling Price	Percentage Profit (+) Loss (−)	Holding Period Weeks
4/24/87	6/19/87	Chemical New York	$41\frac{1}{4}$	$46\frac{1}{2}$	+12.73	8
5/1/87	6/19/87	Texas Utilities	$31\frac{5}{8}$	$33\frac{1}{4}$	+ 5.14	7
5/1/87	8/14/87	Central & South West	32	$33\frac{3}{4}$	+ 5.47	15
5/1/87	6/19/87	Consolidated Edison	$42\frac{3}{4}$	$44\frac{1}{2}$	+ 4.09	7
5/1/87	6/19/87	Chemical New York	$42\frac{3}{4}$	$46\frac{1}{2}$	+ 8.77	7
5/1/87	6/19/87	Bell Canada Enterprises	$30\frac{7}{8}$	$31\frac{3}{8}$	+ 1.62	7
9/18/87	7/28/89	Texas Utilities	$31\frac{1}{4}$	$33\frac{1}{4}$	+ 6.40	97
9/18/87	5/19/89	New England Electric Sys.	25	$25\frac{1}{2}$	+ 2.00	87
9/18/87	1/29/88	Central & South West	$30\frac{5}{8}$	$34\frac{5}{8}$	+13.06	19
9/18/87	2/12/88	Chemical New York	$37\frac{3}{8}$	$22\frac{3}{4}$	−39.74	21
9/18/87	1/29/88	Consolidated Edison	$43\frac{1}{4}$	$47\frac{1}{4}$	+ 9.25	19
10/16/87	6/9/89	Texas Utilities	$30\frac{7}{8}$	$31\frac{1}{4}$	+ 1.21	86
10/16/87	5/19/89	New England Electric Sys.	$24\frac{5}{8}$	$25\frac{1}{2}$	+ 3.55	83
10/16/87	1/8/88	Bell Canada Enterprises	$28\frac{1}{2}$	$28\frac{7}{8}$	+ 1.32	12
10/16/87	9/16/88	CP National	$28\frac{7}{8}$	35	+21.21	48
10/16/87	5/19/89	National Fuel Gas	21	$22\frac{1}{4}$	+ 5.95	83
10/23/87	1/29/88	Texas Utilities	29	30	+ 3.45	14
10/23/87	5/19/89	New England Electric Sys.	$24\frac{1}{4}$	$25\frac{1}{2}$	+ 5.15	82
10/23/87	1/29/88	Central & South West	$31\frac{1}{4}$	$34\frac{5}{8}$	+10.80	14
10/23/87	12/31/87	Bell Canada Enterprises	$28\frac{1}{8}$	$28\frac{1}{2}$	+ 1.33	10
10/23/87	1/29/88	Tucson Electric Power	$54\frac{3}{4}$	$58\frac{5}{8}$	+ 6.62	14
10/30/87	1/29/88	Texas Utilities	$28\frac{1}{4}$	30	+ 6.19	13
10/30/87	5/12/89	New England Electric Sys.	24	$24\frac{1}{4}$	+ 1.04	80
10/30/87	1/29/88	Central & South West	$31\frac{1}{4}$	$34\frac{5}{8}$	+10.80	13
10/30/87	1/29/88	Consolidated Edison	$43\frac{1}{4}$	$47\frac{1}{4}$	+ 9.25	9
10/30/87	12/31/87	CP National	$23\frac{3}{4}$	24	+ 1.05	9
11/6/87	1/29/88	Texas Utilities	$29\frac{3}{8}$	30	+ 2.13	12
11/6/87	5/12/89	New England Electric Sys.	24	$24\frac{1}{4}$	+ 1.04	79

Purchase Date	Selling Date	Company	Purchase Price	Selling Price	Percentage Profit (+) Loss (−)	Holding Period Weeks
11/6/87	1/29/88	Central & South West	31⅛	34⅝	+11.24	12
11/6/87	1/29/88	CP National	25⅝	27⅛	+ 5.85	12
11/6/87	12/31/87	Service Master L.P.	23⅝	23¾	+ .53	8
11/13/87	1/29/88	Texas Utilities	28¼	30	+ 6.19	11
11/13/87	5/19/89	New England Electric Sys.	24¼	25½	+ 5.15	79
11/13/87	1/8/88	Central & South West	29¾	30⅛	+ 1.26	8
11/13/87	1/8/88	CP National	25	25⅛	+ .50	8
11/13/87	1/29/88	Consolidated Edison	43⅞	47¼	+ 7.69	11
12/4/87	12/31/87	Texas Utilities	26¾	27	+ .93	4
12/4/87	12/31/87	New England Electric Sys.	22¼	22⅜	+ .56	4
12/4/87	12/31/87	Central & South West	28¾	29½	+ 2.61	4
12/4/87	12/31/87	Security Pacific	24⅝	25⅜	+ 3.05	4
12/4/87	1/8/88	Consolidated Edison	42¼	43	+ 1.78	5
12/11/87	12/31/87	Texas Utilities	25¾	27	+ 4.85	3
12/11/87	12/31/87	New England Electric Sys.	22⅛	22⅜	+ 1.13	3
12/11/87	12/31/87	Central & South West	28⅞	29½	+ 2.16	3
12/11/87	12/31/87	Security Pacific	24½	25⅜	+ 3.57	3
12/11/87	1/8/88	Bank of New York	25⅞	30	+15.94	4
5/6/88	6/10/88	Texas Utilities	25½	25⅝	+ .49	5
5/6/88	6/10/88	New England Electric Sys.	20⅝	23⅜	+13.33	5
5/6/88	6/10/88	Central & South West	31	33	+ 6.45	5
5/6/88	6/10/88	Consolidated Edison	42½	44¼	+ 4.12	5
5/6/88	6/10/88	Tucson Electric Power	55¾	56¾	+ 1.79	5
5/13/88	6/10/88	Texas Utilities	25½	25⅝	+ .49	4
5/13/88	6/10/88	New England Electric Sys.	20½	23⅜	+14.02	4
5/13/88	6/10/88	Consolidated Edison	41⅛	44¼	+ 7.60	4
5/13/88	6/10/88	Tucson Electric Power	55½	56¾	+ 2.25	4
5/13/88	6/10/88	Potomac Electric	21	22⅛	+ 5.36	4

Purchase Date	Selling Date	Company	Purchase Price	Selling Price	Percentage Profit (+) Loss (−)	Holding Period Weeks
5/20/88	6/10/88	Texas Utilities	$25\frac{1}{8}$	$25\frac{5}{8}$	+ 1.99	3
5/20/88	6/10/88	Consolidated Edison	$41\frac{3}{4}$	$44\frac{1}{4}$	+ 5.99	3
5/20/'88	6/10/88	Central & South West	$30\frac{7}{8}$	33	+ 6.88	3
5/2(88	6/10/88	Potomac Electric	$20\frac{7}{8}$	$22\frac{1}{8}$	+ 5.99	3
5/20/88	6/10/88	BCE Inc.	$29\frac{5}{8}$	$30\frac{3}{8}$	+ 2.53	3
5/27/88	6/10/88	Consolidated Edison	$42\frac{3}{4}$	$44\frac{1}{4}$	+ 3.51	2
5/27/88	6/10/88	Potomac Electric	$20\frac{7}{8}$	$22\frac{1}{8}$	+ 5.99	2
5/27/88	6/10/88	BCE Inc.	$29\frac{7}{8}$	$30\frac{3}{8}$	+ 1.67	2
5/27/88	6/10/88	Service Master L.P.	$25\frac{1}{2}$	$26\frac{1}{2}$	+ 3.92	2
5/27/88	6/10/88	American Home Products	$71\frac{1}{4}$	$75\frac{1}{2}$	+ 5.96	2
11/25/88	1/27/89	Texas Utilities	$28\frac{3}{4}$	$29\frac{1}{8}$	+ 1.30	9
11/25/88	1/27/89	Central & South West	$30\frac{5}{8}$	$32\frac{1}{4}$	+ 5.31	9
11/25/88	5/25/90	Tucson Electric Power	$50\frac{1}{4}$	$12\frac{1}{4}$	−75.62	78
11/25/88	1/27/89	Consolidated Edison	$44\frac{1}{2}$	$46\frac{7}{8}$	+ 5.34	9
11/25/88	5/19/89	BCE Inc.	$31\frac{7}{8}$	$32\frac{3}{8}$	+ .78	25
11/3/89	5/25/90	Service Master L.P.	$21\frac{3}{4}$	$22\frac{1}{8}$	+ 1.72	29
11/3/89	5/25/90	Citytrust Bancorp	$25\frac{5}{8}$	$9\frac{1}{8}$	−64.04	29
11/3/89	11/6/92	UJB Financial	$22\frac{5}{8}$	$18\frac{1}{4}$	−19.34	157
11/3/89	2/22/91	Fleet/Norstar Financial	$27\frac{1}{2}$	$14\frac{5}{8}$	−46.82	83
11/3/89	5/18/90	International Bus. Mach.	$98\frac{1}{4}$	$115\frac{3}{8}$	+17.43	28
1/26/90	5/25/90	Citytrust Bancorp	$11\frac{1}{2}$	$9\frac{1}{8}$	−20.65	17
1/26/90	5/25/90	Service Master L.P.	$21\frac{1}{8}$	$22\frac{1}{8}$	+ 4.73	17
1/26/90	2/15/91	Potomac Electric	$21\frac{5}{8}$	$21\frac{1}{4}$	+ .58	55
1/26/90	12/27/91	Consolidated Edison	$26\frac{5}{8}$	$28\frac{1}{8}$	+ 4.65	100
1/26/90	11/6/92	UJB Financial	$17\frac{7}{8}$	$18\frac{1}{4}$	+ 2.10	145
2/2/90	5/25/90	Service Master L.P.	$21\frac{1}{2}$	$22\frac{1}{8}$	+ 2.91	16
2/2/90	11/8/91	Potomac Electric Power	$22\frac{1}{2}$	$23\frac{7}{8}$	+ 6.11	92
2/2/90	12/27/91	Consolidated Edison	$27\frac{7}{8}$	$28\frac{1}{8}$	+ 2.74	99

Purchase Date	Selling Date	Company	Purchase Price	Selling Price	Percentage Profit (+) Loss (−)	Holding Period Weeks
2/2/90	11/6/92	UJB Financial	19	18¼	− 3.95	144
2/2/90	2/22/91	Fleet/Norstar Financial	24⅛	14⅝	−39.38	55
2/16/90	12/27/91	Consolidated Edison	26¼	28⅛	+ 7.14	97
2/16/90	11/8/91	Potomac Electric Power	22½	23⅞	+ 6.11	90
2/16/90	11/6/92	UJB Financial	18	18¼	+ 1.39	142
2/16/90	2/22/91	Fleet/Norstar Financial	24⅛	14⅝	−39.38	53
2/16/90	11/23/90	Wisconsin Energy Corp.	29¼	30¾	+ 5.13	40
4/27/90	5/18/90	Service Master L.P.	20¼	21	+ 3.70	3
4/27/90	5/18/90	UJB Financial	14	16¾	+19.64	3
4/27/90	5/18/90	Consolidated Edison	24	25⅛	+ 4.69	3
4/27/90	5/18/90	Fleet/Norstar Financial	19	22⅛	+16.45	3
4/27/90	5/18/90	Hibernia Corp.	15⅜	16⅝	+ 8.13	3
8/10/90	4/19/91	UJB Financial	11½	12⅝	+ 9.78	36
8/10/90	11/23/90	Service Master L.P.	22⅝	22¾	+ .55	16
8/10/90	2/22/91	Fleet/Norstar Financial	16	14⅝	− 8.59	28
8/10/90	11/23/90	Consolidated Edison	22⅝	22⅞	+ 1.10	15
8/10/90	11/30/90	Potomac Electric Power	19¾	20	+ 1.27	16
8/17/90	4/19/91	UJB Financial	11½	12⅝	+ 9.78	35
8/17/90	2/22/91	Fleet/Norstar Financial	16	14⅝	− 8.59	27
8/17/90	11/23/90	Service Master L.P.	22	22⅛	+ .57	14
8/17/90	11/23/90	Consolidated Edison	22	22⅞	+ 3.98	14
8/17/90	11/30/90	Potomac Electric Power	19⅜	20	+ 3.23	15
8/24/90	4/19/91	UJB Financial	10⅞	12⅝	+15.09	34
8/24/90	2/15/91	Fleet/Norstar Financial	14⅜	14½	+ .87	25
8/24/90	11/23/90	Service Master L.P.	20	22⅛	+10.63	13
8/24/90	11/23/90	Consolidated Edison	20⅜	22⅞	+12.27	13
8/24/90	11/23/90	Potomac Electric Power	18½	19¼	+ 4.05	13
8/31/90	2/22/91	Fleet/Norstar Financial	15	14⅝	− 2.50	25

Purchase Date	Selling Date	Company	Purchase Price	Selling Price	Percentage Profit (+) Loss (–)	Holding Period Weeks
8/31/90	11/23/90	Service Master L.P.	21	22⅛	+ 5.36	12
8/31/90	11/23/90	Consolidated Edison	21¾	22⅞	+ 5.17	12
8/31/90	11/23/90	Potomac Electric Power	19⅛	19¼	+ .65	12
8/31/90	2/22/91	Hibernia Corp.	13⅜	7⅝	–42.99	25
9/7/90	2/22/91	Fleet/Norstar Financial	15	14⅝	– 2.50	24
9/7/90	11/23/90	Service Master L.P.	21	22⅛	+ 5.36	11
9/7/90	11/23/90	Consolidated Edison	21⅞	22⅞	+ 4.57	11
9/7/90	11/23/90	Potomac Electric Power	19⅛	19¼	+ .65	11
9/7/90	2/22/91	Hibernia Corp.	13	7⅝	–41.35	24
9/28/90	2/8/91	UJB Financial	9⅛	9½	+ 4.11	19
9/28/90	2/8/91	Fleet/Norstar Financial	12½	13⅞	+11.00	19
9/28/90	11/23/90	Consolidated Edison	21	22⅞	+ 8.93	8
9/28/90	11/23/90	Potomac Electric Power	18½	19¼	+ 4.05	8
9/28/90	2/22/91	Hibernia Corp.	11½	7⅝	–33.70	21
10/12/90	11/23/90	UJB Financial	8⅛	8⅝	+ 6.15	6
10/12/90	12/7/90	Fleet/Norstar Financial	11⅞	12¼	+ 3.16	8
10/12/90	2/22/91	Hibernia	9⅛	7⅝	–16.44	19
10/12/90	11/23/90	Service Master L.P.	20⅞	22⅛	+ 5.99	6
10/12/90	11/23/90	Barnett Banks	15	18½	+23.33	6

Appendix **E**

Time Overlay: Price

Purchase Date	Selling Date	Company	Purchase Price	Selling Price	Percentage Profit(+) Loss(−)	Holding Period Weeks
2/4/77	5/19/78	Heublein	28⅛	29	+ 3.11	67
2/4/77	7/28/78	Burroughs	72⅝	78¼	+ 7.75	77
2/4/77	3/13/81	Eastman Kodak	71⅞	80⅝	+ 2.17	213
2/4/77	6/24/77	Chesebrough-Pond's	22⅝	23¾	+ 4.97	20
2/4/77	8/4/78	Longs Drug Stores	28⅞	30⅛	+ 4.33	78
2/11/77	1/26/79	Heublein	29½	31½	+ 6.78	102
2/11/77	11/18/77	Disney (Walt) Productions	38⅜	39⅞	+ 3.91	40
2/11/77	11/25/77	Burroughs	70¾	71⅝	+ 1.24	41
2/11/77	3/13/81	Eastman Kodak	71⅛	80⅝	+13.36	212
2/11/77	5/12/78	Longs Drug Stores	27¾	28⅛	+ 1.35	65
2/18/77	4/16/82	Yellow Freight	33¾	13⅞	−58.89	268
2/18/77	11/18/77	Baxter Travenol Laboratories	33	38⅜	+16.29	39
2/18/77	8/4/78	Longs Drug Stores	28⅝	30⅛	+ 5.24	76
2/18/77	6/24/77	General Mills	29⅜	29⅞	+ 1.70	18
2/18/77	11/18/77	Disney (Walt) Productions	39⅛	39⅞	+ 1.92	39
4/1/77	11/18/77	Air Products & Chemical	26¾	27½	+ 2.80	33
4/1/77	11/25/77	Roadway Express	33	33¾	+ 2.27	34
4/1/77	7/1/77	Burroughs	61½	62	+ .81	13
4/1/77	6/24/77	Warner-Lambert	26⅜	28¼	+ 7.11	12
4/1/77	3/13/81	Eastman Kodak	68⅞	80⅝	+17.06	205
4/7/77	6/24/77	Air Products & Chemical	25¼	25⅝	+ 1.49	11
4/7/77	6/24/77	Warner-Lambert	25⅝	28¼	+10.24	11
4/7/77	11/25/77	Roadway Express	33½	33¾	+ .75	33
4/7/77	7/1/77	Burroughs	61¾	62	+ .40	12
4/7/77	8/4/78	Schering-Plough	36⅛	36⅞	+ 2.08	69
4/29/77	6/24/77	DEKALB AgResearch	26½	27	+ 1.89	8
4/29/77	6/24/77	Heublein	23½	26	+10.64	8
4/29/77	6/24/77	Lilly (Eli) & Co.	38⅛	39¼	+ 2.95	8

Purchase Date	Selling Date	Company	Purchase Price	Selling Price	Percentage Profit(+) Loss(−)	Holding Period Weeks
4/29/77	6/24/77	Schering-Plough	33⅛	35¾	+ 7.92	8
4/29/77	11/18/77	K Mart	29	29⅝	+ 2.16	29
5/13/77	6/24/77	Revco D. S.	15¾	18⅜	+16.67	6
5/13/77	6/24/77	Eastman Kodak	58¼	59⅞	+ 2.79	6
5/13/77	6/24/77	Lilly (Eli) & Co.	36¾	39¼	+ 6.80	6
5/13/77	11/18/77	Richardson-Merrell	20⅝	24⅛	+16.97	27
5/13/77	6/24/77	ARA Services	37	42¼	+14.19	6
11/4/77	11/18/77	Masco	17⅞	21	+17.48	2
11/4/77	11/18/77	Eastman Kodak	51⅛	52⅛	+ 1.96	2
11/4/77	11/18/77	Kellogg	21⅜	21¾	+ 1.75	2
11/4/77	11/18/77	Texas Utilities	20⅛	21⅛	+ 4.97	2
11/4/77	11/18/77	Xerox	47⅞	48¾	+ 1.83	2
1/6/78	5/5/78	Economics Laboratory	20⅞	21	+ .60	17
1/6/78	4/14/78	Winn-Dixie Stores	34⅞	35⅛	+ .72	14
1/6/78	4/14/78	Masco	18⅝	19½	+ 4.70	14
1/6/78	4/14/78	Wetterau	14¼	14½	+ 1.75	14
1/6/78	4/14/78	Emery Air Freight	38⅝	42⅛	+ 9.06	14
1/13/78	4/14/78	DEKALB AgResearch	16½	17½	+ 6.06	13
1/13/78	4/14/78	Revco D. S.	17¾	21½	+21.13	13
1/13/78	4/14/78	Shell Oil	28¾	31⅞	+10.87	13
1/13/78	4/21/78	Economics Laboratory	20½	20⅞	+ 1.83	14
1/13/78	4/14/78	Wetterau	13⅝	14½	+ 6.42	13
1/20/78	4/14/78	Disney (Walt) Productions	35¼	35¾	+ 1.42	12
1/20/78	4/14/78	Economics Laboratory	20	20¼	+ 1.25	12
1/20/78	4/14/78	Wetterau	13½	14½	+ 7.41	12
1/20/78	4/14/78	Standard Oil (California)	35¼	40	+13.48	12
1/20/78	4/21/78	Burroughs	64⅝	66⅛	+ 2.32	13
1/27/78	4/14/78	Disney (Walt) Productions	33¼	35¾	+ 7.52	11

Purchase Date	Selling Date	Company	Purchase Price	Selling Price	Percentage Profit(+) Loss(–)	Holding Period Weeks
1/27/78	4/14/78	Economics Laboratory	19¾	20¼	+ 2.53	11
1/27/78	4/14/78	DEKALB AgResearch	17¼	17½	+ 1.45	11
1/27/78	4/28/78	Sears Roebuck & Co.	24½	25¾	+ 5.10	13
1/27/78	4/14/78	Eckard (Jack)	23⅞	27	+13.09	11
10/6/78	1/19/79	American Hospital Supply	26½	26⅞	+ 1.42	15
10/6/78	8/24/79	Emery Air Freight	22⅝	23¼	+ 2.76	46
10/6/78	8/17/79	Fleming Co.	18⅛	18½	+ 2.07	45
10/6/78	12/7/79	Burroughs	75⅜	81⅛	+ 7.63	61
10/6/78	1/19/79	Emerson Electric	34	37¼	+ 9.56	15
10/20/78	1/19/79	Economics Laboratory	23⅛	24⅜	+ 5.41	13
10/20/78	1/19/79	Richardson-Merrell	23	23⅞	+ 3.80	13
10/20/78	1/19/79	Standard Brands	24¼	25¾	+ 6.19	13
10/20/78	8/10/79	Emery Air Freight	20⅜	22⅜	+ 9.82	42
10/20/78	1/19/79	Colgate-Palmolive	18¼	19	+ 4.11	13
10/27/78	1/19/79	Richardson-Merrell	21¾	23⅞	+ 9.77	12
10/27/78	1/19/79	Albertsons	32¼	40½	+25.58	12
10/27/78	1/19/79	Economics Laboratory	22¾	24⅜	+ 7.14	12
10/27/78	1/19/79	Sterling Drug	14⅝	17	+16.24	12
10/27/78	1/19/79	Squibb	27	32¼	+19.44	12
11/3/78	1/19/79	Economics Laboratory	20¼	24⅜	+20.37	11
11/3/78	3/23/79	Roadway Express	26½	28¾	+ 8.49	20
11/3/78	1/19/79	Richardson-Merrell	22	23⅞	+ 8.52	11
11/3/78	1/19/79	Sterling Drug	14½	17	+17.24	11
11/3/78	1/19/79	Foster Wheeler	30½	33¾	+10.66	11
11/10/78	1/19/78	Roadway Express	24¼	25	+3.09	10
11/10/78	1/19/78	Albertsons	33⅛	40½	+22.26	10
11/10/78	4/16/82	Yellow Freight	23¼	13⅞	–40.32	179
11/10/78	1/19/78	Foster Wheeler	30⅞	33¾	+ 9.31	10

Purchase Date	Selling Date	Company	Purchase Price	Selling Price	Percentage Profit(+) Loss(–)	Holding Period Weeks
11/10/78	1/19/78	Crouse-Hinds	21½	24¼	+12.79	10
3/2/79	3/23/79	Longs Drug Stores	25⅜	27	+ 6.40	3
3/2/79	3/23/79	Petrie Stores	36	37⅞	+ 5.21	3
3/2/79	3/23/79	Baxter Travenol Laboratories	35⅞	38⅞	+ 8.36	3
3/2/79	3/23/79	Minnesota Mining & Manufact.	55⅞	57⅞	+ 3.58	3
3/2/79	3/23/79	Masco	19¾	20⅞	+ 5.70	3
10/19/79	12/7/79	Foster Wheeler	19⅛	25⅝	+33.99	7
10/19/79	12/7/79	Sperry	42⅝	49¾	+16.72	7
10/19/79	12/7/79	Alberta Gas Trunk	22½	26½	+17.78	7
10/19/79	5/30/80	Yellow Freight	16¼	17½	+ 7.69	32
10/19/79	12/7/79	Walter (Jim)	28¾	32⅝	+13.48	7
10/26/79	12/7/79	Alberta Gas Trunk	20¼	26½	+30.86	6
10/26/79	12/7/79	Foster Wheeler	18⅞	25⅝	+35.76	6
10/26/79	12/7/79	Universal Leaf Tobacco	18⅜	20	+ 8.84	6
10/26/79	12/7/79	Masco	21⅝	25	+15.61	6
10/26/79	12/7/79	Walter (Jim)	28⅜	32⅝	+14.98	6
11/2/79	12/7/79	Meyer (Fred)	27⅛	29⅝	+ 9.22	5
11/2/79	9/3/82	Emery Air Freight	18	11⅜	–36.81	164
11/2/79	12/7/79	Foster Wheeler	19⅝	25⅝	+30.57	5
11/2/79	12/7/79	Masco	22⅜	25	+11.73	5
11/2/79	12/7/79	Colgate-Palmolive	14	14⅝	+ 4.46	5
3/7/80	5/16/80	Pay'n Save	19⅝	21¼	+ 8.28	10
3/7/80	5/16/80	Myer (Fred)	20⅜	23⅞	+17.18	10
3/7/80	5/23/80	Gordon Jewelry	22⅛	23	+ 3.95	11
3/7/80	5/16/80	Roadway Express	22	27½	+25.00	10
3/7/80	5/16/80	Economics Laboratory	19¾	21	+ 6.33	10
3/14/80	5/16/80	Pay'n Save	19⅜	21¼	+ 9.68	9
3/14/80	5/16/80	Meyer (Fred)	20	23⅞	+19.38	9

Purchase Date	Selling Date	Company	Purchase Price	Selling Price	Percentage Profit(+) Loss(−)	Holding Period Weeks
3/14/80	5/16/80	Pay Less Drug Stores NW	15¼	18½	+21.31	9
3/14/80	5/16/80	Petrie Stores	23¾	31⅞	+34.21	9
3/14/80	5/23/80	Southland Corp.	21½	21⅝	+ .58	10
3/21/80	5/16/80	Peoples Energy	41	44⅛	+ 7.62	8
3/21/80	5/16/80	Rollins	21¾	24¾	+13.79	8
3/21/80	5/16/80	Meyer (Fred)	20	23⅞	+19.38	8
3/21/80	5/16/80	Ralston Purina	10	11¼	+12.50	8
3/21/80	5/16/80	Southland Corp.	19⅞	21¼	+ 6.92	8
3/28/80	5/16/80	Rollins	20	24¾	+23.75	7
3/28/80	5/16/80	Economics Laboratory	16⅝	21	+26.32	7
3/28/80	5/16/80	Gordon Jewelry	18⅛	20¼	+11.72	7
3/28/80	5/16/80	Parker Pen	14⅜	16⅞	+17.39	7
3/28/80	5/16/80	McCormick & Co.	18¾	25¾	+37.33	7
12/19/80	3/13/81	Petrie Stores	24	31¾	+32.29	12
12/19/80	3/13/81	Air Products & Chemical	41½	42¾	+ 3.01	12
12/19/80	3/13/81	Wheelabrator-Frye	49⅞	54⅝	+ 9.52	12
12/19/80	3/13/81	Emery Air Freight	13¾	16½	+20.00	12
12/19/80	10/17/86	*Texas Eastern	38⅜	29	−24.43	304
8/28/81	10/23/81	Sonoco Products	23	27¾	+20.65	8
8/28/81	4/29/83	Union Pacific	52⅞	55	+ 4.02	87
8/28/81	10/23/81	Eckerd (Jack)	22⅞	25¼	+10.38	8
8/28/81	9/3/82	Emery Air Freight	13¾	11⅜	−17.27	53
8/28/81	4/23/82	Union Camp	48⅝	49	+ .77	37
9/4/81	10/23/81	Raytheon	38¼	40⅜	+ 5.56	7
9/4/81	10/23/81	Emery Air Freight	13¼	13½	+ 1.89	7
9/4/81	10/23/81	Wometco	16¼	18¼	+12.31	7
9/4/81	3/4/83	Sperry	35⅛	35⅜	+ .71	78
9/4/81	10/23/81	United Technologies	43½	45⅜	+ 4.31	7

Purchase Date	Selling Date	Company	Purchase Price	Selling Price	Percentage Profit(+) Loss(−)	Holding Period Weeks
9/11/81	9/26/83	Foster Wheeler	15½	16¼	+ 4.84	106
9/11/81	3/4/83	Union Pacific	49⅝	49¾	+ .25	77
9/11/81	4/15/83	Genstar	21⅝	21⅛	− 2.31	83
9/11/81	10/23/81	Economics Laboratory	18	18⅛	+ .69	6
9/11/81	9/3/82	Hudson's Bay Co.	24½	18¼	−25.51	51
9/18/81	10/15/82	Wetterau	15	15⅜	+ 2.50	56
9/18/81	10/23/81	Halliburton	50	52⅞	+ 5.75	5
9/18/81	10/23/81	Baker International	34⅜	37½	+ 9.09	5
9/18/81	10/23/81	Schlumberger	52¼	54¾	+ 4.30	5
9/18/81	10/22/82	Foster Wheeler	14¼	15⅛	+ 6.14	57
9/25/81	8/27/82	Wetterau	13	13½	+ 3.85	48
9/25/81	10/23/81	Inter-City Gas	7⅝	8½	+11.86	4
9/25/81	10/23/81	Foster Wheeler	12¼	14	+14.28	4
9/25/81	10/23/81	Hudson's Bay Oil & Gas	28⅝	35	+22.27	4
9/25/81	10/23/81	Halliburton	46	52⅞	+14.94	4
1/22/82	4/8/82	Gordon Jewelry	13¼	14⅜	+ 8.49	11
1/22/82	4/8/82	Baker International	30	30⅛	+ .41	11
1/22/82	4/16/82	Central Louisiana Energy	26½	21	−20.75	12
1/22/82	8/27/82	Parker Pen	11⅞	12⅞	+ 8.42	31
1/22/82	4/9/82	Panhandle Eastern	30½	31	+ 1.63	11
6/11/82	8/27/82	Sundstrand	26¼	34¼	+30.48	11
6/11/82	10/17/86	Baker International	24¾	10½	−57.58	227
6/11/82	8/27/82	Air Products & Chemical	28¼	29	+ 2.65	11
6/11/82	8/27/82	Foster Wheeler	10⅝	11⅜	+ 7.06	11
6/11/82	10/15/82	Halliburton	29¼	30¼	+ 3.42	18
6/18/82	8/27/82	Sundstrand	23¾	34¼	+44.21	10
6/18/82	10/15/82	Baker International	22⅝	24½	+ 8.29	17
6/18/82	8/27/82	Big Three Industries	16½	17⅝	+ 6.82	10

Purchase Date	Selling Date	Company	Purchase Price	Selling Price	Percentage Profit(+) Loss(−)	Holding Period Weeks
6/18/82	8/27/82	Air Products & Chemical	26⅝	29	+ 8.92	10
6/18/82	8/27/82	Sonat	22⅜	26¾	+19.55	10
2/10/84	8/4/84	Thrifty	14⅛	17	+20.35	25
2/10/84	1/18/85	PHH Group	27⅛	29⅛	+ 7.37	49
2/10/84	8/4/84	Dun & Bradstreet	53¼	65¾	+23.47	25
2/10/84	8/4/84	American Stores	32¾	37⅜	+14.12	25
2/10/84	8/4/84	Wal Mart Stores	33¼	45¼	+36.09	25
2/17/84	1/18/85	PHH Group	26¼	29⅛	+10.95	48
2/17/84	8/3/84	Rockwell International	28	30	+ 7.14	24
2/17/84	3/7/86	Heileman (G) Brewing	22¾	23⅞	+ 4.95	83
2/17/84	8/3/84	Thrifty	14½	17	+17.24	24
2/17/84	8/3/84	Scoa	19½	25¾	+32.05	24
2/24/84	1/18/85	PHH Group	25¾	29⅛	+13.11	47
2/24/84	3/7/86	Heileman (G) Brewing	23	23⅞	+ 3.80	82
2/24/84	8/3/84	Fishbach	46¾	48½	+ 3.74	23
2/24/84	8/3/84	Kellogg	28⅜	34	+19.82	23
2/24/84	8/3/84	Hewlett-Packard	37⅞	40¾	+ 7.59	23
5/25/84	8/3/84	PHH Group	18⅜	21⅞	+19.05	10
5/25/84	8/3/84	U. S. Tobacco	32½	38¼	+17.69	10
5/25/84	8/3/84	*Bairnco	19.4167	27⅜	+40.99	10
5/25/84	8/3/84	Dun & Bradstreet	51¾	65¾	+27.05	10
5/25/84	8/3/84	Albertsons	23½	26¼	+11.70	10
8/16/85	10/25/85	First Virginia Banks	24⅛	25⅛	+ 4.15	10
8/16/85	11/15/85	Fleet Financial Group	37⅝	38⅝	+ 2.79	13
8/16/85	11/1/85	Security Pacific	27⅜	27½	+ .46	11
8/16/85	10/25/85	Central & South West	24½	25½	+ 4.08	10
8/16/85	10/25/85	Tucson Electric Power	37¾	39⅛	+ 3.64	10
9/20/85	2/27/87	Texas Commerce Bankshares	29⅜	29½	+ .43	75

Purchase Date	Selling Date	Company	Purchase Price	Selling Price	Percentage Profit(+) Loss(−)	Holding Period Weeks
9/20/85	10/25/85	Citicorp	$41\frac{1}{8}$	$41\frac{1}{4}$	+ 1.52	5
9/20/85	10/25/85	Texas Utilities	$26\frac{5}{8}$	$27\frac{7}{8}$	+ 4.69	5
9/20/85	10/25/85	Anheuser-Busch Cos.	$31\frac{1}{4}$	$35\frac{3}{8}$	+13.20	5
9/20/85	5/22/87	Hospital Corp. of America	42	$44\frac{1}{4}$	+ 5.36	87
9/27/85	10/25/85	Fleet Financial Group	$33\frac{1}{2}$	$37\frac{1}{2}$	+11.94	4
9/27/85	10/25/85	Citicorp	$40\frac{3}{4}$	$41\frac{3}{4}$	+ 2.45	4
9/27/85	10/25/85	Eckerd (Jack)	$27\frac{5}{8}$	$29\frac{1}{4}$	+ 6.85	4
9/27/85	10/25/85	Texas Utilities	$26\frac{1}{8}$	$27\frac{7}{8}$	+ 6.70	4
9/27/85	10/25/85	Ametek	$21\frac{1}{4}$	23	+ 8.24	4
9/19/86	10/17/86	Manor Care	$16\frac{1}{4}$	$18\frac{1}{4}$	+12.31	4
9/19/86	10/17/86	Bard	$31\frac{3}{8}$	$32\frac{7}{8}$	+ 4.78	4
9/19/86	10/17/86	Lomas & Nettleton Financial	$35\frac{5}{8}$	$47\frac{1}{4}$	+34.98	4
9/19/86	10/17/86	General Cinema	$43\frac{1}{2}$	$44\frac{3}{4}$	+ 2.87	4
9/19/86	10/17/86	American Stores	$53\frac{3}{4}$	58	+ 7.91	4
9/26/86	10/17/86	Manor Care	$16\frac{3}{4}$	$18\frac{1}{4}$	+ 8.96	3
9/26/86	10/17/86	Lomas & Nettleton Financial	36	$47\frac{3}{4}$	+32.64	3
9/26/86	1/9/87	Pep Boys-Man,Mo.Ja.	$42\frac{5}{8}$	$44\frac{3}{8}$	+ 4.11	16
9/26/86	10/17/86	Bard	$30\frac{1}{2}$	$32\frac{7}{8}$	+ 7.79	3
9/26/86	1/9/87	Hershey	$22\frac{3}{8}$	$26\frac{7}{8}$	+20.11	16
9/26/86	10/17/86	Hershey	$16\frac{1}{4}$	$18\frac{1}{4}$	+12.31	2
10/3/86	10/17/86	Manor Care	$36\frac{7}{8}$	$47\frac{3}{4}$	+29.49	2
10/3/86	10/17/86	Lomas & Nettleton Financial	$22\frac{5}{8}$	$26\frac{7}{8}$	+20.11	15
10/3/86	1/9/87	Hershey	$21\frac{1}{4}$	$23\frac{1}{2}$	+10.59	15
10/3/86	1/9/87	Ames Department Stores	$74\frac{1}{2}$	$77\frac{1}{4}$	+ 3.69	2
10/3/86	10/17/86	American Home Products	$22\frac{1}{4}$	$23\frac{3}{4}$	+ 6.74	8
4/24/87	6/19/87	Ames Department Stores	$31\frac{1}{8}$	$36\frac{5}{8}$	+17.67	8
4/24/87	6/19/87	Meredith	$28\frac{1}{2}$	$32\frac{5}{8}$	+14.47	8
4/24/87	6/19/87	Dean Foods	$26\frac{7}{8}$	$29\frac{3}{4}$	+10.70	8
4/24/87	6/19/87	Super Valu Stores				8

Purchase Date	Selling Date	Company	Purchase Price	Selling Price	Percentage Profit(+) Loss(–)	Holding Period Weeks
4/24/87	9/23/88	Lomas & Nettleton Financial	32	19⅛	–40.23	74
5/1/87	6/19/87	Deluxe Check Print	30⅝	32¼	+ 5.31	7
5/1/87	6/19/87	Hillenbrand	26¼	27⅛	+ 3.33	7
5/1/87	6/19/87	Pep Boys-Man,Mo,Ja	44½	49⅝	+11.52	7
5/1/87	4/19/91	*American Water Works	20¼	20⅝	+ 1.85	207
5/1/87	6/19/87	Meredith	31¼	36⅝	+17.20	7
9/18/87	8/4/89	Ames Department Stores	17½	18½	+ 5.71	98
9/18/87	1/29/88	SmithKline Beckman	57	57¼	+ .44	19
9/18/87	2/12/88	Chemcial New York	37¾	22¾	–39.74	21
9/18/87	5/25/90	Bank of Boston	30½	13⅛	–56.97	140
9/18/87	5/19/89	Bankers Trust NY	46	46¼	+ .54	87
10/16/87	7/28/89	Upjohn	34½	34⅝	+ .36	93
10/16/87	10/7/88	Dow Jones & Co.	36	36½	+ 1.39	51
10/16/87	11/29/88	Bard (C.R.)	35⅜	37	+ 4.59	15
10/16/87	6/9/89	V F Corp.	34	35	+ 2.94	86
10/16/87	9/16/88	*General Cinema	20.9375	21¼	+ 1.49	48
10/23/87	1/29/88	Upjohn	31	33¼	+ 7.26	14
10/23/87	12/31/87	Pep Boys-Man,Mo,Ja	12⅞	13¾	+ 6.80	10
10/23/87	3/18/88	Dow Jones & Co.	33	34⅞	+ 5.68	21
10/23/87	12/31/87	*General Cinema	17	19⅜	+13.97	10
10/23/87	1/8/88	Dayton Hudson	28¼	31	+ 9.73	11
10/30/87	1/29/88	Dayton Hudson	31⅜	34⅞	+11.16	13
10/30/87	1/29/88	Ames Department Stores	11⅜	13⅜	+17.58	13
10/30/87	12/31/87	*General Cinema	16⅛	19⅜	+20.16	9
10/30/87	1/29/88	May Department Stores	32	33⅝	+ 5.08	13
10/30/87	12/31/87	Hewlett-Packard	50⅛	58¼	+16.21	9
11/6/87	1/8/88	Dayton Hudson	30¾	31	+ .81	9
11/6/87	2/19/88	Fort Howard Paper	37½	37⅞	+ 1.00	15

Purchase Date	Selling Date	Company	Purchase Price	Selling Price	Percentage Profit(+) Loss(−)	Holding Period Weeks
11/6/87	12/31/87	General Cinema	18	19⅜	+ 7.64	8
11/6/87	12/31/87	Westinghouse Electric	47¾	49¾	+ 4.19	8
11/6/87	1/8/88	Ames Department Stores	10¾	11	+ 2.33	9
11/13/87	1/8/88	Dayton Hudson	30⅜	31	+ 2.06	8
11/13/87	1/29/88	Ames Department Stores	11⅛	13⅜	+20.22	11
11/13/87	3/18/88	Fort Howard Paper	38⅜	40	+ 4.23	18
11/13/87	12/31/87	Westinghouse Electric	45⅜	49¾	+ 9.67	7
11/13/87	12/31/87	Affiliated Publications	48½	57	+17.53	7
12/4/87	12/31/87	Bank of New York	25⅛	25¾	+ 2.49	4
12/4/87	12/31/87	May Department Stores	25⅛	29⅛	+15.92	4
12/4/87	12/31/87	Morgan (J.P.)	29¾	36¼	+21.85	4
12/4/87	12/31/87	Affiliated Publications	41¼	57	+38.18	4
12/4/87	12/31/87	Bard	29¼	34½	+17.95	4
12/11/87	12/31/87	Donnelley (RR) & Sons	29¼	32⅝	+11.54	3
12/11/87	12/31/87	Wal-Mart Stores	23¼	26	+11.83	3
12/11/87	1/8/88	Bank of New York	25⅞	30	+15.94	4
12/11/87	12/31/87	Deluxe Check Print	23½	24⅜	+ 3.72	3
12/11/87	12/31/87	Security Pacific	24½	25⅜	+ 3.57	3
5/6/88	6/10/88	Manor Care	10½	11½	+ 9.52	5
5/6/88	6/10/88	Pep Boys-Man,Mo,Ja	11¼	12¾	+13.33	5
5/6/88	6/10/88	Clorox	27¾	29½	+ 6.31	5
5/6/88	6/10/88	Gannett Company	30½	32¾	+ 7.38	5
5/6/88	6/10/88	Deluxe Check Print	22¼	24	+ 7.87	5
5/13/88	6/10/88	Deluxe Check Print	22½	24	+ 6.67	4
5/13/88	6/10/88	Ball Corp.	27⅞	30¾	+10.31	4
5/13/88	6/10/88	Equifax Inc.	25⅝	27⅛	+ 5.85	4
5/13/88	6/10/88	Browning-Ferris Industries	23	24¾	+ 7.61	4
5/13/88	10/7/88	Flowers Industries	18½	18⅝	+ .68	21

Purchase Date	Selling Date	Company	Purchase Price	Selling Price	Percentage Profit(+) Loss(–)	Holding Period Weeks
5/20/88	6/10/88	Affiliated Publications	51	58¼	+14.22	3
5/20/88	6/10/88	Pfizer Co.	49⅝	53	+ 6.80	3
5/20/88	6/10/88	Equifax Inc.	26⅝	27⅛	+ 1.88	3
5/20/88	6/10/88	National Service Industries	22⅜	23	+ 2.79	3
5/20/88	6/10/88	Deluxe Check Print	21½	24	+11.63	3
5/27/88	6/10/88	Deluxe Check Print	21⅜	24	+12.28	2
5/27/88	6/10/88	Ames Department Stores	14	16	+14.29	2
5/27/88	6/10/88	Affiliated Publications	50¼	58¼	+15.92	2
5/27/88	6/10/88	Ball Corp.	28	30¾	+ 9.82	2
5/27/88	6/10/88	Pep Boys-Man,Mo,Ja	10¾	12¾	+18.60	2
1/25/88	1/27/89	ConAgra	27¼	31⅜	+15.14	9
1/25/88	1/27/89	Dayton Hudson	39¾	42⅝	+ 7.23	9
1/25/88	1/27/89	V. F. Corp.	28⅛	29⅝	+ 5.33	9
1/25/88	1/27/89	Donnelley (RR) & Sons	32⅜	36⅞	+13.90	9
1/25/88	1/27/89	Rockwell International	19⅜	21⅝	+11.61	9
11/3/89	5/25/90	Citytrust Bancorp	25⅜	9⅛	–64.04	29
11/3/89	5/18/90	Pep Boys-Man,Mo,Ja	11	14⅛	+28.41	28
11/3/89	5/18/90	Anheuser-Busch Co.	37¾	39⅜	+ 4.30	28
11/3/89	11/6/92	UJB Financial	22⅝	18¼	–19.34	157
11/3/89	5/18/90	Walgreen Co.	42	44¼	+ 5.36	28
1/26/90	5/25/90	Ames Department Stores	6⅞	2¼	–67.27	17
1/26/90	5/18/90	Sara Lee Corp.	27¼	28⅛	+ 7.14	16
1/26/90	11/6/92	Marriott Corp.	28⅛	21¼	–24.44	145
1/26/90	5/18/90	Heinz	29¾	33	+10.92	16
1/26/90	5/18/90	Deluxe Corp.	30¼	30⅞	+ 2.07	16
2/2/90	5/25/90	Ames Department Stores	6⅜	2¼	–64.71	16
2/2/90	11/6/92	Marriott Corp.	26⅜	21¼	–19.93	144
2/2/90	5/25/90	Citytrust Bancorp	10⅝	9⅛	–14.12	16

Purchase Date	Selling Date	Company	Purchase Price	Selling Price	Percentage Profit(+) Loss(–)	Holding Period Weeks
2/2/90	2/1/91	Bard (C.R.)	17¾	19	+ 7.04	52
2/2/90	2/22/91	Fleet/Norstar Financial	24⅛	14⅝	– 8.59	55
2/16/90	5/25/90	Ames Department Stores	5⅞	2¼	–61.70	14
2/16/90	5/25/90	Barrnett Banks Inc.	33	35⅝	+ 7.95	14
2/16/90	5/18/90	Donnelley & Sons	41⅜	43⅝	+ 5.44	13
2/16/90	5/18/90	Mercantile Stores	35	37½	+ 7.14	13
2/16/90	1/17/92	Dow Jones & Co.	28⅛	28¾	+ 2.22	100
4/27/90	5/18/90	Marriott Corp.	22	24¼	+10.23	3
4/27/90	5/18/90	UJB Financial	14	16¾	+19.64	3
4/27/90	5/18/90	Fleet/Norstar Financial	19	22⅛	+16.45	3
4/27/90	5/25/90	Dow Jones & Co.	25⅛	26⅞	+ 6.97	4
4/27/90	5/18/90	Loral Corp.	26¾	27⅝	+ 3.27	3
8/10/90	4/19/91	UJB Financial	11½	12⅝	+ 9.78	36
8/10/90	12/21/90	Pitney Bowes	40	40¼	+ 3.13	19
8/10/90	12/7/90	McDonald's Corp.	29⅞	30¼	+ 1.26	17
8/10/90	2/1/90	May Department Stores	44⅞	45½	+ 1.39	25
8/10/90	2/1/90	Hewlett-Packard	37⅜	37⅞	+ 1.34	25
8/17/90	4/19/91	UJB Financial	11½	12⅝	+ 9.78	35
8/17/90	2/1/91	Dayton Hudson	59	65¾	+11.44	24
8/17/90	1/17/92	Marriott Corp.	18⅜	19	+ 3.40	74
8/17/90	2/8/91	May Department Stores	46⅝	48⅞	+ 4.83	25
8/17/90	2/1/91	Hewlett-Packard	34⅝	37⅞	+ 9.39	24
8/24/90	2/15/91	Barrnett Banks	24⅜	24⅝	+ 1.03	25
8/24/90	2/1/91	Hewlett-Packard	34¼	37⅞	+10.58	23
8/24/90	11/23/90	McDonald's Corp.	27½	28⅝	+ 4.09	13
8/24/90	12/7/90	Dayton Hudson	55½	57	+ 2.70	15
8/24/90	4/19/91	UJB Financial	10⅞	12⅝	+16.09	34
8/31/90	2/1/91	V. F. Corp.	19¾	22⅝	+14.56	22

Purchase Date	Selling Date	Company	Purchase Price	Selling Price	Percentage Profit(+) Loss(−)	Holding Period Weeks
8/31/90	2/1/91	Hewlett-Packard	$34\frac{7}{8}$	$37\frac{7}{8}$	+ 8.60	22
8/31/90	12/7/90	Dayton Hudson	$56\frac{3}{4}$	57	+ .44	14
8/31/90	3/1/91	Barnett Banks	25	$25\frac{1}{2}$	+ 2.00	26
8/31/90	12/7/90	Mercantile Stores	$29\frac{7}{8}$	$30\frac{1}{4}$	+ 1.26	14
9/7/90	2/1/91	V. F. Corp.	$19\frac{3}{8}$	$22\frac{5}{8}$	+16.77	21
9/7/90	12/7/90	Mercantile Stores	$29\frac{7}{8}$	$30\frac{1}{4}$	+ 1.26	13
9/7/90	12/14/90	Melville Corp.	40	$40\frac{5}{8}$	+ 1.56	14
9/7/90	12/14/90	Dayton Hudson	$57\frac{7}{8}$	$58\frac{1}{8}$	+ 1.31	14
9/7/90	12/14/90	Knight-Ridder Inc.	$43\frac{3}{8}$	$44\frac{3}{4}$	+ 3.17	14
9/28/90	11/30/90	Marriott Corp.	$10\frac{1}{4}$	$11\frac{3}{8}$	+10.98	9
9/28/90	11/23/90	Barnett Banks Inc.	$17\frac{7}{8}$	$18\frac{1}{2}$	+ 3.50	8
9/28/90	11/23/90	Pitney Bowes	$28\frac{3}{8}$	35	+23.35	8
9/28/90	11/23/90	Capital Holding	$31\frac{3}{8}$	$33\frac{7}{8}$	+ 7.11	8
9/28/90	12/27/91	Browning-Ferris Industries	$30\frac{3}{8}$	$21\frac{3}{8}$	−29.63	65
10/12/90	11/23/90	Marriott Corp.	$8\frac{7}{8}$	$9\frac{3}{4}$	+ 9.86	6
10/12/90	11/23/90	UJB Financial	$8\frac{1}{8}$	$8\frac{5}{8}$	+ 6.15	6
10/12/90	2/22/91	Hibernia	$9\frac{1}{8}$	$7\frac{7}{8}$	−16.44	19
10/12/90	11/23/90	Capital Holding	29	$33\frac{7}{8}$	+16.81	6
10/12/90	11/23/90	Barnett Banks Inc.	15	$18\frac{1}{2}$	+23.33	6

The following purchase prices were adjusted for stock splits as follows:

12/19/80	Texas Eastern	2:1	10/16/87	General Cinema	2:1
5/25/84	Bairnco	3:2	10/23/87	General Cinema	2:1
5/1/87	American Water Works	2:1	10/30/87	General Cinema	2:1

Index

About the Authors

THOMAS J. HERZFELD, president of Thomas J. Herzfeld & Co. in Miami, Florida, is a market strategist, money manager, investment advisor, and widely considered the world's leading authority on closed-end funds. The author of *Herzfeld's Guide to Closed-End Funds* (McGraw-Hill), he has been featured in every major financial publication and on national television, including *Wall Street Week with Louis Rukeyser.*

ROBERT F. DRACH has been a regularly scheduled guest on Public Broadcasting System's nationally televised *Nightly Business Report* since 1979. Founder of Drach Market Research, his background includes two graduate degrees relating to securities analysis and extensive experience in portfolio management. Mr. Drach's writings are utilized in investment programs throughout the world.